THERE WAS A LIGHT

The Cosmic History of CHRIS BELL and the Rise of BIG STAR

RICH TUPICA

PERMUTED
PRESS

A PERMUTED PRESS BOOK
ISBN: 978-1-68261-928-5
ISBN (eBook): 978-1-68261-929-2

There Was A Light:
The Cosmic History of Chris Bell and the Rise of Big Star
© 2020 by Rich Tupica
All Rights Reserved

PERMUTED
PRESS
Permuted Press, LLC
New York • Nashville
permutedpress.com

Published in the United States of America

This book is dedicated to David Bell, who was always a pleasant phone call away and willing to talk about his kid brother, Chris.
I will always be grateful.

And to Nicole and Fiona.

A special remembrance goes out to John Fry and Richard Rosebrough. During their final years on this planet, they encouraged this project, offered up hours of memories and connected me with those closest to Chris. A month before Fry unexpectedly passed away, he agreed to fact check a portion of this book via email. In that same message he offered up a bit of advice: "It is likely to be done right only once, so let's keep it precise, right down the line." I may not have accomplished that, but I will never forget his wisdom.

Chris Bell, 1975.

PHOTO BY DAVID BELL

Author's Note

This oral history contains many original interviews conducted by the author between 2013 and 2018. Some quotes were edited for clarity. To capture additional recollections and give voices to those who passed away before the start of this book, other excerpts were mined with permission from an array of outside publications and journalists. Another key source for *There Was A Light* was hours of raw interview footage from *Big Star: Nothing Can Hurt Me*, the acclaimed 2012 documentary (Magnolia Films). I cannot thank Ardent Studios and the entire film crew enough for graciously granting me that access. See page 449 for a complete list of sources.

TABLE of CONTENTS

"The individual has always had to struggle to keep from being overwhelmed by the tribe. If you try it, you will be lonely often, and sometimes frightened. But no price is too high to pay for the privilege of owning yourself."

—FRIEDRICH NIETZSCHE

PROLOGUE

'A STORY OF NOBLE, HEROIC FAILURE'

"If you're a rock 'n' roll fan, even if you haven't heard of Big Star, you owe them, because I guarantee you: Any band you like did hear of them, and listen to them, and do their best to do as well as they did."—**Mike Mills of R.E.M.**, 2004 Memphis Heroes Awards induction speech for Big Star

In the four decades since the bewildering death of Chris Bell, the steady drum-beat of plaudits, honors and credits planting him among the musical influencers of his generation would have given him great solace. Tragically, he died at twenty-seven years old while living at his parents' house, working a dead-end job as a grocery store clerk, and not knowing the recordings he'd leave behind would go on to achieve the goals he'd obsessed over throughout the 1970s.

After founding Big Star, the Memphis, Tennessee-born guitarist/vocalist led the charge on 1972's highly influential #1 *Record, produced at Ardent Studios. At his side was a triad of fellow Memphians, including former Box Tops front-man Alex Chilton on guitar and vocals, Andy Hummel on bass, and Jody Stephens on drums. With ample assistance and latitude from Ardent founder John Fry, the assembly of audiophiles perfected a hybrid of beautiful British pop and rowdy American rock.*

It didn't last long. Shortly after the LP's release, Chris slid into a bout of clinical depression and exited the band. Big Star carried on without him and, with Chilton at the reins, the band laid down the equally remarkable Radio City *(1974) followed by* Third/Sister Lovers *(1978).*

Chris recalibrated as a solo artist and produced a sonic boom of poignant material—recorded piecemeal throughout the mid-'70s at his home base of Ardent

1

Studios, in London at George Martin's AIR Studios, and in France at Château d'Hérouville.

Despite valiant efforts in his lifetime, Chris saw few triumphs and received minimal interest in his stockpile of solo recordings. After a succession of snubs from labels, in his final days he even took a job flipping burgers—not the archetypal makings of a future rock 'n' roll legend.

Fast-forward to today, Grammy Award winners like Wilco and Beck cover his magnum opus "I Am the Cosmos" in concert, and his international cult following is larger than ever thanks to a series of books, deluxe album reissues and a Big Star documentary detailing portions of his short, reticent life as a rebellious Memphis songwriter.

Carole Ruleman Manning — Photographer, Ardent Studios art designer: Chris died when he was twenty-seven years old. I heard somebody talking about that on the radio one night. It was on a program about all these rock 'n' roll people who died at twenty-seven. There was Hendrix, Joplin, Morrison—a long string of people—and they included Chris. The tragedy of what happened to him after he left the group, combined with that, it's like he just walked into a template for a rock 'n' roll legend.

Terry Manning — Ardent Studios producer, engineer, musician: While Chris was alive he didn't become a star, but over time he has taken on that status. Whether it's a cult status or beyond that, he definitely made it. For the relatively small output he had, the quality is amazing.

Ric Menck — Drummer, musician, Matthew Sweet, Velvet Crush: He died young and left a nearly faultless body of work in his wake. He was gifted and flawed, a sensitive young man wrestling with personal demons and expressing his feelings through song. The saddest part is he never got to realize how much his music meant to people. I think he would have appreciated it more than Alex Chilton ever did.

Andria Lisle — Memphis-based journalist: Chris Bell has a different legacy than Alex Chilton because Chris died at twenty-seven, whereas Chilton went on to create a discography that was almost the antithesis of what he did in Big Star—playing with Tav Falco's Panther Burns, producing the Cramps, and then putting his own spin on [the 1958 Italian pop song] "Volare." Chris Bell is frozen in time, which makes his music and lyricism that much more beautiful and his personality that much more impenetrable.

Mark Deming — Music critic, journalist: Alex had been a rock star before Big Star. He was a charismatic guy and his crazy life made for

2

good copy. Bell, on the other hand, was a genuinely troubled soul, and I have a hard time imagining he could have a career like Chilton did even if he hadn't lost his life. I can't see Bell bonding with Paul Westerberg or opening for the Jon Spencer Blues Explosion like Chilton did, though I bet the sort of folks who gravitate to Nick Drake or Scott Walker might have embraced Bell if he'd been around longer.

Jody Stephens — Drummer, Big Star, Icewater, Rock City, Baker Street Regulars: Chris' profile has certainly increased over the years. You get on YouTube and all types of things pop up for Chris. That's pretty cool. But Chris didn't make any real money from music while he was alive. He passed away in '78, even before the release of *I Am the Cosmos*, his solo LP. I don't know exactly how much money having "In the Street" as the theme of *That '70s Show* brings in, but it's in syndication and sometimes it's on three or four times a night. I wish I would have had a share of that song.

Rick Nielsen — Guitarist, songwriter, Cheap Trick: Right before *That '70s Show* debuted, they wanted either the Big Star song or "Surrender" by Cheap Trick as its theme. They picked the Big Star song. After the first season, the producers said, "Can Cheap Trick do a version of it?"

John Fry — Ardent Records founder, engineer, Big Star's executive producer: When FOX came up with *That '70s Show*, their music supervisor decided "In the Street" off Big Star's first album was the tune that typified the '70s.

Andria Lisle: I thought Big Star's popularity might peak with *That '70s Show*, but their legacy has just grown and grown over the last few decades, and rightfully so. Chris Bell and Alex Chilton produced some incredible material together.

Bob Mehr — Memphis-based journalist, author, *Trouble Boys: The True Story of the Replacements:* Even as big as Big Star is now, I don't know that the average Memphian on the street knows who Chris Bell is. At the same time, there is an awareness of Chris now within the city that's dramatically, exponentially more than it was even a few years ago. Back in 2008, on the thirtieth anniversary of his death, I wrote a story about Chris that ran in the daily newspaper in Memphis on A1, the cover of the paper. At the time, there were non-music people who knew Chris, those who went to school with him or whatever, who were totally surprised and perplexed that a story about him would be on the front cover of *The Commercial Appeal*. They had no idea he was someone who was so highly regarded nationally and internationally or that he had any level of fame or notoriety. In the years since, with the Big Star box set *Keep An*

Eye on the Sky, the *I Am the Cosmos* reissues, the Big Star documentary and all the local press about those releases, Memphians have a better sense that Chris was, and is, an important artist.

While Chris' entire catalog of music has been issued over the years, most exhaustively on Omnivore Recordings' 2017 Complete Chris Bell *box set, his private life remained an unknown tale. Filmmakers Drew DeNicola and Danielle McCarthy-Boles experienced firsthand the secrecy surrounding Chris while interviewing his friends, family and bandmates during the making of 2012's* Big Star: Nothing Can Hurt Me *documentary.*

Drew DeNicola — Director, *Big Star: Nothing Can Hurt Me*: It was a major problem getting people to talk about Chris Bell for the film. We went around to scout out and find people who would be able to tell us more because everyone was very guarded about Chris. We didn't know if it was about his sexuality, or if they were just troubled by the story itself. On the one hand, it seemed like there was this big conspiracy cover-up. It was like, "What's going on in Memphis? Nobody wants to talk to us about Chris Bell." To some degree, that was true. Another thing was that the guy was mysterious, even to people who knew him for years. I definitely had people say, "I won't talk about his sexuality. If you ask me, I will walk out." We had to lay down rules for the interviews sometimes. We also had to rely on a lot of conversation off-camera to help us form what we would try to get on camera for people. In the end, we were like, "We're not here to out this guy. We're here to tell the story and how it relates to the music."

Danielle McCarthy-Boles — Film producer, *Big Star: Nothing Can Hurt Me*: The film introduced a lot of people to Chris Bell and a lot of people who knew Chris Bell were just so appreciative we focused on him. It seemed to be more of a revelation for people about Chris. That was surprising for us. His story is more of a tragic, heartstrings-pulling story: his struggle to be heard as an artist, his issues with his sexuality, and his early death. At the screenings, many times I heard people crying during the Chris Bell parts. I heard people sobbing. It touched a nerve.

Personal demons and ambiguities aside, Chris' solo recordings, and the entire Big Star catalog, have become known as some of the earliest prototypes for alternative rock. Even the promotional methods employed by Ardent to support the band foreshadowed the DIY ethos embraced by countless '80s and '90s indie-rock bands and labels.

Drew DeNicola: The Big Star story is all about sticking to your guns and doing things your way. Not being part of the mainstream, but having contempt for the mainstream. Snubbing your nose at the mainstream, destroying yourself rather than being a part of the mainstream. Driving yourself insane because you feel left out, but at the same time choosing not to be a part of it. That became the dominant attitude in alternative and indie rock. They were doing that before the rest—having that attitude and being a part of the world of outsiders, rejects and beautiful losers.

Barney Hoskyns — British music journalist, author: It's a story of noble, heroic failure. A band that, in a parallel rock-critic universe, was as big as the Beatles. The music borrows from '60s pop but twists it into something so distinctive and, at moments, so heartbreakingly strange. It's almost like they were great because they didn't quite know what they were doing. Or did they?

Sherman Willmott — Memphis-based fan, Shangri-La Records founder: In the '70s, when Big Star was playing here in Memphis, which wasn't often, they were not well known, so the shows were not well attended. There was so much other music going on, they fell through the cracks. There's always been a lot going on here. When I think of Memphis music, I go all the way back to jug-band music and then Willie Mitchell and Booker T & the MGs. There's a broad spectrum of history here and Memphis puts it in your face. But the '80s were not good for the Memphis music scene. We had to start from scratch. By the '90s, things got better with bands like Big Ass Truck, the Oblivians, and '68 Comeback. They fought against this whole idea that Memphis is only about Elvis and music from the '50s. Even in the '90s, people could still not understand how a band from Memphis could sound like the Grifters or, ten years later, Jay Reatard. Now the battle is won. You can be from Memphis and not be rockabilly or blues. Great bands can come from Memphis and not sound like Charlie Feathers, Elvis, or BB King. Big Star was early proof of that.

Drew DeNicola: The Memphis music community is strong, legitimate and true. Big Star is totally a part of that world. People from Memphis don't like to compromise. They have an island mentality, but it's a beautiful thing. Stax had Booker T and Otis Redding. Royal Studios had Al Green. All these studios had their people, the artists who made them what they were. Big Star is that for Ardent Studios.

Robert Gordon — Memphis-based journalist, author, filmmaker: Over time, as Big Star's recognition has come, it's only further implanted Big Star into the Ardent mythos. If you talk to any of the employees there, within minutes, Big Star's influence will come up.

Andria Lisle: Having Ardent here in Memphis is fantastic. It has brought so many successful working bands to town, groups like R.E.M.

and the Replacements—going all the way back to ZZ Top—and then more recent bands like the Raconteurs. It's extremely validating to drive past and say, "Oh, that's where Led Zeppelin mixed *Zeppelin III*."

Robert Gordon: Ardent was a direct reflection of its owner John Fry. It was about clean sounds and clean state-of-the-art equipment. Fry was an engineer and interested in sonic clarity. Ardent has always reflected that and has been on the cutting edge of technology.

Sherman Willmott: In the early 2000s, when *Rolling Stone* came out with its "500 Greatest Albums," Big Star was the most obscure band to have three in the top 500. Being a Memphis guy, it was a real eye-opener for me. It's when I more fully grasped the outside-of-Memphis perception of the band. To have one album in that list would be an achievement, but it's mind-bending for a band that played so few times and sold so few records to accomplish that.

Carole Ruleman Manning: John Fry said the resurgence of Big Star just happened.

Drew DeNicola: It happened organically. It was a total surprise to Ardent.

Jody Stephens: What brought that all about was the guys in R.E.M. mentioning the band early on, Paul Westerberg writing the song "Alex Chilton," Greg Dulli with the Afghan Whigs mentioning the band. A lot of folks kept putting the name out there. People started picking up on it and seeking out tapes. Outside the mentions in the press, it was basically people just passing tapes around, one guy digging it and passing it on to his friend. That's probably why it took twenty years.

Steve Rhea — Classmate, musician, songwriter, Christmas Future, Icewater: There was a network of rock writers all over the world who loved Big Star. It was through them the band's following grew. All the contacts were like a root system of people who loved the music. The rock writers are historians for music that's not only popular now, but for music that has legs. Music that has longevity. Big Star came back around thirty years later because the music has something. It was unique, and the rock writers recognized that, even if the music companies didn't.

Sherman Willmott: Things picked up and they are no longer a cult band, in my mind. There are always new people discovering Big Star, and it's a good starting point for some great other Memphis music—like the Scruffs or the Chris Bell solo record. It's a great stepping stone. I've been a fan for over thirty years and I'm still a sucker.

Drew Fortune — Journalist, author: In 2016, I interviewed Paul Westerberg [of the Replacements] at his house in Edina, Minnesota on a freezing Valentine's Day weekend. After playing me some music in his basement studio. Paul and I were pretty comfortable together. I scanned his CD collection, noticing weird ones like Buckcherry—though that one probably belongs to his son Johnny—but I noticed Big Star, too. As I had always wondered, I asked if Alex Chilton was his musical hero. "Nah," Paul scoffed. "I liked him for those couple years, but I was never wild about him. I like Gene Vincent and the way he looked. I like Johnny Thunders." This admission caught me off-guard, as I figured Westerberg worshiped to a Chilton shrine in his bedroom every night. That was all I got on Chilton and I didn't press. In a sense, it's kind of the perfect tribute to Big Star. Paul penned a love letter, and one of his best songs to a guy he didn't absolutely cherish. Big Star is so good that even if you're not a die-hard fan, the songs can touch you in a place that most bands can't begin to navigate.

Today, there are legions of Big Star fans across the world, many of whom found the band via the Replacements, but longtime Bell/Chilton fans knew the band was special back in the 1970s—in the prime of their obscurity.

Chris Morris — Journalist, music critic: The people who stumbled on the Big Star albums early on were thinking, *This wasn't successful. Why?*

Ivo Watts-Russell — 4AD Records founder, musician, This Mortal Coil: I picked up Big Star's *#1 Record* and *Radio City* around 1975 in a sweet shop on the east end of London. They had a box of American imports set out on the counter. I also scored the other Ardent Records releases, Cargoe and the Hot Dogs, at this place. They didn't typically sell records there. Clearly, they were off the back of a lorry. It was by total chance I found them. It does fan the flames of infatuation when you've heard an album as good as *#1 Record* and no one else has heard it and you can't find it anywhere.

Ric Menck: The first time I recall hearing about Big Star was back in the early '70s when I read a glowing review of *Radio City* in, I believe, *Crawdaddy Magazine*. I recall reading reviews in *Rolling Stone* and maybe *Circus* as well. The problem was that it was incredibly difficult to find copies of the album in the Chicagoland area, which is where I grew up. It took a year or two before I could track it down. When I did finally find them, both Big Star albums were everything I imagined and more. I was instantly smitten. What made them even more beguiling was that it was nearly impossible to find out any information about the band. All

I had to go on were the reviews and the album covers, which I would cradle in my arms and stare at for hours on end.

Matthew Sweet — Singer-songwriter, musician: There was no Wikipedia for Big Star. You couldn't learn about them unless you knew people who knew about them. There were a few magazines like *New York Rocker Magazine* and *Trouser Press* where you could learn some about them, but that's about it. The first time someone told me about them was in the early '80s. I was sixteen or seventeen and worked in this record store in Lincoln, Nebraska, where I grew up. It was an after school and weekends job at Dietz Music. This rockabilly guy with a great record collection came in and heard some of my demo recordings. He told me, "You would really like Big Star."

Mike Mills — Bassist, vocalist, R.E.M., Big Star's Third: R.E.M. was just getting started. I was in college, still trying to sort out all the things you're trying to sort out in college. We were just starting our band, just beginning to write songs and trying to figure out how to go about that. Big Star was always an inspiration. If not exactly a template, then close to it...I felt closer to it [than the Beatles]. I mean the Beatles were something I heard as a kid on my tiny AM radio—they were from England and I was very young. It was this in-the-sky thing that I loved but I wasn't even sure why. By the time I heard Big Star, I was a musician and I knew what they were doing and why it was so much more personal to me. I felt a lot closer to the music. It felt like something I could do. The Beatles, I don't think I could ever do anything like that. But with Big Star, I thought, *I could aim for that. I could do something that might be close to that.*

Matthew Sweet: They were important to me when I was starting to write songs. Early on, I scored a couple Big Star tapes. The first thing that struck me was the guitar playing. At that age, I grew up on British acts like Elvis Costello, Generation X and the Buzzcocks—the bands that made power-pop-ish kinds of records during that punk and new-wave invasion. I was looking for American artists that I related to. That's why I started getting *New York Rocker Magazine* and learned about the dB's and the first R.E.M. 45. I mail-ordered these records. When I was older and had success with "Girlfriend" in the '90s, a lot of people were going crazy for Big Star, like Teenage Fanclub. I always loved them, but never got to be a part of that scene. I loved Big Star, but some of those bands wanted to *be* Big Star.

Chris Morris: Younger generations of bands have followed along that post-Beatles, neo-pop rock path. As a result, the sound has never gone away, it's just gone through these various permutations. You've got the Posies, the Replacements and Teenage Fanclub—all the acolyte bands that have carried that torch. That sound has always been present, but it's been continuously updated and amplified. Those Big Star records are so present for me that chronology doesn't come into play when I'm listening to them. They are contemporary for me, which maybe makes me fucked up.

Alex Chilton — Singer-songwriter, guitarist, Box Tops, Big Star, Panther Burns: I'm continually surprised that people fall for Big Star as they do...I would say there was some maudlin strain running through the records that a whole crew of today's youth would identify with, though I'm not particularly one of them.

Pete Yorn — Singer-songwriter, musician: Very few times have I heard a song and it stopped me in my tracks. I just listened to it over and over, like when Brian Wilson first heard "Be My Baby" and listened to it repeatedly. I heard "I Am the Cosmos," and it just fucking cut right through me. I thought it sounded like some lost Paul Westerberg track. I didn't know what the hell it was. Then I did the research and found out how tragically he died. The thing just hit me. Out of all his songs, that's my favorite. It's a little slower than you think it should be. It has a real emotional fucking intensity that I love—those power-pop melodies. When you let a song be a bit slow it adds this heaviness to a track.

Peter Holsapple — Singer-songwriter, musician, dB's, R.E.M. sideman, solo: A friend from Memphis gave me two bootleg cassettes many years ago. One had a version of *Third* on one side, and Big Star's WLIR broadcast on the other. The second cassette was Chris Bell's solo songs in no particular order, with a couple mixes of a few different songs, probably not the whole album because it wasn't released yet. Both cassettes became integral parts of my listening, but Chris' recordings were just monumental to me, like hearing a missing part of *Radio City*. I will never not sigh when I hear the first chords and notes of "I Am the Cosmos." It is truly one of the most perfect songs ever written and recorded. The pain is so evident, the strain on his voice and the ethereal guitar solo. The handclaps were hugely important in my own songwriting, even the little crunch in the tape that made the cymbals break up a little. The "yeah, yeah, yeah" vocal and knowing it's the same key as the Beatles' rendering of the same words—it's just magnificent, and it's never gotten any less magnificent over time.

Bob Mehr: When Rykodisc released the *I Am the Cosmos* album in 1992, I was just excited to hear Chris' songs with such great fidelity.

I had listened to cassette bootlegs of Chris' Car Records single, and some other tracks that had been floating around for years, but to hear those songs properly and to read liner notes by his brother David Bell, it helped answer a lot of questions about Chris and the Big Star story. But at the same time, it also opened a whole new mystery about Chris Bell as this tragic, romantic figure.

Chris Bell in Nendaz, Switzerland, 1972. This photo was later used on the cover of "I Am the Cosmos."

PHOTO BY DAVID BELL

ACT ONE

MAKE A SCENE

Chris Bell as a toddler.

BELL FAMILY ARCHIVE

CHAPTER 1

THE BELLS — BEATLEMANIA: 1918-1965

The enigmatic roots of Chris Bell and his musical legacy might be firmly entrenched in Memphis's rock 'n' roll folklore, but digging deeper lands you eighty miles south in rustic Oakland, Mississippi, a speck on the map in Yalobusha County. The rural town of a few hundred is where Chris' father Vernon Mortimer Bell, born September 2, 1918, was raised.

David Bell — Brother: Our father, Vernon Bell, was born in Memphis and brought up in this little place called Oakland, Mississippi. It was not even a city yet, just a little stop on the railroad. His mother had problems with her pregnancy, and she died a few days after he was born.

Cindy Bell Coleman — Sister: Right after he was born, Daddy went to live with his grandparents because his father was a traveling salesman and he had to work on the road, so there was no way he could take care of a baby. They raised him until my grandfather remarried, and by then he had been living with them for years. It was like he was theirs. I've got old photos of Daddy in front of cotton gins down in Mississippi.

David Bell: World War II introduced my father to Europe. He was a US B-17 bomber crewmember—134th Bomber Squad in Norfolk, England. That's where he met my mother, Joan Branford Bell.

Joan Branford, was born in Claydon, Suffolk, near Ipswich, on July 5, 1915, to Ernest Womack Branford and Ethel Louise Pullman.

David Bell: Our mother was about ten years older than her brother. I got the impression she was a little headstrong, a little spoiled. Her nickname was Pinky. She was born in 1915, so she was ten years old in the middle of the Roaring Twenties. I remember her telling me she liked jazz, like Louis Armstrong.

Cindy Bell Coleman: Daddy met our mother in England while she was working for the military driving a pharmacy truck.

Tom Eubanks — Vocalist, bassist, guitarist, songwriter, Rock City: Chris was proud of his mother's British heritage. In 1971, when we were recording that Rock City album, we were sitting on his bed working on songs and he said, "It's so weird, I've never been there, but I'm always homesick for England."

David Bell: Growing up in Memphis, all of us as kids heard from our friends how they wanted to come over and hear our mother talk. They were thrilled by her English accent.

Terry Manning: Chris loved his mother to death and was proud of her Britishness. He saw himself as half-British.

Cindy Bell Coleman: Mom was proper. She would be gardening—non-stop gardening. I don't know how she did it. She was bound and determined to create an English garden in our backyard.

Sara Bell — Sister: That's what she worked on from the time she got us off to school to the time she started to get dinner ready.

David Bell: My older sister Virginia and I were both born in Norfolk in England and we lived there for a while. At the end of the war, my father said, "I'm going back to America and you're coming along with me." Chris wasn't born yet. We left on Christmas day in 1945 from either Glasgow or Edinburgh. We were on board what was called a Liberty ship. They were apparently described as rust buckets. My mother was bedridden with seasickness for the entire crossing. I was about two months old when we arrived in Memphis. We lived in an apartment for maybe a year.

Cindy Bell Coleman: Mother told me it was a lovely apartment, especially for being right after the war. It was in a tall building near the entrance of the Memphis Zoo in Midtown.

David Bell: It was closer to the old Medical Center in Memphis, right across from Forest Park.

Cindy Bell Coleman: They were on the ninth floor and nobody had air conditioning. She was used to English weather. She said, "It was so hot, I thought I was going to die." In Memphis, you're talking ninety degrees with ninety percent humidity. She would take the children downtown to the stores just to get into the air conditioning.

David Bell: She told me, in her first summer in Memphis, every day she would go over in her head how she would tell my father that we cannot possibly live here because she would die. It was so hot, so humid. This was an English woman who came from a place where people start passing out in the streets when it's eighty degrees. Luckily, soon after, air conditioning came in. Air conditioning woke up the South.

With a young family to support, Vernon used what he learned in the military and became a dining entrepreneur. By 1947, a burst of prompt successes afforded the Bells' their first proper home at 416 Holmes Circle in Memphis.

Cindy Bell Coleman: When Daddy was a captain in the Air Force, his job was to go around and set up officers' clubs, which is how he got the experience to open restaurants.

David Bell: He bought the Little Tea Shop from a couple of women in January 1946. It was a luncheon restaurant downtown, when downtown Memphis was a vibrant and fun place. It was between Main Street and Front Street, and the Mississippi River was before you. Main Street had huge department stores, jewelry stores and a lot of movie theaters.

Five years after settling in Memphis, on Friday, January 12, 1951, Christopher Branford Bell was born—just one month after the birth of William Alexander Chilton and two weeks before John Andrew Hummel.

David Bell: The day Chris was born we drove to the Methodist Hospital in Memphis. We couldn't go in, but we looked up to whatever floor it was and could see a waving hand in the window.

Cindy Bell Coleman: There were six of us children. Virginia is the eldest, then David, then Vicky, then Sara, then Chris, and I am the youngest.

Sara Bell: Most of our Sundays were spent on picnics and things like that.

David Bell: Our mother would find these picnic places that were not exactly out in the country, but it felt like you were because you were by some little creek somewhere.

Sara Bell: We would take family vacations every summer. We went to this theme park called Tweetsie Railroad in North Carolina on one. The first trip we took a train all around Grandfather Mountain. But most often we all piled into the station wagon. There would be eight of us in there. The car didn't have a third row, but it had the cargo area. Daddy had it wired up back there with a fan, so it would stay cool because two of us would be lying down. We drove to New York and D.C. Another summer we drove to Florida. Chris and I spent the most time together because we were only fourteen months apart.

By the late 1950s, Vernon was heavily involved in another of his passions: pro golf. With a swelling bank account, it became a tradition for Vernon and Joan to fly to the British Open each year. In May 1958, he solidified his own place in golf history when he co-founded the Memphis Open, the PGA tourney later branded as the FedEx St. Jude Classic. Vernon remained the tournament's general chairman for the next twenty-two years, and recruited icons like Arnold Palmer and Jack Nicklaus to play the event. President Gerald Ford made a hole-in-one during the 1977 celebrity tournament. During his tenure, Vernon also masterminded a local broadcast of the competition, pioneering the telecasting of golf. In 1992, he was posthumously inducted into the Tennessee Sports Hall of Fame for putting Memphis on the pro-golf map while raising millions of dollars for St. Jude Children's Research Hospital.

David Bell: In the summer of 1955, we moved into our second house at 4443 Cherrydale Road in Memphis. That's right when our father opened the Knickerbocker on Poplar.

Linda Schaeffer Yarman — Friend: I met Chris in high school because our parents were in the same circle. His father was a big supporter of the Colonial Country Club golf tournaments, as was my father.

David Bell: I can't remember Chris ever playing golf. I did until I was about fourteen. My claim to fame was I made a birdie on one hole. By the time I was fifteen, I gave it up. I was a swimmer and a diver. Chris didn't play sports in school, but he played tennis much later.

Cindy Bell Coleman: Our father was extremely involved in that tournament. The tournament was a big deal for our family. Every year they would have the courtesy cars for the golfers, and nine times out of ten, Daddy ended up buying it, and that would be his new car for the year. He loved starting restaurants and startups, but once it got going and the startup was successful, he was ready to sell it and move on. Golf was his true passion. He came alive during that.

Sara Bell: He was always betting on the golf course at the Colonial Country Club. That's where our membership was. Growing up, we spent all summer long at the swimming pool, except Daddy, who was on the golf course. But my mother told me he lost interest in playing the game. It was probably because he was so much better than most people. He had played in the British Amateur. Golfers don't enjoy playing unless it's with other people equally as good.

David Bell: The golf tournament was never a money-maker for him. Everything he did in golf was pro bono. It was a lot of work, especially when it got to the part where it was on national television. The more successful it got, the more stressed he got.

While the golf tournament grew alongside his restaurants, the Bell family remained at their modest home on Cherrydale in Memphis. The siblings attended White Station, a public school in Memphis, and mingled with fellow neighborhood kids and the swarms of furry pets that filled their property.

Cindy Bell Coleman: Chris built a clubhouse up in the rafters of the garage at the house on Cherrydale, and he would hang out up there. I had a playhouse Daddy built for me out in the backyard. To us, at the time, it was a huge backyard. Half was a play area and the other half Mother gardened. We always had dogs, always had collies. One was named Colonel and one was Captain. Then a cat wandered up. At one point that cat had kittens and we had sixteen cats. They loved animals. We played in the neighborhood, it was that typical kind of growing up. You would go outside and then be home before dark, the type of thing you can't do anymore.

David Bell: I was just a shade over five years older than Chris. As children, we used to go down to Mississippi occasionally, once or twice a year, to visit my father's family. It was rural for us. We were city kids and thought we were in the sticks, but it was always fun to get out of Memphis. Chris was just a regular kid. He loved putting things together and was a big comic book fan. He really liked *Superman* comics.

Sara Bell: When we lived on Cherrydale, Chris was an avid comic-book collector—*Superman*, *Casper the Friendly Ghost* and *Archie*. He wasn't sharing his comics with anybody.

David Bell: Chris surely had a little temper back then. When he was about ten, he impaled me with a dart in my arm. I made him mad. He was wild into comic books, and sometimes I would want to snag one of them. He didn't like that. I'm lucky he didn't hit a vein.

Sara Bell: Aside from comics, he collected autographs of movie stars. In the back of the movie magazines it told where you could write to get autographs. He wrote off for Marilyn Monroe's signature.

While Chris attended elementary school, Joan managed the homestead and Vernon worked long hours.

Cindy Bell Coleman: We could be anywhere in the world and someone would come up to him and say, "Vernon Bell, how good to see you."

David Bell: Our father noticed that trampolining had become wildly popular when I was still in high school. It was the early '60s when he opened a trampoline place called Jump For Joy. It was close to the Knickerbocker. One day at Jump For Joy, he kicked out a friend of mine, Donna Weiss, who was quite overweight. She later co-wrote "Bette Davis Eyes." But our father's main thing was always restaurants and, by the early '60s, he was well established. He had two restaurants going at that time, the Little Tea Shop and the Knickerbocker. Initially, the Knickerbocker was half the size of what it grew into. It was in an old strip mall near our school, White Station. There were other shops in there; one was a shoe store. After three years, he took over that shoe store and expanded the restaurant. It could hold 360 people.

Cindy Bell Coleman: Dad would go into the Knickerbocker every morning, but someone managed it for him. He worked an awful lot.

Sara Bell: He was the ultimate businessman. Daddy would get home around 8 p.m. and have dinner on the ottoman in his chair sitting in front of the television in the den.

Cindy Bell Coleman: We had already had what Mother called "children's dinner." Before Dad got home, we all sat down to a formal dinner in the dining room—Mother at the head of the table. It was set English-style. We had to use proper manners. If you didn't, you got your ears bopped.

David Bell: My mother was sort of the disciplinarian, though my father was the ultimate disciplinarian. When he got home, God help you if you had to deal with that.

Cindy Bell Coleman: He was very much a man's man. He was soft-spoken, but when it came to discipline, he was very firm. All he had to do was give you a look.

During Chris' early childhood in the 1950s, Memphis staked its claim as the home of blues and rock 'n' roll, thanks to Sam Phillips' Sun Records and Elvis Presley's groundbreaking entrance into mainstream culture. In 1964, a teenaged Chris Bell was not enamored of the King in the slightest. Like millions of others his age, the shaggy-haired Brits fascinated him. It was the same for all three of his future Big Star bandmates, including bassist Andy Hummel, who performed in two teen bands before he met Chris: the Chessmen (on bass) and the Swinging Sensations (on keys).

Andy Hummel — Classmate, bassist, Icewater, Rock City, Big Star: I wasn't particularly aware that Memphis was some huge center of rock 'n' roll or one of the places rock 'n' roll was invented. The groups I listened to came out of New York or Los Angeles. The only thing from Memphis that was rock 'n' roll in those days was Sam Phillips' Sun Records, with Elvis and Carl Perkins. I wasn't particularly conscious it came from Memphis. I wasn't a huge Elvis fan in those days anyway. I didn't get into Elvis until much later. They would have contests on the radio all the time, "Who's the best: the Beatles or Elvis?" There was no question in my mind whatsoever. I was a huge Beatles fan.

David Bell: Our family's house on Cherrydale Road was within a mile or two of Elvis's first nice house on Audubon Drive, but Chris wasn't a big Elvis fan. He was interested in music, but by then Elvis was doing all those ridiculous movies. I was old enough to love early Elvis, but Chris wasn't.

Alex Chilton: When I was little I had a bunch of older brothers and sisters—well, I had one sister and a couple of brothers and in the '50s, it was pretty wild there. Everybody was greasing their hair and blue jeans and T-shirts and black boots, with Elvis being around.

Cindy Bell Coleman: I used to see Elvis riding his motorcycle around in our old neighborhood. He would ride down Cherry Road. We used to hear about Elvis buying people cars and one of Sara's friends dated him for a little bit. That's her big claim to fame now.

Richard Rosebrough — Drummer, Alamo, Dolby Fuckers, Chris Bell, Alex Chilton, recording engineer: Most of our crowd was born into the Beatles and did not care about Elvis. We didn't have time for Elvis, except for maybe as a joke.

Alex Chilton: Elvis? Never laid eyes on him. Once when I was fifteen, me and a friend went out and climbed over the wall at his house and knocked on the back door. This bodyguard named The Chief answered the door and talked to us for about fifteen minutes and then drove us out to where we were parked...He said that Elvis and Priscilla were asleep, it was 10 p.m. Nobody cared much at that time [about Elvis], you know. That was 1966.

Steve Rhea: Aside from music heritage, we didn't ascribe anything terribly great to Memphis. We knew Holiday Inn started here. Memphis had entrepreneurs, it had businesses that were started here. That's a great tradition I didn't come to appreciate until many years later. We sort of took Memphis for granted while our attraction to the British music that was coming over expanded.

Andy Hummel: Being in Memphis, there was an R&B influence because of Stax and WDIA, but I don't think many of us were particularly conscious of that. It was just there. For my peers, it was all about AM radio—the Beach Boys, Four Seasons, the Beatles. During our junior-high days you'd primarily just hear what was on the five buttons on the radio in your car. My mother, being the standard '60s suburban house-wife, had one of those gigantic wood-trimmed station wagons. I remember driving down Poplar Avenue coming home from grade school and hearing "I Want to Hold Your Hand" on the radio. It was like, "Wow!" I had never heard anything like that before, with all that harmony, and how upbeat it was.

Alex Chilton: I loved British music. When I first got interested in rock 'n' roll in 1964, it was when all the British music first started coming out. 1964 through '66, I thought music was great. But then in '67, when all this psychedelic California music started happening...people got more pretentious. But '64 to '66 was still three-minute songs and everything was fairly understandable. It was great.

By the time the British Invasion hit, Chris had already dabbled in the basics of pop music on his guitar. But after he witnessed the Fab Four on television, rock 'n' roll engulfed his teenage life. From there, he dug deeper for other British groups.

Chris Bell: At school, people were getting acoustic guitars and playing folk songs, the Kingston Trio and all that. In the states, that's what was happening. The Beatles came out and somebody would get a bass guitar, we would have a couple acoustics and try to do that kind of thing.

David Bell: Before Chris ever thought about picking up a guitar, I specifically remember him liking Brenda Lee. Everybody has always said Chris got into music when the Beatles went on *Ed Sullivan* in February of '64, but, the year before, he took piano lessons for maybe six months and was starting on guitar. Of course, with the Beatles on *Ed Sullivan*, he and a zillion other kids went crazy and got serious about music.

Sara Bell: We were in the den on Cherrydale and all gathered around to watch the Beatles. Even my mother was thrilled. It was unusual for her to show interest in what we were watching, but because they were from England she found it entertaining. She was standing at the back of the room just smiling and, of course, it changed Chris' life.

Chris Bell: I started playing guitar pretty early—I was twelve or thirteen. It was around the time the Beatles were first hitting in the States. That was the only thing up to that point that encouraged me to get into music of any kind.

Steve Rhea: The whole world changed when the Beatles appeared on *Ed Sullivan*. Almost any musician in Memphis will tell you the same thing.

Cindy Bell Coleman: Chris was obsessed with the Beatles.

Chris Bell: They were the only thing that sort of moved me to be interested in rock 'n' roll, or music, guitar playing and such. Before that, music was a side thing, something that went on in the background. That went on for a year or two until I got turned on to some English music, which was like the Who's first album and the Yardbirds. Then I started playing in several electric groups.

While he was nearly two years younger than Chris, future Big Star drummer Jody Stephens was also in awe of the new sounds. The two would meet years later and connect over their love of the Fab Four.

Jody Stephens: Ringo and the Beatles got me into drumming. Charlie Watts was amazing, too. They were the perfect drummers for those bands. A great drummer to me is somebody who fits well into a band and fits well into the songs. Ringo was so creative. Early on, Ringo was doing six one-hour sets with Rory Storm in Hamburg. His chops were amazing. You watch Ringo do shuffles and sing, that's hard as hell. "Help" was a shuffle. There were so many things that were shuffles that made me think, "Why does this feel different to me?" Add to that McCartney's walking basslines, which were probably influenced by Duck Dunn and Booker T.

Steve Rhea: The British Invasion wasn't only about the music. It was about the groups, the fashions, the lingo, the architecture—everything. It impacted us on a lot of levels and created an intense interest. Back then, Memphis was pretty parochial. They didn't think much beyond the city limits, or, certainly, beyond the tri-state area. The British Invasion immediately caused us to think about the world, or at least Europe. And the women: they had beehive hairdos and were wearing the weirdest clothes. Then the Beatles came and just transformed all that. We were totally into what was coming, not what had been. We saw ourselves as avant-garde. We saw ourselves as ushering in a whole new wave of art, music, movies, fashion and ways of thinking.

Carole Ruleman Manning: I had asked Chris if he wanted anything from London, because I was getting ready to go there. He brought me this clipping from the *NME* and said, "Yeah, I want these boots."

Tom Eubanks: Everything was profoundly dead before the Beatles came. There was Fabian, Bobby Darin doing "Mack the Knife," and

Elvis doing his movie scores. Then the Beatles came out and the Kinks hit it big with "You Really Got Me."

Andy Hummel: The neighborhood kids and I would go down to Poplar Tunes, or Pop Tunes, to buy 45s with our allowance. I can remember going to peoples' houses to listen to singles. That's the thing you did. Somebody would have a little record player and a pile of 45s.

Steve Rhea: For the most part, the Beatles were doing whole albums of original material. That was just unheard of. Prior to that, everything was about singles, the old 45 discs. People would have a hit and people would go buy the single for $1. When the Beatles came on, they ushered in album music where you liked every song on it.

Tom Eubanks: Every record Chris mentioned, I owned. I just figured everyone had every Who and Beatles record. He wasn't a big Rolling Stones fan, but I owned all the Stones albums.

Chris Bell: The Rolling Stones were getting very big. The Beatles were still doing well, and some other groups had popped up. Plus, Herman's Hermits was coming over with the Dave Clark Five. That was pretty much dominating the charts in the United States. Up to then, it had been groups like the Shirelles and the Essex.

Andy Hummel: In seventh grade, I got clued in to the fact there were bands, so I pestered my parents until they bought me a bass and started playing in a little garage band called the Chessmen. I was in a band with Jody Stephen's brother Jimmy Stephens, he was one of the singers in the band. That's how I first met Jody. He sat in on drums a few times when our regular drummer wasn't available. We played songs like "Louie Louie." It was typical garage-band sets.

By 1965, Vernon Bell had amassed a small fortune through his dining enterprise. He moved the family to a striking two-story home on a wooded property at 1447 Riverdale Road in Germantown, a countryside suburb of Memphis. The newly built, 4,734-square-foot manor with eleven rooms boasted five bedrooms and four bathrooms. In the backyard was a large pool, which Chris was assigned to clean as his main household chore. At the time, Germantown was still a largely undeveloped, rural stretch, but was rapidly growing. Between 1950 and 1960, the population tripled to over 1,100 residents thanks to subdivision developments. Today it surpasses 39,000 citizens.

Cindy Bell Coleman: Sundays were always a big day at our house. Daddy would bring steak or fried chicken home from the restaurant for the big Sunday dinner. That continued as we moved to Germantown.

We moved there when I was in the fifth grade. There was nothing in Germantown when he bought the acreage out there and built the house.

David Bell: My father could buy the property and build the new house because of his succession of successes. All of his business ventures worked out well.

Steve Rhea: Chris' parents moved into what was then the country. They built a house like Tara in *Gone With the Wind*, a beautiful white mansion with columns in that classic Southern style.

Vera Ellis — Friend, Alex Chilton's ex-girlfriend, John Fry's sister-in-law: That's how it felt to us, like it was the perfect home: Don't go in there, you might get it dirty.

David Bell: Germantown is east of Memphis. We had twenty acres out there. Everybody was excited about the move. Germantown had always been known as this horsey village just outside of Memphis. Of course, now it's one big extension.

Robert Gordon: Back then, it was still rural and rich. You'd see signs saying "Cars 35" and "Horses 10." It was a big horse town. Well, nothing about it was big. It was like you had to go through the country to get there. Downtown Germantown was a wooden store.

Cindy Bell Coleman: Back then, there were the neighbors down the street that were in tiny houses they had been in for generations. The man who lived directly to the right was Mr. McPherson. He was 99 years old when he died. He would tell stories about when he was a little boy and how he heard cannons going off during the Civil War. At our place, we had horses, ponies and a pond out in the pasture. I used to swim the horses through the pond all the time and ride down the road. Where there are now houses used to be riding stables and not too far from us there was a race track. I didn't appreciate it at the time, but it was a neat place to grow up. It was lovely and laid-back. You could just go and wander. Chris would ride occasionally, just fooling around, but that wasn't his thing.

As he entered his freshman year of high school, Chris was transferred from White Station, a public school, to Memphis University School, a private preparatory school in East Memphis. The MUS Owls were known as an elite batch of uniformed students, but that didn't stop Chris from seeking out the school's edgier rock-music zealots, like classmate Steve Rhea. Born July 3, 1949, Steve ultimately collaborated with Chris in two pre-Big Star outfits, the high school garage band Christmas Future and Icewater, an early-'70s studio project.

Chris and sister Sara Bell with their
mother, Joan.

The Bells: (Front row, L-R): Sara, Chris,
Vicky. (Back): Virginia, David.

Vernon Bell with celebrity player President Gerald Ford in 1977 at the professional
golf tournament now dubbed the FedEx St. Jude Classic.

Chris and sister Virginia Bell.

Joan and Vernon Bell aboard the Queen Mary.

(left): Sara and Chris Bell on vacation, 1961. (right): Vernon Bell holding Chris.

Steve Rhea: Chris and I both transferred from White Station to MUS, the best boys' private school in Memphis. We were both public-school kids until the last few years, so we didn't feel like our families were any aristocratic Memphis families or that we had grown up rich, though Chris' family was probably a little bit more well-to-do than mine.

Rick Clark — Journalist, producer, musician, Alex Chilton, Prix, Tommy Hoehn: MUS was the school where rich kids went. MUS is like junior high through high school.

Alex Chilton: Money ruled the entire thing [at MUS]. Whatever kids had the most money had the dominance.

Tommy Hoehn — Singer-songwriter, Prix, solo: John Fry, Andy Hummel, Chris Bell, myself, and Steve Burns [the Scruffs] all went to MUS. It was a little elitist. We were raised on the Beatles, raised away from girls. That strange environment, as much as anything, is what created that [British-inspired] direction, that sound. That was where East Memphis white kids fled to.

While the Bell family was experiencing the perks of the American dream, President John F. Kennedy had already been assassinated, and the Vietnam War was escalating under the watch of President Lyndon B. Johnson. Racial tensions burned across the United States, especially in the South. It wasn't until September 1959 that "Colored Waiting Room" signs were removed from the local Greyhound station.

Tommy Hoehn: It's a curious thing. The race card in the city is one that has molded, from my perspective, the music in this city. The whites ran from the blacks for a long time and tried to carve out their own little music scene.

Alex Chilton: The first time that public schools started to be integrated in Memphis was 1963, and it started with just my grade. They brought maybe twenty or thirty black people to be in our class. It was really tough for those few black kids. It was the very beginning of any type of integration and white flight—all the white kids went off to private schools.

David Bell holding his little brother Chris in front of their childhood home in Memphis.

BELL FAMILY ARCHIVE

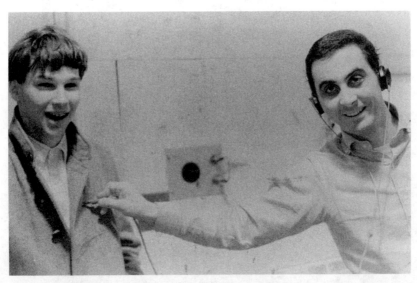

Chris Bell with DJ George Klein of WHBQ-AM and host of *Talent Party*, 1965.

PHOTO BY CAROLE MANNING

CHAPTER 2

THE JYNX — TEEN SCENE: 1965-1966

Chris played in a string of teen bands with a mishmash of friends, some of whom ultimately collaborated with him on a series of projects at Ardent Studios. By 1965, things were getting serious when Chris, a freshman at Memphis University School, met future Box Tops bassist Bill Cunningham and formed the Jynx—his first foray into performing rock 'n' roll in front of high school crowds. As the band's lead guitarist, he tore through the innovative riffs of his idols, like the Who's Pete Townshend and the Yardbirds' Jeff Beck and Eric Clapton. The Jynx were a part of a new wave of Memphis garage bands, though a previous generation had already forged the path across the Bluff City.

David Bell: A big local band in the early to mid-'60s Memphis garage-rock scene was Tommy Burk & the Counts. They were like a half-generation before Chris' band the Jynx. I remember the Counts when I was in high school. They played parties. There was another band, the Gentrys, they had a hit in 1965 with "Keep on Dancing." The Gentrys had Jimmy Hart and Larry Raspberry. They'd have a Battle of the Bands every weekend in Memphis. It was a big, big scene.

Larry Raspberry — Singer-songwriter, guitarist, the Gentrys, Alamo, the Highsteppers: After all the band gigs on Friday and Saturday nights, it wasn't unusual to see all these bands at Shoney's grabbing some food with their audience. It was exciting.

Van Duren — Singer-songwriter, Baker Street Regulars, solo, Loveland Duren: Chris came up in garage bands in the '60s. Those teen bands did everything from Stax and Motown to Beatles and British Invasion. Most versions of those bands did the same type of material.

There wasn't a whole lot of distinction because they'd just play parties. They'd play what people wanted to hear.

Alex Chilton: Some of the older bands were playing some soulful songs, but kids my age were pretty Beatles-influenced.

Bill Cunningham — Bassist, keyboardist, the Jynx, Devilles, the Box Tops: I first met Chris through music at the tail end of '64. Together, with a couple of fellow musicians from my old junior high band, we started the Jynx in early 1965. I would spend the night at the Bells' house. Chris and I became best friends as soon as we met. We hung out all the time. All of us were dreamers. Chris took music seriously. The Jynx would play high school parties almost every weekend for Memphis University School and Hutchison students. We mainly played rich kids' parties by the poolside. It kept us pretty busy. We knew everybody there and they all knew us. I don't know how big our following was across Memphis. I certainly wouldn't consider it significant.

Leo Goff — Bassist, the Jynx: The Jynx name was a takeoff on the Kinks.

David Bell: They wore matching jackets so they'd look Beatles-ish or Kinks-ish. DeWitt Shy was the drummer and his mother booked them gigs. There were some garage parties and shows like that. I was at a lot of their shows because I had a driver's license and I would lug Chris and his equipment from party to party and to his band practices.

Bill Cunningham: We played a lot of songs, but mostly British Invasion covers. It was not Memphis soul music, but we did play things like "Walking the Dog" and several other Memphis-based tunes. It wasn't like we didn't do any soul, but most of it was the Zombies, Beatles, Rolling Stones, Them and the Moody Blues.

Among the crowd at the weekend parties was Alex Chilton, born December 28, 1950, in Memphis. One of four children, Alex's life was different from the jump. At six years old, he witnessed his older brother's tragic drowning, following a seizure, in the family's bathtub. His father, Sidney Chilton, was a jazz musician and his mother, Mary, ran an art gallery out of their home. This Central High School student was an accepted outsider.

Alex Chilton: I was about thirteen years old in 1964. I was a public-school kid, but somehow my family was hooked up with all these rich, society people in town and I started going to their little circuit parties. It was the same people at every party. It was my scene from the time I was in junior high school until the time I quit school to become a rock star.

David Bell: Chris and Alex knew each other for a couple years before the Box Tops took off in '67.

Alex Chilton: Their parents would let them have a big party for all their little private-school friends. It would be around a pool or inside the house and the parents would always hire a band to play. Half the time, it would be Chris' band the Jynx with DeWitt Shy on the drums and Bill Cunningham on the bass, plus whoever was singing. These parties were full of these rich, beautiful kids. Every week there seemed to be one or two parties. That's where I got to know Chris. It was a magical, wonderful scene.

Chris' growing circle of friends spanned beyond MUS. He soon found camaraderie with some fellow mischievous teens at the adjacent all-girls school. Andy Hummel, who transferred to MUS one year after Chris, joined the mix.

Linda Schaeffer Yarman: MUS was next door to the private girls' school I went to, Hutchison School. Andy and Chris both took art classes held at the girls' school. I encountered that whole bunch through mutual friends.

David Bell: Chris' close friends at the time were Carole Ruleman Manning and her friends. They were the female counterparts to all these MUS boys who were rebels, rock 'n' rollers and lovers of anything English.

Carole Ruleman Manning: I had known Alex Chilton since I was twelve years old. I dated him at thirteen and fourteen. I had known Chris since I was fourteen, dated him when I was fifteen and sixteen.

Andy Hummel: It was pretty cool. Those girls were of like mind to Chris and me. The wild childs of MUS and the wild childs of Hutchison's somehow met each other and hit it off.

Linda Schaeffer Yarman: Our inner circle of friends were the odd people out, the rebellious ones at the school. We just loved Chris. He was liked by everybody, but he was quiet, shy and into music.

Cindy Bell Coleman: Chris' room was always completely consumed with guitars and amplifiers, all sorts of music paraphernalia and posters.

Sara Bell: I was into Motown and loved that music. I just didn't relate to what he was doing. When I think of Chris, I think of him in his room constantly playing songs and practicing.

Steve Rhea: We saw ourselves in that school setting as being different and separate from the other guys. However, I was more aware of cliques and snobbery at White Station, the big public school. I was totally accepted at MUS. People respected me for my talent and they did for Chris as well. But they were a little more Ivy League-type.

Alex Chilton: These weren't angry, young poor kids. These were the ultimate privileged class of Memphis. They didn't have anything to rebel against. If they had, they would have been cut out of their parents' wills. That's how these kids were kept under control. I was a bit of an outsider, but it wasn't a huge deal. Surely, all these people had a ton of money and I wasn't one of the richies.

Carole Ruleman Manning: Alex and Chris really did lead different lives. Alex was from an arty, Midtown-neighborhood background. Chris was from an upwardly mobile, East Memphis businessman's child background.

Michael O'Brien — Classmate, friend, photographer: Chris and I lived out in East Memphis and Alex lived in Midtown, the older, historic area of Memphis. East was a new, nouveau-suburban area. The Chiltons' house on Montgomery was a great place to hang out during those teenage years. Alex had very permissive parents.

Andy Hummel: I also lived in Midtown Memphis. It was much more diverse living in an older neighborhood like that. The environment Chris grew up in, out in Germantown, was much different from mine. He grew up on what had previously been plantations out on the countryside. Midtown was generally professional people who lived in those neighborhoods because their father had to get to the hospital pretty quick if somebody went into labor, or the attorney had to get to the court building every morning. In those days they were all in downtown Memphis. There were also horrible shotgun-house neighborhoods just a block away. It was literally that diverse.

Gary Stevens — Classmate, friend: Andy's father was Dr. John Vernon Hummel, a handsome and tall baby doctor. He was well known in Memphis, worked with Methodist Hospital for thirty years. Andy learned a lot about cars from his father, who was an autophile. He was also a gourmet cook and known in the wine circle—very cultured. You would expect that when your wife, Barbara, is Miss America 1947. The music came from his mother, she was a talented pianist and a singer. Andy also loved photography and he was good at it. His father indulged him with nice cameras from Germany and let him build his own photo studio in the attic of their house.

Tom Eubanks: Chris came from a well-to-do family and was a little bit spoiled, but not overly so. He was always trying to bum money from people. Chris would try to borrow money for cigarettes all the time. I knew he was getting a liberal allowance from his parents for basically doing nothing, so I asked our friend John Dando about it one time. Dando said, "Chris is saving up for a leather jacket just like the one John Lennon is wearing on the cover of *Rubber Soul*—it's down at Lansky's."

Linda Schaffer Yarman: Chris was absolutely not spoiled. That is the opposite of Christopher. He was one of the most kind and humble people I've ever met.

Sara Bell: We just weren't raised spoiled, but it looked like we were because of the house. But my friends all had more than I did, same with Chris. They all had the newest clothes and whatnot. Us kids had a car, but there would be three or four of us sharing it. The oldest was required to get everyone else around, so I was usually giving Chris rides to get where he needed to go. We had a Volkswagen Karmann Ghia, that's the one he forgot to put motor oil in and it broke down on the interstate. The motor blew up.

Tom Eubanks: I never saw Chris act in a supercilious manner. He was never disdainful of others or putting anybody down. He cursed some, but not a lot. He was a well-mannered, quiet and somewhat refined guy. We were always just talking about the records we were listening to at the time.

Richard Rosebrough: Vernon Bell was old school. He was from Mississippi and came from humble beginnings. He didn't just give his children things. When they were growing up, they had to earn it. They had to go get a job. It wasn't given to them on a silver platter.

Andy Hummel: Any time I went to hang out with Chris, which I did quite a lot before we got heavily into Big Star, it seemed like a wonderful life he led out there. They had this colonial-style house on this gigantic, wonderful lot. He had three sisters who all seemed like interesting people. His mother was a nice person, plus she was British, which was cool. I never saw much of Mr. Bell, I saw David a little bit. The only thing I ever thought was a little peculiar was Chris had such a difficult time getting his parents to buy him musical instruments, which I never found difficult for some reason. I don't know why my parents were so easy about that because they weren't easy about anything else. I was forced to do music since I was in the third grade. Nobody else in the Bell family was musical at all. In Chris' case, it was kind of an off-the-wall thing.

The Jynx were regulars in the preppy party scene, but the group was not afraid to hit the streets of Memphis, either. The band shared bills at numerous teen clubs that popped up in the wake of Beatlemania.

The Box Tops, 1968 (L-R) Bill Cunningham (organ), Alex Chilton (vocals, guitar), Gary Talley (guitar), Rick Allen (bass), Tom Boggs (drums).

PHOTO COURTESY OF BILL CUNNINGHAM

A teenaged John Fry in his home studio with (future FedEx founder) Fred Smith at the dawn of Ardent Studios, January 1960.

ARDENT STUDIOS ARCHIVE

Chris Bell, Terry Manning, and Michael O'Brien in Ardent Studios' control room.

PHOTO BY MICHAEL O'BRIEN

Chris requesting a Beatles-style cut at his local barber shop.

PHOTO BY JOHN DANDO

Steve Rhea: The teen clubs were always run by these guys nobody knew. They had vacant buildings, so they decided to make money off this phenomenon of teens that needed a place to go. They formed these teen clubs and invited local bands to come in and play for a cut of the door. These places were just wild, crazy and dark. People had dances at Skateland Frayser, places like that. At this time, there are no clubs or Liquor by the Drink [alcohol sales at establishments were restricted until late 1969] in Memphis. There was nothing going on in Memphis nightlife, and then suddenly music ignited everybody. There was a teen club down near the bridge in the Pinch District called the Roaring 60s. There was another teen club in Midtown around Cleveland and Madison called the Tonga Club.

Alex Chilton: There was another one called the Go-Go that was also in Midtown. Those were happening all the time on the weekends. Must have been a fuckin' hundred teenage bands in town, there was an endless amount of teenage rock 'n' roll bands in Memphis at the time. The clubs were almost all white. A couple of bands may have had a black singer here or there, but in general the color line was pretty starkly drawn and almost all these bands were playing British Invasion, white rock 'n' roll.

Cindy Bell Coleman: One of his band's shows was at our sister Sara's sixteenth birthday party out in our backyard near what we called "the wild garden." It was near a grove of trees. My mother planted it like a wild-land garden and it had a little pond. The band set up next to that and played for Sara's birthday party. This wasn't too far from the backhouse.

For Chris, a perk of moving into the new house in Germantown was gaining access to an old one-story house the family christened the "backhouse." Positioned at the back of the property, it was promptly filled with guitars and gear. Chris used the rickety shack as a creative space for years to come. It also served as a secluded haunt to smoke cigarettes and experiment with booze and pot.

David Bell: The backhouse had sat at the very front of the property on Riverdale Road but was moved to the very back of the property when my father bought it. Rather than tear it down or burn it, my father, being frugal, thought, "We'll put it at the back of the property." Then we built our new house in its place. In short order, Chris asked our father if he could use it for band rehearsals. That's when my father had it hooked up for electricity.

Cindy Bell Coleman: The backhouse was his hangout place. They padded all the walls and would practice their music.

Steve Rhea: It was this little clapboard, wood-sided house that had two rooms, a kitchen, and a bath. It was just a cheap, pier-and-beam wooden house.

Tom Eubanks: The backhouse was left on blocks and you could see right under it because Mr. Bell didn't go through a whole hell of a lot of trouble trying to dig footings and build a foundation when he moved it.

Bill Cunningham: It was far enough away from everything that you could turn the amps up, make a lot of noise, and no one would complain.

Terry Manning: We would go out there and almost anybody involved at some point in that revolving door hung out there. We would do photography or set up the amps and play.

Linda Schaeffer Yarman: I was only at the backhouse a couple times. That was their hangout. When Andy and Chris wanted to take a break from music that's when they called me and we hung out together. We would tear across town doing whatever.

Vera Ellis: We acted stupid out in that backhouse. They'd be playing music, smoking a little pot, drinking a few beers, smoking cigarettes, which, back then we were not supposed to be doing. Sometimes we went swimming, too. The Bells had a pretty pool with a lovely waterfall. The only time I went in their house was when someone cut himself and Chris took him inside. His mother got these gorgeous white towels from her gorgeous white house and was taking care of the blood and helping to mend the wound. She was this pristine woman in her pristine home. His mother was always nice to us, but I don't know what she actually thought about us.

Sara Bell: Our mother was pulled in every direction, but I would say Chris was her favorite.

Tom Eubanks: Chris respected his mom. When we practiced in his backhouse, we had to drive back there. I remember him saying, "Hey guys, be careful driving up in here because my mother works her ass off on these flower beds back here."

David Bell: Chris had ideas of turning the backhouse into a studio. He certainly wanted to be able to make all the noise he possibly could. No one was going to allow that kind of volume in the house. When he discovered Ardent Studios a couple years later, he and his friends migrated there.

After Alex and Chris bonded at house-party gigs, the pair decided to work together musically. A Jynx gig would be the duo's first public collaboration.

Chris Bell: In 1965, I first met Alex Chilton, who wasn't really into music at that time, but he started playing some gigs with us.

Drew DeNicola: If anyone was a true musician in the early days, it was Chris. Alex wasn't in the Box Tops yet. He was just a kid who hung out and sang a bit.

Alex Chilton: I couldn't play or anything...I wasn't in any bands at the time. I was singing with some guys in my neighborhood and Chris invited me to audition with their band and I guess he dug it. We rehearsed a few times.

Chris Bell: Alex came and did a couple gigs with us. He didn't take it seriously at all. He just had a mimic, or something he could do with his voice that would make it sound very gruff.

Alex Chilton: It was kind of like imitating black records.

Chris Bell: Sometimes he'd come in and sing like that just as a joke and walk off after two numbers. Alex did talk to me a couple of times about doing a gig. I tried to talk him into joining the group I was with because he could sing quite well.

David Bell: Alex Chilton sang with the Jynx a few times. I specifically remember a gig they had at Christian Brothers High School in Memphis. It was the first time I ever saw Alex or certainly heard him sing. I was knocked out.

Chris Bell: I could see Alex was getting interested in the music, but he was more into Otis Redding and the whole soul and R&B thing.

Steve Rhea: People that knew Alex in high school said he was always different, the James Dean character in your class. He grew up the son of musicians, had a different way of dressing and all of that. He was also just extremely intelligent. Even before he had any kind of success, there was something about how he talked, or just his presence, that was noteworthy.

While he was never an official member of the Jynx, Alex almost sang on the band's sole recording session. The four songs, released decades later as The Jynx's Greatest Hits!, *a ten-inch vinyl via Norton Records, feature Bill Cunningham on bass, Dewitt Shy on drums, David Hoback on rhythm guitar, and Chris on lead. After Alex flaked out on the session, Mike Harris stepped in as vocalist. The* Nuggets-*style tracks, including a primitive take on Van Morrison's "Little*

Girl," were recorded so the band could lip-sync the covers on a local television program.

Alex Chilton: Chris said they had a recording session. I guess I was just scared of the entire procedure. I told him I would be there, but I didn't go. I instead went out and got drunk or something. I didn't go to the session.

Chris Bell: We continued, Alex drifted off. He wasn't very interested in music back then because he wasn't playing any instruments.

Alex Chilton: This was at least a year before I went into the studio with the Box Tops.

Bill Cunningham: The Jynx recorded those songs for George Klein's Saturday afternoon WHBQ TV show, *Talent Party*, which featured local acts as well as nationally known artists.

Steve Rhea: *Talent Party* was a knockoff of Dick Clark's *American Bandstand* on a local basis. Chris and his band went down there. George Klein was a local DJ on WHPQ. He had local acts come in and lip-sync their songs. Klein was interested in the bands playing around Memphis in these local high schools.

Bill Cunningham: I had arranged the studio time with Roland Janes, the producer of the session, at Sonic Studios in Memphis. Travis Wammack was the engineer on the session. Wammack was known for his instrumental hit "Scratchy."

Robert Johnson — Guitarist, singer-songwriter, John Entwistle's Ox, session player, solo: Sonic Studios was pretty cool, just an old beauty parlor kind of place. The building is still there, right down the street from Ardent. He built a control room and put egg crates all over the walls. Everybody and their mammy recorded there because they wanted to be on *Talent Party*. You'd have to submit a tape, and if they liked it they'd let you on the TV show.

Even with a steady flow of gigs and a television appearance, the Jynx called it quits after just over a year. While some of the Jynx members returned their focus to homework, Chris' musical focus swelled. From there, the MUS sophomore partook in a string of cover bands with Memphis pals like drummer Richard Rosebrough, born September 16, 1949, who became lifelong friends with Chris and one of his steady musical cohorts during his mid-'70s solo years.

Bill Cunningham: After the Jynx broke up I moved on to another group called the Jokers, a band already established around town. The drummer was Richard Rosebrough, who went on to play drums for Chris on "I Am the Cosmos." It was after that short time with the Jokers that I joined the Box Tops.

Richard Rosebrough: You can thank Bill Cunningham for introducing Chris to everyone. That was the first link. I first met Chris in my mother's living room back when I was sixteen and playing with the Jokers. Bill, who was our keyboard player, said, "I've got this friend named Chris Bell, I want to bring him by to jam with us." Chris had his red Gibson and one of those old Bassman amplifiers with four ten-inch speakers. After that we developed a friendship. When Chris would come into town he'd stop by my house and hang out. We would jump in the car and go out to the record store and listen to the newest Who and Kinks records. Of course, we would always be talking about the Beatles.

Chris Bell: The guys in those early groups were mostly the crowd who would all end up at Ardent Studios, like Richard Rosebrough and Terry Manning.

Robert Johnson: Terry Manning became an incredible engineer at Ardent and a creative guy. He was probably one of the better engineers to come out of Memphis. Back then we only had three television channels and there were no video games or Internet. All we did was sit in our rooms and play guitar. That breed is totally gone in modern times. That's why a lot of us were great musicians.

THE JYNX

(15) IPS MASTER COPIS HEADS OUT

TITLE	TIME
1- I GO CRAZY	2:14
2- XTP JUST LIKE ME (F)	2:10
3- TP AND MY BABIS GONE (mF)	2:20
4- X LITTLE GIRL	1:55

BILL CUNNIMGHAM   B. CUNNINGHAM
324 9765

Bill Cunningham's original tape box from the Jynx's recording session at Sonic Studios in Memphis, 1965.

"Definitely a Rodin!" comments Art Editor Chris Bell *(in shades)*, as Assoc. Editors Barney Gordon, Frank Crumbaugh, and David Luther muse over their own opinions of this metal sculpture of a World War I ace, which the group found in a secluded alcove of Brooks Memorial Art Gallery while looking for ideas for the cover of the 1969 *Muse*.

A snippet from the 1969 MUS yearbook, detailing Chris Bell's role as arts editor for
Muse, a school publication.

PHOTO COURTESY OF THE MEMPHIS UNIVERSITY SCHOOL ARCHIVE

CHAPTER 3

THE LETTER — THE STUDIO: 1967

After the Jynx dissolved, Chris spent his sophomore year, 1967, casually jamming in one-off garage bands. Chris branded himself as an outsider who smoked Lark-brand cigarettes and had an uncommon passion for not only rock 'n' roll, but also experimental photography and art-house films. Further expanding his sixteen-year-old mind were two landmark albums released that year. In May, Jimi Hendrix debuted with his revolutionary Are You Experienced *LP. A month later, the Beatles unveiled a new world with its eighth studio album,* Sgt. Pepper's Lonely Hearts Club Band. *Chris absorbed these pioneering sounds and studiously hashed out the notes on his electric guitar, a red Gibson ES-330.*

Andy Hummel: Chris and I were particularly rebellious...We didn't want to be a part of that rich white-boy MUS scene. We just became a part of our own scene.

David Bell: Chris going to MUS was sort of a schizophrenic thing for him. On one hand, he liked several people he knew at the school, like Andy Hummel and Steve Rhea, but he also liked to buck the rules. He wanted to be rock 'n' roll, and the boys at MUS had to wear coats and ties.

Andy Hummel: When we were in high school, the only exposure to the drug and hippie culture I had was reading about it in *LIFE* magazine, like everybody else. I don't recall there being anybody in Memphis with particularly long hair or wearing big bell-bottom pants or anything like that. They would have kicked you out of where I went to school if you tried that. You would have lasted ten seconds.

David Bell: Chris would leave the house dressed suitably for his school and have a second set of clothes underneath—striped pants with bell bottoms and a rock 'n' roll-style shirt or something. Then my parents would get these phone calls, "Sorry, Mr. Bell, Chris' attire is not appropriate."

Sara Bell: My mother said Chris was so disappointed because he liked to play basketball, but the school wouldn't let him try out for the team if he didn't cut his hair. That wasn't going to happen.

Steve Rhea: Chris called the normal kids in our class "the Sweater Gang" because they all wore sweaters. There was nothing distinctive about the way they dressed, wore their hair or anything. It looked like they were all twin brothers.

Andy Hummel: We were sort of misfits...We did everything we could think of to put ourselves 180-degrees opposite of our parents. My parents took me out of public schools because they were afraid I was going to knock some girl up in the ninth grade. They really thought that.

Carole Ruleman Manning: Just about all of us felt separated from everything. We didn't want to identify with the mainstream preppy sort at school.

Bill Cunningham: Chris only cared about music, art, and photography.

Richard Rosebrough: Steve Rhea and Carole Ruleman would hang out at the backhouse when they'd do photography. Chris also did a lot of camera work with Michael O'Brien, who later on shot some of the famous Big Star promotional photos.

Michael O'Brien: Chris was extraordinary and sure of himself. He knew what he liked and what he didn't like. When I think back, in contrast to what kids were like in high school, most are unformed and unsure. Chris had a focused direction, which set him apart. He was fun loving, funny, and very witty. He'd make jokes. I never saw a morose and dark Chris. He would come over to my house in East Memphis, and my mother adored him. Chris was probably her favorite person. He was always polite and would always tease.

Andy Hummel: He was elitist as hell, but he wasn't pompous. I don't remember anything moody or confrontational about him at this point. Chris was a leading-edge kind of guy. He was at the forefront.

Michael O'Brien: Chris was a perfectionist. Even the way he dressed was meticulous. He always buttoned the top button of his shirt, which was unusual at that time.

David Bell: He was reserved and quiet, but he was kind of mercurial. Carole said Chris could go from zero to one hundred in about two seconds if something struck him as hysterical or inspired him.

Andy Hummel: We were also into English and Italian movies. They weren't easy to see. They didn't play much in Memphis, but we had an art theater.

David Bell: Chris and his friends went to the Guild Art Theatre. They showed French and English films. I was studying French. It was an influential place for the arty sect in Memphis.

Sara Bell: He loved foreign films, a lot of British titles. He and his friends would go see things like *Georgy Girl*.

Michael O'Brien: He was influenced by *Blow-Up*, the movie. The main character was a fashion photographer in the London scene. After seeing the film, Chris loved the idea of a little spy camera. He experimented with his photos. He had a Minox camera and would use infrared film. There was a thing called infrared slide film. If you put a certain filter over it, you could make these psychedelic-looking pictures. He was technically proficient.

David Bell: He had a scientific and mathematical bent to him. We were endlessly at Radio Shack. It was the place to find affordable microphones for their bands—amplifiers and PA systems, or anything to do with stereos and speakers. We would go to Radio Shack to get a tube. I don't know if he ever built an amplifier, but he wasn't far from it. He certainly could repair them.

Tom Eubanks: Instead of being the usual Southern boy playing football and being a jock, Chris was regarded as the slightly odd, artistic type.

Gary Stevens: He wasn't a social person and a lot of people took it offensively. Chris was just totally shy. That is often misinterpreted as being snobbish or self-indulgent. Chris was neither of those things. He was just socially inept. He didn't speak with confidence. He was a solitary individual and it stood in his way.

Tom Eubanks: But Chris wasn't a cat people made fun of or fucked with, not that he would have fought anybody. He would have just put them down verbally. There was nothing stupid about Chris. He was more cerebral.

Linda Schaeffer Yarman: That's what we liked about him—that artistic soul he had. He wasn't just all out there.

Drew DeNicola: Chris was selective in a lot of his dealings with people and what he was doing musically. He was savvy. He was like, "These are my people and it's us against them." He was sophisticated as a teenager. Later, Big Star was his ultimate creation based on his discriminative taste of every single element of that band. The members were chosen carefully. The sounds were worked over and obsessed over. He used to refer to him and his friends as being like Apple. That was his plan, to have a Memphis version of Apple.

Tom Eubanks: Chris always wanted to put together a band like our perception of the Beatles: four good friends who are making this great music and having a great life.

Chris' passion for the Beatles was invigorated after he witnessed his heroes in the flesh during the band's final tour, which stopped at Memphis' Mid-South Coliseum on August 19, 1966. John, Paul, George and Ringo performed two concerts at the venue. Coincidentally, his father had a monetary hand in bringing the group to town.

David Bell: Our father got us tickets through a giveaway at his restaurant. This was during the band's whole "we're more popular than Jesus" fiasco. I was twenty at the time. I had flunked out of Memphis State and then worked in a factory for six months. I saved all my money and did my grand tour of France, Spain, Italy, and England. I came back with a Parlophone pressing of *Rubber Soul* for Chris in the summer of '66. He was thrilled. I got back just in time for the concert.

Cindy Bell Coleman: After Daddy sold Bonanza, he started his own steakhouse chain called Buckaroo, and that's where he did the giveaway for the tickets. We all went to the concert as a family. I remember looking around at all of the girls screaming and thinking, *Why are you crying? They're up there playing music! What's wrong with you?*

While Chris cheered on the Beatles and dreamed of becoming a rock star, the teenaged Alex Chilton was literally on the verge of superstardom after he garnered attention for his blue-eyed-soul-inspired voice. All of this stemmed from Alex's short stint fronting a popular local garage band called the Devilles. When the original lead singer quit, the Devilles' remaining members, bassist Bill Cunningham, guitarist Gary Talley and drummer Danny Smythe, hired keyboardist John Evans and Alex as frontman. After local DJ Roy Mack connected the band with producers Dan Penn and Chips Moman, the group hit American Sound Studio in Memphis and rebranded as the Box Tops. As Alex defiantly flunked his sophomore year at Central High School, he was simultaneously on the verge of success. By September 1967, "The Letter," the group's second single on Mala Records, reached No. 1 on Billboard.

Alex Chilton: The Box Tops was originally called Ronnie & The DeVilles, and their singer left. Some of those guys had heard me sing with my band of people my age. I was sixteen and they were about twenty. They had a big local band and if I joined their group I could make $100 every weekend.

Bill Cunningham: Alex was called in by John Evans who saw him singing at Central High.

Steve Rhea: You would see them playing all over. Supermarkets might have them play to attract teens. We were the leading edge of the baby boomers, so people exploited the music for some commercial advantage.

Chris Bell: Roy Mack, who was a radio station engineer, got together with Alex and formulated the idea of the Box Tops with an early group called the Devilles.

Alex Chilton: We kept working together. Their manager [Roy Mack] was a big disc jockey in town and he had an in with the recording studio, the big independent producers in town. [Roy] would break their records on the radio, so they had to do anything for him and he managed this band.

Chris Bell: I was over at his house when Roy brought over some tunes by a country artist for Alex to listen to. He brought over the tapes and I remember hearing the tape with "The Letter," which was a country tune. He said, "We want a Motown sound, you know? We got Spooner Oldham and Dan Penn. All you have to do is come in and do that voice you do. We got it all set up."

Alex Chilton: I got with the band and within three weeks we had recorded. "The Letter" was the very first we did.

Chris Bell: They worked out an act, wrote some tunes and put it together. They talked it over with Alex's parents and he left school. He went off and did that...and you know what happened there.

Beverly Baxter Ross — Friend, vocalist, actress: I was a girlfriend of Andy Hummel's from 1964 to '66. I was also Jody's girlfriend from 1970 to '73. I knew Alex before the Box Tops because I went to Central High with him. He was a bad boy. At school, I used to correct him all the time. I would say, "Quit being so ugly, Alex! You are hurting her feelings." That was 1967. He was a bad little thing. His band played in the tenth-grade talent show at Central High. Then suddenly it was the Box Tops—it was, "My baby, she wrote me a letter."

Alex Chilton: We recorded it in March, and it came out in August. And it came into the charts about No. 80 and then it went to No. 59 or something. All these people started realizing it was going to be a real big hit. That was about the time school was about to start, so I managed to blow off going back to school. The personnel on the [Box Tops'] road band changed around...Before the record even came out, two of the guys were gone who had played on "The Letter" and so we had to replace them. We were just barely a shell of a band at that point. The whole established group I joined had fallen apart before "The Letter" came out. They all thought, *Eh, we've made records before. They never went anywhere. This one won't either and we've got to go to college next year.* So they quit.

Bill Cunningham: At the start, after "The Letter" was released, we were not a solid sound. But after a couple dates we pulled ourselves together. The Box Tops was a funny thing in the '60s. Initially, Alex didn't know anyone else in the band, so he pulled me in because we were friends. Danny Smythe, the drummer, was the only guy who was in the Devilles from the start, but we all got to know each other and became friends on tour.

Chris Bell: They started playing the tune on the radio and we were listening to it but didn't realize it was Alex. We were a bit surprised when we found out.

Alex's distinct voice on the "The Letter" made him a '60s pop star, but he often credited Dan Penn for his soulful vocal delivery on the moody Wayne Carson-penned tune.

Alex Chilton: I started singing it softly at first and the producer came out and said, "No, sing it really hard—kind of growl it like this." He kind of demonstrated it for me and I did it the best I could. People tell me they thought I was fifty years old and fat or black. We had a hit record on a lot of black stations with that record because people thought we were black. It's impossible to describe, it has some sort of movement and immediacy about it. "Give me a ticket for an aero-plane, ain't got time to take a fast train." It gives you a feeling of movement. A lot of people were in Vietnam at the time, too, and that was their fondest dream—their ticket out and back home.

Steve Rhea: We were happy for the Box Tops' success and that Alex was such a hit. "The Letter" was the overall number two *Billboard* hit of 1967.

Alex Chilton: It was number one for four weeks. It knocked off "Ode to Billy Joe" from the top spot. What knocked off "The Letter" was "Light My Fire."

Bill Cunningham: In 1967, we played with The Doors in Fort Worth. "Light My Fire" was number one and "The Letter" was number two, or vice versa. They were changing up. The Doors' equipment didn't come in, so their guitar player, Robbie Krieger, borrowed Gary's guitar. We were in a room with them in the back and Krieger was just stoned out of his head staring at the ceiling. On stage, Jim was screwing—with his clothes on albeit—the PA system. He was in his black leather pants, typical Morrison. After playing with The Doors, we ditched our matching-suit look. We immediately went to wearing whatever we wanted.

In February 1968, the Box Tops scored another hit with "Cry Like a Baby," a song co-written by Dan Penn and Spooner Oldham. By April, the sweet and soulful single peaked at No. 2 on the Billboard *Hot 100.*

John Fry: The first song [Alex] did at Ardent was "Cry Like a Baby." The first time I ever saw Alex was when he was sitting on the floor in the control room waiting to do his vocals.

Holly George-Warren — Writer, Alex Chilton biographer: Alex loved it. He got to quit school to go on the road. He loved early touring days with the Beach Boys. It started going sour after his growth as an artist, and he chafed at his lack of artistic control in the studio.

Bill Cunningham: We toured a lot in those days. My mom kept a diary. In 1968, we had six days off. It was a blur. By the time we were flying, after the first three or four months on the road, it became a routine. It was getting up, getting to the airport, getting to the city. We would go do some television miming for a performance, go to an autograph signing at a record store, go to a radio station for an interview, and then do an afternoon show and maybe an evening show. We were lucky to get something to eat. Finally, we would wind down at the hotel and get a little sleep—wake up and repeat. It was all structured. People told us what we had to do and where we had to be at what times.

On October 6, 1967, the Box Tops played their first show with the Beach Boys in Indianapolis at the State Fairgrounds Coliseum. For the next three years, the two bands shared countless bills in big rooms.

Bill Cunningham: As soon as "The Letter" came out, Brian Wilson called immediately and asked for us to be added to a Beach Boys show. Within two weeks of "The Letter" being released we were on a Beach Boys show in Ohio. That was at a coliseum. It was the first one I ever did. I walked out to my bass and picked it up. The stage was so big, I was unaccustomed to it. Once the count off happened, I never heard anyone else. It was like a bass solo for me. This was the tail end of the screaming days, so all the girls were screaming. My clothes were literally

(far left) Chris Bell's high school yearbook photos: 1965 (top), 1967 (middle), 1968 (bottom).

(top right) Linda Schaeffer Yarman, one of Chris' closest friends, poses for a photo.

PHOTO BY CHRIS BELL

(center) Andy Hummel at MUS, 1968.

waving, shaking from the vibrations coming from the voices. That's how strong the screams were.

Alex Chilton: We must have played about one hundred nights with them over a couple of years. This was after Brian Wilson quit going on the road with them, of course. Anyway, they'd all been big fans of "The Letter" and they recorded it, too.

After the Box Tops were nominated for a Grammy Award in 1968 for Best Contemporary Vocal Group, the band's fame continued to grow, as did its bond with the Beach Boys—they even spent an eerie night alongside Dennis Wilson and his friends, the Manson Family.

Bill Cunningham: I was there, too. It was out at Dennis Wilson's house. Manson and his girls were there. It just didn't feel right. It was a typical '60s night; everyone was stoned and hanging out. The eyes of Manson were just so evil-looking. I didn't know until after the murders how evil he was. Manson freaked me out and I wanted to get away. The vibe was bad, so I split. But Dennis, Carl Wilson, Alex and I were all pretty good friends and hung out a lot. I was closer to Carl; he would call and talk to me about my girlfriend problems.

Alex Chilton: I went out to California and stayed with Dennis Wilson, it was there I met Brian. This was 1968. He seemed alright to me, but, come to think of it, I guess he was acting a little weird. The two of us went out to The Whisky and everyone was telling me it was the first time Brian had been out in years. He was doing funny things. Like he started doing push-ups right where we were sitting in the club. Later he was doing some recordings, under what circumstances I don't know, but I got a whole lot of telephone calls from him in the middle of the night. He wanted to record me singing on this thing.

David Bell: Chris and his friends were excited for Alex when "The Letter" took off, but I don't know if they particularly liked the music that much. It was often described as blue-eyed soul and my brother was crazy for the Kinks, the Who, and, obviously, the Beatles. But everyone in that scene was impressed.

Beverly Baxter Ross: No, we weren't impressed. We've got Elvis walking down the street. My mother was Elvis's nurse.

Steve Rhea: It was good dance tunes, but they were playing the music we were sort of against.

Andy Hummel: I don't recall discussing the Box Tops in those days. They weren't particularly something that was on my radar screen. I always kind of liked "Neon Rainbow." I always thought that was a good song, but I was never a real fan of "The Letter."

Carole Ruleman Manning: Alex really did go off into what would have been a lot of young men or young women's dream—to be this huge star. That was while Chris had to clean out the pool on Saturdays. He felt like such a victim because his father used to make him clean out the pool in their East Memphis Germantown mansion. There was something that Chris saw as quite glamorous about Alex's life, but Alex had to live on the edge. He had to be an adult from an early age. Of course, Alex didn't have that Box Tops money for too long.

Holly George-Warren: He was so young when they hit number one. I think he felt he missed out on a normal life as a teen. But it opened the doors to a music career and gave him so many amazing experiences.

While Alex was garnering press from teen magazines and performing on national television programs, back home, Ardent Studios had swiftly made a name for itself in the music industry. Fry founded the studio in 1959, and operated it out of his mother's home at 4035 Grandview Boulevard in Memphis. Born New Year's Eve of 1944, he was still a teenager attending MUS when he launched the earliest incarnation of Ardent. After home-recording a

series of rock and pop singles, in 1966 John opened the company's first legit location on National Street in North Memphis. While Fry came from a wealthy Memphis family thanks to his father's successful career as a developer, his innate audiophile leanings steered him in another direction: the science of sound. This passion was shared with Fry's early Ardent collaborators, including future FedEx founder Fred Smith and future Big Star promo-man John King—all teenaged MUS kids when they formed Ardent.

John Fry: My early interest was in radio. I grew up listening to music in Memphis, and I started to come of age around the time that rock 'n' roll was hitting...We would listen to WDIA, they had just amazing air personalities. Then I started tuning in to distant stations, where you'd get a different geographical perspective.

Steve Rhea: Fred Smith, who runs Federal Express, was in the same classes and in the same friendship with both John Fry and John King. He also has a great affinity for music. It's one of the things that pulls Memphis together and puts us on the map.

John Dando — Friend, sound technician, Ardent Productions, Big Star road manager: John Fry and John King convinced this fellow who had a radio station over in Arkansas called KCAT that they knew every-thing about programming a radio station. They'd go roaring over to

Arkansas in John's old Thunderbird and work as programmers at this radio station in the afternoon. That's where the notion to do a recording studio came from.

John King — Publicist for Ardent Records, Big Star: [Fry] was always reading *Popular Science* and technical brochures from electronics manufacturers. He built a radio transmitter, but the signal didn't go too far.

John Fry: We had a little pirate radio station. Fortunately, it was low-powered, and we were lucky to not be arrested. That interest in radio, the music being played on the radio and electronics, led us to the idea, "Well, if we can do radio production, maybe we can actually record music." We built a studio in my house on Grandview. There was one room that we had partitioned off for a little control room, a moderate-sized studio area and there was this other room sixty or seventy feet away. Somebody had the idea that it was built for my grandmother, so it became known as "Granny's Sewing Room."

Terry Manning: Bands or vocalists would be in that room, which was a decent size, and John would be in the control room across the way.

Jim Dickinson — Producer, singer-songwriter, multi-instrumentalist, solo, Mud Boy and the Neutrons: The studio was in a separate building, with a patio between it and the control room, so, if you were engineering, you couldn't see anything that was going on.

Steve Rhea: John's parents were well enough off to have a swimming pool and a pool house that was separate from their house. John converted the little study into a control room with all the glass and equipment. Then, all the wires went through the roof and came out in the pool house, where they were set up to record music.

Tim Riley — Artist manager, Ardent Studios: Fry was an astute, generous type. People don't often realize it, but Fry was not only an amazing engineer, but pretty much self-taught. If he didn't know the answer to a problem, he researched it and came back with the most amazing answer. He was a bright guy. The business grew and he became successful.

John Fry: The original equipment was junky, homemade, and cobbled together. But finally, from about '61 to '65, we had a fairly decent Altec valve console and an Ampex stereo machine and Ampex mono machine.

Andy Hummel: I'm sure the reason John was head-and-shoulders above anybody else, technically, is he grew up with all of this. He started back when it was on one-track, two-track, and then four-track recorders—purely analog.

John Fry: I read everything I could get ahold of and, what little opportunity I had, I observed other studios. By and large, it was a trial-and-error process.

John Dando: That's a big part of Ardent and John Fry, he figured out how to do things himself...That's the thing about people in Memphis, they are uncompromising. That's what makes the ones who make it great.

John Fry: When we decided that we were going to start to press our first 45s, we had to have a name for the label, and we liked the sound of Ardent. "Hot, fiery, fierce, burning, passionate" was the dictionary definition. "Okay, that's not bad!" 1959 was the first release, by Freddie Cadell. At first, we were only distributed in the local area and we pressed a thousand of each single. We would go in-person to the local stations and beg them to play it.

The first record by the Ole Miss Downbeats, "Geraldine," did get put into regular rotation by WHBQ and made their chart...We were recording 45s and putting them out as well as doing rentals and service recording. It was pretty disruptive. Bands were coming to the house all the time and all my parents ever said was, "Who are all these people? Why do some of them have so much hair?"

John King: From the beginning, [Fry's] parents were very supportive, helping make a fertile, creative place for left-of-center people.

John Fry: My dad was in the building-material business, which is pretty far removed from music. You would ordinarily expect most parents to be opposed to this, like, "What's this loud noise coming from these bands?" But strangely enough, they were supportive. The general routine was, "You can do anything you want, just do it well."

As Ardent's workload increased, John Fry hired two youthful engineers to help run the boards, the now renowned producers Jim Dickinson and Terry Manning.

John Fry: The next step in the garage saga was meeting Jim Dickinson. I met Jim through a guy who worked in music stores named Bobby Fisher. Bobby had come across a local band, and he introduced me to Jim with the idea that maybe Jim would work with them. They originally had another name, but Jim made up a new name for them: Lawson and Four More...I'm not a person who believes in coincidence, it just so happened that the keyboard player in Lawson and Four More was Terry Manning.

Jim Dickinson: My friend Bobby Fisher called me one night in 1965 and asked, "Can you write a song like the Kinks? Can you write one in

45 minutes?" I asked, "What are you going to do with it?" He said, "I found this group and I'm going to record them at John Fry's." I told him, "Take me along or you can't have the song," and that was the beginning.

Steve Rhea: Dickinson was producing and bringing in these off the wall acts and trying to figure out how to be a success. They recorded a few bands that turned up on that CD retrospective, *Thank You Friends: The Ardent Records Story* [2008].

Tom Eubanks: Fry was born with an old soul. He is the kind of guy you expected to come into the studio wearing a white lab coat, like they used to do in England at studios.

Andy Hummel: Fry's most obvious characteristic to most people is he talks just like Jimmy Stewart.

Jim Dickinson: One night, Jimmy Crosthwait was out there banging on a cardboard box with some maracas. Fry asked, "Is he smoking marijuana out there?" I said, "Yes," and Fry said kind of dryly, "Well, I was just curious." He acted like an old man when he was a teenager, but in his own way, he was incredibly hip.

Not long after Ardent cut Lawson and Four More's 1966 single, "If You Want Me You Can Find Me," the home studio was forced to shut down.

John Fry: The thing that occasioned our move from the home studio to a commercial building was the fact that my parents decided to sell that house. At that point, I'm having to make the decision whether this is a hobby or something I'm at least going to give a try as a professional career. I chose the latter and we went out looking for a building.

Terry Manning: When Grandview was being sold, John, Jim and I would go to various locations to look until we found the building on National.

In May 1966, Fry leased a newly built storefront at 1457 National Street in Memphis. The two-thousand square foot space was the first professional home of Ardent Recordings—later re-branded as Ardent Studios. Expensive new gear promptly filled the modest location.

John Fry: We had already ordered a Scully four-track, which was delivered before all the building work was completed. At first the carpenters worked in the daytime and we lashed up something crude and recorded at night...I wish I could say we had a real business plan, but the business plan was, "We're going to try and make a pretty nice studio over here and maybe things will work out." Jim Dickinson was sort of producer-in-residence and Terry Manning became the first engineer other than myself.

Steve Rhea: Terry transitioned from being a musician to becoming an engineer. He began to learn how to use all the equipment and became John's chief engineer.

Jim Dickinson: Manning and I became engineers at the same moment, when Fry went home for dinner one night and didn't return. There was a jingle session and Manning and I wondered, "Are you going to punch the red button, or am I?" To Manning's eternal credit, he suggested we both punch it.

Terry Manning: I was the first employee on the payroll, as engineer or assistant engineer, the one to open things up, file tapes, sweep the floor. In other words, do everything. Mary Lindsay was the receptionist and Jim was, I guess, "director of entertainment." I recall National Street as buzzing fairly quickly.

John Fry: Dickinson came along as sort of an in-house producer and he would engineer frequently. There were periods of time when it was just work and sleep.

Andy Hummel: Ardent was a little storefront. It was brick, had a couple offices, reception area, a control room and one big studio.

Richard Rosebrough: The room over on National was a small room, but great for horns.

Steve Rhea: I began to go over there with Terry. That was like walking into *Alice in Wonderland*. Everything was four-track at that point. It was still basic, but it got to be a lot better.

John Fry: We just had the one studio, so a lot of times it would be Terry working in the day and I'm doing it at night and vice versa.

Terry Manning: On a typical day, I arrived first—well, after Janie the maid. I would start turning everything on, setting up for whatever session might be booked, usually around 9 a.m. If I was engineering, John might come in about 11 a.m. to do office work, some days perhaps not at all. But if John was the engineer, he would be there well before the session started. Many sessions started at 11 a.m. or noon, but it varied a lot. The days were often long. If I were producing a rock band, it might go well into the night.

After Ardent committed to a lease, and had a professional setting, work quickly flowed in to the studio after locals heard of its top-notch equipment, which fortuitously paralleled Stax Records' studio setup. It proved to be a positive situation for both Memphis-based companies.

Andy Hummel: They were also starting to get a lot of business from Stax, their overflow business. Stax recognized the technical excellence John Fry maintained at Ardent, which nobody else did in those days.

John Fry: My first connection to Stax was at fourteen years old, going down to the Satellite Record Shop. They got the good records first, ones the suburban stores wouldn't have. I'm not even sure I knew there was a studio there. The professional contact with Stax began as we were building the studio on National. A fella walked in one day, his name was Welton Jetton. He said, "We heard you were building a studio, this is an input module that we're building for a console we're furnishing to Stax." We ordered a console using the same components, amplifiers and equalizers. At the same time, we purchased our first multi-track machine beyond a stereo machine. We thought we had died and gone to heaven, "We've got four whole tracks!" Welton told the people at Stax, "Hey, I am doing a console for these Ardent people. If you need to do some extra work, you ought to go over there because they're going to have similar equipment and there are people over there who know what they're doing." It's amazing they trusted us. I was twenty-one and I looked like I was about sixteen. I knew what I was doing, but there was absolutely no reason for anybody to think I knew what I was doing. I went from being in a home studio to, "Wow! We're recording records by artists we've heard of and actually get played a lot on the radio." That was a cool thing, but you realize quickly there is responsibility that goes along with this role.

Al Bell — Record executive, Stax Records co-owner: One of the Bar-Kays told me about Ardent, and after Stax separated from Atlantic Records, I went to check it out. The marketplace was saying that Stax was dead—Otis [Redding] was killed in the plane crash—and we woke up to find out that our biggest hit-makers, Sam & Dave, were signed to Atlantic. We lost our back catalog to Atlantic, too, so we had nothing. I found a track on Booker T & the MGs, and I took it to Terry Manning and said, "This feels like a hit to me." Manning played marimbas on it, and the song became "Soul Limbo," one of the records that aided in the resurrection of Stax.

John Fry: From the beginning of 1967 until Stax closed in 1975, we did all their overflow studio work. Ardent did just about every major artist they had at one time or another.

Terry Manning: Al Bell was already one of my closest friends. I had been working at Stax after school during my Central High days, even while the studio was still at John's house. We had been working together on the Staple Singers' records and others, so it was always great for me to be working with him. I was also close to [Stax co-founder] Jim Stewart, so for me it was Old Home Week. Of course, John was close to both already, as well. Stax was then operating at a high level, doing so much recording that they needed a nearby outside studio that they could trust. So Ardent National was the perfect thing for them, at just the right moment. There were months when nothing else could book because Stax was doing so much work there with us.

John Fry: Another early customer was Pepper Sound, the jingle company that became Pepper Tanner. What they did was interesting and uncommon for this part of the county because they would record large, orchestral ensembles. Some of their material was big-band style. I got to engineer some of those sessions. It was scary. I remember doing sessions with forty players; we had twelve microphone inputs and four tracks.

Terry Manning: Every week for quite a while [Pepper Sound] would do these large library advertising editions for radio stations.

John Fry: That was mostly '66 through maybe '69 into '70 a little bit.

Terry Manning: The sessions would often be huge, with forty to eighty union musicians playing at once. There could be a full string section, orchestral horn section, woodwinds, bass, drums, two guitars, two or three keyboards, a large percussion ensemble and all that. I would get thrown in there to engineer this all by myself. The jingles were only a minute long, if that. You had to get your sounds fast, no messing around and no room for error. It made a man of you.

John Fry: The good thing about the jingle company was that it allowed me to record a tremendous variety of genres and instrumentation—country, big band, orchestra—that I would never have seen in the ordinary course of business that went on in Memphis.

Andy Hummel: There would be a small orchestra in there and a bunch of singers gathered around a microphone singing "A&W Root Beer!"

John Fry: Along with the jingles and Stax work, we were trying to record our own artists. The *Batman* TV show was starting, and they were running promos for it on WHBQ. Jim Dickinson conjured up a girl group called the Robins. We bought an old car and had a metal shop put fins on it and turn it into a Batmobile.

With the growing list of high-profile clients, Ardent quickly put its own imprint, Ardent Records, on hold and concentrated on the more profitable Ardent Studios. Releasing local projects like the Robins' single fell to the wayside as bigger names, like James Taylor, passed through the doors over the next couple years.

John Fry: There was a fella named Don Nix. He played in the original Mar-Keys. He played baritone sax, one of the people he went out on tour with was Leon Russell. He was telling Leon about the studio, so one of our first high-profile clients to come from out of town was Leon Russell. Then, Terry Manning had become acquainted with Jimmy Page because the Yardbirds had come to Memphis a number of times and played. Terry kept in contact with him and when they did the Led Zeppelin *III* album, Terry persuaded him to come to Ardent. There is nothing that makes people aware of you as much as a little tiny credit on the back of a record that does well. Between the work we were doing for Stax, and these other high-profile projects, the word was starting to get around.

Ardent Studios at 1457 National Street in Memphis, 1966.

ARDENT STUDIOS ARCHIVE

CHAPTER 4

ENTERING ARDENT — CHRISTMAS FUTURE: 1968

During the autumn of 1968, Chris slogged through his junior year at MUS. He hadn't had a serious band since the Jynx, but his next group, Christmas Future, was in the making. He abandoned the nascent garage-rock sound and explored the psychedelic sounds heard in his expanding record collection. However, it was his first visit to Ardent Studios that thoroughly hooked the seventeen-year-old into the record business.

David Bell: It was through Steve Rhea and Terry Manning that Chris heard about Ardent.

Steve Rhea: I told Chris, "You have to come over here to National and see this recording studio." I took Chris over there and introduced him to John Fry and Terry Manning.

John Fry: I first met Chris Bell in 1968. We had a group of young musicians who started hanging out at Ardent and recording music at night. A lot of them knew Terry Manning. The first time I ever laid eyes on Chris was when I came in the studio one night and he and Terry were sitting in my office. Chris was sitting in my chair behind my desk. He had his boots on my desk and was smoking a cigarette. I was like, *Whoa, who's this guy? What's he doing?*

Steve Rhea: Chris and I would do anything we could to hang out at Ardent. This is all when we were still in high school. I would go over to National and there would be [Stax guitarist] Steve Cropper. They'd be producing, we would be sitting around listening or engineering, whatever they needed us to do. We were like Ardent scruffs.

Richard Rosebrough: Chris introduced me to John Fry. Chris thought John was just the coolest guy he had ever met in his life. We would hang out at Ardent, watch sessions and ask questions. Ardent was an unusual studio because it was very clean, painted with all these pastel colors and had the finest equipment money could buy. Of course, we didn't realize it at the time. I was just eighteen.

Chris Bell: I was spending a lot of time at Ardent Studios in Memphis, a fine studio. I was getting more involved with the technical side of recording and production. It was right after things like *Sgt. Pepper's* and everything was becoming more production-slanted. I was still playing locally, but in between times I was hanging out at Ardent [and] generally learning all about the studio process. All this time I was developing as a rock 'n' roll guitarist, still along the lines of the Who, the Yardbirds [and] Hendrix.

Steve Rhea: I always feel indebted to John for allowing us to have access to the studio, which was pretty much putting creative people in this wonderful playground and then teaching us the science behind the mics, the acoustics, getting us to where we could run the boards and get sounds on tape.

Robert Johnson: I would see Chris at Ardent on National back in the late '60s. He became one of "Fry's Boys," as we called them.

John Dando: It was a lot of odd ducks, real clique-ish anglophiles. There were a lot of talented, intelligent people walking around. John Fry tended to attract a lot of brainy people. He's pretty brainy himself. He made it possible or gave you an opportunity to do a lot of things. If he recognized any skills or desire to learn something, he would let you do it.

Steve Rhea: Chris and I would be at National on a weekend night when everybody else was gone. On multiple occasions, Don Nix would show up with some new tape. One night he came in with Leon Russell. We hardly knew who the guy was at that point. They'd sneak in and do work in the studio, sometimes when we were the only ones around.

David Bell: Many of the young people involved with Ardent Studios were talented. They were learning how to record. That helped change the kind of music they were playing and helped move Chris into being more interested with being in the studio rather than playing live. And what Chris was learning at Ardent he was also trying to incorporate at the backhouse.

Chris' first original recording was laid down with Terry Manning contributing keys, backing vocals and percussion. Chris played guitar and bass, while delivering an insecure lead vocal. It was a promising start that showcased his willingness to experiment with sounds.

Adam Hill — Engineer, producer, Ardent Studios, Big Star archivist: "Psychedelic Stuff" was the earliest tune Chris cut at Ardent. It's the most amateur track he cut at the studio. It's on a four-track tape. That would have been the four-track Scully that's still sitting up front at Ardent today. But even with that, he was doing tape flanging and lots of stacked tracks.

Michael O'Brien: Chris knew so much about music and was generous. I was trying to be a drummer because I desperately wanted to be in a band. He would help me pick out the drum set and then pick out a guitar and try to teach me things, but I was not teachable. One night he was stuck. He didn't have anyone but himself. He said, "You're the only drummer that's around." We went in and worked on a Hendrix song. It was fascinating. He was a great director. He'd say, "You're pushing the beat," Play a little louder" or "That's great! You're sounding like Keith Moon." He was working with someone with no talent, but he could still direct and get what he needed.

Christmas Future would be Chris' final venture as lead guitarist in a teen band, but the group was just the beginning of his sonic relationship with the band's drummer, Steve Rhea.

Steve Rhea: They didn't have a traditional school band at MUS, but students who could informally play guitar, sing or play drums played in the pep band. We put together modern, popular songs and changed them into pep songs for MUS and played them before football and basketball games. At some point, Chris was playing guitar, and I was playing drums. That's when Chris and I first started playing together. We took the Yardbirds' "Shapes of Things" and changed the lyrics around into a pep song. Chris had a Fuzz-Tone pedal. I would look over and think, *This guy sounds like Jeff Beck. He's great!* It wasn't long after that my band, the Strangers, disintegrated. Chris came up to me in the hallway with Vance Alexander. He said, "We're going to form a band called Christmas Future, would you like to play?" I said, "Sure, but we need a bass player." That's when we got Peter Schutt and kicked it off from there.

Peter Schutt — Classmate, bassist, Christmas Future: Steve Rhea and I were in another garage band together for three years and it disbanded with the advent of psychedelic rock. Steve asked me to play bass in the new band. Vance was the singer. It was just me, Chris, Vance, and Steve on drums.

David Bell: Christmas Future was heavier than the Jynx. Music had become much more mature and drug-influenced.

Chris Bell: We got tired of playing like human jukeboxes, playing Sam & Dave, so we started an underground movement in high school to get a group that would just play English music.

Andy Hummel: They played a lot of Hendrix and Cream. It just blew me away. All I had ever done was soul and white-boy punk.

Chris Bell: We were playing school dances with friends, which I hated. All they wanted to hear was soul.

David Bell: Chris hated it when they wanted him to play "Mustang Sally" or "Midnight Hour."

Steve Rhea: Stax was in its heyday and soul music had reasserted itself. That funky soul music was going strong. Motown was also hitting its stride, and those groups sort of edged out a lot of the British bands. We would go to shows and bands weren't playing the British as much anymore. They were playing the latest soul hits, with a horn section and things like that. We reacted to that. We had been vaccinated against that sort of sound by the British, not that we didn't appreciate it.

Chris Bell: Back when that [psychedelic] wave came in, not many people were doing that. Nobody was listening to Jimi Hendrix. They were still pretty strong, at least in the high school scenes, into Sam & Dave, Otis Redding and all that.

Gary Stevens: Christmas Future had somebody in the audience with an overhead projector dropping different colored oils in there. They had a strobe light. It wasn't big-time or anything, but a serious effort at psychedelic music. It was cover material, but it was songs nobody else would dare cover. They were into that movement. Vance Alexander would go to the hardware store and buy the reflective circles people put at the end of their driveways. [Then] he molded them into sunglasses and sold them at school. He called them "freak-out glasses." Jim Morrison and Vance Alexander had to be kindred souls and they looked just alike. Vance acted just like Morrison. He had no hesitation about getting on stage and letting it fly. He wasn't very good, quite frankly, but it was super entertaining.

Andy Hummel: Christmas Future played at MUS in the cafeteria one night when they had a party. I was like, *Wow! Here are these guys that are actually out doing this. How cool is that?* Pretty quickly after that, I quit the R&B band I was in. I just played at home on the old Silvertone.

Michael O'Brien: One day at the backhouse, I heard Christmas Future play "Pictures of Lily" like fifty times in one night. He wanted to get all the parts exactly right. What a great ear he had.

Chris Bell: I was selecting the material for the band to play and basically producing it. I was devoting less and less time to school and study and more time to the studio and music.

Steve Rhea: Christmas Future practiced a lot at the backhouse. We played once, maybe twice, then we kicked out Vance Alexander. At one of the practices there was a big conflict between Vance and me over what genre of music we were going to play. He was into the Doors and all that West Coast acid rock, a road I didn't want to go down. He kept pressing us to go down that road. Vance was a bit of an unstable guy. We ended up in a fistfight. Not a bad one, but we squared off. I hit him, he left, and he was out of the band.

David Bell: Vance was a little bit of a rebel without a cause. He was a good singer, but a troubled kid. He committed suicide either in high school or shortly after.

Even though Chris was learning the basics of engineering at Ardent, Christmas Future remained a cover band and never recorded an original tune. The guys preferred to upset local crowds with their stash of ear-piercing guitars and effects processors.

Steve Rhea: It was all just cover material from England.

Peter Schutt: Christmas Future played one gig in Lepanto, Arkansas. When we played a couple Hendrix songs and "My Generation," the crowd basically made us leave. Chris lit a guitar on fire à la Jimi Hendrix.

Chris Bell: It was a dream for us to go up and play and smash equipment and all that.

Steve Rhea: With that gig in Arkansas, you had kids who just wanted to hear the latest funky soul music out of Memphis. When we showed up, they didn't get it. They were underwhelmed.

Chris Bell: People hated most of it. They'd come up and say, "Please play 'I Feel Fine.'" I knew they were talking about James Brown, but we would play "I Feel Fine" by the Beatles instead. In a way they hated us, but we introduced a lot of stuff to Memphis, the strobe lights and psychedelic music.

Richard Rosebrough: Chris idolized the Who and Led Zeppelin, so he picked up a lot of chords, tricks and moves from Pete Townshend and

Chris Bell (top) and Michael O'Brien (bottom) hanging at Ardent Studios on National Street.

ARDENT STUDIOS ARCHIVE

Christmas Future, 1968: (bottom photo, L-R) Drummer Steve Rhea, guitarist Chris Bell (back), vocalist Vance Alexander, and bassist Peter Schutt (in front).

PHOTOS COURTESY OF PETER SCHUTT

other members of the Who—that kind of attitude. He thought the way Jimmy Page moved on stage was cool. He picked up some patterns like moving his hand after he hit the guitar—theatrics.

Tom Eubanks: Playing live, Chris never gave any indication of the brilliant work he could do in the studio. On stage, he was a slashing-type guitarist.

Steve Rhea: We were interested in how to get textures and fuzz tones and how to sound like Jeff Beck or Jimmy Page. It wasn't like Chris could mimic Eric Clapton's solo on "Crossroads." Chris could just get that edge on guitar sounds, the texture and punch the song needed.

Chris Bell: We would play Led Zeppelin and there were people who enjoyed that. They were first turning on to drugs and we had this tape echo. Nobody else was doing it.

Steve Rhea: We definitely had an attitude. Our job was not to please audiences and try to find songs that would help them have a good time and make them dance. Our job was to play the great avant-garde music we loved from the Yardbirds, Beatles and the Who. Those were the bands we began to focus on and mimic in our music. We were developing down that road as musicians. Once we figured out the audiences didn't get off on that as much as we did, it gradually started to become adversarial. It got to the point where it became a badge of honor if they threw you off the stage or didn't ask you back.

Richard Rosebrough: About that time, Terry Manning was in a band with Joe Gaston on bass and Joe Lee on guitar. They were called the Goatdancers, but they started breaking up.

Steve Rhea: Peter Schutt left and we got a new bass player named Bill Boyce. Terry Manning also joined the band. Terry was leaving his old band and we were happy he agreed to join us because he had a lot of stage experience and could play keyboards and guitar. Christmas Future evolved into this band with Chris and Terry upfront and me and Bill Boyce in the back.

Chris Bell: We did that for a year or so. Some people came and went. One person would go on and do another thing or try to keep up with school.

With Terry Manning on board and Chris' growing connection to John Fry, Christmas Future utilized Ardent Studios' arsenal of high-end hardware and amped up the group's already experimental live sets.

Steve Rhea: John Fry could do a lot of things to modify equipment. He would create a little metal box with a foot switch, what we now know as an overdrive pedal. It wasn't Fuzz-Tone, but a neat sound. He gave us what everybody has now, but nobody had back then: a professional rack, just like at a recording studio. That was our PA. He helped us outfit the sound system, the speakers and all of that. That's what John and Terry brought to our performances: enhancements.

John and Terry put a tape cartridge machine in the rack, which we used during our cover of "Happenings Ten Years Time Ago" by the Yardbirds. There's a point when you get through the second verse where there's a guitar break. As you go into the guitar break, on the record is a slowed-down explosion, which Fry had figured out in the studio by listening to the record very closely. It didn't just go, "Boom!" It was drawn out. John found a recording of an explosion and slowed it down and we put it on the tape cartridge machine. The last concert we played was at MUS. We're up there and the place was jam-packed. We're aware we're going to subject them to a bunch of music that's just going to make them stop and go, "What? What is that? I can't dance to it." But we're knocking them dead. We're rocking out with sounds they'd never heard before. We get to that break in "Ten Years Time Ago" and Terry leaps over and hits the button on the tape cartridge, the explosion goes off in the PA system and Chris goes winging into this great guitar solo. We were in heaven. We're totally offending these people. They have no clue what's going on. We ended on "My Generation." Drums got smashed, everything got turned over. That was the last time that foursome ever played. We weren't asked back.

David Bell: There's a run of about two years there where they went from playing in a garage band as punky teens, to still teens but learning and learning fast. Christmas Future, in a year or two, morphed into Icewater and then Rock City, which finally became Big Star.

Upon entering his senior year at MUS in 1969, Chris and Andy Hummel grew closer. Born January 26, 1951, Hummel was the perfect contemporary to Chris' rising rebellious side. As Hummel told Perfect Sound Forever *journalist Jason Gross in 2001, "We were basically a couple of neurotic little rich kids who went to a private school."*

Andy Hummel: In our senior year of high school we became best friends because we were kind of bad guys. We smoked cigarettes and pot, drank and all that.

Carole Ruleman Manning: I saw Andy as not being as involved in the group of friends. It would have been hard to be as involved as Chris though. Chris was just full tilt. He had this focus with his music that was just laser-sharp.

Andy Hummel: Chris and I first met each other sneaking off to smoke in each other's cars or the back forty of the golf course. We just hit it off because we were interested in the same things: music and photography.

Carole Ruleman Manning: Andy was a really cute-looking guy. You can tell I was an adolescent then because that's just about all I noticed. Andy was attractive and tall with brown eyes and dark hair, kind of like a puppy dog that wasn't fully grown, falling over himself a little bit.

Andy Hummel: When Chris and I first started hanging out a lot together, it wasn't particularly a music thing. I didn't talk to him about starting a band until we got into college. Chris had his own little scene he was already into in high school. I was single-mindedly into girls—stealing the car in the middle of the night and going to pick up girls from the Hutchison girls' school.

Vera Ellis: Chris had a little bit of a crush on Linda Schaeffer, but also a little bit of a crush on me and Carole and Beth Horton. He kind of wanted a girlfriend but it never worked out that way.

Andy Hummel: Did Chris ever have any girlfriends? Not that I know of. I never thought about it much and certainly never discussed it with him.

Gary Stevens: Chris didn't discuss much of anything with anybody. One night, Andy brought Chris over to my house in the middle of the winter. My parents had a beautiful home with a huge pool house. I could tell right off the bat, Chris was extremely uptight and uncomfortable being around me. When Chris got up to go to the bathroom, Andy jumped up and said, "I'm going to go get us some beers!" Andy had a fake ID and looked thirty years old. Chris came out and the first thing he said was, "Uh, where's Andy?" God almighty, I thought Chris wanted to hide in the corner.

Andy Hummel: You'd find certain convenience stores where you could go buy beer and cigarettes. During school, you'd sneak off to smoke at lunch. If there was such a thing as the hippie crew in twelfth grade, I guess we would have been it.

Vera Ellis: All our parents didn't understand the pot and drugs. Everything was new, that's not something their generation had done. They just didn't know what to do with us. All our parents were terrified.

David Bell: Chris got along fine with our mother. He was fine with our father until he became a budding hippie in the late '60s. Earlier on, it was easier for our parents to understand. The swinging '60s and the Beatles had come in. These were just kids with garage bands. They might go out and make a little money. But the older he got, and the more my father saw this wasn't a fad and it was going to last, and the innocent Beatlemania turned into the not-so innocent late-'60s, they weren't so impressed.

Cindy Bell Coleman: I never knew of or heard any conflict or discussion about Chris. One thing about our parents was that anything that happened between them and the kids stayed between them. It was always between the child and the parent, and none of the rest of us was brought into it.

Richard Rosebrough: We would party and hang out at different friends' houses. We started to have drinks. Some were into the hard liquor. I stuck with beer. We were smoking joints and just being unruly and brash.

Andy Hummel: One time I went and picked up Chris. My father had this old 1956 Lincoln, a cool car. He somehow figured out a way to take a cassette player, which, in those days, were big and bulky, and fit it into his glove compartment. I talked him in to letting me take that car one night. I had a couple of cassettes. One of them was Led Zeppelin. Chris and I cruised through this parking lot listening to Led Zeppelin thinking we were the coolest people who ever walked the Earth. We were probably trying to find someone to sell us some pot. We would smoke it if we could get it, but getting it was not a simple matter.

Prior to graduating from MUS, both Chris and Andy were accepted at University of Tennessee. Before they packed up and moved into their dorms, their 1969 summer break in Memphis introduced the eighteen-year-olds to their new favorite drug: LSD.

Andy Hummel: The summer after the twelfth grade is when I first met Alex Chilton. Chris and I went over to his house with Michael O'Brien. That was the first time we ever dropped acid. We had some purple haze. It was the first lunar landing and we sat in Alex's house watching the surface of the moon for hours and hours. It was on television 24/7. It was just this one camera taking a picture of the limb and nothing else happened. It was boring. To be sitting there tripping your brains out, watching this hour after hour, was very strange.

Steve Rhea: I would stay away from that. We had some other friends who were apparently wilder and more into that when we were in high school. Chris was sort of privy to that, but it's like he would protect me from it. Once he said, "Don't ask." He was operating in a couple different worlds then.

Terry Manning (top left) and Chris Bell (both photos) perform a psychedelic set as Christmas Future in Arkansas at a National Guard Armory to a packed house of teens, 1968.

PHOTOS BY DAVID BELL

Christmas Future performs in front of their classmates at
Memphis University School, 1968.

Christopher Branford Bell

Muse Asst. Art Ed. 11, Art Ed. 12; Chess Club 12; Pep Band 11, 12.

Chris is an artist in many fields, most notably in that of music. His instrument is the guitar, and he is a master guitarist. Chris has demonstrated his considerable talents around Memphis, as a member of several prominent bands, both in and out of school. Chris' enigmatic facial expression has been a puzzle to all of us. We don't know what he is continually musing about. Perhaps he is looking forward to his next haircut from his dentist, or to his next D.A.R. meeting. Chris' Brooks Brothers style has won him numerous fashion awards, both at home and abroad.

Chris Bell's 1969 MUS senior yearbook profile.

Terry Manning's *Home Sweet Home* LP,
featuring Chris Bell on guitar

ENTERPRISE RECORDS, 1970

73

CHAPTER 5

UT — LSD: FALL 1969-1970

In the fall of 1969, Chris headed off to the University of Tennessee in Knoxville, a six-hour drive east. His introduction to higher learning proved to be more mind-expanding than he expected, thanks to the readily available batches of high-powered psychedelics floating around campus. Marijuana was also easier to score. For the first time in his eighteen years, he was away from parental supervision.

Andy Hummel: There were a few friends up there we already knew, like Michael O'Brien and Jimbo Robinson. They'd been going to school at UT for a year when we got there. Initially, we lived in separate dorm rooms, but all hung together with those other guys. We all hung in people's dorm rooms, primarily.

Michael O'Brien: I was busy being a photographer for the school newspaper, but they would come over and hang out at my apartment and we would have fun together on the weekends. I would also go over to Morrill Hall where Andy and Chris lived. Their friend John Dando was there, too.

Drew DeNicola: John Dando was not only one of Chris' best friends early on, but later he was road manager for Big Star on two tours.

John Dando: I had known Chris Bell for several years indirectly through his sister Sara. My second year of school is when Chris and Andy arrived at UT. I struck up a relationship with them through Michael O'Brien. I lived in one complex and Andy and Chris lived in the one immediately next door, but I eventually moved in with them.

Andy Hummel: Chris had morphed through dorms. His initial dorm room was just the pits. It was one of those places where you had a great big common bathroom with everybody taking showers in stalls in this big, open deal. It was old and wasn't particularly nice. But Chris managed to get himself transferred over to my dorm room, a nice new one. They were like little suites.

John Dando: Andy and Chris were like little old women living together. They used to fight and bicker. It was always arguments like, "Who's got my cigarettes? Where are my cigarettes?" Just bickering over small things like that. That got amplified later when they were playing [in Big Star]. But they got along well, they were good friends.

Instead of hitting the books, Chris dug into illegal substances and spent many long nights listening to records. Bob Schiffer, their liberally minded New Yorker friend, turned Chris and Andy on to the many war protests cropping up across campus.

John Dando: It was the middle of the Vietnam War. There was a lot of drugs, craziness and rock 'n' roll. It was the height of the Baby Boomers…One day, outside of Chris and Andy's building, at pretty much high noon, there was to be a major eclipse of the sun. We had all learned how to make these kits so you could view it without burning out your retinas. Everybody was doing windowpane acid and building these kits while listening to the latest Led Zeppelin album. All these people lying on the grass just stoned out of their minds trying to watch this eclipse and listening to Jimmy Page. It was just wild. There was no way you could function as a student at that place.

Andy Hummel: It was a strange period in history. That was the year of the Kent State massacre, the Vietnam War was going on—Abbie Hoffman and Jerry Rubin.

Bob Schiffer — Friend, UT classmate: Andy came to school being pretty conservative and soon I had him going to anti-war protests. He basically had an awakening in college.

Andy Hummel: We were becoming kind of politicized because of our friend Bob Schiffer. He was just a screaming liberal. We never paid much attention to politics before, but then we started getting involved. That's when they started having the strikes on campus and saying, "We're not going to class!" It wasn't just the students, it was the professors as well. We didn't go to class for two days. We all went down to some seedy storefront where they were silk-screening the back of your army-surplus jackets with red fists that said "Strike!" and everybody had Che Guevara buttons on. It was a gas.

David Bell: Chris was not terribly into politics, but he was no fan of the war in Vietnam and was kind of worried about the draft. He must have had a low number.

Bob Schiffer: Chris was politically liberal but didn't get involved as much. If there was music at a certain rally, he'd go to that. He would have never served in the military. He was a humanitarian, that's the best way to put it.

Andy Hummel: You suddenly find yourself hanging around all these strange people from New York City and meeting girls who don't all have the same blonde hair and wear cute little skirts all the time. You meet girls with long blonde hair that wear bell bottoms and a lot of jewelry. It wasn't just girls, it was also things like meeting guys like Bob Schiffer. I never dreamed there were guys like Bob on the planet until then. There certainly were none of them in Memphis.

Bob Schiffer: We would listen to music and hang out until 3 a.m.

Andy Hummel: That fall, we were getting more into acid. Because the chemistry labs are right there on site, the acid you got was sometimes way too strong.

John Dando: Chris and Andy had convinced people they were expert drug takers and would test drugs for people…There was so much frenetic madness going on, I don't know how in the world they ever studied.

Andy Hummel: We did manage to get ourselves declared the "pot experts" of the dorm. Anybody contemplating buying some would immediately traipse up to our room and have us try it out…Other than being a pothead and tripping too much, I don't think Chris was showing signs of any neurosis [at this point]. He smoked Lark cigarettes. I always thought that was odd.

John Dando: A curious thing about Chris, and everybody used to notice it, he always had a full-body purple aura every time you were doing acid. It was the most incredible thing. We all would say, "Whew, what is this all about?" Was he the messiah, deity, royalty, or something? When you looked at him there was this purple glow all around his head and entire body. It was incredible to see.

Andy Hummel: We did acid almost every weekend in our fall semester. We usually met on Friday evenings. We would pop it and go play ping pong until it came on. When the cinder-block walls of the ping pong room started to look like it had little worms crawling out of it, you knew you were ready to go. Then we would go drive in the country in Jimbo's car. He had an eight-track player in his car. You could listen to Crosby, Stills and Nash.

John Dando: The whole campus was just covered with people doing acid. That, coupled with the anti-war movement and a police department that was paranoid as hell and poorly trained, made us all paranoid.

Andy Hummel: The environment we were in was very paranoid, with all this political unrest going on and being on a university campus while it was happening. There were constant threats of "this guy's a narc and you're liable to get busted any minute."

John Dando: There were narcs supposedly everywhere.

Bob Schiffer: Dando was an outsider. He was somebody who complained a lot. He was very overweight and that was something that bothered him a lot. He just couldn't relax. There was a lot of stress around him, but he found a way to always be useful and involved.

Gary Stevens: Dando had this Volkswagen Microbus, quintessential early-'70s hippie shit. He wore these Ray-Bans with the bright yellow lenses. When he'd trip, you couldn't shut him up, but he was also one of the nicest people I've ever met.

John Dando: I had a bit of a problem with the acid. It probably led to me dropping out that second quarter. I guess some people made it through, but I had certainly gone berserk. I got so paranoid after a few acid trips that I couldn't function anymore.

Andy Hummel: Because of the quality of acid we were getting up there—it was absolutely amazing—it was a fragile thing. If everything was going fine, then it was the most fantastic experience you can imagine. When things go south, it's the worst experience you've ever had. That doesn't have to happen to you but once before it changes a whole lot of things. There were a lot of people up there who had bad flashbacks and mental problems as a result of doing it.

John Dando: Chris and Andy were kind of aloof and tried to act different from everybody else. They were into this notion they were English, mod rockers. They weren't dressing like everybody else. They weren't going around in tank tops like everybody else was at the time.

Bob Schiffer: Chris didn't like to follow whatever was hot. He was anti-hot.

Michael O'Brien: Chris was funny, almost British in what he liked and would turn his nose up at. He wouldn't be caught dead at a UT football game. He'd be like, "Yeah, we don't want to do that."

John Dando: They weren't hippies, which was sort of the prevailing thing. Chris and Andy were wearing full-length coats and things like that. At that time, Frye boots were the big rage, and they had the best Frye boots. It was a studied sort of thing. They were trying to be cool.

Andy Hummel: Our standard outfit from when we went to college until several years afterwards, even while we were doing Big Star, was we wore Levi's, white Oxford shirts with button-down collars and cowboy boots. That was it. Forever, that's all we ever wore.

While music engulfed Chris' life, along with photography, he dabbled in film-making at UT.

Michael O'Brien: Chris and I made a black-and-white film for an art class called *Zing Went the Strings of My Heart*. It was basically "A Day in the Life of Bob Schiffer." It's very amateurish.

Andy Hummel: We both took photography classes our freshman year. He went one step further and he and Michael O'Brien took a cinematography course. It was an applied course, so they checked out this sixteen-millimeter camera. It had the three lenses on it, so you had to switch to the lens you wanted.

Bob Schiffer: It was mainly Chris Bell's work. It was me, Michael, Andy and Chris, but Chris was the brains behind it. It's all me in the film. It opens with a woman lying next to me. It's a fantasy film.

Andy Hummel: There were shots of Bob cruising around on campus doing crazy things. The climax of the whole movie was, one of them, through the art department, managed to get a girl who did nude modeling. We went to Michael's little apartment and they tried to compose this scene. The idea was, "We're going to set the camera up on this tripod. We're going to show Bob lying in bed and sleeping, because he was getting ready to have a dream. What we're going to do is stop the camera, and then we're going to get the nude model girl to come in and get in bed with him and turn it back on." That was pretty risqué for those days.

Bob Schiffer: Then I come back to reality in a bathroom shaving, and then I'm out jogging. There's a scene with me eating French fries at this dive cafeteria near where we lived. Then I put some money in a jukebox and suddenly I'm a rock star.

With just one shoddily made film on his resume, Chris decided rock 'n' roll would remain his primary passion. It was during this semester that he and Andy collaborated musically for the first time.

Andy Hummel: All this music, Steve Miller, Crosby, Stills & Nash, *Abbey Road,* was just coming out, and, of course, Led Zeppelin. It was all absolutely fascinating to us. We increasingly got to the point where we said, "We've got to figure out a way we can play music." When we went home for Christmas break we said, "Well, we'll bring our gear back with us to UT." Chris had his guitar, I brought my amplifier and bass, and we started playing together in the dorm room.

John Dando: They weren't playing shows or anything, but they did have a couple guitars.

Andy Hummel: Chris had his red Gibson 330. I had a red Gibson EBO bass. The two guitars looked exactly alike. I had this big, old ugly Kustom amplifier. We had this musical connection going and we did that for those three or four months.

Bob Schiffer: They'd be in their room jamming all the time.

Andy Hummel: Of course, in those days, the only way you could make your amplifier sound good was to turn it way up. That didn't last long in a dorm room. We couldn't play much because of the sound problem. People would stick their umbrellas out the window and whack on our window and yell, "Turn it down! Shut up!" Everyone in the dorm wanted to kick us out. We were loud and obnoxious. We were trying to let the musical demon out.

Gary Stevens: Chris talked the manager of their dorm into letting them have a little room down in the basement across from the laundromat to play music in. He and Andy would get stoned and go down there every night with their guitars.

Andy Hummel: Chris and I were inseparable in those days because we lived with each other and pretty much did all the same things. We tried to figure out everything we could about how English rock 'n' roll bands made the sounds they made, who they were and what they did. And, "Gosh, what is going to be on the next Beatles album to come out, how can we find out about it and where can we get that information?" You had to dig to come up with it. It was a joined-at-the-hip effort.

Michael O'Brien: Chris loved George Harrison, I remember him playing "Here Comes the Sun" over and over again.

Chris Bell at Michael O'Brien's apartment in Knoxville, February, 1971.

PHOTO BY MICHAEL O'BRIEN

Andy Hummel and Chris Bell in John Fry's plane.

PHOTO BY JOHN FRY

Chris Bell at UT.

PHOTO BY ANDY HUMMEL

Bob Schiffer: He admired George Harrison. That was his idol. That was his favorite Beatle, no question about it.

Andy Hummel: One night, Chris and I were in our dorm room and said, "What if we just call Apple and see what happens?" We called Apple Records up. Chris was the one on the phone. Somebody answered. It must have been the middle of the night there. Somebody with a John Lennon-sounding voice answers the phone and Chris says, "Who is this?" I guess he caught him off guard. They weren't used to getting a phone call like that. The guy goes, "Uh, Neil Aspinall." It may have actually been Neil Aspinall, or maybe it was John Lennon.

Bob Schiffer: Music was everything to Chris. He was big into Led Zeppelin, the Byrds and Thunderclap Newman. He had all kinds of tastes.

Andy Hummel: The amount of music hitting the airwaves in those days was just phenomenal. The San Francisco thing was going crazy. The English thing was going crazy. Woodstock had just happened. We started going out and hearing the occasional band because the university had concerts and there were little clubs with music. We didn't see a whole lot of live music, but there was a Byrds tribute band that we went and listened to at some club and they all had Rickenbacker twelve-strings. But it was mainly listening to records, especially when we were high. We both had stereos and as many LPs as we could get our hands on.

With no parents to answer to, Chris and Andy made a couple of low-budget expeditions to New York City.

Andy Hummel: We went there with Bob Schiffer and Michael O'Brien that fall. We had enough money to fly up there, but we didn't have enough money to get back.

Bob Schiffer: I stayed at my house, they stayed at a real dive hotel about a mile from my house. We went out around New York—the Village and other places.

Andy Hummel: Bob was like, "No problem. I will visit my dad. He'll give me money, so we can have a good time in New York. We'll all fly home on my nickel." We got up there and didn't have anywhere to stay. We spent the first night in Grand Central Station, but you couldn't sleep there for long because the cops would kick you out.

Bob Schiffer: The cops came in with their billy clubs and told us to get up. It's the closest I've ever felt to a homeless person.

Andy Hummel: Then the three of us went wandering around while Bob went to Brooklyn to see his dad and get this money. His dad wrote him a check, which would have been enough to get us home, but the trouble was, and this never occurred to us, you can't just walk into a bank in New York City and cash a check. It didn't even matter that it was obviously his dad. "No way we're cashing that check. Not unless he's here," they told us. Finally, my mother wired us some money. I called her up. She didn't even know I was in New York. It was like, "Gosh, mom. We're stuck in New York City and we've got to get home somehow. Please wire us some money!"

Andy Hummel: We also went to New York City right after Christmas. It was cold as hell. There was this girl, Beth Horton, she went to Hutchison. She was from Germantown and was good friends with Chris.

Cindy Bell Coleman: Beth was a constant in his life.

Andy Hummel: She blew into town in her Cutlass and said, "Let's go to New York City, I've got a car." We each grabbed a carton of cigarettes and said, "All right, let's go!" We stayed in this awful place called the Times Square Motor Hotel. We all stayed together in one room. I mean, this was a sleazy hotel, at least it seemed that way to us. We pulled the mattress off this bed and there was this long pocket knife under there. We spent three or four days cruising around New York City trying to see everything there was to see and taking pictures. That was the Christmas that John and Yoko put up the billboard in New York City that said "War is Over! If You Want it." A lot was going on.

With guitars in hand, but no place to turn up the volume, Chris and Andy decided to leave UT following their freshman year. In May 1970, the pair headed home to Memphis where they could attend a local college and utilize both Ardent Studios and the backhouse. By that time, John Dando had also dropped out and returned to Memphis.

Andy Hummel: Chris and I went back to school and finished up that spring quarter and came back to Memphis for the summer. We both had our fill of going away for college. No car, living in a dorm room, can't play music and no place to develop your pictures—it was a drag.

Michael O'Brien: Chris left college because he couldn't get anything going musically at UT. I don't ever remember him performing or playing that freshman year. In Memphis, Chris had access to the recording studio and musicians he knew. The culture of East Tennessee, Knoxville in 1969 and 1970, was probably a foreign experience for him. He felt out of his element. I didn't see Chris much after he left because I stayed in Knoxville for the next three years. I never saw the dark side of him.

Andy Hummel: There's this sort of sarcastic, facetious, us-against-the-world elitist mindset that existed back in the early days of Chris and me being in college and subsequently starting up what eventually became Big Star. That was beginning to tail off somewhat as Chris was becoming more real and perhaps expressing more of his inner self artistically. Being elitists in your high-school days is one thing, it's another thing entirely once you've been in college for a year or two. College knocks a lot of that out of you.

Chris Bell: It wasn't much of a college experience. It was a university and we were just getting high or tripping all the time and listening to music instead of studying, which was all I was interested in. After a year of that, I came back to Memphis.

John Dando and Chris Bell, in 1969, pose on campus at
the University of Tennessee, Knoxville.

PHOTO BY ANDY HUMMEL

Thomas Dean Eubanks performed with Chris in two Big Star precursors, Rock City
and Icewater. Under the signature Thomas Dean, he also issued
a 1974 solo single, "Oh Babe."

COURTESY OF BILL CUNNINGHAM

Chris Bell snaps a self-portrait at his parent's house, 1970.
COURTESY OF DAVID BELL

CHAPTER 6

FREE AGAIN — ICEWATER: 1969-1970

While Chris regrouped in Memphis, Alex Chilton was also going through a transitional period. At eighteen, Alex was contemplating his exit from the Box Tops. Fresh off another disappointing tour due to poorly-planned gigs, and while still technically on contract with the dissolving group, he stealthily entered Ardent Studios in 1969 to record solo material and begin doing things on his own terms. While he was the frontman, he was never the leader or creative force of the group, and he was determined to free himself from the constraints of the Box Tops machine.

Later titled 1970, *the Ardent sessions feature the proposed single "Free Again," a standout track reflecting Alex's pursuit of autonomy. The burgeoning songwriter was not only departing an internationally famous blue-eyed soul group, he was also undergoing a divorce from Suzi Greene, the mother of his son, Timothee Chilton, born in late 1968. Pressures were mounting from a few directions, and he planned to escape it all, including many of his fatherly duties. Amidst the stress, Alex felt a creative spark. He practiced guitar relentlessly and soon became a proficient player. He also filled notebooks with both clever ("I Wish I Could Meet Elvis") and poetic lyrics, like the melancholy ballad "All We Ever Got from Them Was Pain."*

Terry Manning: Alex felt that they were imposing their will on him. He would pitch his songs when they were looking for new material and, with one or two exceptions, they would just reject all of them. I would be working in sessions with them, and whenever Dan Penn would instruct him to "sing it like this," Alex would roll his eyes. He would look over at me and we would wink at each other like, "We are the hip young guys." At the time, it was like, "We could do so much better." So, Alex came to me after one session and said, "Let's just do it." That *1970* album did bridge the gap between the Box Tops and Big Star.

Steve Rhea: Alex had been on the road for two or three years. He was different and aware, not only of music, but the music business.

Andy Hummel: We heard Alex was around doing sessions but didn't run into him during that period.

Richard Rosebrough: While Alex was still a Box Top, there was a proposal by Terry Manning to record a demo just to see what Alex could do without the Box Tops. I played drums on just about all of it. It had originals and some covers, like "Sugar, Sugar" and "Jumpin' Jack Flash."

Alex Chilton: "Sugar, Sugar" is closer to the Yardbirds than the Archies. It was sort of a humorous thing, meant to be the heavy version of "Sugar, Sugar." Like Iron Butterfly doing "Sugar, Sugar," real spontaneous.

Richard Rosebrough: I always felt that was Fry's first attempt to get a bona fide artist and develop talent for Ardent.

Carole Ruleman Manning: There was a push to release some of this material. A little bit of a relationship developed between Memphis and New York, people taking trips up there to shop material. John Fry, John King, Terry and I went up and tried to sell Alex's *1970* album. There was a desire to produce and release records.

The album was pitched to a few labels, including Atlantic Records and the Beach Boys' Brother Records, but all prospects fell through. The album sat shelved for decades. Ardent Records finally released 1970 in 1996, and Omnivore Recordings later issued a 2012 expanded version as Free Again: The "1970" Sessions.

Steve Rhea: No record label picked it up at the time, but much of it was still in the vein of the Box Tops. He was still singing in his low register. "Free Again" and some of the other songs could have been straight Box Tops songs. "Free Again" was the song I liked the most. It had "hit" written all over it. Then they put the steel guitar in it and probably freaked out the radio folks and record labels. They were probably thinking, *Is this country or rock?* It never got any traction.

Andy Hummel: Chris and I got a test pressing of the LP Alex worked on with Terry Manning. It was like, "Wow! Who's this guy?" I thought he was like "The Letter" and "Neon Rainbow" and all that. It was chock-full of great music.

Jim Dickinson: In the late '60s, at a particularly low ebb of my career, I considered becoming a rock journalist. I was fascinated by the Box

Tops, so I did this interview with Alex Chilton after it was all over. There was a million-selling record for "Cry Like A Baby" on the wall, and the label had peeled off. It was lying in the corner like a dead moth, surely symbolic to Alex of his career.

Alex Chilton: ["Neon Rainbow"] was right after "The Letter" and it didn't do so well. People didn't recognize the group at all, you know. And then came "Cry Like a Baby," and that was pretty big. Then we did a few things that didn't do so hot. And then we had another pretty big one. "Soul Deep" was big, that was the last big record we had.

Right out of the gate Alex's solo career was experiencing turbulence and a lack of commercial success. Nonetheless, he was introduced into the Ardent family and was encouraged by the artistic freedom experienced at the studio, in comparison to his dealings with Box Tops producer Dan Penn.

Alex Chilton: They kept presenting me with such material that I thought was not all that good, so I was trying to write something better...The material that they came up with for me, I just felt from the start that it was dead wrong for me.

Bill Cunningham: People took advantage of us, no doubt, but there is a lot of wrong information out there, too—statements that we didn't play on anything. That's not right at all. There are songs only Alex and I played on. We played all the instruments. "I See Only Sunshine" is one of those songs. The two of us built it up because we needed a B-side for "Sweet Cream Ladies" [1969]. They used studio guys when we were out on the road, so they could rapidly get a track ready, but it's not like we were never in the studio or were kicked out of the studio. We're all over a lot of records.

Alex Chilton: The Box Tops actually played on "The Letter," but after that our producer said, "You people are too incompetent to do any-thing." We never got it together at all as a band. It was a demoralizing experience. I hated doing it.

Dan Penn — Producer, singer-songwriter: I resent that and don't like it. [Alex] was never oppressed in any way at American Studios by me. The only thing Alex has got any kicks about is that I didn't want to cut some of his stupid songs...and I told him as much. It was for his own good. Later on, he wrote some better stupid songs with Big Star and they were pretty good. Everybody thought I crammed "me" down his throat—not so. I didn't coach him to sing like me. I might have said, "Hey, just a tad more punch" or "a little rougher, maybe?" And I did say, "Say 'aero-plane,' don't say airplane." But that's it, everything else was pure Alex.

Alex Chilton: When the Box Tops first started out, I couldn't play guitar much at all. Only after we had our first hit records did I start playing.

Bill Cunningham: Alex had just started writing songs early on and he tried to get them placed. Dan Penn tended to not pay attention to them. That's one thing that frustrated Alex. Later, he was able to talk Dan into placing them on B-sides, so he got some money from that.

Dan Penn: All my records with Alex, I'm proud of the way I acted. I'm proud of the way he acted. I don't know what all these bitchin's are about...I'm tired of that Alex Chilton sob story.

Alex Chilton: The only reason I stayed was because everybody told me it was such a great thing. I finally got to the point where I wouldn't listen to what anybody said anymore. We never sounded any good because the record had tunes on them that nobody cared for. I hated "Cry Like a Baby." The best thing we ever did was "The Letter." I liked "Soul Deep" and it was written by [Wayne Carson], the same guy who wrote "The Letter."

Jim Dickinson: My initial interest in Alex was because of those records. The second Box Tops album, *Cry Like A Baby,* and the Dusty Springfield record *Dusty In Memphis,* which were made simultaneously, are the high-water marks of pop music in Memphis. I don't think Stax ever came close. Alex won't even talk about that record, though. I mean, that's unbelievable. Of course, it's not the band, it's the American [Sound Studio] rhythm section and they were a fucking *band*. You know, what's the difference?

Bill Cunningham: I left the Box Tops and went to school. I left the last day of August 1969. The band had a few personnel changes right after that without input from the band members. Nothing was our choice and that alienated us a lot. John and Danny, they both quit, mostly because of the draft and Vietnam, they also went to college. I've heard the band disintegrated after I left.

Alex Chilton: One day, I finally got fed up with playing with the Box Tops. It was a distinct day of my life. I said, "Hey, forget it. From here on, I've had it."

Alex didn't officially abandon the Box Tops until February 1970.

Alex Chilton: I guess it was about 1969, during Christmas time [the Box Tops] had a tour booked to go to England and play around in there. [We] got there and looked at the gear we were going to use and the way we were going to travel around. It was this stinky old van, and this junky, old equipment that sounded horrible...We had played a lot of gigs in our time on equipment that wasn't ours, and a lot of it sounded bad. Things were pretty primitive back then in a lot of cases. We had done that enough and I didn't want to start doing it all over Europe. I just kind of said, "Well, look, you guys go ahead and play it, but I'm not going to make this series of dates here." And you can imagine the flap that set off in our management. So anyway, we came back to the States and started doing some more dates into 1970...Somewhere in like January or February, in North Carolina, I said, "Look, I can't do it anymore."

Bill Cunningham: Gary and Alex were over it.

Chris Bell: By early 1970, Alex had virtually reached the end of the road with the Box Tops. He hated the gigs and eventually he walked off stage in the middle of a gig because it was so awful.

Alex Chilton: I wouldn't say I "stormed off the stage," but I know the last gig I played with them did end a little early. I went back to Memphis and hung around there for [four months] and then went to New York that summer.

In the autumn of 1970 Bell and Hummel enrolled at the same Memphis college, though advancing their recording and songwriting skills remained a priority, especially for Chris. The pair, along with fellow music aficionado John Dando, lugged guitars to the backhouse.

Andy Hummel: We had already decided before we got back that we were going to try to do something musically and have a band...We both immediately applied to Southwestern at Memphis, which was a small liberal arts college in Memphis. It's now called Rhodes College.

Chris Bell: I was trying to stay pretty closely involved with music.

Richard Rosebrough: It was the year they left UT and came back to Memphis that all these things really started happening at Ardent.

John Dando: I was just lost when I came back to Memphis. I had nothing to do and nobody to do anything with, so Chris and I started spending a lot of time together at the beginning of the summer of 1970. We struck up a much closer friendship. Chris and I got into the infamous Bell family backhouse. That's when our friendship began to grow. We started getting into all kinds of mischief. We spent a lot of time fooling around at that backhouse.

Andy Hummel: Chris and I started working on Chris' backhouse, trying to fix it up so the kitchen could be a dark lab where we could develop pictures.

David Bell: Chris was into photography. He did some experimental photography, psychedelic prints. He would show me eight-by-tens and I have memories of watching things develop in pans of chemicals. He was also doing a little bit of oil painting.

John Dando: One of the many projects Chris and I got involved in was when we decided we wanted an Altec Voice of the Theater speaker system, the standard PA system that was in virtually every movie theater. We wanted to use it as a big studio monitor speaker in the backhouse. Not having money to buy one, we borrowed one from Ardent and decided to copy it. We traced it to get the measurements off it. We precisely measured everything. It had all these pieces of curved plywood in it. We literally just reverse-engineered one and built this cabinet with glue and nails. We steamed pieces of wood, bent them, made all these precise cuts. We built a knock-off of one, which Big Star used for a long time as their PA system. No one could tell the difference. It worked great.

Andy Hummel: In the front room of the backhouse is where we set up for the band. We moved our musical equipment back there and started playing a little bit. We had big plans for that little shack. It was going to become culture central!

John Dando: Chris was still into the notion of being a Beatle. Between the two of us, we really believed we were building Apple Corps. I guess my role in the Apple fantasy was Mal Evans, the road manager. We saw no limits to what we could do. We were in this backhouse, which had no plumbing, attempting to build a dark room. We laid asphalt tile and put up sheetrock and painted. Anything we needed to buy or do, we figured out a way.

The backhouse may have served as a prime rehearsal spot, but it didn't compare to Ardent. Chris' increased presence at the hit-making studio strengthened his bond with John Fry, who recognized Chris' passion and allowed him to experiment with his own projects at night. And with a growing demand for more able engineers, Fry started an Audio Engineering 101 class specifically created for Chris and his friends.

John Fry: Back then, there were no recording schools. Our studio business was growing, so I started running some engineering classes at the studio. Chris, Andy and Richard Rosebrough all participated in that.

Carole Ruleman Manning: In a way, the backhouse crew kind of moved over to Ardent.

John Fry: I held little classes to try to get some extra trained engineers, so Terry and I wouldn't have to work ourselves to death as we had been. We explained the basic physics of sound, because otherwise you can't understand how a microphone works and you'll always be puzzled as to why you're not getting good results. From the console, we would move on to the outboard equipment—what's compression ratio? What's attack and release time? They were appreciative and, frankly, it benefited us.

Drew DeNicola: Fry is technical about every detail. John Fry had a clear "John Fry method" on how to do things and that's what he taught at the student courses. The engineering courses were like six-to-eight weeks [long]. It wasn't like, "Come on in and I'll show you a few things." John treated it seriously and Chris was in the first graduating class of that seminar.

Richard Rosebrough: There were six people, including Chris Bell and myself. We showed up at 8 a.m. on a Monday to learn how to record. We showed up, usually drunk or hungover, and John Fry had a chalkboard and stood in front of it like a teacher.

Andy Hummel: He was holding classes to teach people the physics of recording. Those classes were much more about that than sitting in the studio and manipulating a console or a tape machine. It was more about, "Here are the physics and engineering principles behind recording so you understand what you're doing before you go in the studio and actually start doing it." He was liberal with his knowledge and expertise. He was all about sharing it with anyone and, to some extent, getting people employment in that sort of work.

Richard Rosebrough: John got a blackboard in there and drew pictures of amplifiers, showed the path an audio signal would follow. He discussed different types of microphones, how a compressor works and why you used a compressor, what equalization was. He made it all simple and understandable. But Fry wasn't a musician. He had the technical recording side of it down, but he wasn't a musician. He couldn't tell you how to play a piano, a guitar or drums.

Terry Manning: The overriding thing I learned from John Fry was to make every effort you can to know the real science and physics of sound, so you can capture it the way you want, or control it as needed, or let things shine through. If you just wing it, you may get lucky and yes, going by the book is a bit rigid to some people. But he did impress upon me that I should know where the sound is coming from, what picks up sound waves in the way you want and how to keep from getting distortion and noise—all the basics of solid engineering. He was just a fanatic on doing it right.

After Chris completed Fry's class twice in a row, he was experienced enough to pick up engineering jobs for some of Ardent's paid clients, which earned the nineteen-year-old additional access to the studio for his personal projects.

David Bell: Chris started doing a fair amount of engineering at Ardent. In fact, it was that time he spent recording with the Memphis Horns that later got them to do the horns on *#1 Record*. I went to the old Ardent on National a few times, but that was the start of me being out of the country for seven years. I had gone to France.

John Fry: Chris was doing some engineering for our clients. He was meticulous about production, paying close attention to detail.

Drew DeNicola: Perhaps he had to prove the validity of rock 'n' roll as a pursuit because his parents didn't fully approve. But the other reason is he was obsessed with John Fry.

Terry Manning: Chris asked me a lot of questions and I helped mentor him a bit, too. He learned quite a lot. Chris had above-average studio skills for being a band member. I don't think he rose to the level of a full-fledged engineer, like being able to work any kind of session: classical, folk and different kinds of microphoning, but he was quite aware of sound.

Adam Hill: He knew what he was doing. Even though some of his later solo recordings were not recorded as well as they could have been, he knew how to run a machine. He knew how to patch in a compressor, he knew how to cut his own vocals, and he knew what levels to cut on the machine. He wasn't as good as Fry, but nobody was.

Chris Bell: Ardent had an arrangement where anybody that had any prospect and wasn't totally awful could come in and work for nothing. Not anybody, but if there was a person who'd been hanging around there, which is what Andy Hummel and I did for a long time, you'd reach the status of being able to go in after hours and record your own songs, or maybe bring in a couple of friends to work with.

Greg Reding — Pianist, guitarist, vocalist, the Hot Dogs: It was an absolute creative's paradise. You were encouraged to go in and work.

Chris Bell: John Fry would let you come in, if you could do something for Ardent—after you'd assembled some masters or something. He'd just expect some repayment for the time you had used.

John Fry: They all had keys to the studio. They could come and go as they pleased. You might say I was a fool for trusting all those folks, but they were responsible. We never had anybody tear up anything. It worked out fine.

Andy Hummel: We had weaseled our way into Ardent. We were actually allowed to go in the studio late at night and fiddle around. Once you start hanging out at Ardent, you're suddenly exposed to a much bigger world. There were all these Stax people there, a group of people you would have never associated with either artistically or personally—suddenly your eyes get big.

Gary Stevens: Chris was always either at home playing guitar in his bedroom, asleep or at Ardent. On his way between Ardent and home, he got into the habit of stopping into my house on Poplar. He knew I stayed up all night, and Andy was usually with me. If he drove by and Andy's car was there, he'd pop in at 3 a.m. with a six-pack of Heineken. Chris always had a reel of tape with him and would say, "I want you to hear this." And it would be the most bizarre shit, a lot of strange sounds.

Chris and Steve Rhea's debut performance on a major-label record came courtesy of his Ardent connections. In 1970, Terry Manning invited them to lay down guitar on the Home Sweet Home *LP — Manning's own tongue-in-cheek solo record. The disc, recorded at Ardent, was released via Enterprise Records, a subsidiary of Stax responsible for Isaac Hayes' earliest albums.*

Terry Manning: I can see Chris walking into National with his Gibson 330, looking at the amps and the equipment with his eyes wide open, just like a kid in a candy store. He knew, just as I did a few years earlier, that this is where he was going to be.

Richard Rosebrough: I also played on Terry's album some. Chris played through his Fender Bassman. He played loudly, and all his parts were overdubbed. He was dressed up in rock 'n' roll essentials: tight jeans, tasteful coat and sunglasses under his headphones. His curly hair was patented and to die for. He was hot and at full stride.

Terry Manning: We all knew each other well musically by then, so when I got the chance to record *Home Sweet Home*, I also asked Chris to come in to play some leads on two or three songs, because I thought he played better lead than I did. They were both, but especially Chris, intrigued by the chance to be in a real studio and create original music. All the things we did later, Icewater, Rock City and Big Star, sort of flowed out of all that.

Richard Rosebrough: Terry also called in Paul Cannon to play his Les Paul on a few selections, but I was not present for that. That was that slick million-note guitar, definitely not Chris Bell.

Terry Manning: Chris was just excited to death to be playing on a record. He played on "Guess Things Happen That Way," "Trashy Dog," and "Wild Wild Rocker." Previously, he also played one small harmony part to my guitar solo on my version of "One After 909." He used a few pedals. He loved his Gibson 330. He also had a Telecaster, but that Gibson was his signature guitar. It was red, and the kind with the Mickey Mouse ears. He almost always used Fender amps.

David Bell: I showed some friends of mine *Home Sweet Home* and they said, "Wow! That's impressive." That's when I first realized Chris was getting serious.

With a bit of sweat equity built up at Ardent, Chris decided to get serious about writing and producing originals with his old Christmas Future mates Steve Rhea and Terry Manning. The trio impulsively chose Icewater as its moniker and started cutting original tunes after hours. Andy Hummel lent a couple basslines to the Icewater stockpile, like "Sunshine," a soft ballad penned and led by Steve. Chris, who played lead guitar, was still doubtful about his vocal abilities and only sang lead on "Looking Forward." The more self-assured Steve mainly handled lead vocals, along with guitar and drum work. Terry contributed bass and keys. Their tracks, particularly "All I See is You," fully mirrored the Beatles' pop sensibilities. Not long after the onset of Icewater, Chris would simultaneously embark on a heavier studio outfit called Rock City, along with vocalist/guitarist Tom Eubanks. But, for now, it was all about Icewater.

Andy Hummel: We hung around Ardent more and more. We started to be able to come into the studio at night. But, at that point, it was mainly the Steve-and-Chris show, with Terry in there some.

Terry Manning: Early on, Chris had no original songs. Then he started writing and got really into it.

Steve Rhea: Icewater and Rock City is the point where we stop playing Beatles and Yardbirds covers and we start writing material. Chris is collaborating with Eubanks [for Rock City], trying to write in that style. It's guitar-driven and very 1970s-sounding, as opposed to what Chris is doing with me when we were writing [for Icewater]...With me, Chris is working more on harmonies and pop-sounding material, not so much heavy and guitar-driven. We're writing songs, some of which are acoustic, some are electric...At this point, I've gone from being a crazy Keith Moon acolyte, to being mellow like Crosby, Stills and Nash. For me, there were a lot of acoustic melodic lines and harmonies.

Terry Manning: When Chris and Steve first came into Ardent, certainly they were wet behind the ears technically, but from my sessions, and then some excellent instruction from John, they quickly became good enough to get a sound down on tape, especially Chris.

Steve Rhea: I wrote "All I See is You" and played the guitar and drums and sang. Chris played bass. The guitar was plugged into a Leslie [speaker]. I hear more of Terry in "Feeling High." That's pretty original and I remember us trying to have a long fade at the end. These tracks were recorded as Icewater. A lot of things we did in that era were kind of tongue in cheek. We were always creating these commentaries on what was going on around us.

Chris Bell: I was pretty heavily involved at Ardent by that time. I had been doing some recording there on my own with Jody, Andy, and all kinds of different people.

As Steve, Icewater's drummer, was shifting to playing guitar and singing, a need for a drummer arose. Enter Jody Stephens. While still a high schooler, Jody made his entrance into the Ardent circle as the drummer for Icewater, and later Rock City. This put three-fourths of Big Star in the same room for the first time. A shade younger than the rest, born October 4, 1952 in Memphis, Jody joined the Ardent family and remains with the company as its Vice President of Production. But for now, like Chris, he was just in awe of the magic happening around him.

Andy Hummel: We needed a drummer. I said, "Oh, I know this guy Jody Stephens who I played with in the ninth grade and he's dating my old girlfriend Beverly Baxter."

Jody Stephens: I was still in high school, but I was playing drums in the first college production of *Hair*, at Memphis State. Andy came to see one of the shows and came up and said, "Hey, we're putting a band together, are you interested in coming and jamming a bit?" I said, "Sure."

Steve Rhea: Jody was invited to come in and take over the drums as I moved more toward guitar and bass for Icewater sessions. When we played live, I was playing guitar and he was playing drums. I graduated at that point to a different role.

Jody Stephens: We were kids back then. The first time I stepped through the door at Ardent, I was seventeen. Andy Hummel introduced me to Chris Bell for the first time around March 1970. We were all outside on a sidewalk somewhere. Andy introduced me, and then Chris pulled Andy off to the side to talk to him privately. I thought, *Wow, that's kind of an interesting way to meet someone.* Chris was a pretty private person until you got to know him. Chris was usually on a mission of some sort, so he was selective of the people he spoke to. Chris was focused on being a musician and writing, being in the studio and all the things that entailed. He kind of lived and breathed it. The next time I met up with Chris was at Ardent Studios at a session of his. He was working with Steve Rhea on "All I See is You." It just kind of blew my mind because they were recording music in a fashion and style that was similar to what got me into music, the Beatles and the British Invasion. It sounded so different from everything else that was being done in Memphis at the time. There were great things happening there. It was like, "Wow, how did you do that?" Ardent was the place to experience that.

Beverly Baxter Ross: If I was at Chris' house, we would just hang out and snack in the kitchen. He'd make me tea and crumpets. But mostly I was out in the backhouse for a lot of their rehearsals because I was Jody's steady girlfriend.

Jody Stephens: I just remember all of us having coats on and a space heater. It was still cold as hell in that backhouse. That's where we met up for the first time to play together. The first time it was just kind of a jam. There were a lot of people there, but there weren't any attitudes. We were just exploring music and trying to have fun.

John Dando: In those days, Chris wasn't as dead serious about music. He was having fun.

Jody Stephens: Steve Rhea was at this first jam, Terry Manning was there with a guitar strapped on, and Chris, myself and Andy. The whole thing was kind of disjointed. I walked away thinking it could probably never be organized enough to get anything done, but I was wrong. The next rehearsal turned out to be more of a band rehearsal with Steve, Chris and Andy. We started working on songs. That was the beginning.

Andy Hummel: Jody was just a really good drummer, that's the main thing. He was maybe somewhat of a calming influence.

Steve Rhea: Jody never smoked dope or did any of that craziness. He's just a down-to-earth guy.

Andy Hummel: He was also a really good chick magnet.

Carole Ruleman Manning: Any female who met Jody immediately thought, "Wow, this guy is seriously good-looking and it's not fair for him to have longer eyelashes than I do." He could have modeled any-where on earth.

Beverly Baxter Ross: Jody was the heartthrob, with Andy following close on his heels.

With Steve Rhea leaving Memphis to attend Southern Methodist University in Texas, Jody committed to drumming for Icewater at a string of local gigs. As 1971 approached, the studio project essentially morphed into a gigging live band, playing mostly covers and a few originals. While Chris and Steve infrequently teamed up musically over the ensuing months for one-off shows and sessions, Chris increasingly performed live with Andy and Jody. Big Star was on the horizon. In later years, Steve became a successful banker and financial planner.

Steve Rhea: I didn't see myself as a rock star down the road, so I chose to go to Dallas to go to college.

Jody Stephens: Steve Rhea, who typically played drums, had to go back to school, which created an opening for me.

Steve Rhea: Years later Jody said to me, "I'm so glad you went to college." He said that because if I hadn't I probably would have been the drummer in Big Star and he wouldn't have.

Chris Bell: I got together with Andy and Jody. We were playing as a three-piece. It was still Jimi Hendrix, the James Gang, a lot of Who songs and a few Beatles tunes.

John Dando: We would put together gigs and go out and play. We would borrow my parents' station wagon and rent a U-Haul trailer.

Jody Stephens: We had trouble with gigs because we played what we wanted to. We didn't do dance material, and in the States, to survive, you had to do Top 40 material.

Andy Hummel: That was sometime during that fall, we were playing fraternity gigs...At the same time, Chris kept another side band going on with Steve Rhea. I don't think they played out but a couple of times, once in Humboldt at the Strawberry Festival.

John Dando: In those days, Chris was into James Gang. He covered James Gang songs before he started Big Star. He was also into Free, bands like that.

Andy Hummel: The influence was very much English with a little bit of San Francisco sound thrown in. We did Hendrix all the time. It was mainly who was good at that time. Clapton was good. Jimmy Page was good, probably better than any of these people. Chris was a huge Jimmy

Page fan, perhaps to a lesser extent, Eric Clapton. I was on board with all that.

Jody Stephens: We were doing Free, Led Zeppelin and Badfinger material at one-nighters.

Andy Hummel: You couldn't do a lot of Zeppelin because that took a lot of technical expertise we didn't have at that point. We did the Yardbirds. We didn't do Creedence Clearwater Revival. I liked Creedence, but CCR was not a Chris thing at all.

Jody Stephens: I can remember covers, like "Funk 49," a Led Zeppelin song or two. We did "Tinker Taylor," the Terry Reid song.

For a short stint, Tom Eubanks stepped in as lead vocalist for Icewater at live shows. While he didn't record with the studio group, within months he'd be in the studio laying down Rock City tracks with Chris.

Andy Hummel: Chris said, "I know this guy Tom, he plays guitar and he sings, let's get him involved." He called Tom and Tom came over... We got Eubanks to come in and play with us, as well, and we became a four-piece for a while.

Steve Rhea: Chris had a great friend in Tom Eubanks, who'd played guitar and sang in a few garage bands with Chris.

Jody Stephens: We had several names, like Tommy Tutwiller & the Twisters, which was by accident. We were set to perform and [Tom] jokingly told the promoter that was our name. We got a good laugh out of it and went along to play the dance and all the tickets had "Tommy Tutwiller & the Twisters" on them.

Andy Hummel: Over time, we sort of coalesced into just a three-piece band with Jody Stephens on drums. Eventually Tom left the band...I don't think we played out with Tom very much. At some point, Tom left because he was off being married and running his dad's lumberyard. By the time we started playing out more, it was just the three of us: Chris, Jody and me. We were playing fraternity houses and mall openings.

Van Duren: The first time I heard Chris play was in 1970. Chris, Jody and Andy were playing as a three-piece called Icewater. They were playing a fraternity house at what's now Rhodes College. It was the end of the night, down to their last two or three songs. There were about three people there besides them. It was in a small room and they were playing so loud, it was unbelievable. Chris was just burning. They were doing a Free tune.

SOUTHWESTERN AT MEMPHIS
MEMPHIS, TENNESSEE

REPORT OF: BELL CHRISTOPHER BRANFORD

CLASS	SEX	HIGH SCHOOL CODE
2	1	

MR + MRS VERNON B BELL
1447 RIVERDALE ROAD
GERMANTOWN TN 38038

PERIOD ENDING		
12-24-70		
MO.	DAY	YR.

FACULTY ADVISOR
RUSSELL

DEPARTMENT	COURSE NO.	SEC.	DESCRIPTION OF COURSE	HRS. CRD.	GRADE	SEM. HRS.	QUAL. POINTS
			SESSION 1970-71 TERM I				
COM A	201	B1	AESTHETICS MASS MEDIA	3	B	3	6
ENGL	205	N1	WORLD LITERATURE	3	A	3	9
PSYCH	201	C1	GENERAL PSYCHOLOGY	3	B	3	6
COM A	DI		NARRATIVE PHOTO PROBS	3	NG	0	0
PH ED	100	A	HYSICAL EDUC MEN	0	F	0	0
		34	34 46 2.3529 2.3529 3.3333 AVERAGE FOR GRADE PERIOD ▶	12		9	21

REMARKS

EXPLANATION OF GRADES:

A-Excellent   F-Failure
B-Very Good   WP-Withdrew Passing
C-Average   WF-Withdrew Failing
D-Passing   X-Incomplete
E-Re-examination   S-Satisfactory

Chris Bell's December 1970 report card from Southwestern at Memphis, now known as Rhodes College.

COURTESY OF THE BELL FAMILY ARCHIVE

ACT TWO

#1 RECORD

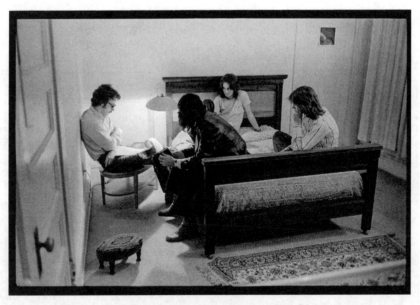

Big Star in Alex Chilton's bedroom, posing for a #1 Record promo.

PHOTO BY MICHAEL O'BRIEN

CHAPTER 7

ROCK CITY — BIG STAR: WINTER 1970-1971

By December 1970, Chris and Steve decided to shop their three-song Icewater demo tape to major labels in New York. While they knew landing a deal was a long shot, Chris' entire crew flew to the East Coast with high hopes, only to be labeled as "Beatles wannabes" by an Elektra Records representative. A few other meetings went nowhere, though the fateful trip served a higher purpose after Chris reunited over acoustic guitars with his old friend Alex Chilton, who lived in the Village.

Steve Rhea: Icewater played one dance in Memphis and then caught a plane the next morning to New York. We took that tape to Elektra Records and some other companies.

John Fry: Alex Chilton had been up in New York for some time. They knew Alex was up there and went to some lengths to seek him out.

Chris Bell: As a reaction to quitting the Box Tops, Alex went to New York to get away from it all and started hanging out in Greenwich Village. He was doing the folk scene with people like Loudon Wainwright III. He went to New York and stayed there for a year and met up with Keith Sykes.

Steve Rhea: Chris stayed at Alex's apartment. Jody, Dando, myself and Andy all stayed at this hotel in Times Square. We were trying to see if anyone would release our songs or give us a budget to go back into the studio and keep pursuing this original material. We didn't get any takers, but we did sort of hook up with Alex at that point.

Robert Gordon: Chris met Alex in New York. They quickly realized they had a Lennon/McCartney kind of pairing and they wanted to further explore that.

Chris Bell: [Alex] talked to me about going to New York with him to do a duo thing, I would play electric guitar and he would play acoustic, like Simon & Garfunkel, or something. He'd been into the acoustic scene and I had been in an electric scene and I didn't want to leave my band...I was none too keen despite his persistence.

John Fry: Chris ultimately approached Alex with the idea of returning to Memphis and joining this band that eventually became Big Star.

Having made a loose agreement to catch up and collaborate soon, Alex promised to check out one of Icewater's shows on his next visit home to Memphis. He wasn't ready to abandon New York. With his girlfriend Vera Ellis by his side, Alex crashed at two different apartments on Thompson Street, pads leased by his close friends Keith Sykes and Gordon Alexander. He also befriended an assortment of musicians, and crossed paths with rock critics like Rolling Stone's Lenny Kaye and Bud Scoppa. One night at Bud's apartment, Alex mingled with his idol Roger McGuinn. He and Vera also attended Vietnam War protests, and were seen at folk, jazz and rock clubs like the Gaslight and Max's Kansas City. More importantly, Alex started performing solo at small clubs.

Alex Chilton: I would play around occasionally with an acoustic guitar. Hang around and play and learn. I knew a lot of folk musicians and was sort of interested in that kind of music, too. But [New York] was happening before that. By the time I got there it wasn't like it was in 1967 or earlier. Sixty-four would have been neat.

Chris Bell: He was starting to pick up some acoustic licks, just learning how to play country music and what was going on in New York at the time.

Alex Chilton: There were still a lot of bluegrass musicians who would come and hang out in Washington Square every Sunday. I fell in with a mandolin player down there and we were good buddies. His name is Grant Weisbrot.

Keith Sykes — Singer-songwriter, guitarist, solo: Alex and I listened to a lot of music and visited record stores quite a bit. He turned me on to Aaron Copland. He also explained electric guitars to me, told me which ones made what sounds. He was a cool cat.

Vera Ellis: He didn't come out of the Box Tops with much money, but he also was giving his ex Suzi and their son Timothee a big chunk of money. We had no money when we lived in New York. Occasionally, we would go down to the strip to Max's Kansas City to hang out. We never went out to dinner or anything like that. Mostly, Keith and Alex just sat around and played music.

Alex Chilton: I wanted to get to the point of playing to where I didn't need a band. I wanted to be able to go to a town anytime I wanted with a guitar in my hand and go into a club and get a job.

Robert Gordon: Keith Sykes, who had a record on Vanguard, was in New York doing the folk thing. Alex was staying on Keith's couch. That's where Chris met him, at Sykes's apartment in New York. Alex wanted to play guitar, he was becoming good at it. He was writing songs, it was post-Box Tops and folk seemed like the way to go.

Alex Chilton: I was confused. I didn't have a style. It was trying to evolve. I had always liked Dylan a lot. I had just quit the Box Tops, so I figured that I may as well make it so I could play all by myself. I didn't need anybody else. I thought I would live in New York and that would be fun, but I didn't play much while I was there. I was so scared and nervous that my hands would tremble too bad to play. I played the Bitter End, the Gaslight, maybe some other places. I learned a lot of bluegrass songs and a lot of those '60s folky things. My writing was evolving. "Thirteen" came from that period.

In preparation for his impending collaboration with Alex, Chris started off 1971 with his next studio-project, Rock City. He wanted to be equipped and organized by the time Alex returned to Memphis and this served as his trial run.

With Steve Rhea away at college, Chris tapped his childhood friend Thomas Dean Eubanks to join the sessions. The songwriting partnership led to the creation of "My Life is Right" and the optimistically melancholy track "Try Again," both later used on #1 Record. Paired with Chris' contributions is a stockpile of Tom's solid rockers like "The Preacher," "I Lost A Love," and "Think It's Time to Say Goodbye." Alongside them was Terry Manning, who contributed production work, keys and backing vocals. Jody Stephens stepped in on drums. Fellow Memphis-based musician Randy Copeland contributed basslines on multiple tracks. Rock City never played a live show, but served a higher purpose as it laid the sonic foundation for Big Star.

Steve Rhea: I didn't have a high confidence level [as the vocalist in Icewater]. Maybe that influenced Chris to engage Tom Eubanks or Chilton and try and come up with a band that could actually get people's attention.

Tom Eubanks: Chris called me up and said, "Do you have any original songs?" I said, "Actually, I do have a few I'm working on." He said, "Well, I need to learn how to use the recording equipment for this project I have coming up with Alex Chilton in a few months, would you want to record them? You can use the studio for free." Chris took me over to Ardent and I got to know John Fry and Terry Manning. It turned out that people liked the songs and that's when Terry got involved.

Terry Manning: Tom Eubanks came in and he had some pretty good songs, he sang and played bass. Chris, Tom and I started putting those songs together and it just sort of morphed into a studio band. Jody played on most of that, we just sort of made a group. Rock City was our first attempt at an actual group album by the backhouse gang.

Tom Eubanks: When we went in the studio, the songs just happened to come together. A lot of that is just luck and faith, but Chris could bring something to the table that just fit right. Terry Manning added little touches to tunes.

Terry Manning: Chris and I tracked most of it and I mixed it.

Tom Eubanks: Jody, once he did his drum parts, was gone because he was just kind enough to play for free. It was the first time he ever recorded...I already had "Lovely Lady" and "Think It's Time to Say Goodbye," which would have come across as more Kinks, if Chris hadn't put so much slapback echo on the guitars. Chris played bass on both of those.

John Fry: These earlier projects, like Icewater or Rock City, I had little to do with. They were proceeding on their own. It does seem paradoxical that we had all this highly organized structure, and then this other activity that was unstructured, but a lot of that comes from the home-studio days.

Tom Eubanks: We always cut in the B Studio, that's where Chris liked to record. John Dando would set up all the equipment, we would play, and then Dando would tear it down. We would go in at 11 p.m. and stay until 3 or 4 a.m., even when I had to be to work at 7 a.m.

Priming his engineering chops wasn't the only perk of these sessions for Chris, he also explored his lead-vocal range on "My Life is Right."

Tom Eubanks: I wrote all the words and then I went over to Chris' parents' house and sat on his bed in his bedroom. I showed Chris the lyrics and he said, "Yeah, I can do something with this." When it came time to sing it, Chris sang it back to me and when he got to the chorus and sang, "You are my life, you are my *daaay,*" he went up to a part a

106

high-harmony guy would sing. I told Chris, "I can't sing it, man. You sing it." I think that had something to do with Chris starting to sing lead on records. I said, "This is turning into more of a group thing, anyway, rather than a record on me."

Having the skillful Terry Manning on hand added some further technical flare to the Rock City tracks, including a makeshift "string section."

Tom Eubanks: We needed string sounds on "The Preacher," but had no money for strings. Terry was doing a string session and got them to record single notes and taped them on the eight-track. For whatever reason, they had an orchestra at Ardent, either for a jingle or a session for Stax. He got different notes and would bring them up on different faders and then operate the faders to make chords, making a string session. That was the dynamic of the Mellotron. Terry used the faders to play the notes. It was absolutely brilliant. I had all the words for "The Preacher." I gave them to Chris and he wrote the music. Even though it's a Beatles-esque lead, that's one of Chris' best lead guitar parts of all time.

Terry Manning: It was Chris who decided to call it Rock City. Down here you see signs that say "Rock City" everywhere, advertising the attraction near Chattanooga where you go up and see the rocks. Their motto was "See Seven States from Rock City," Chris thought *See Seven States* could have been the title. It was a pretty good idea, but when I finally released it [in 2003 via Lucky Seven Records], I didn't end up going with that idea.

Tom Eubanks: After we finished the songs, I was given about twenty quarter-inch tapes of the album and a list of contacts of major record labels. I went about my way cold-mailing the material out; the thing is just a glorified demo. The only label that gave it consideration was A&M. Somebody from there was interested in it, but since it was something they'd received cold in the mail, nothing ever happened with it.

Terry Manning: A funny thing was, I mixed up the mixed tapes inside the wrong boxes, and the Rock City mixes were lost and forgotten for years. I had put them in a box labeled "Tom and the Turtles" and didn't find it until the late '90s.

Tom Eubanks: Back when we were recording, on one of the boxes for the eight-track we recorded on, I wrote "Tom and the Turtles" on it—just to be stupid. Chris wrote "Rock City" on the other one.

Chris Morris: If you listen to the pre-Big Star bands, Icewater and Rock City, there's this kind of slow-moving element, this kind of shifting, viscous quality to the writing. That's Chris, that's not what Alex Chilton

107

brought to the Big Star table. It's also extremely present on *#1 Record*. Then you hear it full-blown on *I Am the Cosmos*, especially on the title song. It's kind of like the sound you'd hear if honey were dripping down the walls of the Sistine Chapel. It's this slow, beautiful, liquid sound. No one else that I can think of before that was doing that. It doesn't hit you over the head like a lot of rock 'n' roll.

Throughout the Rock City sessions, Chris, Andy and Jody kept up Icewater's live act. After a few months, Alex made good on his promise and attended one of their gigs. At the show, held at a Veterans of Foreign Wars hall in downtown Memphis, Chris handled lead vocals and played a mix of obscure covers and some originals. After the set, Alex met with Chris, who'd recently turned twenty. Chris again suggested Alex move home to Memphis and join the band and work on their songs at Ardent, a tempting offer for a man with a batch of new songs. The still-bitter Box Top wasn't keen on the idea of joining another band, but he was impressed with the power trio's live performance. Plus, after Alex's sublet apartment agreement expired, his parents' spacious Midtown Memphis home became more appealing.

Andy Hummel: At some point, Chris had a conversation with Alex.

Richard Rosebrough: They're talking and exchanging song ideas. That's when those two energies started meshing.

Jody Stephens: Chris wanted Alex to join the band as soon as he heard Alex might move back to Memphis.

Chris Bell: Alex came down to Memphis from New York and had heard us play...We spent a couple weeks formulating plans and were excited.

Carole Ruleman Manning: Alex and Chris were such different personalities. It was hard for me to think of them in a songwriting relationship. I didn't see it as something that would work so well.

A second Bell-Chilton meeting happened in February 1971, at Ardent Studios. It further bonded the two songwriters and solidified Alex officially joining the yet-to-be-named band (Chris dropped the Icewater moniker). Together, on a whim, they laid down "Watch the Sunrise." Alex had also already penned "In the Street" and "The Ballad of El Goodo." Chris had his Rock City songs and some new tracks in the hopper. The stars aligned.

Chris Bell: Alex had come along to play in the studio with Andy, Jody and myself. I played him a couple of my tunes and he played some of his and we both dug each other's songs.

Andy Hummel: The first hook-up with Alex was with Chris, Steve, and me—maybe Jody was there. Alex showed up and got out that wonderful

Martin twelve-string he had and played "Watch the Sunrise" and we recorded it. I thought it was an amazing and wonderful song. The guy was obviously super-talented. He didn't sound a thing like he sounded in the Box Tops, which was cool with me.

Steve Rhea: By this time, Alex began to sing in his higher register, but he still had that tried-and-true voice.

Chris Bell: In that rehearsal studio, it was really happening. There was a certain magic about the stuff we were doing.

Andy Hummel: Alex and Chris recognized each other's talent and were drawn to each other. Chris had access to Ardent and Alex had the name. Plus, they were both Capricorns. It just synergized.

Alex Chilton: Chris asked me to join the group and I did, but I didn't have any ideas about a rock band so much. It was a couple years later before I decided how I really wanted to approach things in a rock ensemble.

Chris Bell: Alex had already done [the *1970*] album with Ardent, which wasn't released. It's still in the can. One of the tunes off this album is "Free Again," or something—it was changed around and made into "Give Me Another Chance" for the first album. Anyway, that album fell through and at first Alex was pretty skeptical about Ardent when we formed Big Star because of that experience. I convinced him it would be a good idea.

Alex Chilton: He asked me to join his band and I had been listening to Chris' bands for years at parties, so I was excited about doing that. In '71, when we started recording and practicing, I came back to Memphis from New York and started hanging around at Ardent again.

Jody Stephens: We thought he'd make a great addition. Alex's tastes were more American than ours, although he dug the Kinks and the Zombies, so it was a strange combination.

Alex Chilton: It was a band that got together to play that sort of music. I mean, those guys didn't care for black music at all. You couldn't get them to listen to "Scratch My Back" for anything in the world.

Andy Hummel: The band, except for Alex, was together for about six months before that. Then he came into town and we got him to be in the group and then we started practicing.

Chris Bell: As Big Star was starting rehearsals, Alex decided he would come to Memphis and stay with the group.

Andy Hummel: We hooked up and started playing a lot, almost entirely in the studio. Shortly thereafter it was like, "Alex is going to join the band." Everybody thought that was cool. It took off from there because Alex had some songs.

John Fry: Right from the start, I thought it was great. What they were doing was amazing. I let them have access to the studio as much as possible. I was like, "Hey, I trust you guys. Don't trash the place and make sure you lock everything up and make it ready for in the morning."

Andy Hummel: I guess we talked a little, like, "Here's a guy who can go to any record company and get a contract and record anywhere he wanted to." It was cool Alex decided to hang around Ardent and join up with us. It always seemed a bit odd for me, but certainly fortuitous for us. It remains, to this day, a bit of a mystery as to why he wanted to come and play with us.

Danielle McCarthy-Boles: Alex had been there before, and Chris dreamt of that life. In some ways, Alex was the seasoned veteran and Chris was the naïve, excited dreamer of the two.

The band was still in its genesis when it was promised a recording contract by John Fry, who saw promise in the Bell/Chilton songwriting partnership. Ardent's newly re-launched record label was rejuvenated after it signed on as a rock subsidiary of Stax Records. The first band signed to the label was Cargoe, a Tulsa, Oklahoma-based rock group produced and mentored by Terry Manning.

John Fry: Stax had been talking to Ardent about being the rock brand for Stax. Al Bell, who was the president at Stax, said if we wanted to do that we could have this label and sign all the artists we wanted, but they would do the marketing, promotion and distribution. Of course, we said, "Yes, we would love to do that." Chris and the other guys knew about that and we had already said, "If you get a band together and some material, we will do an album."

Andy Hummel: When the notion was expressed, "Hey, let's record an album," there was a whole new layer of stress added on the band—now we've got to produce a product. You can't just write and record at your leisure. It can't be just fun all the time anymore, there's a work aspect to it.

Al Bell: I considered Fry, Dickinson and Manning to be unique creative geniuses. I had tremendous respect for them and I felt the same way about them that I did about Steve Cropper and Jim Stewart. They needed someone who saw their vision and could turn them loose and I had a sense of the artistry they were seeing. I wanted to help with what assets we had, the way they'd helped us with "Soul Limbo." I thought these guys could do for rock what we did for soul.

Carole Ruleman Manning: There was a need for Stax, they thought, to have a rock and pop presence in the company, a crossover into that market. Ardent, of course, wanted to release some of this product it was putting together. It was a natural relationship.

As Chris and Alex sharpened their growing list of songs, Stax signed a three-way deal with Ardent Records. The world-famous soul label acquired Ardent's manufacturing, merchandising and distribution rights. In an April 1, 1972, Billboard *interview, Al Bell called it one of Stax's "most significant expansion moves in years." The grassroots vacuum Chris operated in was suddenly a part of a bigger machine.*

Steve Rhea: Stax had made a run at having a label that would release pop-type music for years. Terry Manning had his Enterprise label with them. They were always kind of testing the waters, and none of it ever hit. When Ardent made a distribution deal with Stax they were going down a road that had been tried before and John and Terry would have to tell you why they thought it would work that time. Terry Manning was heavily involved over there at Stax, and John believed if we pooled all these resources we could get the job done.

Carole Ruleman Manning: There was so much excitement at Ardent. The excitement of a new company with a new release and a new distribution deal with Stax. While *#1 Record* was being recorded at Ardent, there was a lot of excitement. There was a positive feeling that things were going well. We perhaps had unrealistic expectations.

Richard Rosebrough: John Fry was able to finance the whole thing. It helps to be on John's good side for him to help you out financially. John believed in them and was willing to stay with them from start to finish.

John Dando: Fitting into the Apple mode, John Fry was their Brian Epstein.

Richard Rosebrough: John Fry, Terry Manning, me and the others that followed us, we were all engineers at Ardent. We all had our own pet projects at Ardent. We were all hoping individually for some success. Big Star became Fry's pet band. He liked them. He enjoyed their company. He enjoyed their youth. Fry thought they were writing brilliant songs and of all the bands coming in to Ardent, they had the best chance of making it.

Andy Hummel: If there hadn't been an Ardent, there wouldn't have been a Big Star.

Chris Bell: At this time, we were just playing, jamming together as a band, but we didn't have a name and such. One day, after a session, which John Fry was engineering, we stepped out of the studio for a while and right across the street was a Big Star food market. We thought, "Hey, what a great name for a group." We trooped back into the studio and said to John, "Oh, by the way, we've got a name—Big Star." And that was that.

Alex Chilton: The name Big Star was just sort of a joke. It was the time of glam and glitter rock. The name just seemed to be right for the times.

Andy Hummel: The name Big Star was just desperation. We needed a name, and nobody could think of one. We were sitting out in between the old shack on National and the actual storefront studio, smoking—something—and there was the Big Star grocery store right across the street. Somebody said, "Let's call it Big Star!" I guess it was just a flash of brilliance. All I was thinking was, "That's awfully presumptuous. What are people going to think when they see that in stores?"

The Big Star supermarket in Memphis, which inspired the band name.
ARDENT STUDIOS ARCHIVE

Big Star at Alex Chilton's parents' house at 154 N. Montgomery, Memphis. (L-R) Jody Stephens, Chris Bell, Alex Chilton, and Andy Hummel.

PHOTO BY CAROLE MANNING

CHAPTER 8

#1 SONGS — *#1* TRACKING: 1971

As Big Star attempted to take-off, mainstream rock 'n' roll had shifted gears. In April 1970, the Beatles broke up. Three months later Jimi Hendrix died. Janis Joplin followed soon after. By the summer of '71, Jim Morrison was buried in Paris. Radio had turned to the heavier sounds of Deep Purple and Alice Cooper. On the pop side of the dial were hits by Three Dog Night and the Bee Gees. Still, Chris and his mates stuck to their Tennessee-tinged Brit-rock roots despite the changing trends. It wasn't just the radio waves shifting around the band of Memphians.

Robert Gordon: The wound from Dr. King's assassination was still fresh in the early '70s. A lot of downtown Memphis had been boarded up and never repaired, Beale Street especially. In a way, that was a time when downtown was shutting down and things were moving out east. There was white flight. Polyester was beginning to be an issue, but cotton was still king and kept the economy pretty strong.

Andy Hummel: We were still getting money from our parents to survive on. It's not like we had jobs. You couldn't be at Ardent all night and then school all day and still be gainfully employed anywhere. Alex had already made enough money that his parents put it in some sort of trust fund. He went out and bought his own car.

David Bell: Alex wasn't in school anywhere, but Chris and Andy were both at Southwestern at Memphis. They were university students. Music is what they were doing in all their spare time. I don't know if Chris had a degree in mind or anything, maybe philosophy.

Jody Stephens: I was living with my parents. I moved out for a little while, but we weren't making any money playing in a band. The only way you could pull that off was to live at home.

Andy Hummel: What was going on in our lives at the time was very different for all four of us and was going to create conflict. We were all coming from different directions. I was immersed in going to college. I was doing music on the side in the late evenings. Chris was still trying to go to college, he was just going part-time. He was burning the candle at both ends. Jody was going to college at Memphis State. Alex, on the other hand, was pretty much set that he was going to be a professional musician.

Alex Chilton: We practiced together about three or four times a week for about three months.

Andy Hummel: Around the time we started rehearsing, Ardent had a separate building that was going to be a studio but never was, so they let us use the building to rehearse in. We rehearsed at Alex's parents' house, too. We had the whole band set-up in their music room. They had a grand piano and Oriental carpet in there and we would sit in there and play. Alex's dad was a jazz musician and he did the same thing in there.

Terry Manning: I totally enjoyed hearing Big Star develop. It didn't start out as, "This is an album called *#1 Record* by a group called Big Star." A couple of tracks came from the so-called Rock City sessions, the so-called Icewater sessions, and then when Alex came in, his style and input was added to Chris'.

Steve Rhea: They actually didn't pull any songs from Icewater, but they pulled "My Life Is Right" from his collaboration with Eubanks and used it on *#1 Record*, along with some other songs Chris had done [with Rock City].

Jody Stephens: Alex was definitely the missing piece in the band, as far as providing original songs. When he joined, the quality of songs jumped. I figured Alex would bring in a lot of experience to the stage and presence. I knew he had a great voice. Of course, the first time I heard him sing I knew it was going to be the perfect relationship.

Steve Rhea: Alex shows up and becomes the catalyst. Here's the guy with years of road experience and a voice. When you can put writing, good musicianship and a voice together, then things begin to happen.

Chris Bell: Most of [the songs on *#1 Record*], except for, say, four songs, had accumulated over the past two years. "Try Again" and "My Life Is

Right" I had recorded before Big Star. I had done the tracks with Jody and Tom Eubanks, who wrote half of "My Life Is Right." I did "Try Again" all by myself, I guess. They were pretty much recorded and ready to go. Alex overdubbed a harmony on both of those songs, a little bit of acoustic work for both, and a little slide guitar on "Try Again."

Alex Chilton: Chris and I would have some writing sessions every now and then. He came to my parents' house and had this song that later become "Feel"...It's mostly his tune and I just added one little line on top of his musical structure and that's pretty much the way it went. I would turn up with something I had, and he would make a change or two or give me a line or two or three.

> *I feel like I'm dying*
> *I'm never gonna live again*
> *You just ain't been trying*
> *It's getting very near the end*
>
> — CHRIS BELL, "FEEL"

Chris Bell: I would suggest a few things and changes to Alex's and he would similarly add to mine, but really the songwriting was a separate thing.

Steve Rhea: Chris had a tremendous influence on what Alex was doing guitar-wise, but Alex was always the better songwriter of the two and had all those years of playing in front of a live audience. That came across.

Andy Hummel: We played [the songs] together to learn them and develop the bass, drum and other parts. The songs were tweaked a bit during this process but for the most part they were a done deal when they were brought into the studio. I don't know a whole lot about Chris' writing technique at this point other than he was a guitarist first and foremost.

Ric Menck: On *#1 Record* Chris and Alex's songwriting meshes together beautifully. It's difficult to discern where one leaves off and the other begins. The real difference is with the lyrics. Chris' words are so damn melancholy.

Alex Chilton: I learned to write all these confused, nonsensical lyrics from Chris and Andy.

Jody Stephens: I was never a part of the songwriting process for the first record. Songs would come in and I don't remember witnessing much collaboration, but I'm sure they kind of worked through things. With *#1 Record*, there was thought that went behind the guitar parts for Alex and Chris—they aren't standard strumming parts. They were particular about guitar sounds complementing each other, not being the same but adding some sort of dimension.

Andy Hummel: My perception of those days is that Chris and Alex were musical geniuses.

While Andy is only credited as a songwriter on one #1 Record track, "The India Song," his John Entwistle-inspired basslines seamlessly melded with the original compositions. The Bell/Chilton alliance also motivated Jody, whose signature fills and drumbeats further shaped the Big Star sound. An Ardent Records press release talked up his percussive contributions: "Jody is tall...and reminiscent of an English Teddy Boy. He plays drums with Big Star—not speedy Keith Moon stuff, but more tastefully simple things...Jody never takes drum solos or hides himself behind useless banks of cymbals and skins. While most Memphis drummers were trying to emulate Three Dog funk, Jody developed his own simple, driving beat providing a perfect basis for Big Star's music."

Jody Stephens: What I loved about the band was that I thought the songs were incredible. I didn't write them. I'm not bragging. It just blew me away. I was a huge Beatles freak and I thought, *If I could ever find a band with great songs like that, I would be the luckiest person in the world.* Suddenly, here I am in this band and these amazing songs are coming out. It makes the drumming easy...I can remember the first time we did ["The Ballad of El Goodo"]. Alex probably played through it once and I had the part the first time through on drums. It sounds corny, but it was a spiritual experience, because the part was just there as if I had heard it all before. A lot of songs were like that.

> *Years ago, my heart was set to live, oh*
> *But I've been trying hard against unbelievable odds*
> *It gets so hard in times like now to hold on*
> *The guns they wait to be stuck by*
> *At my side is God*
>
> — ALEX CHILTON, "BALLAD OF EL GOODO"

Alex Chilton: I just sort of did what the original concept of their band was. I tried to present things that were compatible with the concept they already had in place. When I say "they," I guess I'm really referring to Chris. I just tried to get with Chris' stylistic approach as well as I could.

Drew DeNicola: It was Chris' band that Alex joined. Chris was very conscious about who was going to be in the band and what the songs were going to be. It was a concept band he came up with in his dreams.

Alex Chilton: They were oriented toward mid-'60s British Invasion music. The way I saw it, the group was sort of designed to play that kind of music, which left out a lot of things I liked and liked to do. Being a member of a group, you abide by the rules of the group or you quit. For me, there was a lot of jazz music and a lot of black music that I love. Those two categories were pretty much left out of Big Star.

These sessions produced "In the Street," one of his best-known and most profitable compositions, thanks to its use as the TV theme for That '70s Show, *which aired from 1998 to 2006.*

Alex Chilton: "In The Street" is another example of one of the best songs I've ever written.

Andy Hummel: Most of the songs [on *#1 Record*] were sung by the person who wrote it, except "In the Street," which was completely written by Alex but sung by Chris.

Alex Chilton: That was all mine. I guess there's a melody part that Chris sort of did. The way I had put it together, the melody is a little different than what he eventually sang. What he sang was better.

> *Hanging out, down the street*
> *The same old thing we did last week*
> *Not a thing to do*
> *But talk to you*
> *Steal your car, and bring it down*
> *Pick me up, we'll drive around*
> *Wish we had a joint so bad*
>
> **— ALEX CHILTON, "IN THE STREET"**

Steve Rhea: Andy has described the vocals on "In the Street" as this high, Robert Plant-type sound. When they recorded "In the Street" he capoed up on, like, the fifth fret. Alex, when he played it live later on, had no capo at all. It was a completely different key because he couldn't sing that high, but Chris was going for the rafters. "Try Again" was more like the Chris speaking voice. It wasn't a great voice, but it was real. That's what people appreciate about Chris. You can feel all the pain, conflicts.

Andy Hummel: Chris liked having someone like Alex who could sing that well. I always felt that was something Chris struggled with a lot. It got better as the years went along. Alex had a wonderful, resonate singing voice you can cast in many ways. Even then, at that early age, he was amazing with it. You just didn't hear Alex hit notes that weren't on, and Chris appreciated that. On the other hand, Chris was a superb guitar player.

Chris' powerful riffs add the high-octane rock to Big Star's debut, but it's Alex's nostalgic teenage-love ballad, "Thirteen," that's been covered numerous times over the years by the likes of Garbage, Albert Hammond Jr., Elliot Smith, and the Yeah Yeah Yeahs.

> *Won't you let me walk you home from school*
> *Won't you let me meet you at the pool*
> *Maybe Friday I can*
> *Get tickets for the dance*
> *And I'll take you*
>
> **— ALEX CHILTON, "THIRTEEN"**

Carole Ruleman Manning: I like "Thirteen." I don't think it was written about anyone in particular. I knew some of the girls Alex dated around that age, including me, and I don't think any of them got walked home from school.

Alex Chilton: On looking back at that album, I realized something about my own personal development. I had quit the Box Tops, so here I was travelling across the country surrounded by all these businessmen and older influences. I had left my own peer group completely, and in a way I never really advanced past that. What I was writing about on Big Star albums was just going back and trying to catch myself up. I was 21 at the time, but I was writing like I was sixteen or seventeen.

Andria Lisle: Memphis shows through lyrically in songs like "Thirteen" and "In the Street." They paint an excellent picture of teenage life in the provincial South.

Alex Chilton: I remember making up a solo in the studio for "Thirteen" in about fifteen minutes, which is a wild bit of playing. But I was a crummy songwriter, or adept at most. Although, my dad, who was a jazz pianist, taught me a lot about musical theory when I was growing up.

Matthew Sweet: A thing that's very influential to me as a songwriter was the personal nature of Big Star's lyrics. They were personal in a "my

BIG STAR

ardent management 2000 madison ave. memphis, tn. 38104 [901] 278-4052

An Ardent-produced Big Star promotional photo, 1972.

ARDENT STUDIOS ARCHIVE

Big Star goofs off during a promotional photo shoot outside of Alex Chilton's parents' house.

PHOTO BY MICHAEL O'BRIEN

feelings" and "me and you" way. On *#1 Record* they have a great under-standing of sadness and innocence. There's also this feeling of hope and capability in the record. There's a sense of spirituality. There is a sense of hope and purpose.

Alex Chilton: If you're writing anything decent, it's in you, it's your spirit coming out. If it's not an expression of how a person genuinely feels, then it's generally not a good song done with any conviction.

While Alex arrived with songs he wholly wrote, the credits on "My Life Is Right" had some red tape. As the album's production wore on, Chris reached out to his friend and co-writer with a request.

Tom Eubanks: Big Star's version of "My Life Is Right" on *#1 Record* is the exact recording from Rock City sessions. Alex or Chris just added a few acoustic-guitar runs, which I thought emasculated the tune. I am playing bass. Terry Manning is playing piano. Chris, Terry and I are still on background vocals. The Rock City album was cut on an eight-track machine and there were some mix-downs that made it impossible to undo the tune, plus Chris and Alex did not care to re-record it. Listen to Terry's piano on the Rock City version and the Big Star version. It's the same track remixed for Big Star. One morning while they were working on *#1 Record*, Chris calls and says, "We want to use 'My Life Is Right' on the Big Star record and we would like to show Alex as the co-writer." He asked me if they could not list my name as a co-writer. It didn't make me mad that Chris asked me to do this. It kind of hurt my feelings, but I understood why he asked. Chris, as I did, had an infatuation with the Beatles. Did you ever see a Beatles song where John Lennon co-wrote with somebody other than Paul? He wanted it to look like a Beatles record listing "Bell-Chilton," with the odd song written by Hummel. It wasn't a mean-spirited thing by Chris—it was about appearances.

Alex Chilton: It was Chris' idea that we share credit on the tunes, although they were all written pretty much independently.

Tom Eubanks: I told Chris, "No, if you don't want my name on the record, don't use the song." He said, "Well, you'll get all the money." I told him, "That's not the reason I do it. And remember, you didn't have the beginnings of the song. I did. There wouldn't be 'My Life Is Right' without me." I would not agree to that, so it's credited as "Bell-Eubanks."

Alex Chilton: Certainly, [Chris and I] idolized the Beatles and would have loved to do something as great as what they were doing. Our col-laboration, in a way, was kind of like Lennon and McCartney, in that one or the other wrote those songs and the other one maybe threw in the smallest something, if anything at all, although we shared credit for all of them. We worked well together as musicians and both of us were serious about what we were doing...We had a lot of people in our immediate environment telling us how lame we were, but I didn't care about that. We were doing what we enjoyed.

Jody Stephens: It was out of fashion at the time. It was a pretty raw approach to performing. Even the first record, the performances weren't slick performances. It was a little out of keeping with the other things that were in the market at the time. We weren't sophisticated players. Musically or stylistically, we were out of step with what was going on.

Drew DeNicola: Alex said he stopped listening to new music in 1971. He said rock 'n' roll died for him with Led Zeppelin, which is ironic because Chris loved Led Zeppelin.

Andy Hummel: To me, Led Zeppelin was an obvious influence on Chris, especially Jimmy Page. You just have to listen to the right Led Zeppelin. Whenever I listen to Big Star that Chris played on, the Jimmy Page influence was just huge. People always think of Page as the first heavy-metal guitar player and loud electric riffs, but Page's acoustic playing is without equal—that's the kind of sound I'm talking about.

Bob Mehr: It's interesting that Chris loved Led Zeppelin and could peel off Jimmy Page licks. That and he listened to studio playback at epically loud, eardrum-shattering levels. He could also be bossy and demanding when it came to his music. Sometimes, because of the sensitive nature of some of his songs, and the beautifully hurt quality to his voice, we think of Chris as this fragile, timid figure. But Chris Bell's music wasn't twee at all, and as a personality, when it came to his art, he was anything but shy or retiring. Chris had a commanding, boisterous side to his personality, something that existed alongside the searching, uncertain part of him as well.

Adam Hill: The Beatles were the pivot point, but Big Star was listening to the Move, the Kinks, the Who, and Clapton. They had a subscription to *NME*. I was surprised none of them talked about Badfinger, I guess they were more contemporaries than descendants. They name-checked Todd Rundgren more than Badfinger.

Jody Stephens: We loved Badfinger. Procol Harum, I love. I don't know if it's reflected on anything, but their drummer B.J. Wilson was awesome. [Stax session drummer] Al Jackson was a big one for me. Listen to "My Life Is Right" and then "Try a Little Tenderness."

Along with Big Star, the Raspberries became known as a pioneering power-pop band, though Chris said his band was far from an Eric Carmen mimic.

Chris Bell: We never attempted to sound like the Raspberries. They were alright, but Big Star were always more original. I've loved English rock since "I Want to Hold Your Hand," "I Can't Explain," and "Night of Fear." The Yardbirds and Roy Wood were major inspirations. Alex is more into Brian Wilson and early Todd Rundgren. The music was a blend of two channels.

Alex Chilton: I was very into Todd Rundgren when we cut that first album. I was also still listening to a lot of bluegrass and getting into bizarre things.

Andy Hummel: I loved the Carpenters and Chris did, too. He thought they were neat.

Jody Stephens: Chris added a real pop aspect to the band.

Tom Eubanks: I never heard Chris mention the Byrds. To me, with Big Star, the Byrds were an influence with Alex's voice. If you listen to some of *#1 Record* it almost sounds like he's doing Roger McGuinn.

Alex Chilton: The Byrds' [influence] came more from me, as I was learning some country-guitar styles at that time and was listening to a lot of Gram Parsons and Flying Burrito Brothers. You transpose a country acoustic-guitar style to electric and you've got the Byrds.

Steve Rhea: The subject matter of "El Goodo" didn't sound brand spanking new to me because it was all flowing from our general discussion about the Vietnam War, being drafted, the fact that we didn't want to go, and ways to get out of it. Alex put great chords to it. He gave it a Roger McGuinn-style vocal with Chris' high harmony soaring in over that. It was a knockout sound.

Drew DeNicola: On *#1 Record* there are no novelty songs that are not directly related to their lives, aside from Andy's "India Song." It's sort of like how the Beatles have "Taxman" or "Paperback Writer." I don't even think there's a song telling a story about someone else, it's pretty much always first-person.

Chris Bell: We worked on it for about a year, aside from what I had done before we started. We started in the summer, around August of 1971.

Andy Hummel: We got our own, full-blown private reel of tape. We had just been using scraps up until then...Having access to a recording studio at that age was just like heaven. We loved it. We went into the studio whenever we could.

Terry Manning: *#1 Record* was a highly-crafted record over a long period. It wasn't just jumping in the studio and throwing it together. There were many overdubs, many changes.

Alex Chilton: I learned about working in a recording studio. Before that, I had been in a recording studio and sung a lot, but I never really had my hands on all the controls or the making of the sounds in the studio.

Andy Hummel: When we first started, we just had the eight-track recorder. Somewhere in there, Fry got his first sixteen-track. We had the old console, but he replaced that with a new Spectra Sonics console.

John Fry: We thought we had a lot with a four-track in 1966, but by early 1967 it was eight-track, and by 1970, it was sixteen-track. It changed rapidly.

Chris Bell: We started rehearsals and started doing some tracks. I asked John Fry if he would like to engineer for us and he agreed.

John Fry: I was there for a good deal of the first record. I would usually cut the basic tracks. They would set up as a four-piece band and cut the basic rhythm track. They would normally do most of the overdubs on their own, unless something was a little complicated, then I would do it. I would do all the final mixes.

Jody Stephens: Once we began working together, I was intimidated by [Fry's] dead seriousness. Ardent existed because of him. He was the provider, the reason we were able to be creative. Alex and Chris had a vision, which we were able to pursue without reins or over-the-shoulder guidance. Maybe we could have done the same thing at another studio, but Fry's behind-the-board skills were sonically unique. He made Big Star sparkle.

Andy Hummel: What things John Fry didn't personally take care of, Chris was very competent to fill in the gaps.

Alex Chilton: We felt like we could do it ourselves. We didn't want anyone else to mess it up.

Andy Hummel: Chris was in charge. I would pretty well credit him with recording and producing that LP. Of course, he had a lot of artistic help from Alex, but Chris was the technical brains behind it. He was the only one of us at that time who knew how to record. I engineered a little of the later *#1 Record* stuff, but Chris was the main force.

CHAPTER 9

2000 MADISON AVENUE — *#1* OVERDUBS: WINTER 1971-1972

Over the Thanksgiving holiday in 1971, three months into the recording process, John Fry's ultimate vision was realized when he closed the storefront studio on National Street and opened the doors to a state-of-the-art recording studio at 2000 Madison Avenue. Big Star uprooted to the brick structure and continued to fine-tune its twelve-song track list.

Tim Riley: The old studio on National was one studio, one control room with an office up front and a reception area. They outgrew that facility because there was such a demand for John Fry and Terry Manning. .

John Fry: We were busy, so we wanted more than one studio and there's no way in the rented place that we could get a second studio of any size. The other reason was to quit renting. If we're going to be spending money, we might as well spend the money on owning something...We did the last session on National on the Wednesday before Thanksgiving...and were recording in the new studio by the Monday after Thanksgiving. Nobody got much sleep.

Through February, Big Star continued recording at the new facility and then started the mixing process.

Adam Hill: Big Star had tracked almost all the songs on sixteen-track at National Street, they never spent a lot of time doing the basic tracks. By the time they switched to the new studio on Madison, they were in overdub and mix mode. They fiddled with it for months.

Andy Hummel: There were bits and pieces of it that were recorded after Ardent moved to Madison...Moving into the new studio was cool. We had been in this little Podunk storefront place, which had great sounds and was technically flawless, but moving over to Madison made all the difference in the world...To say that Fry pulled out all the stops on the design of the inside would be a gross understatement. They did everything, technically, that you could imagine doing. In A Studio and B Studio, the little pieces of wood on the wall are unevenly spaced. There is a reason for all of that. Nothing in there is an accident.

Drew DeNicola: Ardent was built in the center of Midtown Memphis, which was basically this island of bohemia in Memphis. It's right outside of downtown before you start heading toward the suburbs. It was kind of the mecca. Everything was located within a square mile.

Robert Gordon: Ardent was the place to be. You could walk out the doors of Ardent and go a couple doors down to Trader Dick's, the happening club. You could walk another hundred yards and be in Overton Square. That's where the best clubs in town were, like Lafayette's Music Room. There was TGI Friday's, the first place to get liquor by the drink. It was cool because the only other Friday's in the world at that time was in San Francisco. It made Memphis seem extra hip to have this huge place. The whole front of Friday's had these large windows that opened. All the freaks would hang out in Overton Square, so you could sit in there and watch everyone walk by.

Jody Stephens: On National, there wasn't much mischief to get into. We could go to the Sweden Kream and have a hamburger. The new building was near Overton Square—the party center of the universe. There would be thousands of kids down there because they lowered the drinking age to eighteen. I wasn't partying much because I always had some sort of a part-time job, plus I was going to school and had a girlfriend. On top of that, I couldn't afford the nightlife.

Tim Riley: There was a unique family that hung around Hi Records in Memphis, there was a unique family that hung around Stax, and there was an even more unique family that hung around Ardent. You had these incredible, creative people that all knew each other well. When there was an event, all these people would end up at the same party. It was a cornucopia of creative forces that were just unstoppable. It was always the place to go, especially for pop acts. The black acts wanted to go to Hi and Stax, but the black/white thing kind of diminished as Ardent started doing more work for Stax.

Terry Manning: The Stax sessions were always professional. The players were totally used to being in studio and very comfortable with the recording situation, so everything always went well. It was an incredible school to have been in, with such amazing musicians, writers, arrangers and singers always around. I often can't believe I was lucky enough to have participated in that scene.

Drew DeNicola: The members of Big Star were twenty or twenty-one years old when they were working on *#1 Record*. There were high-end recordings happening all around these kids. If Chris was at Ardent in Studio B working on some backing tracks for Big Star, in Studio A it could be the Staple Singers, Isaac Hayes or Leon Russell—big acts.

Andy Hummel: We staked out B Studio as our own little space. Big Star spent a lot of time in there finishing up that first LP, Chris especially.

Terry Manning: Chris was obsessed with the whole process, so he would come to the studio whenever he could. Alex was only around if he needed to be. Jody and Andy were around when there was something to do on one of the songs, but Chris was there a whole bunch.

Tim Riley: When you walked in to Ardent, by 10:30 a.m., you felt this creative energy throughout the entire building.

Steve Rhea: There would always be somebody up front at the studio. In my day, it was Diane Wall, who was the receptionist and who was hot. She'd greet you and buzz you through. There were some offices, including John Fry's office, behind there. Fry would be in there on a fairly consistent basis, but it's not like he was out wandering around managing people. On the opposite corner, you had Tim Riley's office, plus an attorney for Stax who had an office next to that. Then there was the mailroom with a mimeograph machine, that's where we got our [press kits] mailed out every week. If you kept going around, there was a little lounge area with a Coke machine, right off Studio B...You knew you were cool and were in a wonderful place. There was music going on all the time. If people weren't actively recording in the studio, you were probably hearing music coming out of the studio because some-body was mixing.

Beverly Baxter Ross: Big Star wasn't the only band Fry would give studio time to. He gave a lot of people a lot of time. That started on National Street and continued at 2000 Madison. If he thought a band was worthy, every night all night was open. Every band I knew, just about, got in on that deal. People like Jack Holder, who played in the Hot Dogs, practically lived there. Jack later played with Black Oak Arkansas.

Larry Raspberry: Ardent was a mecca for bands back then. John Fry was the most supportive studio owner in the world.

At Ardent, Chris kept up his board skills by engineering tracks for lower-profile Ardent clients. One of those artists, singer/songwriter Nancy Bryan, recorded an album with Chris, and even cut one of his songs, "In My Darkest Hour." The downhearted track, with Nancy on lead vocals, remained unreleased for a shade over twenty years. Meanwhile, Stax Records engaged Fry and Manning with bigger assignments.

Andy Hummel: Terry was doing the Staple Singers at that time. Ardent had transitioned over from doing just overflow and mixing for Stax to doing serious projects, whole LPs for Stax.

Tom Eubanks: Ardent was like Stax East.

Al Bell: After taking the Staple Singers to Muscle Shoals to cut basic rhythm tracks, we came to Ardent, where Manning helped me capture the vocal sound I wanted on songs like "I'll Take You There" and "Respect Yourself." We built the foundation in Muscle Shoals, then we went to Ardent, where we baked the cake.

Tom Eubanks: Stax's studio was a real rathole compared to Ardent. That's the reason Stax would bring all their records over to Ardent to fix it and master it. But Stax got that funky, raw sound.

Robert Johnson: Ardent was a much cleaner place and more efficient than Stax. The equipment worked better. Stax was just an old theater converted into a studio.

Al Bell: At Stax, we had to take the technology we had, which a lot of people laughed at, and make it work. Fry set up Ardent by the book. Something about the physical environment there gave rise to a kind of closeness that we didn't have at Stax. Ardent was more intimate, and I felt at home there.

Richard Rosebrough: The early Stax days on McLemore Avenue were the golden days when they just had this house band with the M.G.'s. They had kind of poor equipment but had a great time and produced fun records. By the time it got to the Staple Singers and Isaac Hayes, they were shooting for a higher level of involvement with the music business. It stopped being quite so much fun and started being a little crazy.

Carole Ruleman Manning: The more successful artists looked forward to getting out of the Stax environment. It was supposedly pretty wild over there.

Steve Rhea: You might walk into Ardent and there would be Albert King, Pops Staples or Steve Cropper. Or it would be Mavis Staples doing a duet with another Stax artist. They would be in front of the microphones, singing a love song and getting in the right mood. They would have their arms around each other, swaying and singing, having a great time—that was going on all the time.

Robert Gordon: Big Star was always more influenced by British bands, but some tracks, like "Feel," had a Stax influence on them.

John Fry was sonically talented and his connection with Stax brought in substantial revenue for the emerging company, but the Fry family's wealth is what largely facilitated Ardent Studios' rapid growth.

Drew DeNicola: All these Ardent kids got a head start. John Fry started that studio when he was twenty and already had a home studio at the age of fifteen. He recorded a local hit at age sixteen. Fry was programming and running a black radio station at age seventeen. These kids got a real head start. They were turned on by the technology and by the cultural shift, which was rock 'n' roll. It meant everything to them. They had the means and a lot of them had the money, especially John Fry. They had a tightknit group of ambitious, young and fashionable hipsters, basically.

Richard Rosebrough: Ardent Studios was built with a lot of family money. John Fry's family was a privileged family. His father had this successful construction company called Fischer Lime & Cement. John, who was an only child, said, "Well, I want a studio," and his parents said, "Okay, go build a studio."

Andy Hummel: Every city typically has one big company in the concrete business. They get all the business of building the freeways, pouring the foundations of buildings. Fischer Lime & Cement was the one in Memphis...I'm sure the fact that Fry's family was very wealthy enabled him a lot. He could presumably go out and buy whatever equipment he wanted.

Terry Manning: Financially, I doubt if there was ever much of a profit, if any. Fry was fortunate to be in a position that allowed him to finance the studio regardless of profit or loss. He was so kind and giving to so many musicians and artists over the years, helping Memphis music, but there was never a big pile of money being made. Most studios are lucky to break even, and Ardent was no exception.

Tom Eubanks: Terry Manning told me any new piece of gear, the latest, greatest thing, Fry would run out and buy it right away. Gear that was a ton of money back then, but Fry knew what he was doing. He could take it apart and put it back together again.

Richard Rosebrough: We all looked up to Fry. His nickname was "The Massa," a twist on "The Master." He owned us. The feeling back then was that there was an ownership thing going on. Those of us who worked there did not cross him. Whatever Fry said he wanted, that's what we did.

Robert Johnson: One day, I run into Chris Bell. I said, "Hey man, guess what I got? I got a Hiwatt amp." He goes, "Oh, man. No, you don't!" Those amplifiers were impossible to find. This is when they were working on the first Big Star record. I said, "Come on over and look at it." He comes over with Fry, they pull up in that big black car. Fry and Chris come into my parents' living room. I have my Les Paul plugged in and I said, "Here man, play this thing. It's a little too clean for me. I'm not sure I want it anymore." Fry says, "How much do you want for it? Do you want to sell it to us for the studio and Big Star?" I just blurted out a price. Fry reached in his pocket and then wrote out a check. He didn't quibble about the money or anything. Chris and I loaded it in the trunk of Fry's Mercedes. Chris used that amp in Big Star. It's still at Ardent today.

John Dando: There was nobody around here with Hiwatts. They were not available to buy around here. They were ordered in from England. It's what the Who, Yardbirds, and people in Britain were playing with.

Terry Manning: Within most of Big Star's conglomerate group there was nobody who was poor or needing anything. It was a different situation from what a lot of bands come from. I don't know how that affected anything and I'm not bragging about anything. It's just a fact.

Richard Rosebrough: Andy's father was a doctor and Alex Chilton's parents were not poor by any means. Big Star was a poor-little-rich-kid band compared to the rest of the bands in Memphis. There were a lot of musicians and bands that didn't have a penny and their families didn't have a penny.

Beverly Baxter Ross: Jody wasn't a rich boy. He was upper-middle-class but wasn't a rich boy.

Jody Stephens: My dad [John Stephens] came up as an X-ray tech. He got a job at the VA Medical Center in Memphis and eventually headed up the department as an administrator. My mom [Rose] worked there as an assistant.

Robert Johnson: The thing about Chris and Andy Hummel was they had nice cars and all that shit. The rest of us were just working-class people who didn't have that kind of dough back then. Chris would say things like, "Oh, I'm going to the Bahamas with my family this weekend." He was that kind of guy. We would joke and say, "It must be nice, motherfucker!"

Rick Clark: They had the luxury of having a world-class studio to play around in. They never had to go out and road-test themselves or anything. They were an in-the-studio concoction. They existed in this fantasy bubble. I'm not being derogatory, I'm just saying they didn't have to go through the fire anyone else normally would. I'm not diminishing the music. I love the record, the frailness and beauty of it.

Fry's deep pockets aside, it was his trained ear that gave #1 Record *its signature shimmering sound.*

Drew DeNicola: John Fry was only interested in engineering in the beginning of his career, when he first started. Big Star was his high point, the band he put everything into. It was just as much a project for him to show off his chops as it was for the band. A lot of the other big artists who came out of Ardent, Fry had nothing to do with.

Danielle McCarthy-Boles: John Fry was really the fifth member of Big Star.

Adam Hill: Chris was the vision, but Fry executed it. Fry was doing things George Martin was doing without even knowing it. He was on the same plane. *#1 Record* is a testament.

Jody Stephens: He engineered all three Big Star albums and was sort of a translator. He was a George Martin sort. Alex would say, "Hey, I would like to hear this effect," and John would go, "Great!"

Terry Manning: That bright sound on *#1 Record* came from John Fry. He loved crisp high end and had plenty of treble on everything. Alex, his guitar was the Strat, which is quite a bright guitar. He ran it through a Uni-Vibe-style pedal, which cuts bass out. Alex also used a Fender Super Reverb amp, which is also a bright amp. Things started pretty bright and John was not reticent to hold back on the high end on it.

Richard Rosebrough: It was a function of knowing what an AM or FM transmitter was going to do to your record. It was going to lop all the highs off. He added the high top-end in advance, and the result was brilliant and clear-sounding.

Adam Hill: That EQ was a big part of that sound. It wasn't harsh. It added sparkle to it, like those acoustic guitar sounds. You'll never get

Ardent Studios under construction on Madison Avenue, 1971.

ARDENT STUDIOS ARCHIVE

Studio A

ARDENT
Memphis, Tennessee

Control Room A

ARDENT
Memphis, Tennessee

Ardent Studios promotional photos.

ARDENT STUDIOS ARCHIVE

During the production of *#1 Record*, Chris Bell works with John Fry at Ardent. Alex Chilton's then-girlfriend [and John Fry's future sister-in-law], Vera Ellis, looks on in the background.

ARDENT STUDIOS ARCHIVE

From his office desk at Ardent, John Fry snaps a photo of Chris Bell and Terry Manning at his newly built, world-class studio.

PHOTO BY JOHN FRY

close to a Big Star sound without running it through that Spectra Sonics. Fry liked them for a reason and they imparted a sound on those records.

Larry Nix — Mastering engineer, Ardent Studios, Stax Records, L. Nix Mastering: Fry would bring in Big Star's albums for mastering and he'd sit on a stool in front of the high-frequency limiters and crank them up to keep from breaking a circuit in the process. He wanted to get as much high end as he could. I thought he was crazy, but Big Star's sound wasn't like anything else, mostly because Fry was so far ahead of his time.

Richard Rosebrough: Fry had a technique of mixing that astounds me. So many people want to get on the console and plug in this effect and that effect, work with the EQ and change it. He would just manipulate the volume and the balance, mix the sound as it was on the tape. It made it sound real.

Robert Johnson: Fry was mixing one day. I walked in and said, "John, you got this so fucking low I can't even hear it." The knob had zero to ten on it, he had it on two. He said, "In order to mix properly, you need to mix at a low level." When he wanted to crank it up loud, it would go up to three. It's the greatest recording lesson to learn, if you can do it.

Chris Bell: During mixing, Fry tended to be very conservative about the mixing and suppress a lot of things we wanted to bring out. We would do rough mixes. If we wanted the cowbell loud, it was right up front. Whereas when it was mixed, all of that was suppressed. I was constantly fighting during the mixes for more balls in it.

Tom Eubanks: Obviously, from the work he did on *#1 Record*, Fry was an expert engineer because that music still sounds current today.

Adam Hill: Sid Selvidge and Don Nix have both told me, "Fry was the best engineer there ever was." Don told me, "I would go all over the world to cut shit, but I always brought it back to John Fry."

As Big Star finished its basic tracks and transitioned fully into overdub mode, Fry stepped back and Chris led most of the band's late-night sessions.

Chris Bell: While we were in the studio, it was sort of like we were raising hell every night from midnight to 4 a.m. We were just having a good time recording.

Jody Stephens: Chris always had control over *#1 Record*, then John would help produce the mixes. Of course, we would say, "John, what do you think?" And in that regard, he would produce. But for me, it was always Chris in charge of production, and Alex certainly had a voice in that. Even Andy had a creative voice, but Chris was the leader.

Alex Chilton: We cut the basic tracks with Andy and Jody. Chris and I did most of the overdubs. I remember me and Chris working a lot of nights together. We'd sing together a lot and Chris would engineer it all because I didn't know how to engineer at that time.

Chris Bell: We did about nine or ten basic tracks and then started working on them ourselves. I knew how to engineer, so I would just have Alex or Andy over. I would be running the board while they were in the studio or I would run the board and plug in the guitar to an amp that was in the studio, punch record and then go.

Alex Chilton: I guess we were the ultimate guitar band. We spent a lot of time recording our albums, trying to get good sounds out of our guitars, things like that. I don't think anyone will make a guitar band sound as good as we did ours.

Much like their days at UT, Chris and Andy's friendship sometimes led to heated arguments in the studio and elsewhere, occasionally stemming from Chris' tendency to playfully, but sometimes crudely, roast his bandmates.

Vera Ellis: Alex and Chris did have some disagreements, but I never saw it. When we were alone, Alex would say, "Oh, Chris did this," but I don't recall them having any huge screaming matches like Chris and Andy did.

Jody Stephens: Chris razzed Andy in rehearsals. In hindsight, maybe I was saved from that because I was newer to Chris.

Vera Ellis: Chris and Andy were like Fred and Ethel Mertz. Chris and Andy would argue about any little thing, yet they spent most of their time together.

Adam Hill: It wasn't just Chris getting on Andy's case. On the *#1 Record* tapes, you can even hear Alex say, "Andy, did you fuck that up?" He says, "It's really simple, if you don't have it by now, we should just bail on it." It was that kind of thing.

Carole Ruleman Manning: One day they were having a band practice upstairs at Alex's house. Andy got there late, and Chris and Alex just chewed him out. Andy has said he wasn't totally involved with the band all the time.

Richard Rosebrough: The sense of humor around Ardent, mostly with Fry and Chris, was very dry and could be quite insulting.

David Bell: It was so clever, so subtle and so dry. It was quick, sometimes mean. John Fry could be meaner than Chris though.

Ken Woodley — Singer-songwriter, multi-instrumentalist, Alamo, Chris Bell, solo, Ardent Studios employee: Early on, Fry would party like the rest of us. He'd drink and smoke a few joints. He was the first guy I ever seen drink a Heineken.

Robert Johnson: Everybody was smoking pot back then. Everybody was happy and stoned. I hung out around Carole, Terry Manning's wife. She was a pot smoker, but she didn't want to smoke around Terry because he didn't like pot.

Carole Ruleman Manning: In Ardent's atrium, what we used to call "the courtyard," is where we used to hang around, smoke dope and drink at night. We'd talk and bitch about things. There were a lot of people at Ardent, and Big Star was a part of it.

Richard Rosebrough: We were all over the place. One night, we all hopped in Fry's black Mercedes. It was me, Andy, Chris, Alex and Fry, the five of us. We drove out to visit John Dando, who'd landed a job running a huge 50,000-watt AM radio transmitter for WDIA, the black radio station in north Memphis. Dando sat in this little building and kept the transmitter online. We were all fascinated with radio, especially Fry, but that night some psychedelics had been taken. It was just crazy. There was so much electricity going on in that building, you had to be careful with what you touched. Dando was just flipping out and yelling, "Don't touch that, it will melt you! You'll go up in smoke!" We were running around like a bunch of fools.

While Alex and Andy preferred hitting the town, including many infamous nights at T.G.I. Friday's and Trader Dick's, Chris and Fry were more reclusive. The two became close friends and spent countless low-key nights talking music and cranking up Fry's expensive stereo system.

John Fry: I probably spent more time outside the studio with Chris and Andy than the other guys. Chris was a great friend. He was smart, witty and had a good sense of humor. We also spent a lot of time together in the studio, particularly before and during the recording and mixing of #1 Record. We hung out, but never at bars or anything like that. We would hang out and just listen to records. There were more obscure records, like early Cat Stevens and a lot of British bands.

Vera Ellis: We all thought Fry was cool, but he was also just a gigantic nerd. He lived with his mother. They had a beautiful home and gardens. John had his own two-story apartment, but it was in the same house his mother lived in. If you went down the stairs and opened the door you'd be in his mother's house. I went over there a few times, but the guys hung out there more.

Andy Hummel: Fry's house was on a little dead-end street. It was a beautiful house—a big, modern, rectangular prism-looking house with huge windows and all that. John had his own little suite in the back with his own study and music room. It had a separate entrance that was always used when we visited. There was always somebody there visiting. Terry would be there, I would be there, Chris would be there, Alex would be there. Somebody would be there hanging, talking and listening to music...We were a tight band. We hung with each other, dated girls together. We swapped girls, or the girls swapped us, whichever way you want to look at it. It was kind of a cool thing.

Richard Rosebrough: We were all friends. It was like one big family, but Chris and Fry were very close friends. Chris thought John Fry was just the best engineer. He talked John into being Big Star's recording engineer and the mix engineer for the record. That was the only active project John worked on. Fry had done a lot of his most famous engineering work before then, like mixing the Leon Russell record, mixing all these Sam & Dave records—no one ever knew it. It was years before I found out John had this relationship with Leon Russell, who was one of my heroes.

As Chris labored over his band's freshman record, his friend Richard Rosebrough was not only becoming an increasingly talented engineer at Ardent, but he was also drumming in Alamo, a popular Memphis-based progressive-rock band led by keyboardist/vocalist Ken Woodley. The group also featured bassist Larry Davis and guitarists Larry Raspberry and Robert Johnson. Three years later, both Richard and Ken contributed heavily to Chris' post-Big Star solo recordings as the core of his studio band.

Ken Woodley: Larry Raspberry and I went to school together at Treadwell High School. He was two years older than me. I knew him during his Gentrys days. He played all the school dances.

Larry Raspberry: Ken and I lived together on the 4000 block of Summer Avenue when we were in Alamo. It became the practice house. We lived, played and worked together intensely for a couple years.

Richard Rosebrough: Larry and Ken's house was directly behind Ken's parents' house. After Alamo broke up, they both moved out and I

Ardent Studios on Madison Avenue, 1973.

Alamo poses for a 1971 Atlantic Records promo shot. (L-R) Drummer Richard Rosebrough, organist/vocalist Ken Woodley, and guitarist Larry Raspberry. Richard and
Ken later played on most of Chris Bell's solo recordings.

Stax Records co-owner Al Bell chats with John Fry at Ardent Studios. During its hey-day, Stax sent much of its overflow work to Ardent Studios.

ARDENT STUDIOS ARCHIVE

Chris Bell lays down a guitar track while Terry Manning runs the board at Ardent.

Chris Bell at Ardent Studios on Madison, *#1 Record* era.

moved in. That three-bedroom house was affectionately known as the "Action House." Ken had started as a drummer. He was a wunderkind and could play anything that had keys or frets on it. Alamo were part of the mad '70s scene and had plenty of parties at the house. We subscribed to the madness of the time. We did nothing but eat, drink, sleep, date, and play music. Ken was so diverse and talented, he could play Leon Russell and Dr. John just like he could play Stevie Winwood. Ken was my creative leader. I was always on board to do what he said needed to be done.

Ken Woodley: Alamo played almost every fucking weekend at the Shell in Memphis. We opened for Three Dog Night, Allman Brothers and Steppenwolf. Our band received a lot of publicity from that. We had a name around the local scene and would have good turnouts, but there wasn't much else to do on the weekends back then.

Andy Hummel: You have no idea how cool Richard was in those days. Alamo was the San Francisco sound, a big-time band in Memphis who played out all the time. I was in awe of them. Then Richard started recording in the studio. Richard was there all the time. He was quickly emerging as the workhorse engineer at Ardent, which he was for many years.

Greg Reding: I saw Alamo a million times. They sounded like a California rock band that wound up in Memphis. Richard was a laid-back guy. He didn't like to be the center of attention, but he was a phenomenal drummer and just as good behind the board as an engineer. Ken Woodley was another quiet guy, but an amazing musician and songwriter. Ken was a great drummer who could sing and play both keyboards and bass.

Richard Rosebrough: We were working on that Alamo record at Ardent when Fry was in the studio with Big Star recording *#1 Record*. At the same time, Terry Manning was in the studio recording with Cargoe. However, Alamo was never signed to Ardent; we got a record deal with Atlantic Records straight away.

Ken Woodley: The Alamo record was recorded at Ardent before it was even pitched to Atlantic. There was a woman named Linda Alter, a great friend and music fan who worked at Pop Tunes. We got an Alamo tape together and she shopped it for us because she knew some industry people.

Richard Rosebrough: The record was released but the deal didn't go anywhere. Atlantic Records signed about twenty or thirty acts in three months and only chose to promote two or three of them. Everything else fell by the wayside, including Alamo.

Ken Woodley: We thought we'd be big stars and all that. Of course, that didn't happen.

Richard Rosebrough: Alamo would come to the studio and talk about cutting our second album and I would see these kids out in the studio practicing. I would see Chris out there and think, "Oh, they've got some band." I just thought it was a kid band. I didn't realize they were writing and collaborating, getting tight and close with one another.

Ken Woodley: By late 1971, we were almost broken up. I didn't really know Chris until shortly after Alamo ended, then we became friends. We seemed to hit it off well. Both of us were sarcastic—two weirdos.

Chris Bell and Alex Chilton inside a newly built Ardent Studios on Madison.
ARDENT STUDIOS ARCHIVE

Chris Bell works the tape machine at Ardent.

PHOTO BY MICHAEL O'BRIEN

CHAPTER 10

#1 WRAPS — NEON STAR: 1972

With free rein of Ardent during overnight-hours, Chris' nitpicking and fine-tuning of tracks persisted, causing the overdubbing sessions to drag on. His unflinching perfectionism in the studio exasperated Andy.

Andy Hummel: His producing was agonizing, very meticulous and quite frankly a bit overdone in my opinion. Chris spent hours and hours in the studio alone, with Alex, or with the whole band overdubbing, adding special effects and just generally looking for every conceivable way to jazz up the tunes.

Steve Rhea: If John Fry indulged Chris, it was letting him go over and over those songs and just work them to death because of his own insecurities about his voice or whatever. It would have been better for Fry to step in and say, "No, it sounds fine—don't worry about it."

Beverly Baxter: Chris was detailed to the point of being OCD.

Jody Stephens: He was obsessed with the perfect guitar tone and the perfect guitar part. Chris spent hours on those things. He just wanted it to be the best it could be.

Chris Bell: I had some pretty good ideas. I guess I was heavier on production than the rest of them were.

Robert Gordon: Chris had an incredible sense for soundscape. He could take pictures with audio in a way Alex couldn't. From Alex's 1987 *High Priest* album on, his solo records all sound documentary-like, very straightforward. There's not an exciting sonic sensibility. There's a sense of conveying directness. Chris had much more of an ear for sonic excitement. None of this is to demean Alex's talent as a songwriter or musician.

Drew DeNicola: Chris almost treated the rest of Big Star like his staff. Chris was the Phil Spector of the whole thing. They were doing his bidding. Chris wasn't this passive, broken guy. I've listened to three hours of audio tape of those guys recording and what you get in the end is that Chris is absolutely running the show. He was clever and telling jokes. He was a funny, dry-as-a-bone character. One night, they were in the studio with tape rolling and Alex says, "Which way do I stand in relation to this mic?" And Chris says, "Uh…in front of it." There was a lot of that. Alex deferred to Chris in the studio and, to some degree, looked up to him. You can hear it when you listen to those tapes. Alex is nervous. Chris is the one who makes the decisions and makes fun of everybody. Chris was quiet, but also a powerful personality. That's one thing people don't get about Chris Bell. It wasn't as if he was demure and passive.

Andy Hummel: [Alex and Chris] were driven people. They could be very selfish externally, even to the point of being domineering sometimes.

Chris Bell: In a way, we dug each other and respected each other, Alex and I. We didn't set out for a sound. We set out with some plans for an image and what kind of music we liked. We had way different tastes, but we respected each other's tastes. The Byrds, Todd Rundgren and the Beach Boys—Alex was big on all of those. In a way, that caused a nice blend for the first album, because I was more into the Who, Free and the Beatles.

Alex Chilton: He was somebody whose music I dug. I feel like I learned a lot from playing with him and learned a lot about recording. It was a time in my life when I made progress.

John Fry: Starting off, it was very cordial between Alex and Chris. They seemed to play off each other well and work together well. Their interaction in the studio was always good, from what I could see.

Terry Manning: Chris and Alex got along fine in the studio. Chris was a little in awe of Alex because Alex had made it, toured, been on TV and had hits. That was a big deal. Chris wanted all of that. But Chris and Alex had a little bit of a love-hate relationship. I don't mean they literally hated each other, but there was always a little thing between them. Like, "Who's the leader of the band?" or, "Hey, I was a star before this band, you can't tell me what to do."

Andy Hummel: There was a lot of conflict. Anytime you get two people who are that creative and brilliant together, it's going to be a rocky road. But it was mostly very positive.

Vera Ellis: Alex had fame with the Box Tops, been on the *Tonight Show* and all of that, but he was generally a bit difficult. He was always kind of a pain. He wasn't like that with me because I was his girlfriend, but to everyone else he was always a bit of a prima donna.

Alex Chilton: Chris and I worked well together but we had never hung out a whole lot. It wasn't such a personal thing. Chris was trying to be a success in music and I was too. We were sort of united in that, but it wasn't like we had been best buddies.

Bruce Eaton — Journalist, author, *33 1/3: Radio City:* Outside the studio, Alex thought Chris was a little mysterious and he didn't always get where Chris was coming from.

Andy Hummel: I don't recall the two of them hanging out a whole lot. But, we all hung out together—when all four of us were together.

Jody Stephens: We would all stop into the Knickerbocker, Chris' dad's restaurant. Of course, all the female servers there were older ladies in their forties or fifties, and they would dote on Chris. It was always good. We always seemed to share a Frozen Pecan Ball, it was just a scoop of vanilla ice cream covered in chocolate and pecans. All Chris had to do was sign the check and we could leave. That made it doubly fun.

Vera Ellis: We would also go to the movies together. Chris was almost always there. We would go to three movies in one day. After that, maybe stop by the Bonanza Steakhouse, his family's restaurant, and get a steak and a baked potato. We did that quite a bit. Chris was generous with that.

Aside from the relaxed hangouts, the band, excluding Jody, was experimenting with more drugs. What had been just recreational pot, LSD, and booze had snowballed into an amplified usage of mind-warping pharmaceuticals, creating an escalating problem for Chris' mental state.

Richard Rosebrough: We all took pills, usually downer pills. I took Valium for seven years. There was Elavil. There was Carbitral, a heavy sleeping pill. It had a blue band on it. Brian Epstein died taking Carbitrals. There was a psychiatrist's office down in the Medical Center in Memphis. There were a couple doctors there. We had four people from Ardent all going to the same psychiatrist's office.

Drew DeNicola: In Memphis, they were using an entirely different set of drugs from the rest of the country. Elvis's doctor got sued for giving Elvis all kinds of pills. There were doctors like that in Memphis. Everyone was going to see shrinks at the time. They would just go get prescriptions for all kinds of psychiatric drugs. Chris was a big fan of Mandrax, Dilaudid, Quaaludes, and other versions of Quaaludes people were taking. That contributed a lot to the fact that things were emotionally raw for these people. They were taking psychiatric depressive drugs. People have said Mandrax was Chris' favorite thing. It's like a British Quaalude.

Vera Ellis: People were smoking pot and taking some acid, speed, and Quaaludes here and there. Alex or Chris always found it or paid for it. I never had any money. My mother didn't want me to have anything to do with Alex when we were dating. She said, "I know you two just go to pot parties!"

Alex Chilton: I was drinking a lot and taking a lot of drugs, too. Chris' influence was bad, too, because he was always doing Valium.

Robert Johnson: It was Quaaludes for everybody. It was easy to get them. There was one doctor—you'd go see him, give him ten dollars and say, "I can't sleep," and he'd write you a prescription.

Andy Hummel: It was a trying time in my life. Chris and I were both still living at home and going to college while trying to do the Big Star thing. There were a lot of drugs floating around, and I was just trying to figure out where I fit into everything that was going on.

Chris Bell: I was spending a lot of time in the studio overdubbing trying to get the tapes right. Alex was just doing nothing. At that time, I was also going to school and working as an engineer at Ardent...I was trying to do the Big Star thing and it was taking up a lot of my time. Alex, I guess, had too much free time, so he was playing [in a side project] with Richard Rosebrough and Ken Woodley.

Chris' most notorious overdub on #1 Record, *heard rumbling at the 1:20-minute mark on "Don't Lie to Me," required a team of volunteers and roaring engines.*

Gary Stevens: Chris had already laid down "Don't Lie to Me." I was there the night he and Alex did the vocals. Chris kept stopping the tape and saying, "Alex, you're not yelling!" Alex would say, "I don't have a voice left." Chris said, "That's the idea, I want you screaming so it matches the guitar sound." For *#1 Record*, that is the rocker. Listen to the break midway into "Don't Lie to Me," it's got that Theremin and you can hear motorcycles. That's not a sound effect. Chris actually recorded four chopped motorcycles running inside of Ardent. It was brilliant. The night before he did that, Andy Hummel was at my house. It was Saturday night, so we were getting loaded and listening to music. Then he says, "I better get home. I promised Chris I would be at Ardent tomorrow morning at 8." I looked at him and said, "On a Sunday?" He said, "Yeah, I know. Chris is emphatic about me being there." This was going on 2 a.m. Instead of going to bed, we decided to stay awake and bought a six-pack of beer. A few hours later we went to the Arcade Restaurant, had a big breakfast and watched the sunrise. After that, we drove into Ardent at 7:45 a.m. and there is Chris by his old, beat-up station wagon parked next to four motorcycles. We knew the guys on the bikes. They were our friends who all bought Norton 500cc motorcycles from England. We were like, "What the fuck?" We hadn't been to bed yet and Andy still wasn't sure why he was there.

We get out and walk over there. Chris opens the side door of Ardent and says to them, "Can you all get in this door?" They said, "Yeah, of course." He said, "No, I mean I need for you to drive your motorcycles in this door." They said, "Yeah, we'll have to take the steps up in the back, but we can get them in there." Then Chris tells me, "Gary, I need for you to run cable from Studio B out to every corner of the atrium." Chris picked out the AKG mics and said, "Andy, I need you to put the mics down." We were still like, "What the fuck is going on?" Then Chris says, "Hurry, we don't have a lot of time." Finally, I ask, "Does Fry know about this?" Without missing a beat, Chris says, "John's at church. That's why we're doing this now." I look up and hear, "Vroom! Vroom!" There are the bikes driving around the damn atrium. Then, like clockwork, here comes John Fry through the door. I leaned down close to the mic and calmly said, "John's here." Evidentially, Chris picked it up in the control room. John is standing there watching these guys drive motorcycles around inside his studio. Chris busts in and says, "Okay! That's enough. Stop! I don't need anymore." Right then, Fry said, "Chris, I need to see you in my office." Chris disappears, we're all like, "Let's get out of here." We went in the studio to grab our coats and there's Chris walking out of John's office with a big grin on his face. John is behind him yelling, "Open some goddamn windows! That exhaust smells like shit in here." I had never heard him cuss before.

> I know where you've been
> And I know what you've been doing
> Don't lie to me
>
> — CHRIS BELL, "DON'T LIE TO ME"

151

Andy Hummel: Fry had gotten kind of non-involved toward the end of *#1 Record* because we were off doing a lot of the overdubs and work ourselves, but obviously he mixed it. You would never put out an LP without John mixing it, if you had any sense...Around the time we were finishing up the first LP, we were talking about the next phase of that little musical journey. We had to get it released, promote it and go out and play in front of real people. At some point in that, Chris decided to drop out of Southwestern and stopped going to college.

Steve Rhea: We were thinking, "It's all cumulated and surely this is going to take off. We've got a big new studio here, we're a real company. We're not operating out of anyone's backyard anymore. We've got a big label, Stax, behind us, and we've got Columbia behind them." There was a high expectation on Chris' part that this was going to take off and he was destined for success.

Andy Hummel: In my mind, it was just something fun. I didn't think about it much. Then, there was excitement because there was a real LP. Stax was going to put it out and maybe we were going to sell some records. We started having some expectations. I know Chris had high expectations...Sometimes the sun would come out and I would think, "What if people buy this thing and we become rock 'n' roll stars?" Then I would say, "Nah!" and go about my business—go back to chemistry class or something. My motivation was a little different, I guess.

Even Carole, who spent ample time on the sleeve design, was excited to be a part of a nationally released album.

Carole Ruleman Manning: These were the first records most of us had made. John and Terry had worked on records before and had things pressed. But for me, Chris, and for some of the other people this was it, the first thing we had done.

Robert Gordon: The entire lead up to *#1 Record* was that of a sports team that feels confident that it's going all the way—a "can't miss" situation.

Andy Hummel: When the first LP was ready to release, we saw things starting to happen, like, "Oh, you guys need to come in and tell us what percentage of each of these songs you wrote so we can send that off to the publishing company." And, "We need to talk about what your album cover is going to look like. What picture are we going to put on there and what picture will go on the back? And what sort of materials are we going to use to make the thing?" Then it got really exciting for everybody.

With production work finally wrapped up, Chris and Fry celebrated with a trip to Australia, landing in Sydney on December 28, 1971. This wasn't the first trip the pair had gone on. Fry, a licensed pilot, often flew groups of friends to various sunny spots. Chris' appreciation for beachy sites started as a teenager after a 1967 family vacation to Nassau, Bahamas. On the trip, Chris bought a steel drum after he heard "Carrie Anne" by the Hollies. "God knows what happened to that steel drum," David Bell said. "At some point, he probably hocked it like everything else when he needed money." The Bells returned to Nassau in the summers of '68 and '69, but in 1972, Vernon Bell invested in a condo on the island of St. Martin, another destination spot for Fry and Chris.

John Fry: Chris and I went to Australia for a period of about three weeks sightseeing and even looking into their music industry over there. For that trip, it was just the two of us. There was always that kind of craziness going on. We went to St. Martin many times over the years in my airplane, sometimes with a group of friends. I first got a pilot's license when I was seventeen years old. The first trip Chris and I took was to the north part of Fort Lauderdale, Florida, where my family had a small condominium. The St. Martin trips started in the early '70s. The first couple were in a small airplane and it was just Chris and me. By small, I mean it at least had two engines. We were flying over the ocean. There's a possibility of being a shark's dinner if one engine quits.

Richard Rosebrough: Chris could be laid-back but also demanding. John Fry liked to fly his airplane down to St. Martin. That's a long haul. After you pass Puerto Rico, there's a lot of nothing out there for a long way. Chris would say, "Let's get in the airplane and go!" There might be a huge thunderstorm in the area, so there wouldn't be good flying weather, but he just insisted, "Let's go! Point your plane toward St. Martin."

John Fry: That trip from Memphis to St. Martin approaches 1,800 nautical miles. We would do that in two days. We would go as far as Florida, stop, leave there early and try to arrive on the island before sunset because if one would need to ditch in the water the chances of anybody finding you at night are between slim and none. It was an interesting place to visit because St. Martin is divided in half. The island is half-French and the other half is a Dutch colony, which makes for odd neighbors. The attraction back then was that the island was perfectly civilized to support human life, but it wasn't yet subject to the tourist degeneration.

Chris returned to Memphis as Ardent turned its attention to the cover art and promotional photos. The label's promo team hired Michael O'Brien to shoot some publicity shots.

Chris Bell poses with a koala (left) and a kangaroo during a 1972 trip to Australia with John Fry.

Pilot John Fry in the cockpit of his plane.

Steve Rhea and Chris Bell relaxing in St. Martin, fall 1972.

Michael O'Brien: The release of *#1 Record* was approaching and Ardent needed some photography for the launch of Big Star. I did some pictures of the band over at Alex's house. It was shot over a couple days. We shot outside and went up to Alex's bedroom. I said, "What would it be like if the four of you were working on a song?" I tried to put them in situations, one situation where we could get a good portrait of the band. I struggled all day long to get a good shot of the foursome. Then we went to the back of the house and pulled them close to a wide-angle lens and created sort of a strong, horizontal composition. That's when I got that quintessential Big Star promo shot that's all over the place. It's Chris on one side, Alex on the other, then Jody in the back and Andy in between.

Andy Hummel: Michael O'Brien was kind of a key player in this. Before we had Bill Eggleston, we had Michael take Big Star photos. Well, we had Carole first and then Michael came in to do one session.

It was during one of Ardent's marketing brainstorming sessions that #1 Record's *neon star was born. Inspired by the local Big Star grocery store logo, the striking album cover features a neon star sculpture by Ron Pekar, a friend of Alex's. The glowing star, photographed by Carole Ruleman Manning with a Hasselblad six-by-six camera, was hung on Fry's office wall with some black seamless paper behind it.*

Robert Johnson: Carole had started her own design company called Cenotaph, which was inside of Ardent. She did the album cover designs for Ardent.

Carole Ruleman Manning: When I started working at Ardent is when the studio was moved over to Madison...What I did was shoot the pictures for album covers, do the art direction and design, and make sure all the information was correct. From that stage, we would do some promotion...We were all doing something we were interested in. It was making records, making pictures, making covers, and making ads.

Robert Johnson: I went off and got stoned with Chris, Alex and Carole. Then they went off in the studio and Carole said, "Hey, come in the office, I want to show you something." We walked in and there was the neon Big Star lying on the table. She said, "What do you think? This is going to be Big Star's album cover. Isn't it cool?" I said, "Yeah, this is great." I picked it up and it broke right in my fucking hands. I picked it up by the glass. Alex's friend Ron had made it for them for a cheap price. I said, "Oh, no! I've broken this thing." We were so stoned, she just started laughing and said, "Oh, it's no big deal, I'll just get another one made."

With a promotional push in the works, Ardent pressed up "When My Baby's Beside Me" as its debut 45 single. For the flipside, the band re-cut an entirely new, more riotous take of "In the Street."

Richard Rosebrough: The single version of "In the Street" was a real rarity. It was after *#1 Record* was finished and they picked the song to be on the single. This was just one of those "Well, why don't we?" ideas. I was still in Alamo, but they asked me to help out. It has both Jody and I playing drums—all cut live.

Adam Hill: Fry told me someone decided the album version was a little tame, so they decided to re-cut it in a little more rocking fashion for the single B-side. It's the last song on the surviving *#1 Record* reel.

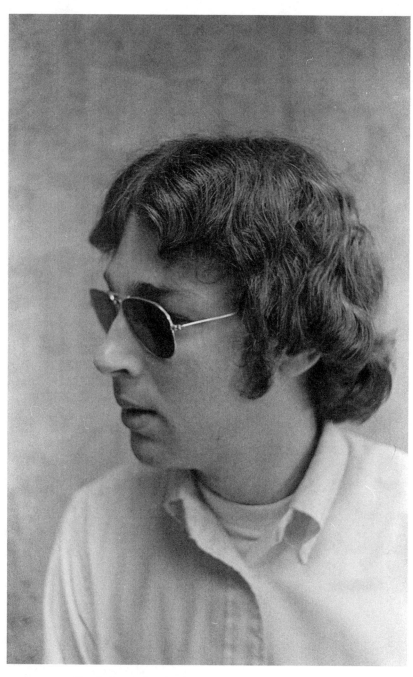

Chris Bell at Ardent Studios during Big Star's earliest days.

As the release of *#1 Record* nears, Big Star poses for a promotional photo at Ardent Studios.

CHAPTER 11

#1 RELEASE — TOUR: SUMMER 1972

The final mixes of #1 Record were completed by the end of 1971, but a series of delays held up its release. The LP, pressed with "the more you learn, the less you know" etched in the run-off grooves, wasn't issued by Ardent/Stax until September 1972, a busy time for Ardent Studios. The Staple Singers' "I'll Take You There," a hit single mixed and overdubbed at Ardent by Terry Manning for Stax, had just reached No. 1 on the Billboard *chart. Chris hoped for even a fraction of that action for Big Star.*

The record's first promotional plug happened locally on the day of its release when WMC-FM disc jockey Jon Scott spun the record over the Memphis airwaves. He also interviewed Alex and Andy. Chris was on vacation in the Bahamas. When asked if a tour was planned, Andy replied, "I believe the idea on that is, after it's been out awhile they'll probably organize a little tour for us to go out on, then we'll come back. It'll slowly get going."

Chris Bell: After we finished the album, Ardent took an age to release it.

Alex Chilton: It took too long. About six or seven months to do all the recording...It took us three months to get the record mastered well.

Andy Hummel: Counting getting the thing mastered, which was the biggest hassle, it took almost a year...We had three places try to master it.

Alex Chilton: We have a lot of strange frequencies on our record, ones they don't usually have to get.

Chris Bell: We said, "Better hurry up or someone will bootleg it." "ST 1006" was a mythical number, that's where that song title came from.

We frightened them by saying, "This is going to be the bootleg album number." It wasn't until the summer of '72 we finally got it out.

John Fry: Chris was happy when the first box of *#1 Record* came in. We opened it up and looked at that nice, shiny-coated paper that we had Stax go through so much trouble to get. It looked just like those British albums.

Carole Ruleman Manning: We wanted to approximate that look. It was horribly expensive, but Stax still let us do it. Stax was not cheap with us at all. We didn't skimp on this album—like the four-color label.

Andy Hummel: When it was finally released, they had a big party at Ardent in the A Studio. We had the release party for Big Star and Cargoe at the same time. They played the LPs over the studio's speaker system. All sorts of bigwigs from Stax and people from Ardent attended. We thought we were going to be rich and famous. Boy, did we have another thing coming.

Carole Ruleman Manning: I heard it over in Studio A. It was so loud in there. John was in there, Chris was in there, Terry was in there, several other people. But the highs on that record—there were so many highs on that record that it truly hurt.

David Bell: I came back to Memphis and Chris played me *#1 Record*. He was enormously proud of it. When he played me that record, I lost it. I cried when I heard that album. He was still, in my mind, my kid brother, but he was twenty-one years old. He recorded a lot of this when he was twenty. I was just knocked out. My impression, from what Chris said, is that the entire band was jazzed. To finally see the finished product was quite nice.

Greg Reding: I thought the first Big Star record was a fucking masterpiece. I've always told people, "If God was a guitar sound, it would be Chris Bell's guitar sound." I loved the record. "The Ballad of El Goodo"—what a hook on that sucker. My God.

Carole Ruleman Manning: When I first heard *#1 Record*, I was absolutely stunned. You could hear all the different things we listened to growing up. You heard the Beatles, the Kinks, some of the Yardbirds. You heard all these influences. It was just such a magical blend of those things that it had its own identity. It was beautiful, and Chris was pleased with it.

Chris Bell: In a way, I was disappointed. I liked almost all the songs a whole lot. I liked Alex's songs a whole lot. Basically, I'm pretty happy with it. There are a lot of things now, after a couple years, that I would like to change or do over.

Jim Dickinson: At the time, I didn't think much of *#1 Record* and *Radio City*. I hear them now; I didn't hear it then. I would like to say that they were brilliant, but I can't.

Larry Raspberry: Big Star's music went beyond me sonically. It was a little intense for me. It felt like music made for the sake of making the best, cleanest recording you could. Some of their gifted writing skills escaped me back in that day. I didn't hear the songs as much as I was distracted by the perfection of the record. I was in a place in my head where the imperfection of the recording is what added depth and character to it. It didn't turn me off, but it didn't turn my head in any direction.

John Dando: One thing that struck me when I first heard the Big Star album was I thought I would hear something more fun to listen to. It wasn't something people were going to dance to. It wasn't the sort of thing you heard on the radio either. It was so serious, and that surprised me because most of the music [Chris] listened to was more like James Gang, and all that. That's what he'd play for cover tunes—more upbeat tunes.

Drew DeNicola: The more you listen to *#1 Record* the deeper it gets. It's complex pop music. In 1972, people were making angry music to be angry, happy music to be happy. There was never any complexity in the emotion. Big Star always had these weird vagaries.

Van Duren: A lot of the early-'70s bands were harder rock and Southern rock. There were other Memphis bands similar to Big Star. Edgewood was one of those bands, but they ended up going into prog rock similar to Yes. But Big Star, in terms of writing and recording, were above everybody else. I'm sure that's due to their access to Ardent for months at a time.

Adam Hill: Big Star didn't fit in with the other local bands. Alamo was jammy. Larry Raspberry was stretching songs out. The Hot Dogs and Cargoe both had that distinct '70s rock sound. When you listen to those bands now you think, "That sounds '70s." Big Star didn't sound really '70s. It's partly the production, it's Fry. He mixed Big Star the way he dreamt of shit sounding. He didn't mix a Freddie King record like he mixed a Big Star record. That was his baby.

Ira Robbins — Journalist, publisher, *Trouser Press:* I was in engineering school in NYC, working for our tiny radio station and Ardent sent us promos. *#1 Record* showed up in a box one day. I liked the cover photo and was impressed by the finish and weight of the sleeve. The music, I must confess, did not do much for me at the time. Power pop was just getting under way. I thought of them sort of as Beatlesesque, which was more prominent at the time than anything as clearly defined as power pop.

Ric Menck: When I first started listening to *#1 Record*, the two bands it reminded me of were the Raspberries and the Beatles, and the softer songs seemed singer-songwriter oriented, almost like James Taylor or someone like that. That's what I thought when my knowledge of music was much more limited than it is today. And when I say it reminded me of the Beatles, I mean it didn't necessarily sound like them, but the music seemed as deep and emotionally satisfying as any Lennon and McCartney song I had heard at that point.

Peter Jesperson — Record executive, Twin/Tone Records co-founder, former Replacements manager: When the Beatles broke up in 1970, it was like somebody had died—a death in the family. It seemed like, "Well, the Beatles are broken up. I guess I have to go do something else now." There was this sense of "everything has changed, and the world isn't as good without the Beatles." When Big Star's *#1 Record* came along, for me, it was the first real sign that it goes on and truly great music is still being made. Slim Dunlap and I used to refer to them as "the American Beatles."

Peter Tomlinson — Fan, music critic: I was eighteen, living with my parents in Edison, New Jersey, and working as a minimum-wage widget-counter in a local warehouse when I got *#1 Record* in the mail. I had been writing record reviews with little publication success, which led me to start up a mimeographed fanzine called *Nix On Pix*. I was so thrilled to get an unsolicited promo album that I put it on immediately. I also recognized the name Alex Chilton, which further piqued my interest. As soon as "Feel" began, I had one of those frozen-in-time rhapsodic moments that come along all too rarely in life. I can still recall it today with utter clarity. It was a real Beatles-on-the-*Sullivan-Show*, life-changing moment. This is what I was looking for in rock 'n' roll, and it was a pretty scarce commodity by 1972. Intelligent, well-crafted, glorious pop. I played the first side obsessively for a month before I even got to side two. My music-loving life is neatly divided into pre-and post-*#1 Record*.

Matthew Sweet: *#1 Record* is such a whole effort. It feels like they tried hard. Not in an overwrought way, but in a way where it's precise when it wants to be. The guitar playing is kind of lovely, and that's different from the other Big Star records. It also has that Americanness in it. More incredibly, coming out of Memphis, a hotbed for rock 'n' roll, it's interesting to hear the British influences. But they still couldn't keep out the Memphis influences, the more riffy, country, rockabilly and even some funky sounds. That all leaked in.

With thousands of records pressed up, it was time to get them in stores and in the hands of radio station programmers and record reviewers across the country. While Stax handled distribution, Ardent Records stepped up its in-house promotion and marketing division to spread the word.

John Fry: Stax was primarily into R&B music...Obviously, their whole promotion thing was geared up to serve the market they were already serving. They let us, at their expense, ultimately create a promotion department. We had three or four people working there. They would work our records to radio and some of the Stax records to Top 40 and FM stations.

Andy Hummel: Fry had set up the in-house promotion shop, which was Courtney Jones, John King and Steve Rhea.

Steve Rhea: While I was still in college in Dallas, Chris began to tell me over spring break about an album he had coming out and he wanted me to come back and work for Ardent. He said he was going to talk to Fry about getting me hired on to help promote the record. I was excited about that because I was close to graduation and had no job prospects...Ardent hired me because I had a huge background in college radio and they knew who I was. Chris persuaded Fry that I needed to be aboard because we were all going to be a success, and if I couldn't be in the band, I needed to be there in some fashion.

John Dando: John Fry got John King to come on and be the promotions director. He was put in charge of promoting these groups, to go after all these college promotion directors and to promote the label.

Steve Rhea: John King was brought in on retainer. He hired Joe Lee, from the old band Lawson and Four More, and he covered the Western states' stations, doing what I had been doing in the Southern region. King was calling stations in the Midwest and Northeast.

Andy Hummel: King busted his ass. You've got to give him a lot of credit. He did everything he could think of. There are all these sort of unsung heroes, even though the whole thing failed. There were a lot of people who did a lot of hard work trying to make it happen. King certainly is one of them; John Dando is another.

Carole Ruleman Manning: John King was quite a presence around Ardent. He was pretty wired all the time.

Andy Hummel: You never knew, when King was talking to you, if he meant anything he was saying or if it was just some huge joke. Still, you would listen to him because he was interesting, and you were trying to figure it out.

John Dando: John King used to run around the halls of Ardent, wearing Weejuns with wedges in them, yelling, "Marketing emergency! Marketing emergency!" It was amazing. He is such a character...King was an absolute wild man.

Steve Rhea: If you mix alcohol, extreme wit, over-the-top love for music and lack of responsibility, then you got John King.

John Dando: King knew everybody in the record business. He knew everything about the record business and all the people working at record labels. He was working closely with Stax trying to promote the label. He was great at wining and dining the record label people. You had to massage these people's egos, and he was good at it.

Steve Rhea: King was the one who later came up with the idea for the Rock Writers' Convention, which was a fabulous weekend in Memphis that Big Star [sans Chris Bell] played at. King was the one calling and cultivating this relationship with the writers. King also decided to go on the road and see some of these stations, instead of just calling them. We went to Chicago, then he went on to Detroit and New York. That was his focus, the huge stations in that belt.

Andy Hummel: King was having some success with Big Star in specific markets they were targeting. Their strategy was not to try and take on big cities like Los Angeles and New York, but places like Phoenix, Tulsa, and what have you. In smaller markets, you could go in and have some influence. They tried that and had some limited successes. They would get the record played for three or four weeks in one of those markets.

Steve Rhea: I would go to work every day, making twenty-to-fifty calls each day to radio program directors. We worked the phones from Oklahoma to the East Coast, from the Gulf Coast up to Kentucky. I was working every rock station in that whole region. I would call and say, "Here's who we are and here's what we've got. I'm going to send you a copy and then I'm going to call you back in about ten days. I want you to listen to this because this is worth hearing." I was relentless about following up and I kept detailed records of who I had called. Pretty soon, I was coming out at the end of a week with pages of radio stations reporting that, "Yes, we have put the song in rotation." We saw some initial success that way. There was also a national "tip sheet," and every couple of weeks or so they would choose two songs that they couldn't decide if they were hits or not. All the 300 or 400 stations would put these songs into rotation and then gauge the reaction. One of Big Star's singles was up against the Doobie Brothers. The Doobie Brothers nudged out Big Star, so Big Star did not get carried forward and put in general rotation. That's the way that system worked.

Jody Stephens: In Memphis, there was WLYX, the Southwestern radio station we listened to. Those guys would play a Big Star song every now and then. WMC-FM 100 was the cool underground-rock station. Whether this was real or not, you could almost hear them getting high at the station and saying, "That was a great song, we're just going to play the whole record!"

Steve Rhea: One day a week, I was off communicating with writers, making up a weekly packet of things to send out. I'm back in the mail-room and we've got boxes of records. We're sending out packets with *#1 Record*. We have hundreds and hundreds of these records going out to radio stations. Ardent also has the Stax promotion network, all these people they employ all over the country that supposedly can get the job done. Then Fry brought on Tim Riley, an independent promotion man in the music business who had an office right there at Ardent. He had big breakthroughs getting records on radio stations and breaking songs that became national hits. He was on a permanent retainer, too.

Carole Ruleman Manning: There were a lot of meetings at Ardent. Tim Riley would have meetings back in his office for promoting the records, back in the southwest corner of Ardent. John King's office was back there. We would have a promotion meeting and decide what we needed to do and that needed to be agreed to by Stax. There was a lot of inter-play between Stax and Ardent. We ran a lot of magazine ads, called around and got stories. I worked with different magazines, like *Billboard* and *Record World*, but we also did things with Marty Cerf's publication, *Phonograph Record*. There was a local one called *River City Review*. There was a variety of regional publications working with us.

Bud Scoppa — Journalist, author, music critic, record executive, Zoo Entertainment: I had gotten to know Alex in 1970 when he spent a few months in New York, but I didn't know anything about Big Star or his involvement in the band when Jon Landau, who was the *Rolling Stone* review editor in the early '70s, assigned me to review *#1 Record*. When I played it the first time, I was ecstatic. The only other initial listening experiences that had excited me to that degree were "Mr. Tambourine Man" in 1965, the first Allman Brothers Band LP in late '69 and Jackson Browne earlier in '72. You can gauge how blown away I was by reading my *#1 Record* review.

"#1 Record isn't revolutionary—the group works within the well-defined forms—it's just exceptionally good. There's not a trace of Memphis soul in Big Star: The group seems to have used the California bands of the mid-Sixties—primarily the Byrds and Moby Grape—as models, but there's a brightness on the up-tempo tunes that seems Beatles-inspired. Parallels are Badfinger and Raspberries, I guess, but Big Star shows more depth and consistency than either of those. A closer parallel is Todd Rundgren, who's equally adept at evoking the Beatles, California rock, and 1965, but even Rundgren hasn't made a whole album as impressive as this one."

—**BUD SCOPPA, *ROLLING STONE***

Ardent's hard work paid off in the form of magazine ink and radio time. Positive reviews rolled in.
"Their sound is full of attractive contrasts and just below the surface subtleties."

—***BILLBOARD***

"Just about every track could conceivably be made into a single."

—***FUSION***

"This album is one of those red-letter days where everything falls together as a total sound. Big Star is into new musical directions but with a firm hold on their roots."

—***CASHBOX***

"This is a group you don't want to pass up, believe me. And you may never hear of them, God forbid. So let's do what we can to make sure they're around for some time."

—***PHONOGRAPH RECORD***

Steve Rhea: We started getting into the music trades like *Record World* and *Rolling Stone*. We were sending albums out to all the press and rock writers, and stories were starting to pop up about who this band was out of Memphis. We're thinking, *Hey! This is going great. We're starting to get a hold.*

Barney Hoskyns: They were rock critics' darlings.

Chris Bell: Ardent did a pretty good job with the publicity. We had nice ads in *Billboard* and *Cashbox* and nice reviews all over. What Ardent did was get records to all the disc jockeys and rock writers and so forth. But Stax did not do much of anything except put out some money for the ads and supported half of the company's activities.

Will Rigby — Drummer, singer-songwriter, the dB's: *Phonograph Record* was kind of championing them. It was the first review I saw for Big Star. They had a giveaway for the single "When My Baby's Beside Me" and "In the Street." You sent in a postcard and they sent you a copy. That's how I got my first Big Star record. It was probably the first Big Star record in North Carolina.

For Chris, the positive press was bittersweet, as rock writers tended to overlook his contributions to #1 Record *and largely focused on Alex being the voice of "The Letter."*

Jody Stephens: Alex was the focal point, and Chris was pissed off about that because the first album was really Chris' project, although he and Alex had done the writing.

Terry Manning: When John King was promoting it to Cameron Crowe, trying to get them to write about it, he'd say, "Alex Chilton from the Box Tops!" Chris would grumble, "This isn't the Box Tops—it's not just Alex." That wasn't the end of the world for Chris, it just irked him.

Jody Stephens: Here's a band called Big Star, which nobody has heard of at the time, but here's Alex Chilton who sang a No. 1 song in the country in 1967, "The Letter," so writers and critics would tend to focus on Alex.

Larry Raspberry: I didn't realize how much Chris played a primary role in Big Star. I was across the hall from these guys at Ardent and I couldn't see any other way than it being Alex's band, with three other talented guys in it. I had to be educated that Chris brought a lot to the creative table. I found out later that frustrated Chris.

Robert Gordon: Anyone who is a Big Star fan realizes today it was more than an Alex Chilton project. You can hear the differences between the first, second and third records. In each of those you hear the personalities. There's no Chris beyond the first one, songwriting contributions aside. There's no interplay between Alex and Chris that's so prevalent on the first one.

Despite the intensity of the promo push, dismal record sales were reported. In hopes of a boost, Ardent Productions hastily planned a makeshift tour for Big Star.

John Fry: We were heavily promoting *#1 Record*, but there wasn't much demand for Big Star shows. The original lineup with Chris played maybe eight or ten shows to support the record from the summer of '72 through the fall.

Andy Hummel: Fry hired a road manager for both us and Cargoe. His name was Vince Alfonso. He came in and got some gigs for us and also looked after the bands. We went out and played a little bit. But first, Ardent bought us some equipment. We were like, "John, we don't have a pot to piss in." We still lived with our parents. For me to be able to go across the street to get something to eat at 11 p.m. so I could keep recording, I had to bum $20 from my mother. I couldn't afford to go buy musical instruments or amplifiers. Fry took the plunge. He said, "If this is going to happen, I've got to do it." He started up Ardent Productions, a different legal entity, whose purpose was to send Cargoe and Big Star on tour to promote our records. John spent a lot of money buying us equipment. We got what Chris and I wanted ever since college—Hiwatt amplifiers. In those days, Marshall Amplifiers were all the rage, but we could never be as plebian as to own a Marshall like everyone else. We had to have Hiwatts. Double stacks, hundred-watt heads. Mine is still at Ardent.

John Dando: We went on a buying spree and bought a lot of Hiwatt guitar amplifiers, which are kind of overkill unless you're playing stadiums. It was too big of equipment for club-sized gigs, which were the type of gigs they were getting. These were little 200 or 300-seat auditoriums—you can't go in there with Hiwatts. They had equipment the Who would use in a stadium. It was just awkward. There were delusions of grandeur at the beginning. They bought equipment based on the notion that *#1 Record* was going to be a big hit...The gear was financed against the band's royalties, which never amounted to much.

Drew DeNicola: These guys were not road dogs. They were "Fry's Boys" and were taken care of financially. We all know the story of the band slogging it away and sleeping in the tour van, but what about this story where they're living like proto-Beatles, but no one has ever heard of them? They're just living in Memphis. That's a big part of why that band ended up being the way they were. They behaved like a supergroup. They wanted legions of fans, but they didn't know what it took, or how much commitment it takes to do something like that.

Alex Chilton: We weren't part of any scene. We were making a record in an insulated environment. If we had tried to get into the rat race or compete with other bands, we would have suffered, but we didn't even bother. We rarely played live.

Terry Manning: Chris wasn't interested much in other local bands. We considered ourselves an island outpost in the middle of the South. We liked British music. We liked Indian music. To a Memphian that was eclectic music, to us it was normal. Chris may have liked some local groups, but he didn't talk much about them.

Richard Rosebrough: Big Star was on its own island. That's something I had a little resentment about. I was a working drummer at the time. My band Alamo had fallen apart, so I would go and do pick-up gigs with other bands. Some of the more common bands got out and worked. They'd drive over into Arkansas for nothing then drive back home and watch the sun come up. Big Star was oblivious to that. They didn't go out and play a lot of gigs. They didn't have a gig every week, or three or four nights in a row down on Beale Street. Big Star played in the studio in their own quiet little palace.

John Dando: Big Star was the apple of John Fry's eye. He wanted to see that group make it.

John Fry: Ardent tried to take care of Big Star, but one thing we didn't have in place was a solid booking system. Everyone at Stax and our place was saying, "Publicity! Publicity! Radio! Radio!" Nobody was saying, "Hey, where's management and booking? Where's the tour?" Beatles toured the world and then became a studio band. I guess Big Star wanted to start where the Beatles left off.

Chris Bell: Most of the gigs we played were really scrappy. It was still down to playing high schools or little halls in small towns.

Andy Hummel: One of the first gigs we got was in Mountain View, Arkansas. When I was a kid and went to summer camp up there, it was just a little town. By this time, because of all these hippies had moved into the north end of the Ozarks, it had become a destination. They had a band shell there. We played that.

Steve Rhea: It was a big venue, an outdoor venue like the Levitt Shell in Memphis. We're backstage and they're tuning up getting ready to go on stage and I notice Chris' hand shaking. Chris, over the years without me noticing, had developed stage fright. He didn't like going out. He was scared to death. He had spent hours and hours in the studio working on *#1 Record*, but I don't think he would have had to spend as many hours if he would have been able to balance that off with more time on stage playing the songs.

David Bell: He had terrible stage fright during the Big Star years, with the few gigs they did. I never saw him having stage fright in his garage bands.

John Dando: Chris didn't have stage fright when he was playing cover tunes with those small bands, when it was just for fun. He was probably just concerned with playing his own material.

Steve Rhea: The only thing I would have recommended to Big Star was they play on stage much more than they did. They over-engineered the first album. It was too inside-out. They didn't take the songs out and test them in live audiences. There's a certain something that happens when you're on stage, you learn a groove and rhythm and come together as a band, instead of layering on pieces. In the studio, there was too much introspection and too much micromanaging of every little thing about the record without enough punch and groove that comes from stage playing.

Chris Bell: I enjoy the studio a lot, but there is nothing like being on stage. There's nothing as good for a band to get you good and tight, which I guess the Beatles are a perfect example of.

Terry Manning: Big Star was great live, but not slick. It was like a rock band playing at a frat house, that's sort of what it was. The later incarnation of Big Star, with Jon, Ken, Alex and Jody, was much slicker. They had a stage presence the original Big Star didn't have. They would have learned that as time went on, but there were not many gigs.

John Dando: They were a studio band and, by that point, had developed a lot of contention between them. I detected a lot of friction developing between Alex and Chris. They didn't seem to be together. They just didn't function as a band very well. It was a lack of practice and playing together.

Andy Hummel: We may not have ever played out enough to get really good at it, but when you get really good, then you're playing "Mustang Sally."

Chris Bell: While I was in the band there were some shows, but not enough to please me, which was one of my arguments. I wanted to get the group out in areas where we had airplay to promote it. We did a few good gigs. One was in New Orleans.

The New Orleans concert, an outdoor show at City Park, dubbed "Political Rally '72," combined candidate speeches with live rock 'n' roll. Big Star opened the event with an 11 a.m. set. The next day, a photo of Big Star performing before hundreds of people was featured on the front page of the Times-Picayune *newspaper.*

Chris Bell: It was rather exciting. We got there the night before the job, and for us it was like the Beatles in New York. There were Big Star songs being played every half hour or something. We did a gig at some pop festival the next day and there was a good reception, a front-page news article and all that.

Steve Rhea: The high point was New Orleans. They had some sort of outdoor concert and had some other acts lined up and they wanted Big Star. They liked the record and were playing it. This is when FM radio was just launching and taking off like crazy. We all went down there, Big Star and their road guy, Vince Alfonso, an Italian guy who came in towards the end. He wasn't hauling equipment; he was just supposed to be the road guy who took care of them and made sure the hotels were right. He was the in-between person. I went down there and ran the sound. We hung around for another night after the concert and then we all came home.

Michael O'Brien: Big Star played in Knoxville one time for a homecoming party at the Student Union, so I did hear a live performance of Big Star with Chris, which was great. It was one of those rare shows with all four of them together. They sounded good, but it was a cold night and they were playing in the parking garage next to the Student Union. It was like thirty or forty degrees outside. They had to re-tune a lot because of the temperature, but they sounded good.

Jody Stephens: It was so cold; we all wore overcoats. Someone in the audience built a fire on the pavement of the garage, which cracked from the heat. The university banned concerts in the garage after that.

Chris Bell: We went down well in bigger places like New York. We played a small outdoor festival once; I don't recall who else was there. It was hard to hold it together. The gigs were depressing because they put us in some bizarre small towns—populations of 400 in Mississippi—where nobody liked pop music.

John Fry: I only saw the original lineup on stage one time. It was in Corinth, Mississippi in a movie theater. I flew to Corinth. It's close to Memphis, probably only seventy or eighty nautical miles, but I flew anyway. The show was attended by few people. The performance and sound were not bad, but there sure weren't any people there to hear it.

John Dando: There was one gig I did not go on because I had a final exam. It was the gig in Corinth, Mississippi. I understand there was a huge amount of bickering going on in the car along the way. That was the thing I could do, [subdue their arguments]. I knew when they were getting ready to blow up or whatever. I just understood that keeping them mollified was just keeping them working. I guess it made me a lackey or a waiter, but if you were going to keep them working you had to keep their little problems under control. They got out on the road with Vince Alfonso, who didn't know how to keep their little egos massaged. There was a big flap over something like cigarettes and they didn't like how something happened down there, somebody didn't treat them the way they thought they should be treated. They came back all hacked off. That's when Chris first said he'd had enough.

The string of disappointing shows frustrated Chris, who was also baffled and exasperated with the lack of album sales. When Big Star played an auditorium in Oxford, Mississippi in October 1972, it was the last time Chris appeared on stage with the band. None of the concerts on this short tour were knowingly recorded, leaving no live audio of Big Star featuring Chris Bell. If a bootleg exists, it has yet to surface.

Jody Stephens: We went down to Oxford in two vehicles. We had a little truck we rented, and the others went down in a car. John Dando was along for the ride, too.

John Dando: I was working at WDIA. They came to pick me up in Chris' Chevy Camaro, so they were kind of low-slung. I walked over to the car to see Chris. He was sitting in the front passenger seat. I looked in at him and noticed he had a fifth of Jack Daniels between his knees that he was drinking straight out of the bottle. I had never, ever seen Chris drink like that. I had never seen him drink much at all. He smoked dope and all that, but I had never seen him drink straight out of the bottle. It was obvious he was in such a state of mind that he was trying to drink that whole fifth of Jack Daniels on his way down to Oxford. It showed when he got on stage. That's when his heavy drinking started. He had on huge dark glasses and kept his back to the audience a lot. He always seemed uncomfortable about singing and he was going to be forced to sing a lot that night.

Andy Hummel: The guitars were so loud nobody could hear anything except the guitars. About thirty people came to hear us.

John Dando: They were awful at the Oxford gig. It was terrible. They looked disorganized and the crowd was kind of sparse. Alex was coming off the Box Tops and was not at all interested in being in a formula act anymore. He wanted to be loose on stage. He didn't want to appear to be a rehearsed, polished sort of act.

Andy Hummel: It was on the way home from that gig that the famous bust happened.

The original Big Star lineup performs in front of an unusually large crowd in New Orleans, Summer 1971.

Big Star performing at Athens State College, now Athens State University, 1972. These rare photos of the original lineup ran in the college's yearbook.

ATHENS STATE UNIVERSITY ARCHIVE

Jody Stephens: After the Oxford show is when Alex, Chris, Andy and Alex's girlfriend Vera were arrested by the Mississippi police.

Andy Hummel: The four of us spent a night in the Lafayette County Jail.

John Dando: I had warned them Oxford was not a good place to do anything that could get you arrested. There was paranoia everywhere about drugs and you couldn't have gone to a worse city to get nailed. It was the center of a major federal drug enforcement thing, the government trained dogs for sniffing out drugs. I said, "We need to be careful going down there." They kind of laughed it off and made fun of me.

Vera Ellis: On the way out there, I road with Dando in the rental, but on the way back I rode in the Camaro with Alex, Chris and Andy. We had just stopped to go to the restroom. I had bought some cookies from the store, I went to the bathroom, then I walked out. Apparently, the cop said I had walked into the restroom with a hypodermic needle. I had some Oreos, that's it. I don't know what the deal was. When the police lights came on, we pulled over. He approached the car and we became scared quickly, because of the way the officer was acting. We had a teeny-tiny bit of a joint left, and they found that.

Jody Stephens: They had long hair and that just pissed people off back then. I didn't even smoke pot. I guess it was just good karma that I came back in the van.

Vera Ellis: At the time, we felt like they had us marked. They saw us at the concert or something. Everything has changed so much now, but back then it was like, "Oh! They've got long hair." Nobody was acting out towards the officer. Nobody was carrying on. We were all just being mellow and trying to make the bad policeman go away. We ended up spending the night in the Oxford jail.

John Dando: Jody and I got back to Alex's house. The band had not made it and they should have made it there before us. Alex's father came downstairs and seemed to be upset. We asked him what was going on, and if he had heard from the band. He'd been called by the police already.

Vera Ellis: They were put together in a jail cell. I was alone on the girls' side. I had my own cell, thank God. It was Alex's father who paid our bail, which was $1,500 each. Someone had to drive out and pick us up because they impounded Chris' Camaro and kept it for a long time.

John Dando: In Oxford, the way you did things there is you hire the right attorney. You pay the attorney fees and he pays off the judge. Chris' father knew some high muckety-mucks in Oxford. He knew the right lawyer to hire to get it expunged immediately.

Vera Ellis: We were written up in the newspaper and my dad was pissed off after his relatives in Mississippi read it. The story mentioned the hypodermic needle, which was just total fiction. Police back then treated long-haired kids like crap because they could. After they paid the fines, it just went away after that, no court dates or anything.

Big Star continued on, but more turmoil was on the horizon.

Andy Hummel: That was our one and only planned and organized attempt for the band to get out and join the initiative to promote *#1 Record*. It was some time after that before it became completely evident that it wasn't going to work.

Chris Bell relaxing at Ardent in between sessions.

ARDENT STUDIOS ARCHIVE

Big Star's sonic mentor, John Fry, in Studio A at Ardent.

CHAPTER 12

DISTRIBUTION DISASTER — RAVE REVIEWS: FALL 1972

By the fall of 1972, the promotional window for #1 Record was nearly closed. Ardent, however, refused to stop pushing the record to critics and disc jockeys. And Stax struck up what seemed to be a promising new distribution deal with the colossal Columbia Records (CBS) via its then-president Clive Davis.

John Fry: When *#1 Record* came out, Stax was in the independent record distribution system, but after about six months, Al Bell went and personally negotiated a new distribution deal for Stax with Clive Davis and Columbia.

Clive Davis — Record executive, former CBS/Columbia president: I had conversations with Al Bell, who co-owned Stax Records, about purchasing fifty percent interest in the company. I decided against that, but did arrange to distribute Stax's releases, which deepened our black-music offerings.

Greg Reding: Columbia didn't need more white or pop acts; they had all of that covered. They just wanted Stax's R&B catalog.

John Fry: [Stax] made this deal with Columbia and took this $6 million-dollar advance, which was a huge amount of money at that time and moved the distribution over. I said, "Oh boy, Columbia! This is going to be great for our music."

Steve Rhea: Columbia was one of the major music companies in the industry at the time. It was pretty much Columbia, Elektra, Warner

Brothers, EMI and Capitol that controlled the distribution. Those are the labels you wanted to be signed with. For Stax to be picked up and distributed by Columbia, that was supposed to be going big-time.

Tim Riley: That's when things started falling apart. It was the wrong marriage between two completely different corporate structures.

John Fry: One thing was, [Big Star] was the kind of product that the distributors didn't expect to get from Stax.

Alex Chilton: Stax Records could never sell a record by a white artist anyway. They were hoping to at that time—it was a new thing for them—but they were over-extended in every direction conceivable. That was just another ill-conceived direction of theirs.

Robert Johnson: Getting Stax to distribute that record was a bad business decision that John Fry made. He did it out of proximity and convenience. They should have gone to New York and got with Epic, Mercury or something. I played with Isaac Hayes, I'd seen what he went through with Stax. I had a feeling Big Star was doomed because of that deal.

Terry Manning: The relationship with Stax was great. The problems came from the outside. Stax, after the Atlantic years, got itself into some distribution problems with Gulf and Western and CBS. Then a bit later there were more problems with the Union Planters Bank situation, so there was almost no realistic hope of success with our product. Plus, it was pure-white pop product, very different from the music Stax had such great successes with. The relationships with radio stations and stores just weren't as strong on our side.

Initially, the Ardent staff was clueless as to why no sales of #1 Record were being reported. They assumed it was being shipped to record shops across the country. Ardent's team soon realized the issue started at the very top of the distribution chain.

Steve Rhea: We were vigorously promoting [#1 Record] and I had page after page of radio stations that were playing the record, but we were dying on the vine. Then I would call the program directors and they'd say, "Do you have any records in the stores yet? We are not getting reports of any sales."

Carole Ruleman Manning: It was like, "What's going on?" We've got all these great reviews. The product is out and Stax seems to be behind it. The record is great. What's going on out there? Something was stuck, but we didn't know what.

Steve Rhea: A decision was made that we needed more promotional help. In retrospect, what we needed was distribution help...The whole time we're promoting the Ardent product, like Cargoe, Big Star, Hot Dogs, and Brian Alexander Robertson, Stax is sending over posters of Isaac Hayes, those are hanging on the wall. Terry Manning was helping Al Bell produce Staple Singers records and they're going crazy, selling huge hits. Stax was totally distracted towards where these big sales were coming from, and they desperately needed them. That was just a microcosm of what was going on in the entire industry. When I would go to New York and meet with the Columbia people, they were all distracted by their million-sellers. All their resources went behind the big sellers, the guys who had the potential to become the Elton Johns of the world. Elton was being touted as the next Beatles at that point. That's what they were focused on, so a little act that was inherited secondhand by a label owned by another label that they had a distribution deal with was not important enough for Columbia to work on.

Chris Bell: There were politics that Columbia would just sooner sell a Columbia album than a Stax album, much less an Ardent/Stax album.

Carole Ruleman Manning: It was [Ardent marketing employee] Courtney Jones who discovered the records weren't getting on sales floors. She would travel as the field-promotion person. She brought it up first, after she started going out in the field. In a meeting she said, "I went into the stores, multiple stores, and they've got our free, promotional albums in there but that's all they've got." Courtney was out in the state of Washington at one time. She went to the stores and was just finding promotional copies. She'd pick it up and say, "Thanks, I'll take this. This belongs to the record company." She asked them, "Why are you just getting these promotional records? Where is the real product?" We must have shipped a ton of those promotional copies.

Andy Hummel: They had these promo kits they'd send out. They did well on that. You've got to give it to John King, he did everything humanly possible to try and make it happen.

Chris Bell: People were writing, asking for records, which shows something. There were people who liked the record and wanted it bad enough to write a recording studio to get it. Stax, Columbia, or whoever could just not get it in stores.

Jody Stephens: I heard about airplay on stations like WNEW-FM in New York and WBCN-FM in Boston. It didn't last long because there weren't any records in the stores.

Chris Bell at the board, 1971.

PHOTO BY MICHAEL O'BRIEN

(L-R) Alex Chilton, Chris Bell, and Jody Stephens working on *#1 Record.*

PHOTO BY MICHAEL O'BRIEN

Chris Bell: Big Star got rave press in *Billboard* and *Cashbox*. There was plenty of airplay, the essential ingredient for any potential to reach fruition, but no records were in stores. It was pointless playing [shows] when the only people who owned the records were DJs and writers.

Andy Hummel: Chris actually got John Fry to call in Al Bell from Stax. We sat down in this room, the four of us, and they were like, "Okay, what are we here to talk about?" Chris asked a couple of questions, three or four. It was meant to be a confrontation, but nothing ever happened. John Fry was very embarrassed by it.

Rick Clark: If you're privileged, you sometimes expect life to operate in a certain way for you. If you think the success of *#1 Record* is a sure thing, that comes from a person who's used to having a life full of certain, nice things.

Carole Ruleman Manning: You can get spoiled or you cannot have a realistic sense of what life is, or how hard it is to achieve certain things, when you just walk into something. Several of us were like that. Chris, Andy and I just sort of walked into this, we hadn't been through anything like Alex had been through, or what Fry and Terry had already been through. When this record didn't sell, it was harder for us. It was a big blow to Chris.

Andy Hummel: He was very depressed and upset about that.

David Bell: Chris was devastated about the lack of distribution, being as young as Chris was, and depression runs in our family. I've had my share of it and he had his. I mean, you can listen to *#1 Record* all these years later and it sounds incredible. *Why weren't they huge?* That's pretty much what he thought. Chris knew what he had done. He engineered a majority of that album and produced about half of it. I can understand how devastated he was when it went nowhere.

Terry Manning: We were all angry with Stax. They just couldn't do it. We tried to do it ourselves.

Drew DeNicola: A big reason Big Star didn't make it was they were functioning on the old model of an independent label: doing it yourself, making music your own way with no one else involved. By 1972, it just wasn't done that way anymore.

John Dando: It was a part of the Ardent ethos to do everything in-house. It was a vertically integrated operation. I don't know if that was good, bad, or gave them a myopic vision of the world. I don't know why they couldn't trust anyone else. For example, they didn't trust anyone else to go out on the road with Big Star but me, [though] there were better people available.

Further complicating matters, Clive Davis, who masterminded the deal, was unexpectedly terminated.

Steve Rhea: It's a comedy of errors here. Shortly after the Stax/Columbia distribution deal we get word that Clive Davis, the man who negotiated the deal with Stax, is being investigated for improper spending on his expense account and they fired him. The head of Columbia, one of the biggest music companies in the world, gets fired. Now there's a new man in charge of Columbia that nobody knows. It just went downhill from there.

John Fry: When the new people came in, like it often happens, they looked around and said, "Well, we didn't like the old guy, so maybe we don't like his deals."

Greg Reding: Ardent's releases were just collateral damage in that whole situation.

#1 Record was not readily available in massive markets like New York and Chicago, and it wasn't getting distributed abroad either. Big Star's early followers overseas used clever methods to obtain the instantly obscure album.

Ivo Watts-Russell: I worked in great record stores from 1972 to 1981. We specialized in imports at the shops I worked at but was never offered the Big Star record by any importers. I worked for Beggars Banquet Records, which sold as many used records as they did new. I never once came across a Big Star record.

Peter Jesperson: I was eighteen and trading records with a guy named Gordon in England. He liked a lot of American bands; I liked a lot of British bands. I found his name in one of the British music magazines in the want ads under "Looking for U.S. pen pal." We had a deal that when a record came out that one of us wanted, the other would airmail it the day it came into record stores. One time he wrote me and said, "I'm looking for a new record by the guy who used to sing for the Box Tops, they're called Big Star." I hadn't heard about it, but thought, "Oh, I like the Box Tops. That sounds interesting." I said, "Okay, I'll keep an eye out for it." I was shopping one day at a store in downtown Minneapolis, it was right in the middle of town called Music City. As you walked in the door, just to the right was a record rack that had room for maybe one hundred records. They called it the cut-out bin. It was all the promotional-only, not-for-sale records with 99-cent stickers. That's where I always went first, to the cut-out bin. I went over there and started flipping through the records. I noticed I was coming to a batch of a lot of copies of the same record. I could tell by the top spine. I get to it and there's the neon star. I picked it up, turned it over, and said, "Oh, this is the record my pen pal was talking about. Great!" I stood there and looked at *#1 Record* and thought, "Wow, this is such a beautiful cover." It had that shiny, laminated look to it, like an import. There was the cool shot of the band on the back with it half-shadowed. I thought, *For this price, I'm going to buy one for myself.* I went back to the rack and grabbed another one. I took it back to my house, put it on the turntable. The first song, "Feel," comes on and I thought, *Oh, my God! This is great.* By the time "In the Street" and "Thirteen" came on, I was absolutely in the bag. I became an evangelist for the band from then on.

John Fry: Even after *#1 Record* came out, I would say that few people in Memphis knew or cared about Big Star.

Rick Clark: I was working at Pop Tunes when *#1 Record* came out. Pop Tunes was the primary record store in Memphis. I don't think we ever sold through the stack of Big Star records.

Drew DeNicola: "No one cared about Big Star." That came from Alex Chilton's mouth. They were weirdos. They were these effete anglophile rockers. They didn't play out much and there wasn't much love in their hometown. The only people that liked them were critics. Back then, there were clear-cut genres, and if you didn't fit in those genres you had no place. Big Star was a casualty of that. The bands critics loved, other than Big Star, were other '60s-inspired bands. They loved the Raspberries, Blue Ash, Badfinger, all those bands. That was also when the MC5 was getting love from critics.

Chris Bell: Big Star did well in New York, New Orleans, and a good bit in Texas, also. It was scattered areas. There was not much support in Memphis, surprisingly. We had a sort of underground following in a way.

Terry Manning: Chris wasn't known in Memphis outside of our little group.

Jody Stephens: We all thought of Chris as a genius, which is what we all thought of Alex. In terms of everybody else, nobody heard of Chris until many years later.

Terry Manning: Memphis music people like Booker T, Willie Mitchell, and Sam Phillips had no idea about Big Star. They weren't checking in and didn't need to or want to. Why should they? They had their thing going. Nothing happened with the music. Maybe if "In the Street" had become a hit single it would have been a different story, but they had no reason to check out a few prep-school kids from Memphis.

Richard Rosebrough: They knew who Alex was because he had hit records. Alex was a known entity. Chris didn't have that track record. Chris didn't go out and actively promote himself or anything like that. He just played and tried to write good songs and get them recorded and sounding good.

Danielle McCarthy-Boles: They were a bit of an anomaly. Certainly, they were not big shots in Memphis. In fact, after the Big Star film [*Nothing Can Hurt Me*] came out, a lot of people from Memphis who grew up during that time said, "I had never even heard of Big Star." They were sort of outliers in terms of the Memphis music scene at that time. If they hadn't been recorded at Ardent and released by Stax, they would have been even more obscure. It was also strange they were on the Stax label, considering they were mostly known as a soul-music label with black artists. They are so Memphis in a lot of ways, but if they'd been in a different city, like New York or San Francisco, they would have done better.

David Bell: A couple years after *#1 Record* was released, Chris would quote biblical passages to me about being accepted everywhere except in his own country. In a way, that's understandable. The powers that be in Memphis didn't give a shit about Elvis until he died. To them, Elvis was just this redneck kid from Mississippi playing the devil's music.

Chris Bell chats with John Fry at Ardent Studios near the large windows facing the
atrium. Later, Chris injured himself after he kicked through
one of the large panes of glass.

ACT THREE

I GOT KINDA LOST

Chris Bell, 1973.
PHOTO BY JOHN DANDO

CHAPTER 13

DISILLUSIONED — QUESTIONING: WINTER 1972

As 1973 neared, despite a disappointing tour and album release, Big Star refocused and collaborated on a batch of new songs for a hypothetical sophomore LP. On the surface, the band appeared to be back on track.

Andy Hummel: As the *#1 Record* effort and its very lame tour wound down in mid- to late-1972, new songs had already been written, both separately and jointly, mostly the latter...Some writing occurred in Alex's bedroom. I know we did "What's Going Ahn" there. Ditto for "Life is White" and "Back of a Car."

Chris Bell: The three of us did "Back of a Car," "O My Soul," and "Way Out West," which Andy wrote, but I wrote some of the bits in there. We arranged them, and I was happy with how they were coming along.

Alex Chilton: Chris, Andy and I got together several times for writing sessions and some of those things were more cooperative efforts than anything on the first record.

Infighting and heightened emotions soon dampened the brief creative streak.

Chris Bell: There were terrible arguments between the band. Alex had, in a sense, left and was playing with other guys while the album was still being recorded...In a way, we were sort of drifting apart. Plus, Andy was encouraged by some people at Ardent that maybe "India Song" was the best song on the album and he ought to go solo. It was bad news.

John Dando: The fact that Chris was around the band all the time, plus all the stress he'd been through working with them in the studio, had made it almost intolerable for him to be around them.

Chris Bell: Everything became political, resulting in bitterness and even a fistfight in rehearsal.

Jody Stephens: Chris and Andy did get in a physical fight one time during a band practice at Alex's parents' house. Chris just kept picking on Andy.

Andy Hummel: Chris was being an overbearing asshole. We were trying to work up acoustic numbers and I hadn't played acoustic guitar before. Jody and I were trying to sing, doing a lot of things we hadn't tried to do before. Chris was like, "Why aren't you doing that?" and "You aren't trying very hard." I finally had enough of it.

Jody Stephens: Andy calmly put his bass down incredibly rationally and said, "I think this is it for the day. We can rehearse again tomorrow." Andy headed out the door and Chris made some barbed comment. Andy whipped around, stomped over to Chris and just socked him.

Andy Hummel: In those days, I was a much more confrontational, easily pissed-off person. I socked him in the nose, and then we wrestled for about thirty seconds, and that was it.

Jody Stephens: It didn't really hurt Chris, so it can be funny. The look on his face, it was pure shock. His glasses didn't come off but were askew on his face. There was an incredible look of disbelief and then Andy walked out the door.

Andy Hummel: We ruined Alex's mother's antique Persian carpet. Chris bled on it. You can't get blood out of Persian carpets.

Jody Stephens: After Andy left, Chris turned around, walked over and grabbed Andy's bass, a Gibson Thunderbird. He picked it up and broke it into three pieces.

Andy Hummel: It was a choice, original Gibson Thunderbird that I had been looking for forever—because who played a Thunderbird? John Entwistle, of course. Fortunately, Robert Johnson was able to fix it.

Jody Stephens: The story continues with Andy kind of stalking Chris at Linda Schaeffer's house.

Linda Schaeffer Yarman: I was with Chris after the fight happened. Chris was hanging out with me in our guest house until the early hours of the morning. Andy came over, saw Chris' car at my house and got mad. Later that night, when Chris got in his car to leave, he saw his guitar in the back seat with holes in it. Andy had stabbed it with a screwdriver during Chris' visit that night. We never saw him but knew it was him.

Jody Stephens: It's a Yamaha acoustic. Andy poked four holes in it. I actually still have that guitar.

Linda Schaeffer Yarman: Chris and I were both livid. Chris went home, and I drove to Midtown to Andy's parents' house and nailed a note to his front door with an ice pick, I couldn't find a nail. It was 2 a.m. I told his parents what Andy had done and how he needed to buy Chris a new guitar. I can't believe I did that.

Jody Stephens: Right after that, Chris goes out to the guitar shop and charges a guitar to Andy. I thought, "How do you charge a guitar to someone without their permission?" But I guess that happened. Andy wound up with the Yamaha with the holes in it, then I was looking to learn guitar, so Andy just gave me the guitar.

Ardent Records accepted that #1 Record was a flop. Fittingly, the last effort to push the record, the mis-pressed "Don't Lie to Me" and "Watch the Sunrise" 45 mistakenly plays "Thirteen" on the A-side.

David Bell: They were still optimistic about pushing *#1 Record* until about the very end of '72. Around the end of the year is when Ardent said, "No more." By then it was obvious the record wasn't going to be a hit.

Ira Robbins: Power pop has always had the distinction of rarely being popular. Add Big Star to the commercial failure, or obscurity, pile with: Shoes, dB's, Kursaal Flyers, Pezband, The Nerves, Paul Collins' Beat, and Dwight Twilley.

Terry Manning: Looking back, [Ardent] was an island in a sea of rhythm and blues, in a country that didn't want the music that we wanted to make. It was an isolated situation.

David Bell: Anybody who's connected to the business knows you can create the most glorious piece of art, but if you don't have a big machine behind you pushing it, nobody will know about it.

Carole Ruleman Manning: After *#1 Record* failed, there was emptiness at Ardent. There was a loss that sort of woke some of us up to the harsh realities of the music business. It was a dark time.

Paired with the disheartening blow of a failed album, Chris' escalated use of prescription psychotropics and alcohol propelled him into a severe bout of depression and paranoia. In the depths of addiction, he distanced himself from John Fry and his bandmates, who noted an alarming change in his disposition.

Steve Rhea: At some point, from when I joined Ardent to the waning months, I realized that Chris and I were not the high school buddies we had been. A lot of things had changed for him. He was frustrated. He was insecure about almost everything at that point. He had a lack of confidence. That totally contrasts with Chris back in high school. Something happened.

Richard Rosebrough: Chris started drinking more and was in more depressive moods. He would get mad or have something on his mind that he wouldn't tell anyone about. I never knew what he was thinking.

Andy Hummel: It wasn't until roughly the time the album was released and started tanking that Chris started getting down in the dumps and freaked out about it all...That was a factor in Chris' emotional problems he started having around this time. The guy poured his heart and soul into this thing. He felt kind of betrayed.

Bob Schiffer: Chris fell apart for a while. He was the only one in the group who fully understood how bad they were getting fucked. They should have been one of the great groups of the 1970s, no doubt about that.

Chris Morris: The failure of *#1 Record* fucked him up badly. It sent him into a crashing depression. It paralyzed him for a while. You could tell he was already sort of a tortured guy, but he went into a tailspin after the Big Star album.

John Dando: Chris drank and drugged himself into oblivion.

David Bell: Chris was hanging with the wrong crowd and trying to self-medicate. There had been lots of press about Clapton and all of them. He'd been led into it during the fashionable days of LSD and all that.

Andy Hummel: Chris was a bright, seemingly happy guy with a total dedication to his music and musicianship when I first met him. In fact, his compulsiveness about it is one thing that ultimately drove us apart. He became so intolerant and demanding that I just couldn't handle him anymore. Of course, I was too far the other way. I just wanted to raise hell and party. He was so intense. The failure of Ardent and Stax to get the first record into stores totally freaked him out. That, along with the emotional turmoil going on in his love life at the time, just broke him down and he became what we would now call clinically depressed.

Commercial failures and drug abuse aside, confusion in Chris' personal life weighed on the twenty-one-year-old. Never having a serious or steady girlfriend, rumors of his homosexuality quietly circulated among his circle of friends. Over the years, the speculation varied from Chris being in love with John Fry to simply being closeted and lonely. Chris, who had slowly become a Christian during this chaotic period, never came out or spoke publicly about his sexuality, though it's become a part of his equivocal rock 'n' roll folklore. His close confidants speak cautiously about the matter, or not at all.

Rick Clark: Chris' rock 'n' roll crazy demise, his spiraling down, was something that arose purely from his toxic blend of born-again Christianity, illegal substances, and sexual-identity conflict.

Richard Rosebrough: The Big Star story is often painted as a rock 'n' roll band that had a huge initial failure and then thirty years later found success. The story, the real story, is much deeper, much more tragic. There was a big energy that drove that whole project, the whole band. At first it was a positive energy, but it just got messed up. This whole story is just as much about John Fry as it is the band, but that's not often woven into the story.

Holliday Aldridge — Lesa Aldridge Hoehn's sister, Jody Stephens's ex-girlfriend: There were rumors that Fry and Chris had a thing, an affair, or whatever you want to call it. It wasn't an affair because neither of them was married—a love affair. I did not see that. They did not act like a couple in front of us.

Andy Hummel: I don't know if it's going to benefit anyone to go into that can of worms because that's not just one can of worms. It's hard to have that conversation without it getting really broader. From my standpoint, I can't talk about that from any personal experience whatsoever, because they were repressed times. Whatever people were doing behind closed doors, certainly no one ever shared it with me. In those days, I was very overtly heterosexual so people who weren't probably wouldn't share that sort of thing with me.

Richard Rosebrough: Chris was not seeing success with his music, but I also think he had a broken heart. He had turmoil deep inside. He was also drunk all the time. As I later found out, he was taking a lot of drugs, too.

Alex Chilton: I never knew anything about his gayness until after he quit our band. But we had a good working relationship and there was never a harsh word spoken between us. Looking back on it now, I see that some of the things he said did indicate some tension, but they were so cryptic that all I could do was just look at him and nod.

Carole Ruleman Manning: Nobody talked about homosexuality. That was like, "Shhh."

Richard Rosebrough: It was pretty hush-hush. There were people who knew but they were very close to him, close to the circle. But there are a lot of folks who were close to Chris who still don't have any idea. In a way, that's not unusual, growing up in the period we all grew up in. Things today, for younger people, are completely different than they were for people my age. It was a closed society back then.

Robert Johnson: There were all sorts of rumors going around. I can't ever say I ever saw anything, but everyone knows Alex swung both ways.

Tommy Hoehn: He was confused. I don't know how gay he was. I will say that when he embraced all of this, the more he embraced it, the freer he became for a while.

Richard Rosebrough: Chris did talk about his problems with me, but there were only like two or three conversations we had. Around that time, I was in the hospital. He came down, brought a joint, and we got high in the hospital room. We talked that night. I said, "What's going on?" It was a lot of personal issues. We're talking about questionable sexuality and confused sexuality and maybe being gay. I don't know how that manifested itself with Chris. He was conflicted. Jealousies cropped up, insecurities. It shook things up a bit. He didn't know how to confront them, deal with them. and let them be a part of his life. They were issues that should have been small, but they grew to be out of control. Chris would bury. He wouldn't talk about his emotions, but you could always tell that his feelings ran deep. He wore his heart on his sleeve, but he never talked about it. When you have a problem and you don't talk about it, it becomes a bigger problem.

Jody Stephens: The homosexuality thing? I've heard people talk about it later but that was a surprise to me. Not that it mattered, not that I would have cared. Back then there were never any discussions or comments or anything that would lead me to think that. He dated Linda Schaeffer, so I don't know.

Linda Schaeffer Yarman: Yeah, we dated. I would pick Chris up, or he would pick me up, and we would go by the Knickerbocker and steal wine. The waitresses would sneak wine out the back. It was a very close, soulmate kind of friendship.

Richard Rosebrough: We always thought if there would be a normal relationship that it would be with Linda Schaeffer.

Terry Manning: All I can say, as far as I knew at the time, there was never any hint of that or anything said or done that would have hinted toward that. You think he'd say something. But you hear that all the time, "Yeah, he was gay." Maybe he was. And other people can say, "He definitely was." As far as I knew, that wasn't a part of anything. I do know, at one point, he was making eyes with the same girl I was at the time. We had a little bit of a romantic rivalry of who was going to get her.

David Bell: He never confided in me with that. I always felt, if he would have, it would have been to me. But that's maybe too egocentric. He may have to other people. He was someone who could keep secrets. He didn't go there. I've never heard of where that rumor came from, but if you want to say he was "questioning"—yeah.

Chris' mental state became perilously unbalanced. His increasingly hot-blooded visits to Ardent became a problem. While most of his anger was pointed at Fry, Chris had also grown resentful of Alex.

John Dando: Chris had several major blow-ups at Ardent with John Fry. He just totally flipped out, just couldn't keep it together anymore. It was a building storm. He was impatient.

Jody Stephens: There were some pretty bad experiences. It was stormy.

Tommie Dunavant — Friend, Earl Smith's widow: Chris did some pretty erratic things. I'm not sure his personality could have dealt with success if Big Star had found it.

Alex Chilton: Chris was having difficulties with the label and there were some personal bad feelings between him and some people there because he was taking some drugs, like downers, which make some people a little paranoid.

Richard Rosebrough: Alex thought Chris was a little too emotional and some of his behavior was a little uncalled-for.

Robert Gordon: The psychodynamics at Ardent were more than what Alex bargained for and that probably had a lot to do with how things later played out.

David Bell: Chris' doctor distributed more pills than anyone. In hindsight, that was absolute malpractice. He was seeing all these Ardent people at the same time. That's just ridiculous. They were so young. I don't think it helped Chris' situation.

Richard Rosebrough: The idea that Chris eventually left the band because he was upset about the record distribution problems is only part of the story. Chris could sometimes want things to go his way and he'd make it difficult for you if you opposed things going his way. This is my own view, but Fry got tired of Chris' antics and tried to push Chris away, and at the same time he pulled Alex into a friendship. Alex seized the opportunity, moved in and said, "I'll be friends with John Fry now." There was nothing more to it than playing politics...Alex manipulated things to run Chris out, so it could be just Alex's band. He was an opportunist. He wanted to make friends with the people in control of that band, which is the hierarchy—John Fry.

Alex Chilton: Chris had a way of being so cryptic and mysterious at times that I didn't get the point of what he was talking about...As long as I knew him, I'm not sure he opened up to me or anybody else. It's funny because he comes to me and says, "I'm having trouble with John," and then goes to John and says, "We're having trouble with Alex."

Vera Ellis: John Fry had purchased a car for Chris and he ended up giving it to Alex and there was some jealousy there. It was an MG—British racing green.

Andy Hummel: Even early on, after Chris and I had come home from Knoxville, sometime in the time we were working on the first LP, there's absolutely no question John Fry and Chris were really, really good friends, very close to each other. They did a lot of things together. They flew together. They traveled together. But there came a period, cruising along through all that, where it seemed like Alex started hanging around with John a lot. I don't think it was a long period of time, but for a while he did. Throwing any question of sexuality aside for a moment, when you are nineteen or twenty years old and you're really good friends with somebody and then somebody who you feel a little rivalry with anyway comes along and is usurping your relationship with that person you held as special—that could upset anyone.

Alex Chilton: I was very concerned with myself and nobody else and I just took over. It was strange. I was an outsider, I just came in. I was just thinking of myself in those days. I didn't think of Andy or Jody or Chris. I would write things and we would perform them, that was about it.

Tommy Hoehn: Alex is sort of a hard person to get along with. My take on Big Star was that it was Chris' band and Alex stole it from him. That's not to detract at all from Alex's talent, but Chris is the one that had the Beatle thing going.

Alex Chilton: I'm a pretty self-centered person, but I wouldn't say I was a megalomaniac.

Terry Manning: Alex had been a star since he was like fifteen years old. He toured the world, had stage presence, looked great and knew how to carry himself. He had his whole flippant attitude. Even back then, Alex had the "I'm me, fuck you" thing about life, as he should have. He was kind of the Marlon Brando of rock music.

Jim Dickinson: When Alex went to New York with Keith Sykes, he came back a different person, and that person was vulnerable. During the first Big Star album, he gradually got his strength back and took the band over.

Chris Bell: Alex's personal ambition changed his mind [about the band].

Alex Chilton: There are several schools of Big Star cultists, most of which are based in England, and one of them sees me as a Machiavellian guy who stole Chris Bell's band from him.

Cindy Bell Coleman: Chris was frustrated with Alex. He made him a little miserable.

Carole Ruleman Manning: As the band was breaking up, several things happened. One is when Terry and I went on our honeymoon to England, Germany, and Italy. On that trip we picked up a black Mercedes, the one just under their limo, for John Fry. We drove it around and then had it shipped back to Memphis for John.

Robert Johnson: John Fry bought a black 1973 5.0-liter coupe Mercedes, the most expensive, fastest, four-door sedan in the world. It was a 300SEL 6.3, a big car. It had a huge V-8 in it. Back then, the Coke machine at Ardent had the glass longneck bottles. Chris got into a fight with Fry about something. He was pouting around and went outside. He took one of those Coke bottles, cracked it on the brick wall of the studio, and then went and scratched "PIG" on the hood of Fry's car. Chris was pissed. I never saw Fry's reaction, but Fry never said much of anything.

Richard Rosebrough: John took it in stride. John is very controlled, never raises his voice. He doesn't get angry the way other people would by ranting and raving, screaming and throwing things.

Adam Hill: Fry would avoid confrontation. Not because he was scared, it was more of an "I'm just not going to worry about that" thing. He was a smart guy.

Carole Ruleman Manning: I thought this was just something in their personal relationship. I couldn't imagine why on earth he would ever do that to John's car.

Drew DeNicola: Chris could be incredibly impulsive and destructive. He could be super mellow and then go to extremes.

Richard Rosebrough: There were some incidents with Chris I witnessed firsthand, like the day Chris kicked through a huge glass window at Ardent. It all happened early in the morning, 9 or 10 a.m. He was working in one of the studios. Ardent has an atrium right in the middle where all these plants are. There are azaleas, crepe myrtles, and there's a fountain there. This atrium is surrounded by glass and there's a hallway there where all the studios are. Chris was working in A studio with John Fry. I don't know what they were doing or what they were working on, maybe they were just in there talking. All I know is Chris got mad, really mad. He stormed out of that studio, walked into that hallway and there was that glass wall sitting there. Chris just hauled off and kicked the double-pane glass.

Terry Manning: He smashed out one of the large plate-glass windows inside Ardent right by the Coke machine, as well as a pane or two in the back door. I cleaned up blood and broken glass all night.

Richard Rosebrough: He broke his foot, broke his ankle. He kicked it pretty hard. The next time I saw him he was on crutches.

Terry Manning: Luckily, Chris had boots on or he might have lost a leg.

Jody Stephens: Like Andy, I was going to college, had girlfriends and worked, so I wasn't involved in these issues. But when somebody kicks out a huge five-by-eight window, you know something is going on.

Terry Manning: Another time, Chris got mad at me for something he thought I had done to another band I was working on. I hadn't done what he thought. He started yelling at me and was out of control. We even had a physical fight right in the Ardent parking lot. Another time we were talking, and he was so depressed. He told me he wanted to kill himself, like maybe run out into the street and have a car hit him. I tried to talk him down a bit and joked, "You should only get hit by an expensive car, maybe a Rolls or a Mercedes." Wouldn't you know it, right then, a new Mercedes came rolling down the street.

Richard Rosebrough: After a certain point, it was weird with Chris. He ended up like a hurt dog. He would go off and be by himself.

Carole Ruleman Manning: I was going out of the office area at Ardent, through the hall, and Chris was coming the other way, but we almost bumped heads. It was one of those awkward moments where you think, "Golly, he's crying, I'm embarrassed that he sees me." He's thinking, "Oh, she saw me crying," that sort of thing. Finally, I said, "What's happened? What's wrong?" He just muttered one word, "Alex." I just knew instantly this was major, major trouble for Chris. I knew it wasn't anything Alex was doing. It was just him being Alex. I don't want to say domineering, but Alex had a strong personality that did tend to dominate relationships. I made the decision to be nice to him and just listen to him. I wanted to get into this thing and find out what was going on, what had been said in the studio, but he made it clear he didn't want me involved in that.

Alex Chilton: Some people have tried to say there was a feud between us or something. But you have to understand, the relationship between Chris Bell and myself constituted a very small part of my life. It covered only a year, or a year and a half. It's not something I think about often.

Chris Morris: They just couldn't work together in a partnership, which was tragic.

Alex Chilton: Any problems I ever had with Chris were strictly under the surface of what he was thinking. I mean, I wasn't having any problems with anybody…Chris was a very secretive person, a very mysterious person. But his personal problems weren't my concern.

Andy Hummel: [Chris and I] had some conflict…Alex and I spent a lot of time socially together. I wasn't spending much time with Chris. It got pretty crazy. Alex and I started partying down and raising a lot of hell in that time frame…One night, we were blasted out of our brains, it must have been 2 a.m. We went down to American Studios—Dan Penn and Spooner Oldham were in there. We were going to try and play music, which was hopeless. There wasn't any way I was going to be playing anything when I was that blasted. We were staying up all night being crazy, hanging out at Alex's apartment with the girls. We just partied a lot. Alex is an extremely interesting guy socially. He is fascinating. He was big-time into astrology in those days. He had an ability to carry on interesting conversations with diverse groups of people. He was amazing at that. You were never bored. They were the kind of conversations where people got to know each other well.

Richard Rosebrough: Alex had a lot of girlfriends. Alex had a lot of friends, period. Alex could go to a bar or meet someone on the street and establish a close personal relationship with them. He'd make them feel like he was their best friend. Then, Alex might just change into a different mood, and he'd just walk away and leave you. I assume his personal relationships could be that way, too.

John Dando: For me, when Alex joined the group, it was such a terrible turning point. When we were first doing those things out of the backhouse and playing with Chris, it was all a lot of fun, it was innocent. We were all having these fantasies of Apple. Somewhere along the way, when they went in the studio and Chris got into playing with Alex, working with Alex and getting under the pressure of doing that album, it became deadly serious. It became obvious Chris had gone through some terrible ordeal.

CHAPTER 14

HOSPITALIZED — RADIO CITY: WINTER 1972-1973

As summer turned to fall, Chris' personal problems extended beyond the studio and into his home life. After flying home from Italy, David was shocked by the depth of his younger brother's depression. In an effort to lift Chris out of his slump and separate him from his bad habits, he invites Chris to return to Italy with him.

David Bell: I was living in Italy from 1971 to 1975. I said, "Whatever it is, come on over to Italy with me and have a good time, try to sort yourself out." Chris came over for the first time in the fall of 1972.

Richard Rosebrough: He needed to be rescued. He needed to stop drinking and stop taking drugs.

David Bell: During that trip, Chris was inconsolable and drank a lot of bourbon. I thought, "This is a wash, it didn't help him at all." He was still in a fairly depressed mood. We also went to Switzerland during that trip, and that's when I shot that photo of him in the Alps, the one used on the *I Am the Cosmos* album cover. That's one good thing to come from it.

Chris recalled one encouraging facet of the gloomy expedition in a 1975 interview: "That's when we just started getting turned on to the scene in Europe." Chris also made a monumental decision: He would leave Big Star. On November 16, he returned to Memphis with the news, though he had already made ominous calls to a few close friends while still overseas.

John Dando: When Chris left the band, it seemed like all hell broke loose. I had phone calls from Chris from numerous places in Italy.

David Bell: Chris probably threatened to leave Big Star a couple times, but he left for good around December 1972, not long after he returned to Memphis.

Chris Bell: Ardent killed us spiritually and as friends...I phoned Alex to tell him I had left.

Richard Rosebrough: We all saw it coming...There was real competition on musical and personal levels, and it started to be hard for them to all get along.

Chris Bell: Things were coming to a head with me and Alex. I had spent a lot of time and effort in producing and overdubbing our recordings and tried to get things as complete as possible. As well as polishing up our songs, I still had things like school and my engineering duties at Ardent to occupy me while Alex was just hanging around taking it easy. Andy, too, was being, shall we say, enticed or encouraged to sign as a solo artist and that was causing problems, too. With this background, I felt it was best if I left the group.

Alex Chilton: I remember Chris coming to me and saying that he was having trouble with John, and, for that reason, he wanted to split from Ardent and go somewhere else. I just thought it wasn't such a good idea. Chris kind of presented it to me in a way that if we would follow him away from the record company that we would stay together. I was more interested in staying where we were. I hadn't learned much about the recording studio at that time and I was very much interested in doing that.

Andy Hummel: Chris leaving the band was an extremely complex affair involving disappointment with the way the release, promotion, and sales of the record had gone. Plus, there were a lot of personal problems he was having at the time.

John Fry: It was just kind of a confluence of circumstances that pushed him right to the brink.

Alex Chilton: Somehow, Chris got it into his head that we and all these people were against him, which wasn't true at all. He got upset with the people at the label and only marginally with us because we were still there. We didn't storm out the way he did.

Things that I'd done before are gone
I can't believe I'm on my own

— CHRIS BELL, "I GOT KINDA LOST"

Tom Eubanks: After Chris left the band, he probably expected everybody to say, "Oh, no! Don't quit!" When they didn't do that, it made it even worse.

John Fry: I don't think there was hostility toward Chris. You're going to think I'm lying, but I never talked to Chris about the issue and I never talked to the other guys about it. As I look back on it, it seems incredibly stupid, but I've got cases of the stupids before and I may get one or two again. I honestly don't think there was any unwillingness on the part of Alex, Andy and Jody, to say, "Hey Chris, come on back, let's give it another try."

Andy Hummel: I did communicate with Chris some during this period, but it was all very negative. Like, "Andy, do you have a gun? I need to borrow it."

Chris Bell: I was pretty depressed about the way things had gone with Big Star because I had made a tremendous personal investment into the group and didn't see myself getting into anything as good as that again. To me, the combination of the four of us, regardless of our personal difficulties, was the epitome of what I could get into musically, as far as creative input from other members. I didn't think the first album was the greatest thing ever done, but I felt like, with the group, the second album would have been phenomenal.

Richard Rosebrough: One of the first things Alex said about Chris after Chris left Big Star was, "Chris has just gone nuts and I don't understand what's going on. He's behaving strangely."

Steve Rhea: Chris was different. He was cordial and nice, but he was kind of like a guy who'd burned out too many brain cells or something— just the way he was talking to me.

John Dando: Chris stayed in touch with my mother quite a bit. They were good friends, and I was always good friends with Chris' mother. At one point, I called home and my mother said she heard from Chris and he sounded bad. She said, "You need to give Chris a call," and I did. She said Chris sounded like he was getting progressively worse. That was troublesome for me.

David Bell: My brother was near rock bottom.

John Dando: He had a wry sense of humor. Chris and I would just get hysterical laughing all the time—until Chris started going downhill. He and I used to have a great time doing anything. We could work on anything and just get beside ourselves laughing. As he became more and more depressed, I don't think he lost his sense of humor necessarily, but the joy kind of went out of it. I felt bad because he pulled me up after I came back from UT and was here all alone, then I had to watch him go downhill, and I couldn't pull him out of it.

In late November, a well-oiled Chris headed to Ardent with the plan of erasing his history with the band.

Tom Eubanks: Chris gets so upset and he goes down to Ardent and erases those Big Star *#1 Record* tapes. He was like, "Hey! It's my band. Everything about it was me, like getting the people together, but nobody gives me credit for it." It was an emotion you'd attribute to being a young man.

Terry Manning: The only thing Chris erased was the multi-track masters. They were destroyed and I'm glad they were. It's the best thing that could have ever happened. I wish everyone who has a good album would erase their multi-track masters once it's finished. Then all these labels can't go back and post these remixes and isolated vocals online. That was not intended by the artist.

Richard Rosebrough: I saw Chris delete those *#1 Record* multi-track master tapes. I was doing a session in the B Studio, which is by the back door of Ardent. I heard Chris knock on the door. I opened the door and he was standing there with his long coat on. He had a reel tape under one hand and a drink in the other. He was drunk. I suspect he'd also popped some tranquilizing pills. He was sloshed out of his mind. I said, "Hey Chris, how are you doing?" He just said, "I'm fine." He walked right past me over to the A Studio. I went back in the B Studio and tended to my session for three or four minutes. I just didn't have a good feeling about things, so I walked over to the A Studio to check on him. The sixteen-track masters to *#1 Record* were easily recognizable to all of us because of all the leader tape and little markings. I saw he had it on the machine at thirty speed and all the tracks were in red. I thought, *He's erasing this tape!* I said, "Chris, that's the master, man. Are you sure of what you're doing?" He casually said, "Yes. I'm quite sure." I said, "Are you OK?" He said, "Yes, I'm OK." I just kind of stood there for a second and thought, "I don't think I'm going to get involved in this." I went back to the B Studio and called Fry, so he would know what was going on. Fry said, "I'm sorry you got involved in this."

After he belligerently argued with Fry, Chris drove back to Germantown and returned to his bedroom at his parents' home. There, he swallowed many prescription pills and laid down on his bed.

David Bell: Everything seemed to be falling apart with the band, and my brother had apparently tried to do himself in...He had attempted suicide at least twice during these years and had been hospitalized as a result.

Drew DeNicola: It all happened in a short period. Chris had come back from being in Europe with his brother and then he quit the band. He had a fight with John Fry, went home, came back to Ardent, erased the tapes, went back home, took a bunch of pills, fell out of bed, knocked his head, someone in the house heard that and took him to the hospital. They pumped his stomach and put him in the psych ward.

David Bell: It was an intentional overdose. It was very serious. I never knew what it was that he took. He was in his bedroom and then he was taken by ambulance. I came home for Christmas and my father met me at the airport. He said, "We've had some trouble at home." After I found out what it was, I thought, *What an understatement.* I visited him at Baptist Hospital where he was admitted for something like three weeks. He had a dulcimer. He was playing Joni Mitchell songs from *Blue*. He was recovering.

Andy Hummel: I went to visit him with John Fry. We took him a tape recorder and some headphones. I made him some tapes. That seemed to help a little bit.

John Fry: It was bad for a while. He was at Baptist in Memphis on their psychiatric floor for a short time and then he was at Mid-South Hospital, a psychological and rehabilitation facility. The whole thing lasted maybe from Thanksgiving until just after the new year. He was out of Mid-South in January. It wasn't until May or so of that following year we were talking again.

David Bell: With Chris, I don't know if it was bipolar or just simply depression. I've had my own depression. I've had one incident of mania—that was before they started recording *#1 Record*. It was as bad as they get. I was suicidal. It was horrible. I had known depression, so by the time he was suffering from it, I could at least commiserate. We talked a little bit about his depression, because I had dealt with it. But even with that, Chris wasn't incredibly chatty about it.

Sara Bell: When I think of Chris, I remember him being so sweet and kind. He was easy going. I don't think he was miserable all the time, but he didn't share anything with me if something was bothering him. I don't necessarily remember happier times. I'm more remorseful because of the way the last few years of his life made me sad.

Andy Hummel: You always assume when people have emotional problems that some of it is because of the environment they were raised in. It was always a mystery to me what was wrong, if anything, with the way Chris was raised because he seemed to have an idyllic home life.

Carole Ruleman Manning: An argument could be made that Chris had a problem with depression all along. He did tend to be somewhat withdrawn part of the time when he was in a group. He would join in, start laughing, and tell a joke, but he did seem to have somewhat of a depressive nature. I hate that he had to go through that, whatever was deeply bothering him. I hate that he had to shoulder whatever that burden was.

John Dando: After he tried to commit suicide, he would call me from there from time to time. There was such a destructive cloud hanging over Big Star at that point. I don't look back at that period as being a positive part of my life. It was about watching people go through pain and degradation.

Terry Manning: After leaving Ardent, I couldn't listen to any Big Star music for over twenty-five years. I could not even listen to it. There was so much angst and raw emotion of a non-positive kind involved, just as much as there was happiness and fun. The whole thing was kind of a mental quagmire to me. Eventually, I did get it back out and listen to it, and was able to hear the happiness, the excitement, and creativity that I loved then and now.

Drew DeNicola: These two powerful forces, Alex and Chris, with use of this studio, came together for this brief time, made this record, and then everything kind of split apart. But they continued to live in the shadow of *#1 Record* and those expectations. They had to move forward and figure out their artistic trajectory in response to that period. Both of them, after being spurned by the industry, became rugged individualists artistically. They made their most personal music after that. They were sort of reluctant outsiders.

Following his release from the hospital, Chris divorced himself from the Ardent crowd and sequestered himself at his parents' home where he slowly wrote a batch of songs for his uncertain solo venture. Big Star slackly carried on as a trio. They were essentially inactive for a stint, aside from three consecutive late January dates at Lafayette's where they debuted "Back of a Car, "O My Soul,"

*"Way Out West," "I Got Kinda Lost," and "There Was a Light." Alex spent ample
time cutting loose sessions at Ardent with a rotating cast of musicians. Jokingly
dubbed the Dolby Fuckers (an inside-joke reference to Alex's confusion over the
purpose of Dolby Noise Reduction), the late-night sessions supplied the roots for
Big Star's first post-Bell LP, Radio City.*

Jody Stephens: Working as a trio after Chris left was a drastic change,
and we weren't ready for it. Big Star played a week at Lafayette's, a club
in Memphis, and we were pretty awful, so we decided to pack it in.

Andy Hummel: During most of that period I was either in the studio
or partying with Alex. I was still going to college and in between girlfriends at that point.

Jody Stephens: Alex had actually formed [the Dolby Fuckers] between
[*#1 Record* and *Radio City*] albums and some of the cuts on *Radio City*
are actually that band. "She's A Mover" was Richard Rosebrough on
drums and Danny Jones on bass. So was "What's Going Ahn" and "Mod
Lang." Andy and I played the rest.

Andy Hummel: The Dolby Fuckers were playing at that time. They were
recording in the middle of the night. With the Dolby Fuckers, the only
common thread was Alex, but it was mostly Alex and Richard Rosebrough. It started out with them being in the studio all night.

Richard Rosebrough: Those late-night sessions with Alex usually took
place in B. That was our favorite: warm, in the pocket, feel-good. Most
of the vocals on *Radio City* were done with a microphone in the control
room. We were all engineering our own recordings by that time.

Andy Hummel: It was the whole crew there recording. We would be
there as much as we could and stay there as late as we could, before we
got too exhausted. A lot of it was just jam sessions.

Alex Chilton: When [Chris] left our band, we were going to hang it up.
It was only sort of an afterthought that we made a second album at all.

*In the spring of 1973, King masterminded the first and only Rock Writers' Con-
vention, a Memphis convention held May 25-26, 1973. To add some legitimacy
to the soiree, King also hatched the National Association of Rock Writers. Both
fizzled after the first year. Still, it was mission accomplished. King conveniently
booked Big Star, minus Chris Bell, as the entertainment. Writers from* Creem,
Fusion, *and* Rolling Stone, *among others, were flown in on Stax's dime for
this convention that celebrated their profession. The hand-picked guest list comprised the likes of Lester Bangs, Lenny Kaye, Richard Melzter, Nick Tosches,*

and a sixteen-year-old Cameron Crowe. The $40,000 shindig helped solidify rock journalists' love for Big Star for decades to come.

Jody Stephens: There was a dormant period. We had actually split up, and then came the Rock Writers' Convention in Memphis and we reformed, temporarily, just to play that after not being together for six or seven months.

Andy Hummel: The Rock Writers' Convention—that was one of John King's strategies for trying to promote the various records at Ardent. His key contact for all the rock writers was Jon Tiven. It was held at Lafayette's Music Room, which was next to T.G.I. Friday's down on Overton Square.

Peter Tomlinson: I had heard about rock critics being invited on lavish record label-sponsored junkets, but I scarcely imagined lowly fanzine editors like myself being included. It was my first plane ride, my first hotel stay, and my first of three Big Star live shows. The ostensible purpose of the trip, to establish some sort of rock critics' union, interested me not at all. My aim was twofold: meet and hang out with the critics I admired, and see Big Star.

Andy Hummel: Nobody had ever paid attention to rock writers before, so they were all immensely flattered, I'm sure. They rented out Lafayette's and threw them a big party with free drinks. Then we got up and played.

Steve Rhea: It was one of the most exciting nights of my entire Ardent experience. They played all the songs from *#1 Record* and some from *Radio City*. There were all sorts of punk guys who were into all the obscure British bands, everything we had been into. It was the perfect audience. Big Star is playing, it gets to a fever pitch at the end, and they run out of songs. Then Alex yells out, "Do you want to hear 'The Letter'?" The whole place goes, "Yeah!" They had never played it before. Jody said they never rehearsed it or anything. Alex just strikes into "The Letter" and they pick it up and follow along and everyone just went nuts. That was the end of the concert. It was exciting.

Peter Tomlinson: I don't remember Meltzer's infamous introduction, ["Well, puke on your momma's pussy! Here's Big Star!"] and I honestly don't recall much of the individual songs, save the impromptu "The Letter." But for an under-rehearsed band missing a key member, they were damn impressive and rocking. I danced!

Jody Stephens: It was sloppy, but there was a lot of energy, and they went absolutely berserk.

Bruce Eaton: After the Rock Writers' Convention, John Fry thought, based on the reaction to the band, it would be worth another shot. Alex said, "Why not?" And then the rest of the band went along.

Jody Stephens: We decided to stay together for *Radio City*.

Bruce Eaton: There was enthusiasm, but it was tempered somewhat by the failure of *#1 Record*. There was not the unbridled optimism that stardom was right around the corner, but John Fry believed in the band 100 percent and was ever the optimist. Alex was intrigued by the idea of heading up a project by himself rather than sharing with Chris, and this was an immediate opportunity.

Jody Stephens: [Back then] you would tag things with "city." If you're in a rock 'n' roll band, it's "rock city." If something bad happened, it was "drag city." We all thought this was a radio-friendly album, so— *Radio City*.

With some of the tunes Chris contributed to just before he left the group, paired with the Dolby Fuckers tracks, the Chilton-led Big Star was ready to knock out Radio City *by the fall of 1973. Jody, then twenty-one, stepped up and performed lead vocals for the first time on Andy's composition, "Way Out West." The standout single, Alex's "September Gurls," is the album's immaculate pop hit that never was.*

> *September girls do so much*
> *I was your Butch and you were touched*
> *I loved you, well, never mind*
> *I've been crying all the time*
> *December boy's got it bad*
>
> **— Alex Chilton, "September Gurls"**

Alex Chilton: Ardent was saying, "Look, we're getting a lot of good response from this album, we just didn't sell any. But you got to do another one. Just look at all those critics, they love you." We had a bunch of material. A lot of it was written with Chris.

John Fry: From some of the demo tapes that we turned up when we went looking for recordings for the [2009] box set, you can pretty well conclude that Chris had a major hand in writing "Back of a Car" and "O My Soul," though he's uncredited on those. Those songs were on Big Star's four-song demo that was recorded not long before Chris left the band. The other two songs on the demo were "There Was a Light" and "I Got Kinda Lost."

Alex Chilton: On *Radio City,* [Chris] wrote parts of "O My Soul." Most of the lyrics after the first bit are his, but I don't care for those words. I mean, "You're really a nice girl..." Fuck! I would never say that. I would be more inclined to say, "You're really a rotten person, but I like you anyway"...I guess I was just too lazy to write some new lyrics for it when we recorded it. "Back of a Car" is another song Chris had a hand in writing. The words were mostly Andy's, and my chord changes. Chris kind of came up with the opening bit of melody, but the rest of it is mine.

Andy Hummel: ["Back of a Car"] has Chris written all over it. I think the concept of the song, the verse, chord changes, and the initial words were something he came up with. But we collaborated in turning it into a song.

Alex Chilton: We made an arbitrary decision—Chris and us—which was that we took those songs, and didn't cut him in on them, and he [took] some things we had helped him on, for which he didn't cut us in on either. I know Chris didn't want to be cut in on any of the songs on the second album, as far as credit or money goes.

Andy Hummel: The break between Chris and Big Star was clean in the sense that, "Okay, the break is now. Chris is no longer in the band, there is going to be some negotiation of which songs we have in our catalog—some are going to Big Star, some are going to Chris."

Andy Hummel: We started from scratch when we decided to do *Radio City* after he left...When we started formally doing *Radio City*, it was like, "John, you're going to come engineer it, right?" And he did, which was neat because we hadn't had the benefit of his undivided attention in a while.

Bruce Eaton: The classic Big Star sound, the first two albums, is the John Fry sound.

Andy Hummel: We recorded everything we had. We had written a few new ones and recorded them as well. But we didn't have enough for an LP, so we started playing around in the studio and that's where "Daisy Glaze" came from. That was just farting around in the studio until we came up with something. Then Alex went off and wrote some words for it and we had a song. Then we added the Dolby Fuckers tracks to the mix.

Alex Chilton: The doing of *Radio City*—we did it in a month, two months, three months. All in all, start to finish, this record was done in a disciplined way like normal recordings are done. Not like the first record—done over a year, three nights a week at off hours.

Andy Hummel: Alex and I did lots of demo-type stuff in the middle of the night with whoever was around. I usually ran the studio and Alex played the music. When we were ready to do a real band track, we would get John to record it, if necessary, and then spend the next month or so doing the overdubs ourselves.

Alex Chilton: I don't think [*Radio City* is] quite as well done as the first one. But, to me, the good way the record sounds is probably because of [John Fry], who did a lot of the engineering and mixed it down for us. I mean, on the first album, Chris kind of sat there with John Fry for hours and mixed these things down, but it was John who was responsible, experienced, and knew how to make things sound good. We could give him our ideas, and he would execute them. It was the same on the second album. It was me sitting there with John, while John more or less mixed these things down.

Alex may have been in creative control of Big Star, but his private life had started to unravel in a few directions, including his failed romantic relationship with Diane Davis Wall, Ardent's office manager. His substance abuse issues had also grown into a battle he'd face for years to come. Nevertheless, Alex's creative output ascended.

Alex Chilton: The music business is a funny place to be. You can start out with certain intentions and quickly get bogged down in quicksand, and I've seen my share. But there were a number of reasons why I was drinking. I had grown up where both parents were drunk a lot, so my role models were very alcoholic. I also had troubles in my career and in love, and all those things combined sent me off on a journey into escapism. *Radio City* was definitely the time of my uncertainty and tension.

Holly George-Warren: He'd drank and experimented with drugs since he was a teen, but it became a problem in the mid- to late-'70s.

Steve Rhea: Alex was probably the deepest one of the lot. He was always talking about his theory of life, or how he had a firm conviction that every great rock 'n' roll talent was born under the sign of Capricorn. "You Get What You Deserve" was sort of an outflow of things he used to talk to me about, that life is sort of inevitable—a destiny thing, and you get what you deserve. So many of the things we talked about worked their way into songs. His infatuation with Diane Wall became "September Gurls."

Terry Manning: *Radio City* was Alex's baby.

Bruce Eaton: On *Radio City,* the songwriting stretches out, pushes traditional boundaries in places. An inexact comparison would be that *#1* is *Beatles for Sale* and *Radio City* is *Rubber Soul*. *#1* always sounded a bit too trebly to my ears and, sometimes, a bit too cluttered. I don't know if that was Chris' influence as he, by reports, belabored over the tracks and did a lot of tinkering. *Radio City* is a bit more stripped down and better for it.

Greg Reding: Chris Bell was the Brian Wilson of Big Star. He had the sonic vision, the melodic vision. When he left, it was painfully obvious he wasn't there anymore.

"Radio City...isn't lacking in self-assurance. It is, however, lacking in the sonic ingenuity and perfectionism that marked *#1 Record*. It's in the area of pure sound that Bell is most missed; his stunning vocal arrangements and roaring multiple guitars gave the first album an intense, almost otherworldly quality that was tremendously affecting in its own right... [*Radio City* is a] diverting 1965-style rock record, in which Chilton puts his worship of idiosyncratic heroes Ray Davies and Roger McGuinn to good use. He and his colleagues deal with the loss of sound expert Bell by taking a recorded approach that is often intentionally stark and like the actual sound of early recordings of the Beatles and Kinks." —**Bud Scoppa, Phonograph Record**

Bruce Eaton: The influence of Chris is undeniable and unavoidable. But *Radio City* is primarily Alex's record. Alex was still finding his musical identity and *Radio City* was an important step along the way.

Peter Tomlinson: Sonically, *#1 Record* and *Radio City* share a secret weapon: the superb mastering skills of Larry Nix. Thanks to him and John Fry, those albums shimmer and shine like aural jewelry. *Radio City* is a different kind of animal, not inferior by any means, just different. Chris' absence is keenly felt, but as a launchpad for Alex's solo career, it's pretty peerless.

Bob Mehr: Even though Chris isn't credited on *Radio City*, he's kind of the ghost in the machine.

Alex Chilton: We kept up the tradition that had been set on the first record for the second record as much as we could, but I had no clue about what songwriting [style] I wanted to do. I knew what musical structures I wanted to play but putting lyrics with it was not my strong suit in those days. I tried but I don't think I ever succeeded with the *Radio City* album. I don't think there's one good song of mine on that record. To me, the only good song on the album is Andy's ["Way Out West"]. I definitely prefer *#1 Record*. There are four or five tunes on that record I think are really good.

Andy Hummel: If there were ever a Big Star song that had major potential as a hit, ["September Gurls"] would be it.

David Bell: There were some bad feelings there, but I do know Chris felt *Radio City* was a terrific album. He had only good things to say about it.

Andy Hummel: I wasn't so stupid that I didn't like our music. We were good. There are some cool songs on there. It's surprising nobody listened to it at the time.

With its iconic "Red Ceiling" album photo shot by Memphis-based photographer William Eggleston, Radio City *was released in February 1974 via Ardent/ Stax. Like* #1 Record, *the track list snubbed pop trends of the era. On the rock end of the spectrum, KISS had just released its debut LP and Rush followed soon after with its debut. Within weeks, both the Ramones and Van Halen played their first gigs. On the adult-contemporary plane, the top hits of '74 were Barbra Streisand's "The Way We Were" and Terry Jacks' "Seasons in the Sun." Big Star didn't mesh with any of it. Ardent Records once again suffered from distribution drama and the record didn't hit stores. Chris' concerns about Ardent sticking with Stax/Columbia proved correct. Still, positive reviews from rock critics started to flow in and, in a May 1974 interview with Jon Tiven for* Circus Magazine, *Andy had some prophetic foresight: "Even if we don't connect with the population," he said, "at least we'll go down in history."*

Alex Chilton: I'm not sure what was all going on, but corruption was rampant at Stax at that time.

Al Bell: By the time we got the Big Star records out, my attention was focused on saving my life and defending myself against multiple business and personal assaults.

Alex Chilton: I know that CBS, at the exact time our record came out, put a complete clamp on distributing any Stax records and would not move one Stax record from the time our record came out.

Jody Stephens: We got more press but sold zilch. *Radio City* sold 4,000 copies and the first one 2,000. Nobody could buy them. There were no records in stores even though we got a lot of airplay.

Peter Holsapple: I found a copy of *Radio City* right after it came out at a big department store called Zayre. Oddly, it was a promo copy but was shrink-wrapped.

Phillip Rauls — Photographer, *Radio City* promotion executive: I worked *Radio City* and went to both New York and L.A. promoting the album. Both trips were with Ardent's John King. Ironically, WBCN in

Boston was one of the only major-market radio stations who gave the album decent airplay. The Ardent staff worked the album pretty aggressively and did get decent secondary radio airplay, but sales were nothing significant. Personally, I thought "Back of a Car" was an excellent track and promoted it with a pretty strong effort, but there were too many other stronger records out at the time and, subsequently, the album was overlooked by a vastly over-flooded marketplace.

John Lightman — Big Star's second bassist: There were these stacks of albums sitting on the floor of Ardent, and they were having a hard time getting anything done with them.

Ben Hamper — Author, Michigan-based radio DJ: My brother-in-law worked at the big rock station, 105, in Flint, Michigan. This was in 1974, I was about eighteen. He said, "Yeah, they throw out a bunch of albums they don't plan to play." They skimmed through them and only saved the ones they could sell at the used record store." Most of it ended up in the dumpster. I was like, "Man! Grab some for me." He gave me about forty albums. Most of it was dreck, but one of them was *Radio City*. I had been a Box Tops fan, so I recognized Chilton's name. I thought, "Could this be the same guy?" I put that on and immediately it hit me. I was blown away because I was already a fan of Badfinger, Raspberries, Flamin' Groovies, all of that. I couldn't believe that brilliant of a record was headed for the dumpster behind a radio station.

Jody Stephens: We got no money from the records, so we had to work. Andy had been going to school, I worked in a bar, and Alex was living off his Box Tops money.

Andy Hummel: By the time we got to the end of the recording of the second LP and they were going into the studio to mix it, I was to the point where I had a choice. I could go finish college and get my degree, get a real job and have a real life or keep doing this crap. We didn't make any money on it and it didn't have any prospect of doing so. We put out another LP—why would that be any different from the first one? The real decision came when they released the thing and they were making plans for the band to go do a little tour up in the Northeast. I said, "Well, I guess I could go commit to do that, or I could just go register for my senior year in college." I said, "I think I'll go register for my senior year in college." And I'm glad I did.

Unlike Chris, who never completed his degree, Andy earned a bachelor's degree in English literature from Rhodes College in 1974. He later enrolled at the State Technical Institute at Memphis and earned an associate degree in mechanical engineering technology in 1978. That year, Andy embarked on his engineering career and moved to Fort Worth, Texas. One year later, he married his wife Patti. By 1990, with three children in tow, the Hummels moved to Weatherford, Texas. During his successful thirty-year career, he became a senior manager at Lockheed Martin Aeronautics Company.

Andy Hummel: We live in a restored, by us, Victorian house a couple of blocks off the courthouse square in Weatherford. My wife and I spend much of our leisure time obsessing over our house and garden. I also own a restored, very hot 1987 Harley Davidson Softail, which I obsess over equally.

John Dando: Andy did the right thing getting out of the band. He wanted a more proper life, and he was programmed for that. Andy predicted he couldn't be an old rocker someday. He wanted boats and cars.

Beverly Baxter Ross: Andy was a genius. He designed the ergonomics for fighter jets for Lockheed Martin. He wasn't willing to be the starving musician.

Andy Hummel: That was the end of phase one in the history of Big Star.

Minus the band's founding members, Chris and Andy, Ardent Records booked spring 1974 dates for Big Star across the Midwest and East Coast. In place of Andy was bassist John Lightman, a fellow Memphian.

John Lightman: I was born in Memphis in 1949; I was a little older than Alex. We first met in late 1973. I was playing with a revised group called Omaha, which featured Jimi Jamison [vocalist of Target and Survivor]. It was a great cover band and we were starting to do original material. We were playing at Lafayette's Music Room one night and Alex was there. He was out that night actually looking for a new bass player. When we were on break, Alex approached me and introduced himself. At the time, I was not familiar with Big Star.

Lightman quickly learned of Alex's passion for astrology—an interest he never abandoned. He was known to frequently carry a copy of Sacred Symbols of the Ancients, *a book subtitled:* The Mystical Significance of Our Fifty-Two Playing Cards and Their Amazing Connection with Our Individual Birthdays. *Alex used the method to gain insight into people he'd just met.*

John Lightman: Right away, Alex asked me what my sign was. I told him Scorpio. Later he told me they were destined to have a Scorpio bass player. At that time, Alex was into numerology and the Chinese horoscope. He was into these cards that were the precursor to tarot. Each card represented certain birthdays of the year. That night was the first night I met Alex. He called me the next day and asked me if I wanted to join the band. We started to rehearse in the big studio at Ardent. I don't know if he consulted with Jody or not. I had the feeling he never consulted with Jody because it seemed like Jody never warmed to the idea of me being in the band. Jody and Alex hardly ever interacted while I was around. One time, Alex and I were talking about rhythm sections. I told him, "You and Jody fit together well." He said, "I think you're out of your mind. I've always thought of Jody as Chris' drummer." Most bands I had been in, the band members talked about music in one way or another. I never heard Alex and Jody talk about anything, but there was camaraderie between Alex and I.

When it came time to learn the songs from #1 Record *and* Radio City, *Lightman recalls a lax Alex.*

John Lightman: Alex, being wise, said, "Listen to the records to get a sense of how the songs go, but just come up with whatever." Alex wanted to hear what my knee-jerk reactions were to the songs. Sometimes, you come up with cool stuff that way and Alex knew that. Plus, I was pretty cocky back then. I thought I was more accomplished on the bass than Andy Hummel. I wouldn't say that now. Also, Andy played with a pick. At that time, I was a snob, but since then I've learned to play with a pick because it's a different sound and some of my favorite players use picks.

After Lightman's debut with Big Star at Eli's, a small club on South Cooper Street, the trio played at Lafayette's in January 1974. From there, with encouragement from John Fry, the semi-rehearsed trio headed to the East Coast to promote Radio City. *Lightman recalled, "There were stacks of that record in the halls of Ardent because of that distribution problem." A reluctant John Dando stepped in as road manager and sound technician.*

John Dando: My involvement was to go on the road with Alex, Jody and John Lightman. I was working for Ardent Management. It sounds kind of cold, but it was purely professional. It was a job. There was no love in it. I would have rather been someplace else than on the road with Alex. I liked being out on the road, I liked traveling, but you didn't have fun taking Alex Chilton out on the road. I've heard John Fry use this expression about the whole bunch: It was "adult day care."

John Lightman: We were going out for the first time on the road, to play the radio show and Max's. We were at the airport, and I asked Alex what the sleeping arrangements were, where we would be staying and so on. I was just curious. He said, "Jody is sharing a room with Dando and you and I are going to share a room." I said, "Okay, that's fine." Then he turns to me and says, "I want you to know: I am not now, nor have I ever been a homosexual," like he was McCarthy or something. I thought,

"Why would you tell me that?" He didn't say it with any kind of irony, or tongue-in-cheek. He was very serious. Maybe he thought I was thinking he was going to hit on me because we were in the same hotel room. He wanted to clarify or put my mind at ease. Alex sometimes would have effeminate ways in how he moved or talked, or whatever, but that doesn't necessarily mean a guy is gay. Either way, I wouldn't care if he was or not. I just knew Alex had lots of girlfriends. He very well may have had sex with guys, too, but not only did he not talk about it, I never even thought about it.

On March 13, 1974, about three weeks after Lightman joined the band, Big Star arrived in Hempstead, New York for a radio session and interview with WLIR 92.7-FM. The tracks were cut direct to two-track at Ultra-Sonic Studios and were released in 1992 as Big Star Live *by Rykodisc.*

John Lightman: The first time we went out, we did the WLIR radio broadcast and then drove to play Max's Kansas City in New York City. We played there four nights in a row. That was our first trip. We just went to those two places. We went straight from the airport to WLIR. We were exhausted because we had been up since early that morning. When we got to WLIR, we did a soundcheck and wanted to go rest and get some food, but they wouldn't let us leave. At least it gave us time to run through the songs and rehearse a bit. I still wasn't too familiar with the songs, and you can tell on a few, like "O My Soul." It's a pretty complex song structure. The parts are not intuitive. It was supposed to be a D chord, but I hit the A chord. It wasn't awful, but you can hear Alex hit his low-D string really hard the second time. It was his way of saying, "It's a D!"

At their four-night run at Max's Kansas City, Big Star surprisingly headlined above the Butts Band, a group featuring John Densmore and Robbie Krieger of the Doors. Actor Ed Begley Jr. performed a set of stand-up comedy as well. Billboard *critic Sam Sutherland praised Alex for his "aura of fragility" on the opening tunes "Ballad of El Goodo" and "Thirteen." "Despite some rough edges...the set was a triumph," he wrote.*

John Lightman: Max's was a small venue upstairs. That's where the bands played. Downstairs was a restaurant. When we first got to Max's, we were downstairs in the restaurant and in comes David Clayton Thomas of Blood, Sweat & Tears. Alex, who probably didn't really know the guy, shouted, "Oh, here comes that asshole David Clayton Thomas." He was always trying to get a response out of people. David turns around and glares at the table. He looked straight at me because he thought I said it. I looked back at him like a deer in headlights. He, in general, flipped off the entire table—gives us the gesture and walks off. Later that night was the first time I experienced Alex's prickly side. We were on a break after our first set, and I was in the back of the club because a small group of college kids were talking to me about my prized 1960 Fender Jazz Bass. I hadn't realized Alex and Jody were back on stage and ready to play. I heard them firing up their instruments, so I started heading up towards the front. Next thing I know, Alex says into the mic, "We need a bass player up here. Johnny Lightnin', where are you?" Then he says, "This is what happens when you get a Jew in the band." He said that on stage into the microphone as I'm walking up to the front. I just let it slide off my back. I didn't engage that at all. It was just Alex being a shit.

John Dando: Alex could be pretty cruel. Alex didn't give a shit. He did what he wanted to do. I wasn't that close with Alex; he wouldn't confide in me or anything like that. He was your worst nightmare if you had him as an artist. My job was to go out and have a successful performance at some place, and Alex is your worst nightmare if you're trying to put on a successful performance, because he doesn't care.

John Lightman: Dando was a little high-strung. The first time we went out, I was off to the side hanging out with Alex. Dando, who seemed agitated, was nearby talking to the club manager. Alex looked at me and said, "You see why we can't have him as our road manager." That hit me out of the blue. Alex and Dando didn't vibe well, plus Alex could be hard to get along with. Even people that were his friends, he would have two sides with them. He could say the absolute shittiest thing at the worst time to embarrass them, for whatever reason. I was not familiar with alcoholism at that time, but that year I saw Alex deteriorating. He was getting more and more messed up and less dependable. He wasn't drinking during the day at rehearsals, but he was during the night hours. He would say, "We are going to have a rehearsal at 2 p.m. at Ardent." Jody and I would be there at 2 p.m. waiting. Then Alex comes bopping in about 5:30 and says, "I'm here, but I don't have my guitar, what do you want to do?" Well, what could we do? We can't have him play air guitar. If you couldn't find Alex at Ardent, he was having a drink next door at Trader Dick's, the wildest bar in Memphis. One night we were hanging out there and this guy was just incensed. He came up and grabbed Alex by his collar and pulled him off the ground. He was really mad. Apparently, this guy was up on a ladder and Alex was standing right there. This guy falls off the ladder and instead of Alex breaking his fall, he just laughed and stepped to the side. He let the guy fall down and hurt himself, so this cat was ready to beat the shit out of Alex. Luckily the situation was defused.

After some late-night bonding sessions at the bar, the trio hit the road in late March, playing as far north as Canada, as well as dates across the Midwest and

East Coast. John Dando returned as road manager, but this time brought along an assistant, Paul Jobe.

Jody Stephens: That tour was like two-and-a-half or three weeks. That was about the longest we were ever out for. Other than that, it was just a few dates here and there.

John Dando: They started out in Boston, went to upstate New York. We crossed through Canada into Michigan and then back to Memphis... The way you had to get things done in those days was to find college promotion people on campuses. John King developed a strong network of those people. Those are the people who got Big Star off the ground. They were fiercely loyal to Big Star. Any gigs we got, in any of the clubs or wherever, were always tied to some college promotion person getting those gigs.

The mini-tour kicked off March 31, 1974 in Cambridge, Massachusetts at the Performance Center, a mid-sized venue in Harvard Square that closed months later. The Big Star crew was initially thrilled to open for the headliner, Badfinger, but was quickly discouraged after they arrived at their hotel in Boston to bad news.

John Lightman: On that second outing, all of our gear was stolen right off the bat. The whole van was stolen. Before we left for Boston, John Dando and Paul Jobe stopped by my house to pick up my amp and bass. They were going to drive up to Boston before us with our equipment. We were going to fly in. Dando comes by and says, "I'm here to pick up your stuff, we're driving it to Boston." He loaded up my amp and then asked, "Where's your bass?" I told him I'd rather take it with me on the airplane, but he assured me it would be safer with them. He kind of pressured me into handing it over. When they get to Cambridge, it's pouring down rain and the parking lot is full. Instead of parking under the canopy and unloading the equipment into the hotel right away, they instead found a parking spot in a far, dark corner of the parking lot. They locked it up and went inside. They left all of our equipment in the rental van unattended. Idiots. After our plane landed, Dando and Paul pick us up from the airport and drive us back to the hotel. Immediately, the first thing I say is, "Where is my bass?" They look at each other and say, "Let's go, it's in the parking lot." I went off on them. We get to where they parked and there is nothing there. I went numb. We reported it to the police. The thieves just thought they were stealing a van, they had no clue they had hit pay dirt with all that expensive equipment inside: a Les Paul, a Martin, Jody's drums, my acoustic amp and 1960 Jazz Bass. I was in shock. That was the only bass I'd ever owned, and it had a lot of sentimental value to me. My father bought it for me and my brother to

Big Star, after Chris Bell's exit from the band, poses for new promo photos in downtown Memphis.

PHOTOS BY CAROLE MANNING

learn on. The fact it was stolen really hurt me. In return, Ardent bought me a shitty $300, made-in-Mexico Precision Bass. It was terrible.

After playing two sets on borrowed equipment at the Badfinger show, Big Star headed to Lansing, Michigan to play the Brewery, a popular club near Michigan State University. Alex had played this now-demolished club in the summer of '69, when it was called Grandmother's, with the Box Tops.

John Dando: We went to East Lansing, to some place called the Brewery, for a week-long run of shows. They got fired after the first night.

John Lightman: The Brewery's booking guy was going to cancel us because there were hardly any people there. It was very empty.

Mark Boone — Michigan-based musician, keyboardist, Uprising: I played in the opening act in East Lansing. We were called Uprising. Alex was a rude, arrogant ass. His performance was lame and his attitude caused them to get fired by the club...I've also opened for Johnny Thunders, who had an attitude, but nowhere like Alex's. Big Star is what he thought he was.

John Dando: The specialty of the house was fried mushrooms. Alex started eating those fried mushrooms on stage while he was trying to play. At times he couldn't sing because his mouth was full of fried mushrooms. He would turn away from the crowd when he was supposed to be singing, things like that. He didn't care about playing to an audience, he was playing for himself.

John Lightman: I just thought it was Alex being Alex. He'd already seen everything, being on tour with the Box Tops. That's why he got into punk music. Once you learn all the riffs and rock 'n' roll clichés, it takes the mystique out of it. You become what Jim Dickinson would refer to as a "puke." You just regurgitate what other people are doing. Alex wasn't interested in playing puke music.

John Dando: A college newspaper writer [Dave DiMartino at *The State News*], wrote a glowing review of Big Star in the paper, so the promoter who fired them came back and demanded they play out the full week in East Lansing.

John Lightman: More people started to come out over the next few days. We played "Baby Strange." We did an impromptu "Wild Thing" one night. "Till the End of the Day" by the Kinks, "Jeepster." Alex did "Motel Blues" acoustically by himself. Outside of that, Alex kept it together on that tour. He was not drinking much, we were not taking drugs. Alex and I were smoking pot, that's it. In Lansing, we just hung out smoking in our hotel room at the Holiday Inn, which was close to the venue. We were pretty lazy.

The week in East Lansing marked the start of Alex's notorious relationship with Andy's ex-girlfriend, Elizabeth "Lesa" Aldridge, a second cousin of William "Bill" Eggleston and future musician in her own right. After a few months of casual dating, Lesa and Alex were inseparable. A few short years later, Lesa made her own mark on the Memphis music scene after she co-founded the Klitz, a pioneering all-female punk band. But, for now, she was Alex's muse and partner in crime. At the same time, Lesa's younger sister Holliday Aldridge paired up with Jody. Both were seen hanging out at Ardent Studios during Big Star rehearsals.

John Lightman: Holliday was just like a little puppy dog. Jody would walk in with his drums and she would have one small, light object. She was cute and wanted to help, the total opposite of Lesa. Lesa was wild. My friendship with Alex corresponds with the start of his relationship with Lesa, who now goes by the name Elizabeth.

Elizabeth "Lesa" Aldridge Hoehn — Guitarist, vocalist, the Klitz: I got to know Alex during *Radio City*, when Chris was breaking up with Big Star. That's when I first fell in with Andy, Alex, and Jody. Chris never warmed to me, I can't tell you why, but Alex and I liked each other a lot. There was an immediate chemistry. However, I did date Andy Hummel before I dated Alex, which was a lot of fun. Dating Andy was maybe the most normal thing I experienced back then. Andy would call me up, come pick me up in his car, open the door for me, take me out to dinner. I had got a guitar when I was thirteen, so Andy and I would play songs, some Carole King covers. He would play guitar and I would sing. It was traditional dating I had missed out on, having dropped out of high school and being a hippie in Princeton, and then France for a year. It was so sweet and innocent. But I don't remember actually breaking up with Andy. I just remember kind of shifting over to Alex.

This brings me to the East Lansing, Michigan show. Alex was on tour with Big Star. It was Jody, Alex and John Lightman. Alex had called me. At that point, we had already gone on a ballroom-dancing date. He picked me up in his convertible—he didn't open the door for me. Anyway, he called me from East Lansing and asked me to go over and get his acoustic guitar from his sister in Memphis because he wanted to add that into the set. So I flew up to Lansing with the guitar to join him on the tour, just as the girlfriend, I didn't perform with them or anything. He had a radio interview there and I went along. It was pretty cool. We had a lot of fun in the station wagon with all the equipment…It was an unusual way to quickly get to know somebody. From there, Alex and

I stayed together for seven years. The rest of my life was just jumping in—sex, drugs and rock 'n' roll. No boundaries and all that.

John Dando: On that tour, I came back to the hotel one night and he and his girlfriend [Lesa] were drawing on the wall with crayons. It just wasn't a fun experience to be out with them.

John Lightman: Alex had a young child, Timothee, who came back into his life around that time. That's why they had crayons, because they were coloring with his son. That's why they were drawing on walls, because that's what a kid would do. They both got really into primitive art, because primitive art is very childlike. Back then, Alex claimed Timothee was not his son—other people say he is definitely Alex's son.

John Dando: Just a lot of bad things happened. I got robbed in New York in the hotel room. We had the truck stolen in Boston.

John Lightman: Big Star had a curse. Alex went through what would be a guitar collector's ideal collection. A Les Paul, a Strat, a Martin, a Firebird, a twelve-string Martin. They were all stolen one right after the other, but it didn't seem to faze Alex whatsoever. More than one of them was stolen out of the closet at Ardent. He'd just put it in the closet, he'd come back to get it and the guitar would be gone. Then he would put another one in there.

John Dando: Seemed like a lot of things happened that weren't much fun. That was the last tour I was with them on. After they stopped promoting *Radio City,* there were no more Ardent-sanctioned tours.

Phillip Rauls: It was my impression that Big Star might have unintentionally desired to be just a studio band and didn't want to compete with the big boys by aggressively working the gig circuit. The few times I saw them in clubs their live sound was incomplete and lacking, too many dead spots. Compared to what was going on in the real music world, Big Star was a studio band, tons of overdubs and fine-tuning. Problem was, they could never produce that great sound in person.

Still, the three-piece band played periodic shows, like the documented May 19, 1974 performance at the Levitt Shell in Overton Park. The loose show was released in 1999 as the Nobody Can Dance *CD, which also comprised the rehearsals from the WLIR session.*

John Lightman: A funny thing about that Levitt Shell show was that nobody was allowed to dance. The Memphis Park Commission was worried about people getting too rowdy. You can hear him announce it on that album at the start of the show. Alex, on the fly, decided to break into "The Letter." I didn't know we were going to do that. I was able to follow him until the monitor went out, then I just played an A. That's all I could do. I cringe hearing it now.

Chris Bell: The few times I saw Big Star as a trio they weren't too hot. Alex was straining to carry the load with Jody Stephens on drums and a new bassist, John Lightman. It just wasn't the same and they had to disband.

As the band struggled to find its footing on stage, Alex decided to look for a lead guitarist with the skillset of Chris Bell.

John Lightman: Alex was a great guitar player. He wasn't a hot licks guitar player, like Jimmy Page, he was more like George Harrison, very precise and clean and melodic. He was saying he was having trouble playing rhythm and lead at the same time. Hendrix could play a combination of rhythm and lead, but that was not Alex's style. He was having trouble going back and forth, so Alex said, "We need another guitar player," which was like the original lineup. He was concerned more with the guitars than the vocals. The first to try out was Van Duren. He had auditioned at Ardent. Right when he gets there, while we were getting our equipment ready to start jamming for his audition, Van sits down at the piano and starts belting out some Paul McCartney songs. I was cringing for his sake because people used to compare Alex and Chris to Lennon and McCartney, with Alex being Lennon. Alex hated that. He didn't want people making that comparison anymore. I thought to myself, *Van, you picked the wrong stuff to do.* We played for a while, but Alex wasn't knocked out. Van was talented, but he wasn't a lead guitarist at that time.

Alex wanted a lead guitar, someone who could play as well as Chris, and I knew Evan Leake could play that well. I was friends with Evan, so I brought him into the band. I was on the verge of quitting when Evan got in the band. I felt I was wasting my time, and Alex's drinking was becoming more of a problem. The reason I quit was one day Alex says to me, "My attitude about music is: I can take it or leave it." He was precisely like that. He didn't give a shit. He was bored with Big Star. It was depressing and dark, but Alex was still writing. He played a couple songs for me. One was "Jesus Christ." I didn't have a phone at the time, so I quit in person. I just said, "I have to stop doing this." Alex said, "Well, what Jim Dickinson says is, 'If they want to leave, let them.'" He was very much under Dickinson's influence at that time. Evan also left shortly afterwards. Right after we quit is when the *Third* sessions started. When they started that album, there wasn't really a band. A lot of people justifiably view that as an Alex solo record.

Andy Hummel.

COURTESY OF THE ANDY HUMMEL ARCHIVE

Richard Rosebrough and Lesa Aldridge.

PHOTO BY ANDY HUMMEL

CHAPTER 15

I AM THE COSMOS — SHOE PRODUCTIONS: WINTER 1973-1974

While Alex, Andy and Jody were in the studio laying down Radio City, *and the Ardent Records team promoted the Hot Dogs'* Say What You Mean *LP, Chris focused on going solo without the label's support. By late 1973, he even ventured far beyond Memphis in search of Big Star's earliest, most vocal supporters — the rock writers.*

Richard Rosebrough: Chris was excited about music again, but he still had conflicting feelings as well. He had a lot of anger and frustration. He had a broken heart. He had a lot on his mind.

Chris Bell: I just stayed away from music for a while because I was going through depression and drinking all the time, being an alcoholic. Gosh, for about the first six months of 1973, I wasn't involved with music at all. I kept writing a few tunes, but I just took a job working for an air freight company [Federal Express].

David Bell: Around fall, Chris went to Los Angeles for a couple months. He was following leads, I suppose. He was trying to drum up some interest and talking to some rock writers.

Chris Bell: After I left Big Star, I was being encouraged by a lot of nice guys—rock writers like Greg Shaw, Marty Cerf and Bud Scoppa with *Rolling Stone*. They were turning me on to people. In a way they brought me up, brought my spirits up about my music and were saying good things about what I did with Big Star. Right before I went to L.A., I was getting fed up with Memphis and I wanted to get back into the music scene. There was not much happening musically in Memphis, so I thought I would pack up my bags and head to the big city.

Bud Scoppa: Chris called me out of the blue—we had never met—and asked if he could crash at my apartment in L.A. for a few days. It was just a few months after I had moved here from New York to go to work at A&M. He showed up at my place in Beachwood Canyon nursing a cold, but otherwise he seemed sharp and focused and determined to play at the Troubadour the following Monday despite being in less than optimum voice. We hung out and talked, but I don't recall anything of significance in our conversations. On Monday night, I took him to the Troubadour and he signed up and proceeded to perform three or four songs solo on acoustic to polite applause from the sparse crowd.

Chris Bell: I started to do some individual gigs in L.A. The Troubadour was the first solo gig that I ever played. It was a very nervous experience. I was terrified, because usually I'm able to hide behind a wall of amplifiers with three other guys and I was not that excited about becoming a James Taylor or Paul Simon. I'm more interested in rock 'n' roll music.

Bud Scoppa: The Troubadour show was a Monday Hoot Night, which he did with a bad cold. It was less than a resounding success, but at least he'd made it through the mini-set. Chris headed back to Memphis the next day, so nothing came of the trip.

Chris Bell: While I was in L.A., it seemed like I was sure to find something, but most of the people I was meeting were rock writers, so I didn't get too heavily involved with actual musicians. I was there right around Christmas. I came home for Christmas after meeting several people and contacting some record company people. I even went back to L.A. for a couple weeks, but nothing was happening. I was pretty broke, so I decided to head back to Memphis for a bit.

Steve Rhea: He was totally a broken guy. He stayed out in California and then came back with orange hair.

Every night I tell myself,
"I am the cosmos,
I am the wind"
But that don't get you back again

Just when I was starting to feel okay
You're on the phone
I never want to be alone

— CHRIS BELL, "I AM THE COSMOS"

David Bell: I first heard him play, acoustically, "I Am the Cosmos" and "You and Your Sister" in early '74. He played them on a Gibson Sunburst acoustic. That same guitar is what he played in D-tuning on "Speed of Sound."

Richard Rosebrough: Chris started playing a lot of acoustic guitar. A lot of the songs he wrote were written on an acoustic guitar. Eventually, he was just as at home with a six- or twelve-string acoustic guitar as he was with his Gibson electric. He also played a Telecaster sometimes.

With his L.A. ambitions behind him, Chris arrived in the Bahamas on January 8, 1974, for a vacation. During this period, he also moved out of his parents' house to a rental home on Midland Avenue not far from Richard Rosebrough's pad on Marne Street. The pair often rehearsed Chris' new songs along with bassist/keyboardist Ken Woodley, but the trio never developed into a proper gigging band. Over the next couple years, Chris would work with a shortlist of Memphis musicians at various studios with the goal of recording a full-length record in mind.

Chris Bell: I started work on my own album, not using a permanent band but getting various people to come along and do sessions.

Jody Stephens: I can't say why Chris never put together his own steady live band. Chris had an affinity for being in the studio, for one. He liked that whole creative process. It's rewarding. It's one of the few things you can account for your efforts for the time. You have a record of it.

Chris Bell: I got together with musicians in Memphis and the only problem then was most of them were all involved and trying to get something going. The scene in Memphis, as far as music was concerned, was everybody was starving there. If they could latch onto a band that was doing a club gig and make some money, then they didn't want to venture into anything else. I was trying to approach several people on the basis that I would like to work with them, in a sense, in the way Harrison and Clapton were working at the time—or Lennon, or anybody, with a series of musicians. It appealed to a lot of people, so I was working with all kinds of combinations in the studio. Richard Rosebrough plays drums on most of the tracks. Ken Woodley has helped me out a great deal, he plays bass guitar and organ for me.

Richard Rosebrough: Chris just loved Ken and I have the greatest love and respect for Ken. He's a talented guy. Ken could play just about any instrument. He started out as a drummer and then a keyboard player. He played a Hammond B-3. Then he learned guitar. We needed bass guitar on that session, so he played bass guitar on that session. He's multi-talented and that's what we needed.

Robert Johnson: Ken Woodley was always a little strange. He was a loner, a little moody. Richard was a little bit of an odd character and focused on engineering. He knew how to record. He was also a great drummer for a white guy. He kind of pounded like John Bonham. Richard was a hard hitter who got a good sound out of his drums.

Richard Rosebrough: Chris never suggested any drum parts to me. He'd just say, "I got this song and it goes like this. I've kind of worked this pattern out." Even on "I Am the Cosmos," he let me do my thing. In retrospect, of course, I was taking my Valiums, and he was taking pills and drinking, so sometimes our tempos and the energy levels of the songs we played ended up being a little slow.

After some rehearsals, Chris' solo LP was informally underway in late January 1974 after he booked time at the now-defunct Shoe Productions in Memphis. The studio was located at 485 North Hollywood Street. This was his first recording venture outside of Ardent since the Jynx cut tracks at Sonic Studios. The freebie session came courtesy of Shoe's co-founder Warren Wagner. There, Chris cut "I Am the Cosmos" and an early, rough version of his poignant, acoustic ballad "You and Your Sister." The trio also laid down the riff-driven rocker "I Don't Know." While the Shoe staff engineered its share of rock and pop records, a 1975 Billboard blurb noted its specialty was producing advertisements for commercial radio stations: "ID packages for rock and soul formats, as well as custom jingles and narrative skit commercials."

Richard Rosebrough: Chris went to Shoe instead of Ardent because of his falling-out with John Fry and a falling-out with Big Star. He felt he'd been kicked out of the family. He also wanted to try another studio. He called me and Ken Woodley up one night and said, "I got some songs I want to cut, we're going to do it over at Shoe." I thought, "Wow, I've never cut over there before. That would be something different." I asked, "Why are you cutting over there?" Chris said, "Warren has offered me some time. I just want to cut at someplace different."

Ken Woodley: Chris wouldn't talk about it. He just set it up and said, "Let's go to Shoe." It didn't really matter to me. I thought both studios sounded great.

John Fry: Chris was never not welcome at Ardent, though he may have felt so for a while. It's wrong to think he was banished—a period of self-exile is more accurate.

Richard Rosebrough: The two principals over at Shoe were Wayne Crook and Warren Wagner. Warren was the contact with Chris. He physically built the place, built the console in his garage. He had a one-inch eight-track machine.

Warren Wagner — Producer, engineer, Shoe Productions owner: The way Chris ended up at Shoe in the first place was because we hung out one night. I used to hang out on Madison Avenue at a place that's known for its hamburgers: Huey's. We were sitting at the bar talking. He said he liked what I put together over at Shoe. I said, "Why don't you come over and we'll do some recordings?" Within the next day or two, Chris calls and we end up in the studio one night, just he and I. We were going over some of his songs; he made some acoustic recordings and then we got a band over there with him. We ended up doing "I Am the Cosmos" in one night, in just a few takes. We probably didn't do more than two takes on the thing. I know there weren't a lot of Bell sessions though—two or three sessions with guitars and bass.

John Fry: I never heard a word about why Chris went to Shoe instead of Ardent. I had no idea what was going on over there or what Chris was doing. I learned subsequently that Richard Rosebrough was coming into Ardent and taking Fairchild Limiters, like 660s and 670s—Beatles' stuff—over to Shoe. I was like, "Okay, Richard. You're a good guy, but don't you know what those are worth?" They sell for over $30,000 these days. Back then I just bought them on a whim. They left mysteriously in the night and were returned promptly so no one noticed.

Warren Wagner: I did sense there was some animosity between Chris and Ardent, but I didn't go into it with him. I co-owned Shoe Productions, but I also did some moonlighting over at Ardent for John. I had known Chris for years before those recordings, back to the garage-bands days in high school.

Richard Rosebrough: Shoe's building was originally designed and intended to be a seven-story building. They built the foundation and the basement but then something happened. They stopped building it, so you had a one-story building with a huge foundation and thick concrete walls. You had to walk down into it. Once you got inside, you didn't hear the planes going over, the traffic outside—you didn't hear anything. It was like operating in a cave, but they were operating a business in there. They were producing jingles. They had good singers on staff, people who were songwriters and could write and score a catchy jingle.

Warren Wagner: Shoe was not just a "jingle company." Some of the artists that recorded there were Lou Rawls, Paul Butterfield, Levon Helm, Dr. John. We also had Jimmy Griffin, formerly of Bread, who we signed to our little label along with Terry Sylvester of the Hollies. We had the Duck Band who played on "Disco Duck," they were basically the Blues Brothers—Steve Cropper, Duck Dunn and Willie Hall—and that's only a few. Shoe wasn't a sterile environment.

Richard Rosebrough: Warren was a good electronics guy. He could figure things out. He got some amplifiers and faders and built a little board.

Warren Wagner: We didn't have the kind of cash John Fry had—Shoe had to improvise. I built the recording console. It was 24 inputs in and sixteen inputs out. It was quite the deal. That's what we used on the Bell sessions. It was different from Ardent. I don't see any comparisons between Ardent and Shoe other than some of the parts I used on the console were derived from designs of a Spectra Sonics console they had in the B Studio at Ardent. Spectra Sonics was in Memphis, so it was natural that I would copy it. I made my own faders, for instance. They were expensive, so I had certain parts machined. I basically mimicked those Spectra Sonics faders for $5 apiece instead of $75 apiece.

Richard Rosebrough: Shoe had one common area, with desks and everything, and that's where we set up our band equipment. It was a big room, probably three to five desks for daily business, we just kind of pushed things over. We had a sound shield that we pushed between the drums and guitar amps, but there were a lot of little offices in the area of where they were recording.

Warren Wagner: There was no glass or window looking into the studio at Shoe. The studio was actually put together in some offices—we made one of them a control room. In one of the offices, we cut a hole for the Steinway Piano to be able to slide through so the keyboard was on the studio wall, but the actual soundboard where we miked it was in another room in an office. I put Chris in one of the office rooms and the drummer was out in the main studio area. Ken, the bass player, was out with Richard.

Richard Rosebrough: I was playing my drum kit on Chris' songs. I always played my own drums. I was playing Fibes drums. They were fiberglass shells. The first time we saw Elton John, his drummer was playing that kind of drums. The next weekend we went out to the music store and there they were. I said, "I'm going to buy them!" They were kind of shitty.

Ken Woodley: Richard was so easy going and an excellent drummer. He wasn't any more neurotic than the rest of us.

Unlike his fresh reels of tape at Ardent, Chris went the frugal route at Shoe and opted for a slightly tattered reel gifted to him by Warren. Today, the ethereally brooding track, "I Am The Cosmos," produced with a $0 budget, is considered a pioneering alternative-rock classic.

233

Adam Hill: Warren was friends with Chris and was doing him a favor. Chris being Chris, he didn't buy a new reel.

Richard Rosebrough: We recorded "Cosmos" on a one-inch eight-track and on scrap tape that had three splices in it. Warren loaned Chris the tape. It was pieces of one-inch tape that were all spliced together, pretty bad splices, too — you could hear the splices go by.

Warren Wagner: Shoe did a lot of jingles to keep the doors open so we had tape reels that had splices in them. Since it was free, I grabbed Chris one of those reels.

Adam Hill: John Fry would call it a "shoddy splice." It wasn't done with the utmost care and attention. It wasn't seamless — it was haphazard. The splice is in the middle of the guitar solo when Richard is pounding the cymbals. That's why you can hear it: the cymbals are just awash and when you have an interruption in that, it draws your attention. Now it's just a part of the recording, part of the story.

Warren Wagner: I did a mix of "I Am the Cosmos" with the delayed echo and compressors at Shoe. The only logical way to cover up the splice was to drown it in echo. Any engineer would have done the same thing, given the technology available at the time. It doesn't sound much different from the other mixes later done by [producer] Geoff Emerick and John Fry.

John Fry: I did a mix of just the eight-track original of the song for the [2009] Rhino reissue of *I Am the Cosmos*. Every time it would hit a bad splice, my co-engineer, Adam Hill, said I jumped up in my chair. The overdubs on sixteen-track and Geoff Emerick's mix cover the flaws completely.

While his previous experience in the studio with Big Star ended on a bad note, the low-pressure Shoe sessions, technical warts and all, were an optimistic start to his solo project. Chris, now twenty-three years old, was elated about the sounds captured on "I Am the Cosmos."

Richard Rosebrough: Chris was fun to work with at Shoe. He always had a smile on his face, a kind of evil grin — the "cat that just ate the canary" expression, but he wouldn't talk a lot. He was this shining star over in the corner of the room. He was excited to be in a different studio with different people, playing his own songs.

Ken Woodley: He was quiet and could sometimes look a bit stern. He could also be a perfectionist. He'd say, "I know you can do better than that." I'd be like, "Chris, I just learned it!" But we always got along great. I wasn't a part of the Big Star clique, the people he'd grown up with, so we were friends on a different level. I never saw him throw a tantrum or anything like that. If he got upset, I'd see it in the way he spoke. He'd grab his hair and mumble, "I can't believe this shit." It was basically just him muttering to himself.

Warren Wagner: Chris was great during the sessions. He wasn't temperamental or anything. I gave him some free time because I liked him and I wanted to be a part of it. Chris came prepared. He had his own amp settings and so forth, I miked it, and that was pretty much it. It wasn't like, "Let's record it and see what it sounds like, then come into the control room and we'll listen to it." It was, "Set everything up, let us know when you're ready." One funny thing about Shoe: If you left the studio door open, we had a big entrance hall that was concrete. We put a mic in that hall and it was just like an echo chamber. It had a twenty-foot-tall ceiling. I recorded that as a track and got a nice live reverb on the drums. We used that and tape delay and echo after the tape delay. It was pretty much a standard set-up as far as miking the drums and Chris. We used a U 87 for his voice and one of those Neumann pencil mics for his guitar.

Richard Rosebrough: Chris would turn it up just as loud as he could. He'd get this piercingly bright, brilliant sound. It's all distorting and melting down, but it's just a dynamite sound. Of course, you run that through compressors and equalize it on the board and it sounds as big as it can be. Warren Wagner was the engineer on that session, he played an integral part in this.

Warrren Wagner: My part of it was assessing what we were going to do and deciding the best way to mic everything and place everybody. The main thing is to make sure it sounds good over their headphones.

Richard Rosebrough: The sound in the headphones was just brilliant. I was used to the monaural headphones they had over at Ardent — they had stereo headphones over at Shoe.

Warren Wagner: Breaking it out into a stereo sound where you can give them two separate mixes in their headphones was important in terms of how they'd feel the music and their fellow players.

Richard Rosebrough: They had my cymbals miked-up so they were very bright and loud. They put a little tape delay and a lot of echo on it so there was just this huge sound in the headphones. That contributed to closing our eyes, going into dreamland and playing what we played.

Interior shots of Shoe Productions, where Chris cut his earliest, post-Big Star solo material.

The exterior of the now-defunct Shoe Productions,
485 North Hollywood Street, Memphis.

(right) Producer Warren
Wagner, owner of Shoe
Productions, engineered
the now legendary "I Am

the Cosmos" session.

*ALL SHOE PHOTOS COURTESY OF
WARREN WAGNER*

Adam Hill: Everything about "Cosmos" was thought-out. He wasn't winging it. If you listen to the solo, that's not an improvised blues solo like Page would do. It's not your standard blues-box bends. With "Cosmos" he went in there with a game plan.

Ken Woodley: Chris knew what he wanted and tried to get it in the studio. That's what you hear when you listen to his music — it's exactly what his ears wanted it to be.

Jody Stephens: It starts with, "Every night I tell myself, 'I am the cosmos, I am the wind,' but that don't get you back again.'" It just comes in so heavy. Not as people define "heavy" these days, but emotionally heavy — instrumentally, too.

Rick Clark: The music is so huge, but intimate at the same time. And it's such an utterly, insanely personal opening lyrical sentiment. In a way, it's arresting to listen to. You can't help but to connect emotionally on some level, but at the same time you're also hearing a train wreck.

Richard Rosebrough: All of his songs have kind of a pleading quality to them, almost a morose, sad tone to them. It's hard to explain.

Matthew Sweet: "I Am the Cosmos" has this otherworldly glow coming off it sonically from a lot of harmonics blending together. It's very multi-tracked and has a specific sound to it. The sound is cosmic. Our bodies are made entirely of matter from stars that exploded. In an intuitive sense, he knew he was the same as everything. I care a lot about science and physics. I try to find ways to get those ideas into my songs more, but with "I Am the Cosmos," it's the pinnacle of that idea. Also, he's aware he can't change the thing that's hurting him most. It's trippy, probably because he'd done acid. It likely opened up his mind to that kind of concept. It's all about feeling. Steve Jobs was so obsessed about that; he said taking acid was one of the most important things he'd done in his life.

Terry Manning: I didn't say this to Chris at the time, but "I Am the Cosmos" is the best emotionally driven pop song ever written. It's just amazing to me. The dichotomy of dark and light, yes and no, happy and sad — all in one song — is just astounding.

Warren Wagner: Today, I live in the hill country outside of San Antonio. Shoe Productions is long closed, but the building is still there. There's a guy who distributes blues records from there. I visited the building recently and the guy told me people come up all the time, ring the bell and ask, "Where was 'I Am the Cosmos' recorded?" These people are from England, Germany, all over the place.

Ken Woodley and Chris Bell.

Chris Bell at a dinner party in Torino, Italy, October 1974.

PHOTO BY RICHARD ROSEBROUGH

CHAPTER 16

BORN AGAIN — CHÂTEAU & AIR: SUMMER-FALL 1974

With a few new tunes etched out, and a growing list of songs that needed to be recorded, Chris' creative spark was relit, but this time around he lacked the financial backing of Ardent and the support of a stable band. For the first time in his career, he was on his own. While his depression subsided, his drug and alcohol abuse persisted. Simultaneously, Chris entrenched himself in Christianity. Soon his friends and family noted a prominent crucifix around his neck and Holy Bible in his hand. This drastic spiritual transformation surprised those close to him.

David Bell: We had grown up in the Episcopal Church, but Chris didn't particularly care for it then. I did. I was at home there, but left it behind in college. It was through him that it was renewed in me. Anybody who knew Chris knew of his conversion.

Richard Rosebrough: He was very much with the Lord. That was the biggest surprise. I thought, "Well, where did that come from?" He went full tilt into that, but he'd also gladly accept a vodka tonic and was always smoking cigarettes.

Van Duren: Chris became what we called back then a Jesus freak. He discovered God but was still eccentric, chain-smoking, drinking, and all the other things he did. He layered that with religion.

Carole Ruleman Manning: When we were young, sixteen or so, Chris wanted to go to Christmas Mass and meet his parents there. I had stopped going to church when I was twelve, but I was impressed Chris wanted to do that. I know he wasn't a saint, but he tended to ponder things that were a little more esoteric than other people.

David Bell: He and his friend Earl Smith went down to this spiritually alive church called St. Andrews by the Sea in Destin, Florida and were saved. It's where he had his baptism. It didn't wipe everything out of his life as far as troubles and drugs, but it certainly helped him get on a more even keel.

> *There was a light*
> *So dear to me*
> *I wanted to live*
> *There was a time*
> *So near to me*
> *I asked you to give your life to me*
>
> — CHRIS BELL, "THERE WAS A LIGHT"

Tommie Dunavant: Before Earl and I started dating, Earl had a born-again experience with Chris. They bonded together and went to church. Chris, Earl, and all of them went down to St. Andrews because it was kind of a spiritual place to go. Chris and Earl had that experience with the Lord at the same time. They frequently talked religion and were passionate about it.

John Fry: Earl and Chris had been great buddies. Earl was a strong Christian person and knowledgeable. Earl helped get Chris' faith reactivated or jump-started.

Richard Rosebrough: Earl Smith was a member of the very well-to-do Federal Express family. He was a cousin of Fred Smith. Earl was a real hippie with really long hair. He was always on the fringes, experimenting with drink, drugs, and new spiritual concepts.

David Bell: Chris and Earl were the same age, or close to it. They met in eighth or ninth grade. Earl was in love with Chris' musicianship. He said Chris was the closest thing to a Beatle he'd ever seen. Earl was a real rebel and he liked that my brother was, too.

Danielle McCarthy-Boles: "Born again" is different now than it was in the '70s. It was a different kind of Christianity movement back in the day. Now you think of Bible-thumping extremists. In the '70s, it was more like, "Yeah, man. Jesus was a cool dude—hippies for Jesus."

David Bell: Chris was fairly liberal overall. He participated in some Vietnam War protests in college, but he talked more about worldwide politics and worldwide economies and what he foresaw multinationals doing in the future. He talked about how it wasn't a great thing, like the beast may arrive from all that. He liked to philosophize a little bit, but it was like futurescape or "What's the world going to turn into? Is it going to be a super conglomerate and who is going to run the world?" That sort of thing.

David returned home for a summer vacation and noted Chris' newfound devotion to religion. He also observed his brother's lingering dark side.

David Bell: During the course of four or five trips to the States to visit family, I saw a slow deterioration in Chris. He had occasionally sent me demos, which showed that he continued to grow musically and lyrically, but on the personal side, his sadness was a constant source of concern to me. It culminated in a horrific scene during a trip home in the summer of 1974. After a night on the town, I returned home and walked into my brother's room to find him pulling, with his teeth, on a rubber tourniquet with a syringe in his hand. I froze. Not wanting to harm him in some sort of struggle with the needle, I stood and watched.

Alex Chilton: Many people I grew up with in Memphis developed raging drug problems long before I did, and lots of them went the junk-to-Jesus route. That was always peculiar to me, but Chris was one of them.

David Bell: As far as I know, Chris never did heroin. That was Dilaudid, which was bad enough. It just freaked me out. I've seen so many times over the years where people write he was hooked on heroin, which is just not true.

Richard Rosebrough: Chris never did heroin. I was with him when he put a needle in his arm and that was Dilaudid, a heavy-duty pain medication. I even did it with him. It wasn't pleasant to me at all. I didn't know Chris was using it until the night we did it together. I had no idea, but Chris had been putting needles in his arms. I was like, "Chris, don't do that!" Of course, he talked me into doing it. I was the type of guy who'd try anything once or twice. I always regretted it. That was the only time I put a needle in my arm.

David Bell: Seeing him with the Dilaudid was the genesis of me trying to get him out of Memphis again, and away from drugs and focused on music. That was the nexus of dangling a carrot and saying, "Let's go record." I wanted to get him away from any sort of access to drugs.

Drew DeNicola: Once David saw Chris kind of going downhill, he decided to take him to Europe. He said, "Let's give him real profession-al-studio treatment, get him with the best people and see how he does."

David Bell: [I told Chris], "We should go to France to do some record-ing at the studios of the Château d'Hérouville where Elton John had recorded *Honky Château* and *Goodbye Yellow Brick Road*." I somehow had to make him feel like a star, like someone on the verge of discovery, especially with his recent track record of uniformly fabulous reviews for *#1 Record*.

Richard Rosebrough: John Fry and Chris, well, their friendship fell away for a bit. Chris was on his own and he was struggling. Suddenly Chris didn't have that backing he was used to having at Ardent, but David Bell had some assets and offered to help Chris.

Over the next few months, David Bell fronted the cost of the European trip and contacted Strawberry Studios, which operated out of the historic 18th century Château d'Hérouville, an estate located an hour outside Paris. By early August 1974, as President Richard Nixon resigned and Gerald Ford took office following the Watergate scandal, the Bells received a letter from Strawberry that confirmed their studio reservation for the following month. Invited along for the ride was drummer Richard Rosebrough.

Chris Bell: How did we arrive in Europe? Well, my brother David was living in Italy and he came home the following summer. He had become interested in the whole music scene and became, more or less, a manage-rial figure. The immediate result being that David, Richard Rosebrough and I flew to France to cut the album.

David Bell: For lack of a better term, I became his manager.

Terry Manning: David basically became Chris' guardian, almost a men-tor in a life sense.

David Bell: I just believed in the music. I was just knocked out from the get-go when I heard *#1 Record*. This is a kid five years younger than I am. I was so impressed with him from an early age, the backhouse days, which is why I now wear hearing aids. The volume just destroyed my ears.

Richard Rosebrough: David lived over there in northern Italy and he'd brought Chris over there, trying to help him out. Of course, this time they took me with them so they'd have a drummer—half of a band.

Chris Bell: My brother, in a way, sponsored myself and Richard Rosebrough to go over to Strawberry Studios to work because I had talked about it with him—plus he was very keen on France.

Richard Rosebrough: David was able to scrape together some money to hire out the studio. It was right out of a dream.

Sara Bell: Chris didn't know how to manage money. He was terrible at that. He never had a nickel and was always borrowing money. I would find out he was trying to borrow from my husband at the time, so having David's support surely helped him out a lot.

Richard Rosebrough: David was a little bit older and had a sense of responsibility. He didn't have a drug problem or drinking problem. He loved Chris more than anything in the world and he would have done anything for him.

David Bell: At this point, it was more a case of the blind leading the blind, I'm afraid.

Before departing on the big trip, Chris covertly took his eight-track Shoe tapes to Ardent and transferred them to sixteen-track. Along with the new tunes he planned to cut in France, he also carried his existing tapes, including the "I Am the Cosmos" reel, to continue the mixing process. He and Richard arrived in Milan on September 24, 1974.

Richard Rosebrough: We were over there about four and a half weeks. A lot of it was traveling.

David Bell: He and Richard flew into the Milan Malpensa Airport. It was halfway between Milan and the town I was living in, Varese. They stayed in my apartment in the north of Italy while we did a little tourist business. I took them down to Rome shortly after they arrived and stayed at a hotel called the Leonardo da Vinci. I remember Chris writing lyrics on some of the hotel's stationery and writing letters. Chris had never been to Rome. When he was there before, he was so depressed he wasn't up for it. Richard hadn't been there either and I wanted to make sure they had a good time before they started working at the Château.

Richard Rosebrough: We spent over a week in Rome. We got a private tour. A taxi driver drove us out to the countryside and showed us real Roman ruins, the real bricks. We spent a lot of time in St. Peter's. It was incredible. There was so much artwork. I could have spent days there. Then we took a train to Torino. There was a family there that invited us to their vineyard and they held a party in our honor, the American musicians.

Richard Rosebrough shot this photo at Château d'Hérouville during the
Chris Bell sessions, 1974.

David Bell: Several Italian industrialists, guests of the party, continually asked Chris to play some songs. He complied, and after finishing one number during which everyone continued to talk, he began playing Joni Mitchell's "People's Parties." Singing in English, the Italian guests never understood the return of the insult. However, a teenage son of one of the businessmen got up and left in disgust.

Richard Rosebrough: There was plenty of wine to drink and all this delicious food. Chris drank too much. He got drunk and everyone laughed, "Oh, he had too much wine!" It was an amazing time. We had gone to northern Italy, gone down to Rome, we had gone to Torino. For a couple weeks, we were tourists. But unfortunately, Chris was still kind of depressed. He drank a lot and always had a vodka tonic or gin and tonic in his hand. He would also have a bottle of pills in his pocket, some Tranxene. We all had medicines in those days. I always had a bottle of pills in my pocket, too. Everybody told me, "Richard, your pockets rattle!" I would have Valiums on me. Aside from that nonsense, there were a lot of arguments between David and Chris. They were two brothers who cared about each other but just didn't always get along. David would annoy Chris sometimes and Chris could be annoying to be with, too. It was just brother shit.

After they arrived in Switzerland, Chris and David had a particularly heated argument. A fuming Chris stormed out of the hotel room and hopped on a train, arriving solo in Denmark on September 26, 1974.

Richard Rosebrough: Chris and David had this big, big fight. Chris just stormed out and said, "I'm going to get on the train. I'm going to Copenhagen." He was drugged out of his mind. He just picked up his guitar and walked out. I said, "No! please don't go!" I tried to calm him down, and he said, "Richard, you just don't understand." Chris left and was gone for four days.

David Bell: I don't remember what he and I were fighting about or what pissed him off, but something did. He could be incredibly spontaneous. I wasn't worried about him, per se. I knew he could take care of himself. He went to Copenhagen and went through France. He met a couple in a dining car while on the train; they were the ones who had a "Fight at the Table." That's what inspired his song.

> *It must be getting past midnight*
> *And now I'm starting to scream*
> *She really put up a good fight*
> *I think this must be a dream*
>
> — CHRIS BELL, "FIGHT AT THE TABLE"

After Chris cooled off, he headed back to Switzerland where David and Richard waited for his return. The guys headed straight to Paris the following day for their first recording session on October 1.

David Bell: The next morning we took a train to the studio. Arriving the following day at the station in Pontoise, some forty kilometers from Paris, we were met by people from the Château's studio who drove us to the village of Hérouville.

Richard Rosebrough: We went over to Strawberry Studios—well, that's what we thought it was called. When we got there, it was called Château d'Hérouville; it had changed names but was the same place.

Château d'Hérouville's studio was situated in an enormous two-wing, two-level mansion in a small country village, and still stands today. The tranquil estate is encircled by fields, hills, and a nearby church. Famously nicknamed the "Honky Château" after Elton John's 1972 milestone LP, the manor was constructed in 1740 in the Oise Valley and saw multiple owners in its time. In 1962, the property was purchased by music entrepreneur and composer Michel Magne. That same year, he was nominated for an Academy Award and Golden Globe for his score for Gigot, *the Jackie Gleason film. By 1969, Michel had turned the French estate into a commercial recording studio. By the time Chris checked in, Michel and the business had suffered financial problems, forcing him to move to the south of France and leave others to operate the Château.*

In 1984, Michel committed suicide in a hotel, and the studio closed the following year. In its heyday, many rock icons strolled the Château halls, a fact not lost on the awestruck Chris, David and Richard. Perks at the Château included a pool, large kitchen and dining room, tennis court, ping-pong tables and a five-acre park. Its distinctive, austere Roman-style architecture, some of which was painted by Vincent van Gogh, was dubbed "one of the sacred spaces of British pop music" by The Guardian *in a 2013 retrospective. Legendary stories took place inside and outside the walls of the famed studio. During a 1971 visit, the Grateful Dead played an intimate gig to a few locals on the grass by the pool. When David Bowie and Brian Eno were lodged at the twenty-plus-room mansion, they reportedly encountered numerous eerie and supernatural happenings. Alleged paranormal activity aside, Château d'Hérouville, with its medieval-style chandeliers and towering wood-beam ceilings, was known for both its inimitable design and astonishing natural acoustics. Leading the Bell sessions was Claude Harper, an engineer with an impressive résumé that started in 1964 at EMI Studios, the famous room eventually rebranded as Abbey Road Studios. There, Claude was a tech engineer, working sessions with the Beatles and other major acts. He was also tapped to help build the Fab Four's iconic Apple Studio. Chris was elated to spend a week with him. The plan was to record at least two of Chris' moodier songs, "Speed of Sound" and "Better Save Yourself," along with "Make a Scene," a punchy rocker.*

> *You hurt me yesterday*
> *I didn't know what to say*
> *You didn't have to be so mean*
> *You didn't have to make a scene*
> *You don't have to be so cruel*
> *You made me feel like a fool*
> *I heard some things about you*
> *They said you was untrue*

— CHRIS BELL, "MAKE A SCENE"

Claude Harper — Engineer, EMI, Apple Studio, Château d'Hérouville: I was working at Château d'Hérouville when I got a message from the guys in the office saying, "There are some guys coming over from the United States."

David Bell: Our engineer, Claude Harper, had been a technical engineer at Apple in London. He was an English guy who spoke perfect French, which amazed me because the English were not known for that. We recorded there for four or five days. While they were recording, we had rooms at the Château. We had room and board, so we ate and slept there.

Richard Rosebrough: We had phoned ahead to the studio about some of the equipment we needed. I couldn't pack my drums on an airplane, and Chris couldn't take an amplifier, so we ordered all of that in advance. It was all there. They had nice equipment provided for us.

Claude Harper: Richard requested a certain drum kit. He wanted transparent tom-toms, for some reason. The whole backline, the drums and amps, was hired in. They brought their instruments with them. We used a small Auditronics desk and the sixteen-track was a Scully two-inch. For mics, I used Neumann U 87s on all the tom-toms, overheads, and for the vocals.

Richard Rosebrough: I'm a drummer first, but I'm also an engineer. I walked in expecting to see all this fabulous equipment and sitting there was an Auditronics console. Auditronics is good, but not a top-of-the-line console. It's also designed, manufactured and built in Memphis, about a block and a half from where I lived. I just got on an airplane and flew 4,500 miles or whatever to Paris to record in this special place and there's this board built around the corner from my house.

John Fry: It's kind of funny, when Chris got to the Château they had removed the Elton John desk. David Bell said it "looked like a toy." They replaced it with an Auditronics desk from Memphis. It seemed to Chris that Memphis was following him around.

Richard Rosebrough: Still, Chris thought he was in heaven. He thought, *This is a real studio,* because it looked Gothic and was built in an attic in this giant room. It had this big metal, black chandelier hanging from the ceiling and these huge one-piece windows that opened-up and let the outside air from the French countryside come in. We were there in September, so the weather was mild. It wasn't cold or hot, it was perfect and beautiful. We set up all the equipment they supplied for us and we did most of our big recording that first day we were there.

Claude Harper: We recorded upstairs because the other studio wasn't working at the time. The studio was a bit shambolic. I went there in '73 and the guy running it basically ran out of cash.

Richard Rosebrough: The older studio, that place had just been ransacked. Our studio was in another part of the complex that was up on the upper level. It was much smaller, much more comfortable. Elton John's piano was still in there.

Claude Harper: The Bell sessions were in the studio upstairs called "Chopin," that's where Elton John did *Honky Château* and *Goodbye Yellow Brick Road*, Bowie did *Pin Ups*, Pink Floyd did *Obscured by Clouds,* and T. Rex did *The Slider*—along with a whole load of others. The studio downstairs was named "George Sand," after the French writer. The studios were named because, apparently, George Sand and Frédéric Chopin used to have illicit meetings there.

David Bell: Chris was excited, and I was just kind of bouncing off the walls during the first session.

Claude Harper: Chris was quite hyper and buzzing. It was basically just Richard and Chris in the studio. Chris did vocals, guitar, and bass parts. I've actually got a quarter-inch tape of what we did that evening.

David Bell: Claude and I were watching Richard play his fills in "Better Save Yourself," [and] our mouths just dropped open. Richard also had access to all sorts of percussion instruments. He played one that looked African. It was a long, spear affair with cymbals all up and down it that he'd shake. He also used it on "Make a Scene."

Claude Harper: We did some interesting things with "Better Save Yourself." Basically, because it was quite short, we copied the drums and the backing track and basically made a loop. Then we played it back onto the sixteen-track and overdubbed on top of that.

Richard Rosebrough: We laid those tracks down and he did some lead guitar overdubs, acoustic guitar overdubs, and sang. He also overdubbed that synthesizer [on "Speed of Sound"] that got out of tune.

Adam Hill: There was an English film called *Speed of Sound* about breaking the sound barrier, that's where Chris got the title. He plays an open tuning on that. Chris was no stranger to open tunings on his guitar. Open G is the most obvious. Keith Richards and the Black Crowes use it—a lot of blues guys, too. Chris used them as well. "Watch the Sunrise" from *#1 Record* is in open G, that song came from that "Country Morn" tune Chris wrote. "Try Again" is in open G. That song is a milestone in Chris' catalog. "Speed of Sound" is in open D, which isn't as common as open G. That's a big part of that ringing sound. He's got a lot of those open strings ringing with every chord, so there's a common tonality that runs through it. It's a little bit droney, not to mention the heavy subject matter.

> *I remember the first time*
> *You said you loved me*
> *I waited all weekend*
> *You never called me*
> *So you find him attractive*
> *So what if he is*
> *You'd like some excitement*
> *We could go to St. Kitts*
>
> — CHRIS BELL, "SPEED OF SOUND"

Chris and Richard wrapped at the Château on October 7, but decided to continue working on the tracks at their next destination: London. Luckily for them, their new friend Claude had high-profile connections.

Chris Bell: The engineer there [Claude] had previously been with Apple and he put us in contact with Geoff Emerick, a truly great engineer at George Martin's AIR London Studios.

Claude Harper: Richard said, "We're going to be going to London, do you know anywhere we could do some mixing?" I went, "How about I call Geoff Emerick?" I pick up the phone and, luckily, I got Geoff, who was busy working on *Venus and Mars* with Paul McCartney. I had a chat with him and then I put him on the phone with Richard. He was nervous, like, "Uh, Mr. Emerick, sir." They started chatting, booked time, and then went to London.

It may have been Beatles producer George Martin who designed AIR in 1969 in Central London, but the late Geoff Emerick also has a storied history engineering the Beatles and is still praised for his groundbreaking work on Revolver, Sgt. Pepper's Lonely Hearts Club Band, "The White Album" *and* Abbey Road. *For Chris and Richard, it was a dream come true to work within the Beatles' inner circle. On October 8, they arrived at London Heathrow en route to AIR, one of the four studios Chris utilized for his solo album.*

Chris Bell: We rang up Geoff and went over there to mix some tunes. He helped mix the tracks we had done.

Richard Rosebrough: That was one of the high points of my entire life.

David Bell: Certainly, with Geoff, Chris was not at all introverted. I was amazed at how forward he was. If I had been in his place, I would have let myself be led by someone who'd been the Beatles' engineer for six or seven years, but he knew exactly what he wanted. He would sit at the board with Geoff and work knobs. He wouldn't just let somebody else do it. Chris knew what he wanted and had no problem telling Geoff, "No, I don't want this" or "Could you do this?" He knew what was in his head and he knew his way around a recording console, but he also knew he was working with someone with an impressive track record and who he'd loved throughout his teenage years. He understood Geoff had great experience with the group he most admired and had obtained sounds for the Beatles he'd always dreamt of. Later, Chris wrote me a letter and told me that our trip to London was worth it and a success based solely on Geoff's mix of "I Am the Cosmos."

As the European trip neared its final hours, the last day in London ended with a big bang.

David Bell: Geoff Emerick did some mixes for three or four days at AIR Studios. At the end of that is when we met Paul McCartney at EMI.

Claude Harper: Sometime after our sessions ended, I get a call from David Bell. He was back in Italy at the time. David said, "You'll never guess what happened. Chris had a premonition when he left the United States and was coming across to Europe that somehow he was going to meet Paul McCartney, but he wasn't sure how."

David Bell: On our last day at AIR, an acetate arrived from EMI and we were treated to a preview of [the Wings single] "Junior's Farm," which, interestingly enough, had been recorded in Tennessee. With a not-so-subtle grin, Chris asked Geoff if he needed a tape delivered to EMI studios that night. Not so coincidentally, Geoff was going to be doing a final mix of "Junior's Farm" there with McCartney. At first, Geoff seemed a bit ill at ease with the proposal, but said we might stop by for just a few minutes.

Richard Rosebrough: Unfortunately, I was not there for that. He met McCartney on the last day. I had just gone home the previous day. I was homesick and wanted to get home to see my dog, so I had left. I guess they secured a tour down at EMI.

David Bell: Geoff got us into Abbey Road that night. We came in and he was in the studio where the Beatles had done all their recordings. The console and engineer's room sits way up high and you look down onto the studio. We were talking with Geoff for about ten minutes when we heard all this ruckus and in came Paul and Linda. We talked with them for quite a while, then they had to do something, so we went to [Studio 1] where they recorded "All You Need Is Love." This was a studio that could hold two symphony orchestras. It was enormous. We tooled around there a little bit and then we came back to [Studio 2] and talked to Paul and Linda for a while longer. A lot of the conversation had to do with recording techniques. Chris asked Paul about getting particular sounds and vocals, that sort of thing. Chris was quite interested in "Lady Madonna." Paul and Linda were extremely friendly and cordial, likely because Emerick introduced Chris as a client of his from AIR. With that kind of groundwork, it was like, "I'm talking to another musician." Then they had to get back to work. We went out in the hallway and my brother had a look on his face that was transcendent. Chris looked like he had seen God. If anything was worth anything out of that whole little odyssey, it was that.

Chris Bell: It was the singularly most heavy moment of my life.

David Bell: He felt he had arrived. "One down, two to go," he said, in reference to Harrison and Lennon. Apparently, he had no interest in meeting Ringo...The mixing ended, and it was time for us to go our separate ways. He returned to the States and I to Italy.

On the evening of October 16, Chris boarded a jet back to Memphis with plenty of stories to tell.

Richard Rosebrough: When Chris got back to Memphis, he told everybody about meeting Paul. He was proud of that.

Drew DeNicola: Chris responded to the experience. He liked working with the best people and using the top-notch equipment, so that pushed him forward.

David Bell: Afterwards, Chris didn't know what he was going to do next. I didn't know what I was going to do. He took up flying, he tinkered with that, but we both knew he still wanted to pursue music.

you said that you loved me
But where are you now
I wanted all week end
But you never called

So you find him attractive
so what if he is
you'd like some excitement
wt could go to St. kitts

{ So it goes, on and on
my love grows, yours is gone

If there is a reason
I'd like to know why
Its just an existence   A stupid existence
A solitary lie   Well it's just a lie

{ There's something I want you to know
I told you this once before
Don't want you to see him no more

Once again you let me down
Broke my heart –

There's a light in the darkness
It's only a glow (It doesn't seem far)

the plane goes down it will not land
pilot's dead a broken man

00192 ROMA · VIA DEI GRACCHI, 324 · TEL. 38 20 91 · TELEX: 62182

Chris Bell's handwritten lyrics to "Speed of Sound."

255

GRAND HOTEL
LEONARDO DA VINCI

I walk the street
I'm all alone
I just can't think
~~what's gone wrong~~ what I've done wrong
I know your mind
he treats you nice
It's suicide
I tried it twice
I know your mind
he treats you nice
It's getting late
And I know you want to go

Chris Bell's handwritten lyrics to "Better Save Yourself."

256

1. Get Away
2. Oh Yea
3. Speed of Sound
4. So Dear
5. A Fight At The Table

CALL
255 8251

1. Make A Scene
2. You and Your Sister
3. I've got Cancer
4. Shoulda Gave Your Love
5. The Cosmos

An early tracklist concept Chris Bell scribbled in his notebook.
Note: the never recorded track, "I've Got Cancer."

Alex Chilton.

PHOTO BY ANDY HUMMEL

CHAPTER 17

THIRD — SISTER LOVERS: FALL 1974-1975

While Chris fixated on Europe, the lingering members of Big Star stuck it out at Ardent Studios. With some Chilton originals on deck, in September 1974, Alex and Jody entered Studio B and started laying down what eventually became Third/Sister Lovers. *This time around, both John Fry and Jim Dickinson signed on to help produce and engineer. For further reinforcement, a roster of seasoned local players, including string arranger and multi-instrumentalist Carl Marsh, added an ethereal glow to the sessions. Guitarist Steve Cropper, of the Stax Records House Band and Booker T and the M.G.'s, contributed guitar on a sparse cover of the Velvet Underground's "Femme Fatale." The tracklist was unlike anything Big Star had previously released. The virile riffing of "Kizza Me" and the curiously jovial "Thank You Friends" are paired alongside the tenderness of "Nighttime" and utter hopelessness of "Holocaust." The high-spirited "Jesus Christ" and Demerol-induced "Big Black Car," an abstract ode to John Fry's Mercedes, further complicate the moody track list. Unlike the first two Big Star LPs, after* Third *was completed, it was pitched by Ardent Productions to a string of outside labels. After Stax had fallen into dire financial problems, Fry terminated Ardent's partnership with the struggling soul imprint in June of '74. After that, Ardent Records folded, though Ardent Studios carried on. By the end of '75, Stax Records was forced by a bankruptcy judge to fully cease operations. It was the end of an era for Memphis music.*

John Fry: Certainly, Stax wasn't the only successful music enterprise here, but it was by and large, in the '70s, the mothership. So much revolved around that, and so much of the reason for all these players, artists and producers to be in Memphis was because Stax was in Memphis. It was a big employer and then just abruptly went under. That was the mid-'70s event that was kind of like the Titanic going down. Our record label was gone, and our biggest customer was gone.

Chris Bell: Ardent, as a label, folded because it just got really bad. Manning and Fry got into some big arguments...I guess financially they could just not hold it together and [Stax folded], too.

Al Bell: If Stax had been able to survive its economic assassination, then Ardent would be one of the world's legendary rock labels. They would have been awesome, and I really regret that.

John Fry: Alex and Jody had already been through two albums that had been commercially disappointing, and during the recording of *Third*, Stax was going out of business, so it's sort of a picture of Midtown Memphis in 1975. Just two years prior we had so much energy and promise, and now prospects seemed bleak.

Third/Sister Lovers didn't come easy, especially for Alex. At twenty-three, his drug and alcohol problems sent his life into a nosedive. Still, he entered a musically prolific streak while his dysfunctional love for Lesa Aldridge quickly grew. Lesa even partook in some of the production and creative process on Third. *With Jody still dating Lesa's sister Holliday, the album's alias,* Sister Lovers, *stuck. During a 1975 interview in London, Chris Bell relayed his thoughts on his former band's third outing. "The last thing I heard, Ardent is still trying to market Alex's new album," he said. "Well, they're calling it a Big Star album, even though it's just Alex and Jody. When I was there, they were calling it* Sister Lovers *because Alex and Jody were dating sisters and one of the chicks sang."*

John Lightman: When I was still in Big Star, I went over to see Alex and found him at Trader Dick's one day. He was in a booth with Lesa and a couple of other people. He told me, "We're changing the name of the band to Sister Lovers." I said, "Okay." He wanted to call the band that, not just the album. That's the reason *Third* is sometimes called *Sister Lovers*. Everyone at Ardent nixed the idea. Why would you build up a reputation as Big Star and then change your name? It didn't make sense, but Alex liked it because of the Aldridge sisters.

Holliday Aldridge: It was called *Sister Lovers* because of me and Lesa. We were dating the two guys in the band. First, I had seen the Big Star album with Jody's picture on the back and thought he was the hottest guy I had ever seen in my life. Then, when I was sixteen, on Valentine's night 1974, I was at home and it was a school night. I was in tenth grade. Lesa called me from Trader Dick's. She wanted money because she was drinking with Alex and Jody. She asked me to come and meet her. It was probably 10 p.m. I had to go ask Daddy for twenty dollars. She was like, "Jody's here! You have to come meet him." I met them there and Jody and I totally hit it off. It was love at first sight. We stayed together for a few years. He was my first true love. I skipped eleventh grade by taking summer school, so I could graduate a year early, because I was dating Jody and didn't want to be in high school.

Lesa Aldridge Hoehn: To me, Alex looked just like Romeo. It turns out, he was my Heathcliff. He was the most charismatic person out of all of us. Alex was intelligent, fun and endearing. He could be so sweet. I was head over heels for him, but he could turn on a dime. He was terribly insecure in relationships and, therefore, jealous. If I was a psychiatrist, I would say he was kind of messed up. His brother died when Alex was a child, plus the rock star stuff after "The Letter" changed him. He was insecure, but not about his music. He didn't ask for affirmation with his songs. He never asked, "Is this good?" It was more in his relationships and trust issues. That kind of went back and forth with the two of us.

John Lightman: Lesa is very intelligent, creative, and personable. She could make friends with people much easier than Alex, who was rather aloof and suspicious of people. Lesa was more open and friendly and that made Alex both jealous and envious of Lesa, because she was getting more attention.

Lesa Aldridge Hoehn: When we started out, he could trust me. I adored him. I would not have looked another way. But it turned into silly things. We would go out to a bar and I would people-watch. He'd think I was looking at other men, but I wasn't. We had some great recording sessions, but our sweetest times were just the two of us watching *The Thin Man* and eating dinner together. We did better alone together.

Holliday Aldridge: Unlike Alex, Jody is straitlaced. He didn't get drunk or didn't do drugs—just not a partier. He'd drink, but I'm talking one drink. He's still kind of a goody two shoes. That's one of the reasons we eventually broke up. I was getting into some wildness and partying with my sister and he didn't approve. Jody was close to his mother, he was a mama's boy and was close to the rest of his family, too. For years, we went to church on Sundays and had Sunday dinner with his folks. We also spent many nights at Richard Rosebrough's house. After our first date, we hung out there until 6 a.m. We also had a lot of fun with Alex and Lesa. We were all friends. Everything was good at first. The four of us did a lot of things together and spent weekends together. Alex and Lesa were a cute couple, but then Alex started having these drinking rages and there was horrible fighting between them. Alex was kind of abusive. Jody was more upset by that than I was. At first, the rages were not directed right at my sister. Our parents' house was in the Central Gardens area of Midtown, the nice side. It had this front door that was beveled glass and Alex broke it. He threw something through it because Lesa wouldn't let him in because he was drunk. Then he would pay for the damage and say, "I'm so sorry." Typical for abusive behavior. They're so sorry hours later and they'll never do it again.

It wasn't just Alex who stirred up problems at Ardent. By Sister Lovers, *the studio had attracted a new batch of rowdy hangers-on, mostly during the nighttime hours when the studio was free of paying clients.*

John Dando: A different element had started to come along that hadn't been a part of that earlier Ardent crew. They didn't have the same ethics. I came at odds with those people. I put a night guy on the door, so we didn't have the door just propped open at night allowing people to wander in and carry out $2,000 or $3,000 Neumann microphones, which was happening.

Ken Woodley: I don't know if everyone had keys, but you'd just go to the back door and knock. Sometimes things would get ripped off. It was hard to tell who was doing it. You'd try to track who was coming in. We had a lot of headphones stolen.

Carole Ruleman Manning: Things were just too far gone. Any efforts to rein them in didn't work too well. This place needed a little bit of a cap on it. It would get so wild it was frightening.

Holliday Aldridge: I got a phone call that Alex was beating my sister's head against concrete at Ardent Studios' parking lot, so I raced over there. By the time I got there he's acting like nothing's happened and my sister is covering for him. It was just horrible. It got physical. That was later when Lesa and I had apartments in Midtown. She lived almost across the street from Ardent on Madison and I was on Maury Street.

Andy Hummel: By the third album, Alex and Lesa were going steady. They had the most turbulent relationship of any two people I've ever met in my whole life. They couldn't live without each other and they couldn't live with each other. Lesa and Holliday became a part of our group. Lesa and I were best friends for a long time.

Lesa Aldridge Hoehn: Andy was a doll and we remained close friends even after we broke up. He and Richard Rosebrough did a lot of hanging out, and they were always there for me when Alex was being a brat and mean to me. Several times Andy came and got me in his Jeep. I would say, "Andy, marry me! Take me away from all of this." Unfortunately, he didn't.

Holliday Aldridge: It was Scotch or gin, or both, that made Alex a mean drunk. Of course, Lesa was defending him and enabling him. She would blame those particular liquors for their nasty fights. I separated myself from it, but those episodes were not prevalent. There were so many more good times than bad times with Alex.

Alex Chilton: In my life, I've never had an easy relationship with a woman that didn't degenerate into some kind of deception or some really bad feeling between people who ought to care about each other. I've never had anything that was very easy for very long.

Regardless of his stormy lifestyle, Alex was in total control when it came to his newfound vision in the studio. With Jim Dickinson by his side, he felt comfortable exploring ground not possible when Chris was in the band.

Alex Chilton: The other members of Big Star were pretty opposed to doing things in a spontaneous manner because they wanted to be like a mid-'60s British group, so I tried to fit into that mold. As the group dissolved bit by bit, I did other things, maybe even as a reaction, but I was influenced by rockabilly, things like that, although the Anglophilic influences remained.

Drew DeNicola: Big Star changed every time they made a record. It was like a collection of recordings made at Ardent Studios with various people. It's interesting that Alex sort of dismantled the Big Star sound that Chris created while Chris continued to hone that sound.

Alex Chilton: The third record was never meant to be a Big Star record. That was only a marketing decision made by record companies who got the rights to the thing later.

Jim Dickinson: [*Third*] was just something somebody wrote on the test pressing. The actual title Alex discussed at the time to name the record was *Beale St. Green.*

Alex Chilton: Each of the [Big Star] records are different. The first one is the real group. The second one is just the three of us trying to carry on in some fashion and the third one is just saying, "To hell with the whole thing. Let's do something completely different." Jody and I stayed together for the third record just because I didn't have the heart to say, "Hey, get lost."

Jody Stephens: I was kind of puzzled, myself. At that point, it was in Alex's hands. It was more like an Alex solo project. I wrote one song. My contribution was I brought in a string section for the song I wrote,

"For You"...Other than that, it was just Alex having a real cathartic experience.

Jim Dickinson: The record is about the decomposition of relationships, including the professional relationship with John Fry, and the one with Lesa Aldridge, who most of the record is about.

Alex Chilton: I was coming to a period of being on my own and couldn't rely on other people to write for me and to help me put my projects together like I had with Big Star. We had all kind of helped each other do things.

Tom Eubanks: Chris needed somebody like Alex to write with. Look at all those years he spent on the songs for that *I Am the Cosmos* album. That represents a lot of years. I'm kind of the same way. Both Alex and Chris benefited from working with each other.

Alex Chilton: I had always felt when I was trying to write a tune [that] I was groping for something I couldn't find, so I decided to start trying to live my life in some different ways...I was drinking a lot and taking a lot of drugs and just writing these confused, morbid, and maudlin sorts of things...All the Big Star records are just me learning how to be a songwriter. I don't think [*Third* is] any more or less confused than the other two—it's just more sickly.

Bud Scoppa: I'm struck by the contrast between Chris' earnestness and striving for shimmering beauty, which are clearly extensions of his work in Big Star, and Alex's delight in deconstruction and sarcasm. I find *Cosmos* far more compelling than Alex's records during that period, although *Third*, considering it as a Chilton record, is fascinating in the depth of its perversity.

Jim Dickinson: Chris was a mimic and I think Alex goes way beyond that. People who say the opposite are just obsessed with the mystery of Big Star.

Bob Mehr: In a weird way, Alex's experience with Chris also colors *Third/Sister Lovers*. Chris' studio style was far more formalized and precise than Alex liked or preferred, probably. The loose quality of *Third*, the chaos of it all, was itself a kind of reaction to his time working with Chris.

Jody Stephens: It was more fun being in the studio with all four of us. On the first two albums, we were well-rehearsed. We had a nice run up to it, especially *#1 Record*.

John Lightman: There are five different bass players on *Third* because they didn't have a steady bassist since I had quit.

Alex Chilton: The first two albums were meticulously planned, but Jim Dickinson showed me you can work with wild abandon and have a good sound, too. Some songs weren't performed well, and I didn't sing them with much conviction or arrange anything special on them either. I hoped Jim would have some advice, which he did, like on "Holocaust." All the wild and crazy stuff was Jim's projects. He has a talent for making subversive music. Anytime anyone had a sort of deep impulse, he'll encourage it. His aesthetic is that "it's better to reign in hell than serve in heaven."

Jim Dickinson: The crazier it was, the more I tried to do it. Possibly we didn't go far enough.

Alex Chilton: ["Holocaust" is] just something I wrote. The music is the same as "Mrs. Lennon," by John and Yoko. I mean, I didn't do that on purpose. I realized it afterwards.

> *Your eyes are almost dead, can't get out of bed*
> *And you can't sleep*
> *You're sitting down to dress, and you're a mess*
> *You look in the mirror*
>
> — ALEX CHILTON, "HOLOCAUST"

Jody Stephens: We would record a song and it would be sweet and pretty, and then Alex would go back and throw the bass out of tune and do something wild and wacky to screw it up...It was Alex kind of working this thing, to the point where he thought it was a true reflection—this is what he was feeling.

Alex Chilton: [Dickinson] just did this crazy conglomeration that was totally confused and then came in there and organized it in the mix. I had never seen anybody do that and it astounded me. I learned more about music in fifteen minutes watching him do that than I learned all the rest of my life.

Jim Dickinson: Maybe I was a little brutal in recording some of it, but the psychodynamic of a record had become important to me by then.

Alex Chilton: Dickinson's a genius, man. That was a turning point in my musical existence.

Jody Stephens: I was grateful to have Jim Dickinson producing. He was a good positive force and John Fry as well. He always instilled confidence. It was going to work out because Fry was behind the board.

Jim Dickinson: People have accused me of indulging Alex on *Third*, but I don't think I indulged him enough. He didn't have any bad ideas and we were able to get consistent performances out of him. I'll never forget the first day. Alex just plugged into this old amp and turned everything up the whole way. There's John in his suit and tie, and he just took the mic in front of the amp and moved it across the room, fifteen feet away—where no one would have put the microphone in 1974. That's the sound...It's not a record, it is a group of recordings.

Alex Chilton: ["Jesus Christ"] was fairly diabolically planned out. I just thought I would like to do a Christmas song, so I copied the lyrics out of several different hymns. I went through a hymn book and picked out several phrases and threw all those into the verses. I couldn't think of anything more clever to say for the hook line than what it says.

No matter how slapdash Alex claims the songwriting process was during Third, *it made a lasting impact. Twenty years later, both Jeff Buckley and This Mortal Coil covered "Kanga Roo," a surreal pop gem born from an early-morning session.*

Lesa Aldridge Hoehn: Alex and I would be there alone at 3 a.m. He let me engineer "Kanga Roo."

Alex Chilton: What's cool about ["Kanga Roo"] is the way it's performed. The first verse of the song is good, but starting at the second verse, it lays a couple of eggs. The way the music sounds on that is truly revolutionary.

Lesa Aldridge Hoehn: He taught me how to use that fat, two-inch tape on the reel-to-reel. It was a fun and sweet night. We spent so much time at Ardent. Everybody still had keys. We weren't necessarily three sheets to the wind, because I remember some of it. It was our after-hours hangout place. It was a creative place to be. There were also not-so-good times in there. When Alex took me in there to sing "Till the End of the Day," Alex told me Fry said he liked it so much that Fry mixed my take himself. In terms of insecurity, that upset him. That was hard for Alex. Rather than being happy for me, or wanting to share, it turned into a competition.

John Lightman: They would have a fight and Alex would go and erase all the tracks she'd sung on.

Jody Stephens: They had some blow-ups. Lesa Aldridge rammed into John Fry's car. Lesa was in her car; Alex was driving John's Mercedes. It was total disregard for anyone else.

Alex Chilton: [One night at Ardent] we were drunk and had a fight. She threw a drink at me and there was gin and tonic in the faders. I was getting very destructive in a lot of ways then, which I was trying to capture on record. I loved the sound of a microphone falling down, things like that.

Jim Dickinson: Alex's big complaint was that he was excluded from the mix, which he was.

Adam Hill: Jim Dickinson described Fry mixing *Third* as Fry throwing paint around a canvas. It didn't matter if it was sheer distortion or a beautiful string section, Fry treated them all on their own merits and made it work.

Steve Rhea: I see *Third* as a total work of art, the ultimate sound textures without any of the normal conventions of having verses and choruses following any constructed shape.

Richard Rosebrough: I liked *Radio City* and thought *#1 Record* had more sparkle to it. But most of my friends, people who were not involved with it, they talk about *Third* as if they were talking about *Pet Sounds* or something. It means everything to them. It was a life-changing record for them.

David Bell: [Chris and I] heard a bootleg of the *Third* album in London. Both of us thought Alex had gone over the cliff into a land of drugs.

Chris Bell: Alex [had] gotten into some decadent stuff, sort of socially and musically. His musical influences [leaned] toward Lou Reed and the Velvet Underground.

Adam Hill: Chris was not a guy who just wings shit and then never revisits it again. That's what Alex was doing during *Third*. You could see how Chris thought Alex was off on a Lou Reed tangent.

John Hampton — Drummer, Baker Street Regulars, Ardent Studios engineer: I met Alex when he was not in a good period. I didn't care for Alex much back in the day, God rest his soul. He was not a happy camper and he was into making everyone else not happy, as well.

Tommie Dunavant: There were several times I was around Alex and he was a little off the wall. In fact, he kind of scared me a little, coming from a small town. Chris never scared me.

Ken Woodley: In the studio, Alex was kind of like working with an alien. Chris was kind of like working with a person. I don't have anything against Alex, he was just eccentric.

Jody Stephens: I hung in there just to get a little more studio experience. There were some pretty dark moments that are still hard for me to process.

Greg Reding: I heard Alex cut himself and bled all over the console at Ardent and, at some point, somebody else took a leak in the corner of the control room. My God, Alex Chilton, that guy didn't give a flying rat's ass about a career. It didn't matter to him one way or the other. I was thinking, "You little shit! You came out of the gate with the record of the year. You're a fucking legend."

Jim Dickinson: I know that last Big Star record was hard for John Fry. He said to me towards the end, "You have to mix what you've got, I can't take this anymore. It hurts too much." He said Alex was treating him like real shit.

John Fry: Chilton was having issues, and the record was made under difficult circumstances. The thing that got my goat most was one day when they had some homeless guy in the studio, staggering around, about three sheets to the wind. They had headphones on him, overdubbing something. I said, "If this is what we're going to be recording, don't ask me to do it. Tell me when you're done, and I'll mix it."

Jody Stephens: We did a live broadcast in Memphis. Alex had brought his [friends] along, people he could spit on and they'd scream for more. I just got sick of it. He was quite an ogre. I saw him one night and it was as if he was reverting to a Neanderthal man: His shoulders were hunched, I could imagine slobber coming out of his mouth. One minute he was mild-mannered and the next he'd grow fangs. He didn't have a smack habit, no habit of any sort, but he was really into downs.

Alex Chilton: Heroin? Oh no, nothing like that, no drugs as good as that. I took whatever pills were around at the time, things like Valium and Seconal, Demerol, and Mandies. Whatever was there, I drank it or took it.

Holliday Aldridge: One night, Jody was meeting me at a party at Marcia Clifton's house. I had taken a downer of some sort that Bill Eggleston gave me when I got there. By the time Jody showed up, I was just loopy. I was getting sleepy and Marcia said, "Oh, take a shower, it'll make you feel better." When Jody walked in, I was coming down the stairs in this dress. I arrived in jeans, but Marcia had given me a dress to wear. I go walking down the stairs and start thinking, "Oh, I forgot to take off my underwear when I took that shower." My underwear was soaking wet. Jody was not happy and left the relationship shortly after. I don't blame him. Jody is one of the sweetest people I've ever met. I saw him ten years ago and said, "What was I thinking?" I should have just married him and lived happily ever after. But he was a bit of a fuddy-duddy and I needed to have fun in the '80s. By the time the '80s were finished, he was happily married to his wife, Diana.

Despite the chaos surrounding them, Third *was completed after Dickinson and Fry signed off on a final mix featuring fourteen tracks. In February 1975, Ardent pressed up 200-300 promotional copies and distributed the LPs to A&R reps and record executives across the country.*

Jody Stephens: There was a clear point [when *Third*] was finished. We had nineteen songs—that was enough. There wasn't a clear point when it was released. We had an initial white-label pressing we sent out to record companies.

John Fry: We made test pressings of *Third* for the purpose of shopping it. Really, to avoid carrying tapes around and make it look a little more like a release.

Alex Chilton: Ardent had ceased to function as a real record company and so they were trying to sell it to other record companies. They were trying to sell the third Big Star record, or whatever you want to call it, to a record company, which wasn't easy.

Jim Dickinson: Everybody knew Stax was going out of business. We were [initially] making [*Third*] for Stax. Nobody wanted Stax to put it out because their records were getting lost, so we figured if we kept working on the record, Stax would go out of business and then we would own it, which is what happened. But then we owned it, and nobody wanted it.

John Fry: Stax was gone then, and we owned the masters, so we just vigorously shopped that to every label in the country and they just did not know what to make of it. We would go to New York, go to Los Angeles and sit in these people's offices while they looked bewildered as they listened to the music.

Alex Chilton: I think Jerry Wexler said, "This record makes me very uncomfortable." They got no positive responses from that.

Jody Stephens: John tried to sell this melodrama to several labels but there were no takers. It was too real.

Jim Dickinson: We couldn't sell it because nobody wanted it...People shut the door in my face.

For the moment, Third *was shelved. Big Star unceremoniously disbanded. The band wouldn't reform until 1993, when Alex and Jody were joined by guitarist Jon Auer and bassist Ken Stringfellow of the Posies. The melodramatic love saga of Alex and Lesa lived on for a few more tumultuous years. By 1978, Lesa (guitar, vocals) was busy gigging and recording with the Klitz alongside bassist Amy Gassner, Gail Elise Clifton (vocals, keys), and drummer Marcia Clifton.*

Lesa Aldridge Hoehn: Alex and I never actually broke up. I left Memphis when I was twenty-five in 1980. I left because it got too hard—too much drinking. I was ready to get married and settle down. I was tired of the whole scene. It was an unhealthy environment with Alex, and I was starting to grow up. My mother had come back from living in Bangkok, which is why Alex wrote that song "Bangkok." She came back to the United States and I decided to move in with my mom and brothers. I didn't realize I was leaving Alex at that time, but I guess I was.

Many years later, in 2010, just after Alex had passed away, I sang two songs at the Shell in Memphis for an Alex tribute show. The night before, we were at Ardent rehearsing and I heard John Fry's unmistakable voice pick up the phone in the front office. I thought I needed to apologize to John Fry, because I was a jerk at times and it sometimes affected him. I went in there and reintroduced myself. We shook hands. I said, "John, I want to apologize for having been a jackass back in the day." He looked at me, thought for a second, and said, "You know, we were all jackasses back then." I loved him for that. It was nice closure.

In 1975, former Jynx member Bill Cunningham reunited with Chris Bell and arranged the string section for "You and Your Sister" at Ardent Studios.

COURTESY OF BILL CUNNINGHAM

Big Star promotional shot, 1974 (L to R): John Lightman, Jody Stephens, and Alex Chilton.

PHOTO BY CAROLE MANNING

ACT FOUR

THERE WAS A LIGHT

Chris Bell in David Bell's Volkswagen at Stonehenge.

PHOTO BY DAVID BELL

CHAPTER 18

BACK TO ARDENT — LOOKING FORWARD: 1975

By 1975, Big Star was dead in the water, but Chris remained optimistic about their small but loyal fanbase across the pond, and he hoped to piggyback off that grassroots buzz. But first, he had work to do at home. Since he returned from Europe in the fall of '74, his artistic confidence was boosted, and he was eager to get his growing stockpile of tapes to A&R reps. For the time being, he'd resumed living in his upstairs bedroom at his parents' Germantown home. With his record still in the works, Chris decided to strengthen his solo catalog and self-engineer a few new songs at Ardent Studios. With no proper backing band in place, he called in favors from his ex-Big Star mates Jody and Alex. The once awkward tensions had diminished and even Andy Hummel, who'd just retired from music, agreed to lend Chris a hand.

Richard Rosebrough: When Chris was back in Memphis, we worked together some more. He was still estranged a bit, but he started going to Ardent in the middle of the night.

David Bell: Chris did have a bitter taste in his mouth as far as Ardent goes. He felt it was Ardent's fault that everything fell apart and signing to Stax was a stupid idea, that it should have been released with a different label. But he got past it and started to record there again.

John Fry: I had no idea what he was doing. Even after Chris returned to Ardent, he didn't talk about what he was doing much. I have no idea why he didn't share all those solo recordings with us. He kept a lot of this to himself.

David Bell: Chris felt Ardent was the past. The base we were working from was Big Star's reputation in England. That was the springboard for trying to get his solo career off the ground.

Richard Rosebrough: I went over to Ardent with Chris sometimes and the two of us would record. He would go in with Ken Woodley and the two of them would record. Sometimes he would put a session together with a whole band's worth of people. Usually, you would find him over there at 2 a.m. with microphones brought into the control room. We would plug headphones in and sit behind the console and record. I even set my drums up in the control room, so I could reach the board.

Adam Hill: These sessions were quick affairs. He didn't sit around getting sounds for four hours and then cut. It was like: Here is the amp, put the mic in front of it, and let's go.

The zenith of this timeframe is Chris' final in-studio collaboration with John Fry, who engineered and mixed the final version of "You and Your Sister," the now classic track featuring Alex Chilton's harmony vocals. Also laid down at Ardent was "There Was A Light," with Jody Stephens on drums and Andy Hummel on bass, and "Fight at the Table," a piano-rocker featuring Jack Holder of the Hot Dogs and Jim Dickinson on keys.

Richard Rosebrough: Chris was using the A Studio a lot. He cut "Fight at the Table" in there. The B Studio was popular at night, so he would go into A and lock the doors. He mixed "You and Your Sister" in there with Fry one day on a whim.

John Fry: The first solo song of Chris' I heard was "You and Your Sister." Chris came in one morning and said, "John, I have this thing. Would you mix it?" I said, "Well, sure." It just so happened I had just spent all this time patching things together and was set up for a mix for somebody else. Everything was all ready, and we started and were done in around forty-five minutes.

Adam Hill: The acoustic guitar sound on "You and Your Sister"—that is the sound Fry taught everybody to get on the Spectra Sonics. John said Chris sheepishly showed up out of the blue. It was typical Chris. He didn't call ahead of time, he just showed up, and it just so happened he was ready for a big-time, full-on client mix.

They say my love for you ain't real
But you don't know how real it feels

All I want to do, is to spend some time with you
So I can hold you, hold you
Your sister says that I'm no good
I'd reassure her if I could

— CHRIS BELL, "YOU AND YOUR SISTER"

Richard Rosebrough: Then Bill Cunningham came back and did some string arrangements on "You and Your Sister" and "Better Save Yourself." Bill had gone to school and got a master's in music. He played concert bass in a big symphony orchestra and knew how to write charts.

Bill Cunningham: I never saw Chris when I was on the road during the Box Tops days. When I got back in town, I was working with the Memphis Symphony Orchestra and was doing sessions for Stax on Isaac Hayes records and things like that, playing upright bass. We were coming out of some session at Ardent with my bass when Chris stopped me in the hallway. He said, "Hey, there are some songs I have been writing and I would like for you to write some string arrangements like George Martin does for the Beatles." I told him, "Chris, I'm not George Martin, I cannot write like him, but I will do what I can." On "You and Your Sister," I played upright bass and conducted the string section. I brought in some friends of mine that I had been working with. After I finished, and the string players were gone, Chris and I went in the booth together to listen back. Chris was telling me, "I bet Alex will come in and sing backup on this." On "Better Save Yourself," I was playing what they call the Col Legno technique, which is using the wood part of the bow as opposed to the string part of the bow. That song had so much going on, I couldn't think of anything to write for it—there was no space. It didn't call for anything, but Chris insisted something else should go there.

I'm off the street, I'm all alone
I just can't think, what I've been doing wrong
I know your mind, he treats you nice
It's suicide
I know, I tried it twice

— Chris Bell, "Better Save Yourself"

Bill Cunningham: He almost didn't seem like the same Chris in some ways. He seemed a lot quieter. It was almost as if he'd been injured emotionally somehow. He wasn't at all like that before. But he was still Chris, it wasn't like a total personality change. The last time I ever saw Chris was when we were listening to the playback of the string session and he was doing a rough mix. I left Memphis in 1975 and started playing in the White House Orchestra for Ford and then for a couple years under President Jimmy Carter.

Jody Stephens: I first heard some of Chris' solo tapes around this time. I played on a few things like "Get Away," "I Got Kinda Lost," and "There Was A Light," but Richard Rosebrough was Chris' primary drummer.

There wasn't much difference from working with Chris in the *#1 Record* days opposed to working with him as a solo artist. He still seemed to have a pretty clear vision of where he wanted to go with his songs. He was still a perfectionist. There were several different versions of "You and Your Sister." There were a couple versions of "Get Away." I played on one and Richard played on the other. He was after just the right guitar sound and melody line, but he was also still looking for just the right delivery in his voice. He would change his voice from time to time. "Though I Know She Lies" doesn't even sound like him.

By mid-'75, Chris had most of his solo album in the can. His tendency to over- work songs with countless overdubs and mixes prevented him from signing off on a final mix.

Chris Morris: The *I Am the Cosmos* album took years to complete, if it was ever really completed.

Van Duren: I spent some time with Chris when he was working on his songs. I showed up to the studio and hung out with him while he was mixing. He mixed extremely loud, louder than you can possibly imag- ine. He was always doing it over and over. My impression was he was trying to get a deal and was going to keep working on it until he did get a deal. He'd go back in and change something, add something, take something away. It was ongoing.

Adam Hill: He kept reworking those solo tracks even after he mixed them with Geoff Emerick. In the case of "Better Save Yourself," after Emerick mixed it, Chris put the stereo mix on two tracks of two-inch, sixteen-track tape and then overdubbed the harmony and an acous- tic guitar.

Barney Hoskyns: *#1 Record* was more polished and crystalline, thanks mainly to John Fry. *Cosmos* is more homemade and indie-sounding, notwithstanding the input from Geoff Emerick. It's closer to early dB's or Let's Active, both of whom were obviously and massively influenced by Bell.

Adam Hill: *#1 Record* had Fry wrapping it all up in a nice package. It's clean, bright and cool. Listen to "You and Your Sister," it sounds sparkly, like *#1 Record*, because John Fry mixed it. Beyond that, a lot of Chris' solo recordings are cloudy. Overall, some of the guitar sounds are pretty gnarly. Not only on the Shoe tracks, even some of the songs he cut himself at Ardent. Everything is fairly indistinct, but when you listen to "Look Up" or "There Was A Light," it was obviously cut at Ardent— especially "Look Up" because it has Ardent's Mellotron. "I Am the Cos- mos" was cut at Shoe, which was a homemade board with no EQ. They cut it on an old piece of tape on a machine that probably wasn't aligned. That's why "Cosmos" is so swirly and cloudy—there's no definition in the recording process.

Chris Morris: His solo album comes from an exceptionally dark place. The comparisons to Nick Drake's *Pink Moon* are extremely apropos. Even in songs that seem to be upbeat and talking about spirituality, he's questioning himself. There is nothing mysterious about what's going on in those songs, or the ones he fronted on *#1 Record*. He's talking about his own personal turmoil. He talks about fights and depression. He's reaching out for God, for Christ, but it's not working for him. It's all on the surface and that's why it's such a flabbergasting record. It's like he's in the room with you. At the same time, the record is methodically crafted. There are beautiful guitar solos and the songs are elegantly written. It's not weird spontaneity. It's all meticulous.

Randall Lyon — Memphis musician, scenester: Chris had the modern guitar sound. He had intuition of the acoustical space in recording. He heard all that stuff that surrounds the sound and gives it a three-dimensional quality. Like "Make a Scene," you'd hear that shit and it would sound like a Beatles song.

Chris Morris: The Beatles were always present in the music, in both Big Star and Chris Bell, especially Chris Bell—it sounds like George Harrison is playing. The tone, the way the solos are constructed. He absorbed those influences completely, but it's not like he's miming it. He made them his own.

Adam Hill: The Beatles influence comes through in Bell's harmonies. That's part of it. It's the little production touches more than it is the straight songwriting. It's more of the studio things than a chord change. Like putting the strings on "You and Your Sister"—that's "Yesterday." Putting the phaser on "Cosmos"—that's "Lucy in the Sky with Diamonds." Even with the Jynx recordings, it was garage rock, but it's early British-rock influenced. Chris had a cat named Prudence. It seeped into everything.

Bob Mehr: I'm not entirely sure power pop is an apt description for Chris' music per se. I don't think Chris was trying to make what we consider power pop. His music, particularly after *#1 Record*, had a depth and majesty, and a reach, both spiritual and philosophical, that was a lot more serious than typical power pop.

Adam Hill: Whether it's Chris Bell, Badfinger, or the Raspberries, the term power pop diminishes the work. It's just good songwriting.

Ric Menck: "I Don't Know" and "Make A Scene" are probably my favorite Chris Bell rockers. To me, those songs are the definition of power pop.

Mark Deming: Calling Bell's body of work power pop is a little confining, especially since I hear as much hard rock in tunes like "Better Save Yourself" and "Get Away." Power pop is upbeat and sunny, it gives people the wrong idea of what to expect. While "singer-songwriter" tends to give people an image of someone like James Taylor, at face value it gives a more accurate idea of what to expect from Bell's music, especially given the confessional nature of his lyrics, which often wrestle with powerful themes. Your average power pop guy is not going to cop to attempting suicide, especially more than once, like Chris does on "Better Save Yourself."

Chris Bell poses inside the London flat he shared with his brother David in 1975.

CHAPTER 19

LONDON — BERLIN: 1975

Over the 1974 holiday season in Germantown, the Bell brothers resumed discussions of launching Chris' music career and seeking a recording contract. The timing was good. David allowed the lease on his apartment in Italy to expire, freeing him up to move wherever the music required. By early 1975, David also cashed out his share of a lucrative real estate business, giving him a financial cushion for future adventures. The brothers booked flights out of Memphis with Chris' tapes in hand. Their first stop, on February 26, was the sandy beaches of St. Martin. There, for a few weeks, they even considered looking into music opportunities on the island, especially since they had access to their family's vacation home. While the Bells had enjoyed a timeshare condo on the island throughout the early '70s, by 1974 Vernon Bell had built a three-bedroom, one-story beach house with a beautiful view.

Cindy Bell Coleman: Our parents had shopped around and found the beach property. They ended up buying a lot-and-a-half down there. Our father got a good deal on it because part of the beach had a huge, old shipwreck on it. That part of the beach was not preferable to most people, but it was going to be at the end of the lot. It didn't block our view, so we didn't care. Eventually, a hurricane blew in and got rid of it.

David Bell: Chris loved going there. When we were first there it was a lot more primitive than what it's become now. It was a simple open house with sliding glass doors, but it had a great feature of a covered porch on the sea side of the house. It was on the beach, Long Bay in St. Martin. You got beach sounds and the whole nine yards. We would go out and sightsee but being right there on the beach with the spectacular view, it was pleasant to just be at the house. There was always a nice breeze.

Cindy Bell Coleman: Everything opened up, so the windows were open most of the time. It was right on the water, so you'd just run ceiling fans and that's where you got your air circulation. The front was a large, open-air room, then there was the master bedroom with a bath and two other bedrooms with a bath. Of course, there was a kitchen and dining area.

David Bell: The house was on what's called the Lowlands. There is a tiny part of the Dutch side that's in the Lowlands, but for the most part that's the French side. Not too far away were restaurants. Shopping was a big deal because you had duty-free shopping there. One day, Chris took me out on a little Sunfish boat; I was scared to death. It was almost akin to when he took me up in a little airplane and I thought, "My little brother can't do this. We're going to crash!" I thought we were going to get attacked by sharks because we were so far out. But being the clever thing he was, he knew how to sail.

Cindy Bell Coleman: Chris was also getting more into painting. He had a bunch of his own paintings in his room at home, but he also did some oil paintings for our mother and they were hung at the St. Martin house. "Water Lilies" was my favorite of his.

During their February vacation, the Bell brothers initially stayed at the family's beach house, but then headed to a rental in Grand Case, a small village on the French side of the island. It was there they both agreed to give up on the island and fully commit to an extended stay in London. "We were talking about different ventures that we might get into on the island," David recalled. "But in the end decided that since we had such a good reception in England, our best chances lay there with his music." On April 13, 1975 the Bells made the thirty-minute flight to Antigua, where they picked up a non-stop to London. The next day, they touched down at London Heathrow and checked in for a five-week stay at the Senator Hotel on Westbourne Terrace in London. "I don't know what's going to happen yet in London," a cautiously optimistic Chris told a rock journalist shortly after they arrived. "I would like to meet some other musicians." The move to England was a dream come true for the twenty-four-year-old, and on top of that, his continued dedication to Christianity had inspired him to curb his substance-abuse problems. Things were looking up.

David Bell: For Chris to be in England, period, was like being in a movie for him.

Chris Bell: I've wanted to live in England for ten years, at least, and I'm half English anyway. I think I'm drawn halfway to England and halfway to the States.

David Bell: It was a fun trip, but this wasn't just a visit. We went there with the intention of trying to get a record deal, as the previous October proved to be something of an inspiration. We met some journalists and other music industry people and felt England would be a good shot for shopping tapes.

Chris Bell: The markets in France and Britain are more receptive than the States. The United States is pretty closed. If you play R&B or soul and are good and tight, and maybe sound like the Average White Band, then you might get a contract. But, if you're different, they tend to be a bit wary of you. The people we encountered in France had heard Big Star and seemed perceptive about what was coming out of Memphis with Don Nix and Jim Dickinson. At Strawberry, we would pick up magazines and read articles about bands you would never hear about in the States, people I know from Memphis, Texas, and Tulsa. I was impressed. They are receptive to new sounds.

Max Bell — British rock critic, journalist: At this time, Big Star were already about the biggest cult group ever, but that didn't mean they ever sold fuck-all albums. I bought their records when they came out, but to be fair, apart from me and the guy who ran Harlequin Record Shop, not many others did.

Chris Bell: I would like to do some gigs here and throughout Europe, in the United States, also. The people who played on my album with me, Ken and Richard, are pretty keen on Europe. Richard was here last time working with me and would love to do gigs. It's just a matter of getting it together. I miss performing live a great deal. It's one reason I don't go to hear a lot of bands play, because you start to ache for the stage when you're just sitting out there.

After the Bell brothers settled into their hotel, the first order of business, from April 21 to 23 and on April 28, was to return to AIR Studios in Oxford Circus where Chris continued to mix "I Am the Cosmos," "Make a Scene," "You and Your Sister" and "Better Save Yourself." Also mixed was the freshly recorded "Look Up," an homage to the power of Christianity.

David Bell: Chris was still wanting to work on different tracks, so we arranged more time to mix with Geoff Emerick at AIR. For a few weeks, while he was doing that, we stayed in London at the Senator Hotel, a funky little hotel near Paddington. For transportation, at first, we were Tubing it in the London Underground. But then I got a letter from my former real estate partner in Italy saying I needed to come back and sign some papers that hadn't been signed for the dissolution of my part in the company. As sort of a parting bonus, I was gifted an older Volkswagen, a little company car. I drove that Volkswagen back to London. After we had wheels, we drove out to

Salisbury Lane and saw Stonehenge; this is back when you could still go up to the stones and touch them. Through it all, Chris was much happier and more positive. He was all business. He was in a situation that was totally conducive to not being depressed. His mood was 100 percent improved. There was a prospect on the horizon, however dim it was. This was also on the heels of his spiritual awakening with Earl Smith down in Destin, Florida. That religious conversion informed the rest of his life.

John Fry: He had a deep faith in Christ as Lord and Savior.

Linda Schaeffer Yarman: We talked about his drug problems, but after he became a Christian, my understanding was he was pretty much off drugs. He may have still smoked pot, that's what he told me. If he was doing anything else, he was hiding it.

Tommy Hoehn: The perception of a lot of people that had known Chris prior was that he'd replaced drug use with Christianity. Perhaps that was the case. I know he believed that he had been healed from drug abuse.

David Bell: From that point on, he smoked a little bit, but I never worried about hard drugs. I feel certain that was not a part of his life anymore. He even quit smoking cigarettes around this time. He quit cigarettes before I did. He'd poke fun about it. He'd tell me, "It smells like old farts in this car. It's terrible."

Linda Schaeffer Yarman: A misconception of Chris is that he was just a tragic figure grasping at success but never got it, or that he couldn't control his demons. I didn't see that. I saw that Chris was successful emotionally and wanting to go the solo route. From what he shared with me, he was at peace.

By May 19, the Bells relocated to a more spacious, but still small, basement flat near Queensway at 28 Kildare Terrace in London. The rental, where they stayed for the next four months, had French doors leading to a garden where David shot promotional photos of Chris. He later recalled that Chris "looked like Jimi Hendrix," thanks to his long, curly locks, colorful scarves, and rock 'n' roll threads. Back in Memphis, Chris often shopped at Chelsea Ltd., a hip clothing boutique in Overton Square that specialized in colorful British apparel.

Andy Hummel: As he got out of Big Star, Chris became more style-conscious and let loose a little bit. For a while he even had his afro.

Richard Rosebrough: He always had just the right shirt, boots, hat and coat.

Cindy Bell Coleman: Chris always had curly hair, but I used to iron his hair for him. Of course, when his hair was shorter, it didn't show as much. Then he grew it out into that horrible afro thing. I told him, "That's terrible." I loved him with his short hair and mustache.

Bob Schiffer: Chris' big thing was wearing British clothes. There was no better dresser. If any of the Big Star guys had style, it was him.

David Bell: Living with Chris was alternatingly fun and maddening. He was constantly making us late to places but was always interesting to be around. I learned as much from him as anyone else in my life. He was very much a reader. He had a lot of religious books sitting around, some esoteric religious books that were not the normal sort of thing you'd find on a Sunday school list. He read a book by a Chinese man about his Christian life in China. He would also read old Greek and Roman literature. But we would go out on the town some, too. We bought tickets to a musical called *John, Paul, George, Ringo...and Bert*. It was a retrospective of Beatles songs. Back then, theatre in London was still affordable in—'75 you could go for like five pounds. But for the most part, Chris' mind was on music. He even met some musician friends, too. He'd meet up with them and was also writing new songs on his Gibson Sunburst acoustic.

Chris Bell: I'm trying to get a label now because my brother's been financing me here and he's not a millionaire. We're trying to get a record company to back me just off what I can play for them, so I can go in and finish the tracks...I've got about an album's worth of tracks down on sixteen-track masters. I've got about eight mixes, but only three or four that I would consider final mixes. I've got about six tracks that need overdubbing and mixing.

David Bell: My typical day was trying to get contacts and talking to people on the phone, trying to set up meetings with A&R guys, shopping tapes and trying to interest people. You're a salesman, in essence. All the press and other contacts came through our friend John Tobler, who we met over there. He introduced us to all sorts of people. John was a press officer with Columbia Records. Through him, we obtained lists of A&R men at virtually every record company in England.

The well-connected John Tobler, who befriended the Bells during their time in London, also facilitated some press for Chris, who was interviewed by a few British rock magazines in 1975, including New Musical Express, Dark Star, Fat Angel, *and the* Omaha Rainbow. *They are the only known interviews with Chris.*

John Tobler — Record executive, CBS Records, journalist: I was working for CBS Records as press officer, but I was also an ex-journalist, so I knew many of the notable British writers of the time, like Nick Kent, Charles Shaar Murray, Richard Williams, and Allan Jones. It was Max Bell, from *NME* at the time, who suggested the Bell brothers come to see me due to my work on *ZigZag*, a respected magazine covering American music.

David Bell: Chris did a lunchtime interview with Max Bell of *NME*. There were introductions to various press people who had been Big Star fans. They helped fan the flames of interest.

Max Bell: I knew Chris during an important and intense period. He was obviously a mass of contradictions. He was at ease around me and my wife in London. We got on like a house on fire. He liked me because I had written about Big Star, but also because I interviewed Alex and I didn't just stand there and take Alex's mood-swinging bullshit. By the way, I loved Alex too. I spent good time with him. His attitude towards me was: He knew I worshipped the ground he walked on, but I was feisty. To know Chilton at all during the period he hung out around the Camden Town clubs, you had to be au fait with his moods. I talked to Alex at length many times. He could get cross, but he would come back. Chris wasn't like that, and when I told Chris what Alex was like, it was hardly news to him.

John Tobler: I suppose I saw the Bells about ten times. I wasn't working with them, but merely made friends with them as London is a big and sometimes difficult place. They first came to meet me at CBS and later to my house, which was in Surrey, about thirty miles southwest of London. My first wife was heavily into religion at that time and she tried, with some success, to involve them in talks of religion. David Bell was far more self-confident than Chris, who always seemed quiet and rather uncertain. David was much worldlier than Chris. I do remember they referred to Alex Chilton as "Bobby Box Top."

Max Bell: Chris' brother was a fantastic guy. He was so earnest about Chris' genius. Not sure if that was the right zeitgeist for those two, but Chris was desperate for a break.

David Bell: We weren't getting bites left, right, and center from record companies, but we were happy just to be there—but there was down time, for sure. Chris would bake a lot, especially bread. We ate carbs, carbs, and more carbs and then watched a fair amount of television. He was first getting into tennis around then, so that summer it was non-stop Wimbledon. He started playing tennis right after he moved back

Chris in Europe and (above) holding his beloved copy of *The Dead Sea Scrolls*, 1975.

PHOTOS ON 286-287 BY DAVID BELL

to Memphis in the fall. But we had a few leads going. We were talking to Charisma Records. Jerry Gilbert at Charisma was very helpful. Also, Phillips and Decca. Chrysalis Records was another promising lead.

Chris Bell: When I was in L.A. a year back, I had met Andrew Lauder from United Artists because Marty Cerf had spoken to him about some of my tapes he'd had. Andrew was kind of anxious to do something, so it's beginning to look like I may do something with UA. When I was in London, I talked to Andrew and he seemed pretty excited about doing a single release on one of my tunes called "I Am the Cosmos" that I did in Memphis.

David Bell: We also chatted with Rocket Records, Elton John's label at the time. The A&R guy at Rocket kept telling me, "I want to get this to Gus Dudgeon." He'd been Elton John's producer; he did all the huge hits. To this day, I don't know if Dudgeon ever heard it or not, but Chris was at least meeting a lot of musicians over there. He had started playing a few gigs and was getting contacts with other musicians and people in the business.

Jim Lord — American singer-songwriter, solo: My manager Peter Holdforth introduced me to Chris at CBS Records in April 1975. I was on that label at the time. He said, "Here's an American guy you should know." My manager was British, so I was doing a tour in Britain he'd set up for me. I met Chris somewhere in the middle of it. We were both solo guys and hit it off well. We were intertwined at the time with that genre, with that folk scene, which was enormous in England back in the '70s. I was staying with Peter at his flat in Fulham and Chris would come by a lot to do some jamming. We also hung around all the pubs in London. We would go have a couple pints, it was a part of that culture. We also had some hashish because it was around. We weren't doing anything heavier, it was fairly innocuous. We were more into the music.

Through his new friends, Chris booked some modest paying solo performances at folk clubs across London, playing a mixture of originals and cover songs. He became close friends with Jim Lord, and even spent nights hanging out at Peter Holdforth's house in Fulham while David was out of town.

Peter Holdforth — English concert promoter, Jim Lord's manager: I had made a few contacts while running folk clubs in Portsmouth and post-1974 in London, and Jim Lord thought they might be useful to Chris, who was wanting to play more shows. Around this time, John Tobler at CBS agreed to produce a tape for Jim Lord at AIR Studios, so Jim invited Chris to provide electric backing at the session.

Jim Lord: Together, we did some recording on two-inch tape. I don't know where the hell the tapes are, but we recorded a couple of my tunes. Chris played second guitar on it. He was a great player, talented kid. If we had a little more time in London, we would have put together an acoustic band. Our personalities and music were compatible.

Peter Holdforth: On the strength of what appeared on the tape, Chris was invited to provide electric backing for Jim at a gig he did at the Cabbage Patch, [promoter] Theo Johnson's club in Twickenham.

Jim Lord: He played guitar for me a couple times, one night it was at the Den of Folk in Gosport, which is near Portsmouth.

Peter Holdforth: Chris did come down to Portsmouth with us once. He was quiet, almost withdrawn, but he came alive in smaller groups and that's when you'd witness his great sense of humor. Several of our women friends were very taken with Chris. When I played them *#1 Record*, they couldn't believe a shy, retiring young man like Chris contributed to a sound like that. Chris was meeting all sorts of musicians, like the Scottish singer-songwriter Dave Keir who taught him how to play jigs and reels.

Thanks to Peter, Chris also shared a stage with folk musician Tim Hardin, best known for writing "Reason to Believe" and "If I Were A Carpenter." Sadly, at the May 21, 1975 concert, the renowned American troubadour was in the clutches of a heroin addiction—one that took his life five years later.

Peter Holdforth: Chris was backing Jim Lord when he supported Tim Hardin at the Centre Hotel in Portsmouth. This concert was plagued with difficulties. The auditorium was under half-full, leaving me short of income. Tim Hardin also turned in a sub-standard performance that night. He rambled on instead of singing and even forgot the words of "Reason to Believe." He never did get paid his full fee, not that he deserved it.

Jim Lord: I sang "Reason to Believe" with Tim. I sang lead and he sang harmony. Chris was playing guitar. It was a kind of great, twisted-around version.

Peter Holdforth: At least Jim and Chris were well received at the show. I particularly recall Chris' inventive lead breaks on Jim's songs "City's Bribe" and "The Bowery." A week or so after that show, Jim went back to the United States, but I kept in touch with the Bells. Outside of his performances, we would spend Tuesday nights at the Chelsea Drug Store, the music bar on King's Road. After one of these evenings, we went back to Chris and David's flat to watch a football match. The wine flowed, and I spent the night on their sofa. The next morning, I was paying the price for my previous night's excesses, and Chris prayed to the Lord to relieve my hangover.

By May, Peter launched his own weekly folk night at the Half Moon in Putney. Aside from folkies, the popular London venue had previously hosted rock royalty like the Who, the Yardbirds and the Rolling Stones. Peter's weekly songwriter-focused series, which Chris played from May 7 until the third week of July 1975, introduced him to many of the local folk heroes.

Peter Holdforth: I ran the Half Moon folk shows in Putney with Pete Gladdis, a friend from Portsmouth who worked for the Ministry of Defence. Chris did a half hour or so depending on how many musicians we had on any given night. He was there whenever he was available and generally Chris kept Wednesday nights free.

David Bell: Chris was a little scared at first, had some stage fright. When you have three other people with you on stage, it's one thing. When it's just you and your guitar, it's another kettle of fish.

Peter Holdforth: The Half Moon was a regular haunt of Ralph McTell, who lived nearby. Bert Jansch was there a lot and would come in to listen to Chris. There was a poster featuring Bert's *L.A. Turnaround* album on the wall and he'd lean next to it with a pint of Guinness in his hand with a roll-up hanging out of his mouth. People coming through the door would do a double take. When Chris played, he used his Gibson Sunburst and performed his own songs, like "You and Your Sister," but mixed in covers of America's "Sister Golden Hair" and "Lonely People." He went over well.

David Bell: He played some Big Star songs, like Andy's "Way Out West." I never heard him do "Cosmos" on stage. He'd do "You and Your Sister," "Look Up" and "Better Save Yourself." There were some covers, too. Larry Norman, who was a Christian artist, had a song called "U.F.O." and he would cover that. Joni Mitchell's "River" was another; he loved that song.

After he gained some traction in the folk circuit, Chris soon landed another slot at the Crypt Folk Club, a popular series held in the crypt at the historic St. Martin-in-the-Fields in Westminster.

Peter Holdforth: The gigs worked out well for Chris. He picked up several bookings on the back of these appearances, including one at the Cabbage Patch. And while I handled Wednesday nights at the Half Moon, Friday nights were quite lively and run by a bubbly Scot named Bill Knox. Chris played there regularly, too. At those Friday shows, there was a recurring headlining act with a singer named Declan Mac-Manus, who soon went solo and changed his name to Elvis Costello.

David Bell: Once Chris started getting more gigs for a little bit of money, we both felt better about it. Through other musicians, and various contacts like Theo Johnson, who had a booking agency, we would find out about clubs where you could get a gig on a weekend or maybe a Tuesday night. He was happy doing it. Nobody was forcing him. Later, some music writer wrote something like, "It's a pity Chris was playing those places because A&R hadn't been in folk pubs for years." That was never the point. We weren't thinking somebody was going to walk in the door and discover Chris. It was more just to be a journeyman musician. It was just him and acoustic guitar.

Three months into the London excursion, on July 21, Chris flew back to Memphis for a six-week homecoming. The trip home was productive thanks to further sessions at Ardent Studios and icebreaking conversations about a potential Big Star reunion. After Chris witnessed firsthand enthusiasm from British rock journalists, he figured a U.K. Big Star concert would cause a media buzz. Yet Chris was still hesitant about working under the Ardent umbrella. In 1975, he told a journalist: "There are chances of Big Star working together again, but I would say the chances would be enhanced if Alex could divorce himself from Ardent Studios. In a way, I sort of resented what they did and didn't really see going back to that after I had seen what happened with Radio City. But Alex is still pretty well hung up with Ardent because of his contract. It keeps money coming into him, I guess, and he feels fairly secure."

David Bell: Chris returned to Memphis from late July to early September, during which he managed some studio time. He talked to Jody Stephens and Ken Woodley about coming to London to tour as Big Star.

Ken Woodley: We talked about it, but I only had fifty cents to my name, so it was only talk. He would ask me about it from time to time. We both wanted to leave town and play music. Staying in Memphis didn't seem to be great for Chris. If he'd been out on the road playing, he would've been a different person.

David Bell: He also contacted Alex Chilton to discuss fixing Alex's latest album, [he was recording *Bach's Bottom* with producer Jon Tiven] and even the possibility of them working together again.

For a short time, Chris' reunion hopes remained cautiously high. "If Big Star could overcome some personal difficulties, if we could get it together, I know we could do something very well," he told a British music writer. Alex, on the other hand, wasn't as eager to revisit the past.

Alex Chilton: I don't know whether he wanted to work together or not. I don't remember that being the case. I mean, musicians get together to do things all the time, on all sorts of bases. I personally had no intentions of ever getting together in a band with anybody again, pretty much.

David Bell: He met with Alex a couple times and realized there was no way it was going to happen.

The Big Star reunion, at least for Alex, wasn't viable, but Chris and Jody agreed to keep the plan on the table and scout for a replacement for Alex.

Bernie Kugel — Publisher, *Big Star* fanzine: Chilton couldn't see Big Star coming back in any way. When you talked to him about working with Chris or any of the other Big Star guys, it was just kind of a negative thing. He was like, "Oh, you and a hundred people in New York who go to CBGB bought the albums, and all you fanzine guys bought the albums, but I never made any money off it. Why should I care about it?" He was negative about the whole Big Star thing.

On September 5, 1975 Chris concluded his Memphis trip and returned to Europe with Big Star still on his mind. That same week he wrote a letter to John Fry that detailed his idea of hypothetically replacing Alex with either Keith Sykes or Tommy Hoehn. Neither happened. The letter also brazenly proposed that he and Fry re-record #1 Record from the ground up, so they could retake the rights from Stax and improve the tracks. Fry didn't take him up on the grandiose idea. Regardless of the failed Big Star relaunch, Chris refocused on performing solo gigs across London while David kept pursuing record label leads. However, some of the label reps didn't think Chris' Beatles-influenced pop songs were in step with mid-'70s hits.

Chris Bell: I still listen to the radio sometimes, bands like Bad Company. We were big on Free before Big Star started—we played all their tunes. I listen to a lot of what's happening here now [in 1975], but it seems the Top 40 here is some punk-type music. They seem to go for novelty here. I still enjoy a lot of things I hear, but a lot of it's American. I enjoy Clapton's [*461 Ocean Boulevard* LP]. I haven't heard all of Led Zeppelin's new album [*Physical Graffiti*]. I heard a couple tracks and it seems like they are doing the exact same stuff, which is a disappointment. I was very keen on Sparks when I first saw them.

Drew DeNicola: Chris was playing proto-Beatles and everyone was tired of that. It wasn't cool music to play in '74 and '75. They were turned down over and over by labels. It's just not what they were looking for and it wasn't getting airplay.

David Bell: On top of that, the funds I came out of Italy with were dwindling, and our A&R contacts had grown short.

John Fry: Chris and David made a lot of efforts to develop relationships with labels over there. None of it ever did work out, but some of it did look promising from time to time.

Max Bell: That would never happen today. If Chris Bell turned up today at an independent record company, he would be feted.

David Bell: If everything had worked out fine in '75, he would have been happy to live in England. If there had been some record contract and success in the music business.

Max Bell: Over here, he became a candidate for doomed rock stars. He wasn't one of those. The romanticism that surrounds Chris obfuscates his songwriting abilities. Yeah, the times made it hard for him. Yeah, he never got his dues. Chris was quite naïve, but he was not daft. Those Big Star boys were so brilliant. I guess they loved and hated each other with abandon. Must be problematic to be ahead of your time. For fuck's sake, they were just young musicians.

Chris kept busy writing songs and working a steady calendar of pub gigs across London, but the low pay wasn't enough to live on and the financial pressures worsened by the day.

David Bell: I was his manager and bankroller for that almost-year in England. In some ways, it brought us closer together, but there were times with conflict because things weren't financially panning out. Once or twice there were some arguments. When you're the one footing the bills, you're worried about, "When are we going to start to see some money come in or pan out?" Also, when Chris went back to Memphis for those few weeks, he came back to London and told me our father asked him, "When are you two going to stop all this business, come back home and stop wasting money?" You start feeling the strain and think, "Hell, all we're doing is spending money. I don't know how long this is going to last."

Terry Manning: Chris had a strained relationship with his dad because Vernon was a stern, strong business guy. I don't think his dad ever fully approved of Chris doing music instead of getting into some sort of business career.

Sara Bell: Our father wasn't involved in Chris' music at all, but at the same time I don't think he discouraged him from doing it. I'm sure he

Chris Bell performs an outdoor show on the steps of the Crypt Folk Club, 1975.

PHOTOS BY DAVID BELL

wished he'd go on to a more stable career as he got older, but he didn't put those demands on him.

Richard Rosebrough: His dad sometimes ragged on him. He'd say, "You should get a real job and stop playing guitars and listening to records." On the other hand, his mom, Joan, was generally supportive of anything they wanted to do.

On top of their depleted bank account, when the brothers arrived in Germany for a string of October gigs, things worsened after David's car was burglarized and the two lost $1,500 worth of clothes and other personal items.

David Bell: One lucrative night at a West End casino, fortune smiled and afforded us a trip to Berlin. We had heard from the musicians' grapevine that gigs were to be had for foreigners with guitars. We set out in the Volkswagon Beetle for the first night's stop in Amsterdam. My brother delayed our departure long enough to make us miss the ferry at Dover. As a result, we arrived very late in Amsterdam. The desk clerk at the hotel warned us not to leave anything in the car, as the neighborhood was rather seedy. Exhausted, we both decided to trust the universe and were subsequently robbed of everything in the trunk of the car. I guess I just had a psychological reaction to that. I felt sick as a dog, so they sent for a doctor who came over and gave me a shot. My dear, beloved brother left me sick in bed at the hotel. He went and got on the train and went to Berlin; we had a list of clubs to play there. Chris got on the train and off he went by himself. I told him, "Leave a note for me at American Express and let me know where you are and how to find you." Of course, he didn't do that. Luckily, I had the same list of clubs, so after I felt better, I just went around to all of them. One night, after I had been in Berlin for two days, I found him in the green room of a club, he was about to go on stage. I felt like I had been lost on Mars and suddenly found my long-lost compatriot cosmonaut. By the grace of God, I found him. I could have killed him. There weren't cell phones back then, but there were ways to contact me. He should have left me a note at American Express. He found himself a hotel room at the famous Pension Funk in Berlin, so I joined him there and we stayed for just under two weeks.

For the following ten days in Berlin, Chris played clubs across the city, though the cash guarantees offered by venues were not as lucrative as anticipated.

David Bell: The pub gigs were quite easy to come by, but unfortunately did not command a very large purse. On one of our last nights, we stopped by the largest and best known of the clubs and asked for a spot during the break of the featured artist—some German with a record out whose picture was plastered all over the entrance to the club. The management was quite accommodating, and Chris was given fifteen minutes during the break. He was introduced and came to center stage with three white spotlights shining on him. The superb German audio equipment, together with a talented engineer, produced a short set that should have been recorded for posterity...He was enjoying himself and I was on cloud nine. It sounded so good and so exactly what I wanted him to be experiencing...When Chris was treated like a professional, he rose to the occasion brilliantly.

The Bells had a good time in Berlin, but after a series of low-paying gigs, they checked out of Hotel-Pension Funk and headed back to their London flat at 28 Kildare Terrace. The long drive home included a French detour to the Château d'Hérouville on David's birthday, and bottles of champagne were popped in celebration. On October 26, the brothers arrived in London to some bad news.

David Bell: We lost our flat we had on Kildare Terrace because I didn't ensure a re-upping for another three months while we were gone on the trip to Berlin. That's what cinched it for not being able to renew on that apartment. Next came a series of nights spent at bed and breakfasts. The end of the line was near, but we were not ready to give up just yet. He kept writing some new songs, too. He wrote "Though I Know She Lies" in London. That was in October or November, towards the end of the time we were there. He was always picking up his guitar and working songs over. He wrote one called "I've Got Cancer." It was never recorded. I'm sure the title was just poetic license.

As the end of the year approached, Chris and Jody relit talks of reuniting Big Star in grand fashion. This time, his promoter friend Peter Holdforth devised ideas along with the Bells.

David Bell: In the late summer, toward the fall of 1975, Chris started talking to a couple different people and looking at venues for a Big Star reunion, with or without Alex.

Peter Holdforth: After my Half Moon [folk series] stopped in August, we only saw each other once after that, although we kept in touch on the phone. Our last meeting was in November 1975. We were discussing renting Hammersmith Town Hall, a 1,000-seat auditorium in West London, as a venue to launch a reformed Big Star in London. The idea was to have an audience consisting of music journalists, record companies and television staff. We were sitting on the stage in the assembly hall at Hammersmith when David asked Chris how many of the band members could be persuaded to uproot themselves from Tennessee to London. He thought Jody Stephens would be agreeable as would John Lightman and Ken Woodley. When David asked about Alex, Chris went quiet and said, "No — not Alex."

David Bell: Jody liked the idea, but, by that time, Andy had left the scene and the right people couldn't be convinced.

Peter Holdforth: A few weeks later, David called me and told me that they had decided to abandon the reunion project and were going home to Memphis.

After countless meetings over the previous eight months, the last two most promising A&R bites, Rocket and Charisma Records, went nowhere. A deal wasn't going to be signed. David later recalled in the 1992 I Am the Cosmos *CD liner notes: "The list of A&R men grew progressively shorter, as we seemed to approach the end of the tunnel without the proverbial light." On November 26, 1975, they packed their bags and flew back home.*

David Bell: We called it off and went back to Memphis because of my dwindling funds. In the end, nothing came of the trip, but Chris wasn't discouraged by that. He wasn't expecting to be signed to a label within six months. He had the discouragement of nothing happening with the first Big Star album, so he was a little seasoned by that point. He made a comment about how at least it would be a good time to be back in the United States because the '76 Bicentennial was coming up. He figured there would be opportunities musically, for shows. He was always thinking about the commercial end of it.

While Chris struck out in London, his former mates—sans Andy Hummel who wholly retired from music—experienced similar struggles. Jody Stephens partnered with Van Duren for a short time, cutting the poppy "Andy, Please" at Ardent. The duo even caught the ear of Rolling Stones producer Andrew Loog Oldham, though the project failed to gain momentum. Across town, Alex Chilton's professional and emotional tailspin continued as he exited Ardent.

Alex Chilton: I made a contract with Ardent where they'd have to give me a pile of money to renew it that year. It was like the third renewal year and I had made the first and second renewal for no large amount of money. But with the third, I had some advance money coming to me and they didn't want to pay it. They wanted to pay it to me a little bit at a time. I just thought, *This is not for me*, and I dissolved my relationship with them. I was fast going broke. I mean, I'd had money since I was in the Box Tops. I had money in the bank, but around about 1975 it was running low. The only thing I knew to do about that was drink and do drugs more and more.

Chris Bell in Europe, 1975.

PHOTOS ON 298-299 BY DAVID BELL

David Bell.

Chris Bell rehearses with his acoustic in London, 1975.

DEAR JOHN,   SEPT. 4, 1975

Thanks for your recent letter.

I have talked to Jody about the gig and he seems enthusiastic. Would you be willing to fly them to Washington? I think we could scrounge up some B.A. "Poundstretcher" round trip excursion fare tickets from there, or at least pay for a good portion of them. We are considering Keith Sykes or Tommy Hoehan as a "replacement" for Alex.

We are on our way to Berlin, I will send you an address for there as soon as I have it. You can send me any information on the Joleker Factory at that time. How would I introduce myself? We got ripped off for about £1500 worth of clothes from the VW trunk last night.

Now - another favor. Thanks for the records, by the way. I'm sorry the package was so expensive. NME is ready to publish an interview, but no photos. I left my Scully briefcase in Atlanta, and although multitudes of promises were made, Earl has not mailed it yet. Would you gather any Big Star pics you have, preferably some of them after I left (or the one you gave me in August, with me cut out of it) and send them post haste post adum dictum valedictore miraboli to NME c/o Features Editor NEIL SPENCER. (I look too ugly in that early B.S. photo you gave me) 128 LONG ACRE. LONDON WC2 They are holding up an interview on account of the lack of any photos other than the obvious album cover arrangement. This press will be important, for the gig and for all of us as individual artists.
I will be in Berlin till the end of October, then back to London.

                            Love,
                            Chris

P.S. This may sound wild, but if B.S. re-recorded #1 Record, would that solve any problems with re-release? I recall that James Taylor did that with some of his tunes when he switched to Warners.

A 1974 letter from Chris Bell to John Fry, his former producer. Written while living in London, Chris discusses reforming Big Star.

Tommy Hoehn: I started [hanging out with Alex] on the heels of that period, during the "Walking Dead"-era. Alex was as down as you can get.

Alex Chilton: I was getting really intense, wondering just why I was so unhappy.

Tommy Hoehn: He moved in with me and we lived together in a bit of a haze for about a year...I was aware [of Chris Bell's suicide attempts], we had discussed it. He cut his wrists, cut them pretty good. Alex did the same thing. Alex did it after I lived with him. Sometime after that he hacked his wrists up. I made jokes about him looking like Franken-stein...Alex was sitting on the floor in my den, I walked in behind him and he was sitting there crying. I said, "What's wrong, Alex?" And he said, "It's the lowest I've ever been in my life." And it was. People thought *Sister Lovers* was garbage. They thought it was crap. Critics hated it, most of them. He was a drunk, an addict, and couldn't get arrested in the city.

Alex Chilton: I just laid up between '74 and '76 and made some crazy recordings. Like these records that Jon Tiven puts out, like *Bach's Bottom*. That was done in '75.

As Alex moved on and gradually cleaned up, his Third *tapes remained shelved. He didn't seem to mind. Aside from Alex losing interest, Big Star's one-time mentor John Fry also underwent a life change as he gradually stepped away from the mixing boards and made Ardent Studio's business and financial dealings his primary focus. However, Fry hit the studio for a few one-offs in the later '70s—most notably his engineer work in 1977 on the Scruffs' dynamic power pop debut,* Wanna Meet the Scruffs?

John Fry: Post-Stax, there were a lot of fears about the record business in Memphis, which fortunately proved to be groundless, as events played out. I didn't want to get entirely divorced from the studio or music business, but there was a period when I came close to making my primary occupation aviation. I had a commercial pilot's license and got involved in a flight-instruction business, which diverted my interest to some extent until the late '70s. A lot of times people think I'm being a curmudgeon, but when the 24-track and 48-track era came in, most recording projects had strayed far from what I was used to.

Richard Rosebrough: Fry, by that point, already had his recording days and was ready to retire from recording and do something else.

John Fry: I got to the place later in the '70s where just about all I wanted to do was remix work. I didn't want to track sessions...It was getting to where we had more and more good engineers. Terry Manning was in and out of town. Richard Rosebrough had become an excellent engineer. John Hampton and Joe Hardy were starting up. We had several of the Stax recording engineers that came looking for employment, too— William Brown, Robert Jackson, Henry Bush and Ron Capone.

Ken Woodley: John Fry gave free rein to many local musicians to experiment and record at Ardent. It was wonderful. Then came the point where Fry said, "We have to start making money." After that, things changed. But the time we did have was so special. A lot of good stuff came out of that.

Jim Dickinson: *Third* was the last record John Fry worked on top to bottom, although he mixed some after that. John was, hands down, the best engineer I ever worked with.

Sept. 15, 1975

Dear John,

How is it going? Something sort of interesting has come up.

A friend of mine, Peter Holdforth, showed David and me a really nice concert hall on the second floor of the Hammersmith Town Hall the other day. He said, as he works in the building for the London Borough (sp?) of Hammersmith, that he could get it cheap, and had been thinking of doing a concert (promoting) there for a good while.

As we were sitting, reflecting on the situation (naturally David and Peter were talking about putting "Big Star" on) it occurred to me that you had mentioned releasing #1 Record and Radio City here in order to recoup some of the funds dropped on Big Star; hopefully to smooth out some friction on the contract releases as well. If we could get Jody, Van, and maybe Keith Sykes over to do a few dates, I can generate quite a healthy bit of press, which could coincide nicely with the re-releases, or generate interest in the releases as far as companies are concerned. David and Peter want to do a date around the end of November or beginning of Dec.

Zig Zag (sort of a British "Circus" or "Creem") is doing an interview with me in 6 wks. Max Bell at NME is ready to go as soon as I can get those O'Brien negs. that carol has + contact sheets of all B.S. pictures that Andy has. John Tobler at C.B.S. wants to help; he's in the press dept. there, and can help with all sorts of stuff, including a C.B.S. act for a second group.

I don't think that anyone is interested in a Big Star reformation at ~~this point, and certainly Alex is in no shape to do anything~~ Furthermore, this would have to be seperate from anyones plans for Jody & Van or me, individually, as far as what Twen and oldham have in mind — strictly a promotional vehicle for whatever is left to eke out of Big Star. What do you think?

It would seem that payola is not peculiar to the music biz. Radio Newsreel (BBC) reports that Lockheed, under cynic sub-committee investigation, admits to making "bribes" of up to $100,000,000 (can that be real?) to foreign officials (namely South Africa) in order to "compete with American and foreign manufacturers," but justifies the transaction with note that the contributions are not written off as losses, but charged back to the respective buyers, thus making it a "profit." Do tell —

Is there a copyright or any sort of contractual tie-up now on Big Star; the name and/or the four sides and/or any of the members as a unit?

Write soon, to AIR, I may be going to Germany Oct. 5 for a month to play gigs — Shades of Hamburg & the Star Club.

Love,
Chris

Chris Bell's 1975 letter to John Fry, written while Chris was living in London, regarding a possible Big Star reunion without Alex Chilton.

304

8-21-75

Dear John—

I hope this can tide you over 'till next week at which point I will send 3 or 4 more mixes—Alex is singing back-up on "You And Your Sister"— it's a rough mix but I think it's finished and it's the best vocal work I've done on it. "Make a Scene" is #2, I'm not real sure about it— try to listen for some saxophone (bass) in the break followed with a good sax solo after the break (like in "Deel"). Last is the final mix of "Cosmos" (Emerick mixed #2 & #3) with which I am very pleased.

Anyway, I'll send "Light at The Table" (needs a vocal, guitar + piano) + "Get Away" + Speed of Sound next week—

let me know how you feel about these tracks—

Chris

An August 21, 1975 letter from Chris Bell to producer Jon Tiven, who agreed to help Chris shop his solo tapes to labels.

COURTESY OF JON TIVEN

ACT FIVE

WELCOME TO DANVER'S

Chris Bell, Danver's Restaurant manager, poses in front of his parents' home in Germantown, Christmas 1977.

BELL FAMILY ARCHIVE

CHAPTER 20

SIDEMAN & DANVER'S — ATLANTA: 1976-1977

Ensconced at his parents' Germantown home, Chris resumed life as a Memphian. Months of rejections prompted him to shelve his solo tapes and retreat from the studio, at least for now. He spent a bulk of March 1976 relaxing in St. Martin and serving as a sideman in bar bands.

David Bell: Everything involving his solo career seemed to be put on hold after he returned from England. As for my direct participation with his music, by the time we came back, that was also on hold. Both of us knew we were going to be getting involved in other things. I had moved back to Memphis, but after a few months I moved to Denver for the next year and a half. We wrote to each other, saw each other on holidays, and generally commiserated on the state of musical affairs, and his desire to get back into the business.

Danielle McCarthy-Boles: Without John Fry or David Bell in his corner, Chris would lose focus on his music. He needed a champion in his corner, or someone to spur him on.

David Bell: In the background, there was always music. He made occasional forays into the studio to test his ability.

John Dando: He wasn't grasping as high as he had in the past, though he was still doing some recording.

Without music at the forefront, Chris wholeheartedly refocused on tennis, often playing and training multiple times per week. For a slender, unathletic type who rebelled against jocks in high-school, this was a personality about-face for the twenty-five-year-old. His old friends were puzzled when they encountered him donning sporty tennis apparel and carrying a racket. Even while he patronized tennis courts across Memphis, Chris could not abandon rock 'n' roll, especially his passion for performing live. Within weeks of his return from England, Chris connected with Van Duren and promptly formed the Baker Street Regulars, a bar band named after the Sherlock Holmes characters. The group played Van's and Chris' original tunes along with some semi-obscure covers. For the first time since his Icewater days, Chris played music just for fun. Van, a few years Chris' junior, was part of a new brigade of Memphis-based, Brit-inspired songwriters.

Rick Clark: There was a tight group of people that were around the Ardent bunch, a nice group of Memphis power-pop bands and songwriters. It wasn't just the Big Star guys; there was Malarkey, Van Duren, the Scruffs, and Tommy Hoehn. They all worked together and recorded at Ardent and Shoe.

Terry Manning: All those guys weren't in our original Ardent group. It was a second wave of British-loving local guys. They had a similar aesthetic to what they liked and wanted to play. They all had a lot of talent.

Van Duren: We were all pretty much brushed aside by the local music community. It was like a square peg in a round hole. Even today, it's still a similar attitude. If you're not doing the same old shit, like "Mustang Sally" and "Brown Eyed Girl," you'll struggle. Chris wouldn't do that, neither would I. We were a small slice of the musical pie. A lot of the other bands in '76 were just at the beginnings of disco, which was the death nail in Memphis for a long time, and one of the reasons I eventually left.

David Bell: Chris didn't like disco very much, but he thought it might be good for music. One time he told me, "Well, it gets people dancing."

Van Duren: There was also the fringe-jacket scene left over from the early '70s. There were heavy bands and the black scene as well. It was a hodgepodge. There was a lot of competition for gigs. People wanted to go out and party. What we were doing required a little bit more thought.

Larry Raspberry: Memphis was still a viable scene in the mid-to-late '70s. The Bar-Kays and all those guys were live-playing bands, as were Jaguar, Target, the Hotdogs and my band, Larry Raspberry and the Highsteppers. You could hear great music all over the place. There was still Overton Square, which had Lafayette's Music Room and Solomon Alfred's, the meccas of live music.

Chris Bell: The Memphis scene [was] below starvation level with folks moving off to Nashville.

Robert Johnson: By then everyone was into all sorts of drugs. Cocaine was running rampant, along with the marijuana and booze. It wasn't like the '72 days, where everyone was just smoking pot and being normal.

John Dando: Memphis in the mid-'70s got to be an ugly scene. They were all banging their heads against the wall trying to make it. It got to be sad watching it all.

As Chris and Van began booking shows for the Baker Street Regulars, Jody Stephens also joined the band. Rounding out the lineup was local guitarist Mike Brignardello.

Van Duren: Mike was on guitar and bass. Since then, he's become a top bassist in Nashville and has been for decades.

Mike Brignardello — Bassist, Baker Street Regulars, session player: I grew up in Memphis, then hit the road immediately after high school in the early '70s. I was in a little club band and learning about being a musician, then I came back in the mid-'70s. Big Star had come and gone in my absence, but I heard about them when I got back. They were local heroes, already a semi-cult band. One of the first guys I met when I came back to Memphis was Van Duren. We hit it off and started playing together. He was the guy who hooked us up with Chris and Jody.

Jody Stephens: We played out a few times as the Baker Street Regulars. It was Chris, Van Duren, Mike Brignardello and myself as a four-piece.

Van Duren: The Baker Street Regulars was the name when the band first started. Chris thought of it. In December of '75, we started to get together and rehearse, but we had been kicking around the idea of forming a band for months before that. I first got together with Chris the day before Thanksgiving 1974. I remember the exact date because that night George Harrison's tour with Ravi Shankar came to the Coliseum in Memphis and I went to the show. But, that day, Chris, me and Jody Stephens met downtown at the Little Tea Shop, which Chris' father still owned. We had lunch, which Chris was able to comp, and we discussed forming a band. Fast-forward a bit and Chris went to Europe with David for a year. In the meantime, I saw him a few times when he was home visiting. We would meet up at bars in Overton Square to catch up. The first time I went out to the Bells' house, Jody took me over there for our first rehearsal. We turn off down this street and it turned into this winding driveway. You couldn't even see the house from the street, the property was so huge.

Mike Brignardello: Chris lived in, to my eyes, at least back in the day, a full-blown mansion. I remember turning down the driveway and driving, and driving, and driving, and thinking, *You've got to be kidding me! He lives on this estate?* I had grown up as a poor kid in Memphis. He had us set up and play in the living room because his parents were overseas for like a month. I was like, "Who goes overseas for a month?" Chris was not about any of that. I'm not even sure he noticed because he was so wrapped up in music. I don't think he knew how privileged it all was. He wasn't flashy or anything like that. Not knowing Chris, when I first met him, I thought he didn't like me. He was so serious, a man of few words. He and Jody had played together in Big Star, and he and Van Duren had a history, but I was the new guy, so I thought he wasn't digging me. Of course, I found out years later that was just his personality.

Van Duren: Chris was different, obviously upper crust. I come from a blue-collar background, so that was a new world for me. He was from privilege and he acted that way sometimes, but he could also be quite humble. He always had a twinkle in his eye, much like Alex in a way. Sometimes you couldn't tell if he was putting you on or being serious. As for Jody Stephens, he's an old friend, we met years before, in 1969 when I was sixteen, through my friend Beverly Baxter. Jody and Beverly were both in the University of Memphis's theater production of *Hair,* the first production of it outside of Broadway. Jody played drums in the production and Beverly was an actress and singer. They became boyfriend and girlfriend for a while. That's how I first met Jody and started playing music with him.

Mike Brignardello: We practiced in a corrugated-metal storage room. It wasn't insulated or anything like that. We'd just roll the door up on hot, humid Memphis days and rehearse. My girlfriend got that photo of us in there. I thought it perfectly summed up where we were at. We were hungry to play. We'd sweat through those rehearsals.

Van Duren: It was pretty miserable in that twenty-foot-by-ten-foot mini storage. Those things were brand new in 1976. It was on Lamar Avenue and was the first of its kind in Memphis. One day, Chris showed up two hours late for rehearsal. He walks in wearing these tennis togs with the sweater wrapped around his neck and says, "Sorry I'm late. Tommy Hoehn and I had a vision on the tennis courts." I didn't know if it had to do with his religious beliefs, or if I was supposed to take him seriously or not. I was a little bent out of shape, but I just laughed when he said that. It wasn't the first or the last time he was late. He operated on Chris time. Even so, by January of '76, we were out playing.

On February 4, 1976, Chris attended Joni Mitchell's concert at the now-demolished Ellis Auditorium in Memphis. The evening didn't end well after Chris left his gear inside his car at the arena's packed parking lot on the corner of Poplar Avenue and Front Street.

Van Duren: He took his mom's station wagon to that show. He had his 1950s Fender Bassman four-ten combo—an amazing amp—in the backseat. He also had his double cutaway Custom Telecaster with a natural maple finish—an amazing instrument. He had them just sitting in the back of the station wagon while he was in the concert. Of course, somebody broke in and stole all of it. After that, Chris would borrow Keith Sykes' Telecaster a lot. Those pictures of us playing together, that's Keith's guitar. He'd use that or his old Gibson 330.

Chris committed to a series of gigs across the city with the Baker Street Regulars. The band landed shows at now-defunct venues, like Aligahpo's on Highland Street by the University of Memphis, Procapé Gardens, known for its signature stained glass windows behind the stage, in Midtown on Madison, and the High Cotton Club, just south of Overton Square.

Van Duren: We played those three clubs about three times each, but the first gig was in the springtime in Oxford at Ole Miss, at a fraternity party. We did originals and some cover material, but the covers were Beatles, Bee Gees, and a lot of fairly obscure things at the time, like Todd Rundgren. We played things nobody had picked up on yet, especially in Mississippi. We threw in my songs, some Big Star songs, and a few of Chris' songs. We'd do "I Am the Cosmos," "Make A Scene," and "Fight at the Table." We learned Chris' songs by listening to what he was calling demos, what later emerged as his solo album. He probably would have worked on those songs for ten years. I'm only halfway joking about that. He never stopped working on those tracks.

John Hampton: Fry was showing me around on my first day working for Ardent on July 7, 1977. I walked into the A Studio and Chris just had the speakers blasting. John gave him a look like, "Son, turn that down."

Van Duren: I believe the only time Chris played a lot of his solo material with a band on stage was with our band. It was a wonderful experience, even though when we played gigs we were pretty much ignored. That's probably why we didn't play much in the six months we were together.

Jody Stephens: There just wasn't much of an opportunity for the Baker Street Regulars to play. Not even Big Star could find a proper booking agent, or a proper manager. That's why we didn't play too often. There just wasn't a demand for it.

Van Duren: Big Star was still unknown in Memphis. I just loved *#1 Record*, I thought it was phenomenal beyond words, but we didn't have people showing up to our Baker Street Regulars gigs and saying to Chris, "Wow, you were on *#1 Record*! Can I have your autograph?" But we did land some shows. There was a spot out in southeast Memphis called The Underground. It was built into a hill so one side of it was underground. Chris showed up late to that show. We were supposed to start playing at about 9:30 p.m. and go until 1:30 a.m. This was an April or May gig, Richard Rosebrough was filling in on drums. I'm not going to say the place was packed, but there were forty or fifty people in the room. It's like 9:25 p.m. and Chris isn't there yet. The rest of us are all set up and soundchecked for about an hour. Finally, he walks in. He's got his Gibson 330 in one hand—no case, just his guitar. In his other hand is a Fender amplifier he's borrowed from somebody. He sets the amp up and then sits down on the edge of the stage and starts changing his strings. I was not happy. I've always been one of those people who wants to keep working. He had his own world. Let's face it: He's a rich kid. I'm not going to say I resented it, but I didn't understand it. He didn't need the money, and I did. Plus, the gigs were few and far between. But aside from that, Chris was amazing on stage. It seemed so effortless to him, like there was no thought going into it. I've rarely seen anybody who could match that with him. He played loud but with such finesse. I learned so much just watching him do things, like open tunings. Being a Joni Mitchell fan, he loved her open tunings and worked with several.

In April 1976, the band changed its name to Walk 'n' Wall and, soon after, Jody stepped down. "I got very disillusioned," Jody told journalist Steve Burgess in the August 1978 issue of Dark Star Magazine. *"I dropped out of the music business and worked as a waiter. Then I played with lots of other bands trying to save money to get [to England]." From there, future Ardent Studios engineer John Hampton stepped in behind the kit. His brother, guitarist Randy Hampton, also briefly performed with the fluid lineup. Richard Rosebrough filled in on drums for most out-of-town gigs.*

John Hampton: Jody quit the band and then I started playing drums. That was my official getting-to-know Chris. We rehearsed quite a bit together as a band and played a couple shows...This was a great rock band. It was part Big Star, blended with the best Brit-pop covers around and Van's Paul McCartney-meets-Paul Carrack lead vocals.

Van Duren: We played at least one private event, one of them was Chris' sister's wedding reception. That was the first week in June 1976.

John Hampton: One of Chris' million sisters were getting married and we were going to be the music at the reception. Having met some of his sisters, this felt more like someone was doing Chris a favor, as his whole family seemed to be a bit too conservative to want us. Then again, if we kept to Beatles covers, obscure Rundgren and Badfinger, and threw in Chris' and Van's originals, we might just pull it off. The gig was Saturday night at 8 p.m. Randy, Van and I were there an hour early, our usual thing, but no Chris.

Van Duren: Of course, Chris shows up late. In hindsight, Chris was hilarious. Hampton was on drums that night. It was a nice country club setting and we're all set up.

John Hampton: Chris was late as crap, but eventually he comes walking in wearing a white shirt and white tennis shorts with a sweater tied around his waist. He also had a Telecaster over his shoulder and was holding a Fender Concert amp. As Van approached Chris, to bitch about his timing, Chris had already plugged in the amp and the guitar into it. *Oh, hell. He just maxed out the knobs.* In slow motion, as Van's mouth opened to speak, a sound straight out of hell came out of the amp. It was the first lick of Zeppelin's "Heartbreaker" solo. Van kept talking as Chris' eyes combed the room, surely to see how many girls were covering their ears. About sixty percent. *Good work, Chris.* With Van now talking at him, Chris decided there was too much top end, lowered the treble on the amp and played the lick again, this time with a little more conviction, which is exactly how Jimmy Page starts the solo. Chris blazed through the rest of the solo, note for note, but he added good where Page went bad. Van gave up, and as the end of the solo got near, Chris once again peruses the room, which by now had all but cleared out, pushed out by the sheer volume. Finally, when he saw my approving smile, he smiled back. I guess we both had a little anarchist in us.

Van Duren: Hampton was just freaking out. He just loved it. Chris was playing that note-for-note, deadpan, staring everybody down. Finally, he cracked a smile. This is still daylight and he wasn't smashed or anything. That was Chris. He was messing with everybody there.

John Hampton: The gig went from there without a hitch, but that solo was forever burned into my synapses. It was as if he was showing everyone how good he could be if he chose to be, so back off. Quite the statement.

Richard Rosebrough: There was another gig in northern Mississippi. John Hampton was the regular drummer but this night I subbed. It was at a Holiday Inn, Howard Johnson's, or something. My bass drumhead, the back head, broke. It started splitting as soon as we started playing. It was breaking quickly, and I didn't have a replacement for it. I still had two more hours I was supposed to play on that drum loudly. We taped it

Van Duren and Chris Bell performing in 1976 as the Baker Street Regulars at Procape Gardens, 1782 Madison Avenue, Memphis.

PHOTO COURTESY OF VAN DUREN

Jody Stephens and Van Duren, 1975.

PHOTO COURTESY OF VAN DUREN

Baker Street Regulars rehearsing in a metal storage unit, 1976. (L-R) Chris Bell, Mike Brignardello, Jody Stephens, and Van Duren.

PHOTO BY BEVERLY BAXTER ROSS

up with all this gray roadie tape. I was just freaking out. We took a break and I told Chris, "Man, my bass drum is broken. I just don't know what to do!" He said, "Have you tried praying?" I said, "No! But it's about to break." He said, "Well, let's pray." We got down on the floor, behind the bass drum, and we had a little prayer session.

Van Duren: That was the last gig we did with Chris and Richard. By then, Chris had already started playing lead guitar with Keith Sykes because our gigs were sparse. Our band was not getting anywhere, and we were all chomping at the bit to do something else. By June 1, Chris left to concentrate on his new job at Danver's, his dad's restaurant, but he kept playing with Keith because those were better-paying gigs. After he left, Mike, John and I continued Walk 'n' Wall as a trio through the summer. Unfortunately, we never recorded anything with Chris when he was in the band, didn't even record a live show. The only recording session I ever did with Chris was the first version of my song "New Year's Eve." Jody and I brought in Chris to play electric guitar. Some of it was re-cut and ended up on my first album.

By early June 1976, Chris committed to a stacked schedule of paying gigs with the Keith Sykes Band. Keith, Alex Chilton's old friend, was a seasoned singer-songwriter who debuted in 1969 with a self-titled folk LP on Vanguard Records. The ensuing years saw him transition into cutting rock 'n' roll albums, garnering some national success in the later '70s and early '80s, including a 1980 Saturday Night Live *performance, and tours with Jimmy Buffett.*

Keith Sykes: Chris played lead, I played the rhythm. He could play his behind off, too. Plus, he could figure out songs off records better than me, so he would show me things. We were just a rock 'n' roll dance band. We would play Chuck Berry-style songs and some old Elvis songs, but we pretty much played my originals.

John Dando: I saw Chris perform more when he was playing with other people, like Keith Sykes. He was pulling himself up a bit and seemed to be enjoying performing. There was a realization on his part that Big Star was behind him. It seemed to me that he'd given it up.

David Bell: I never saw Chris play with Keith Sykes because they were always touring down on the Gulf Coast, in different towns in the south, like Mississippi, Alabama, Georgia and Florida.

Keith Sykes: We played clubs about every weekend, at least three weekends a month. They were just bars, places people go to listen to music, drink and eat. We were not making much money, but we played a lot.

Ken Woodley: Chris and I both played with Keith. We were his pickup guys. It was a paying gig, but $20 is kind of like working for free after you play for five hours and load equipment.

Keith Sykes: I bet we played between fifty and one hundred shows with Chris, so we had a lot of time to sit and chat. Chris talked a lot about music, a lot about Led Zeppelin. He's the first guy I ever met who talked about Led Zeppelin like they were some cult or something. He asked me, "Do you think Jimmy Page sold his soul to the devil?" I laughed and said, "I have no idea." He was a cool cat. When we got together, Joe Walsh had just joined the Eagles. Chris told me, "Joe Walsh can't sing worth shit." Joe Walsh has a fabulous rock voice similar to Chris', so it was odd he said that.

By the end of 1976, Chris' time in The Keith Sykes Band concluded after a string of shows in Alabama.

Keith Sykes: The last time we worked together, we went to Mobile. We stayed at the cheapest motel I could find because we'd play this place called Thirstie's for two weeks at a time. So my wife and I went out one afternoon in Mobile, we got back to the motel, and Chris was gone. About five minutes later, the phone rang. It was Chris. He said, "Hey Keith, God told me to stay at the Holiday Inn." Basically, he said he talked to either Jesus or God, one of the two, and they told him to go ahead and get a room at the Holiday Inn. He said he would pay for it himself. Not long after the Mobile thing, Chris left the band, or maybe I thought it wasn't working anymore and found someone else. That was it. It was amicable. After the band, I just saw him occasionally. He asked me to come over and record a song I wrote called "Stay With Me." I played acoustic guitar on it. He always liked that song.

Chris' departure occurred amidst his movement into a full-time management job at Danver's, the thriving Memphis-based burger joint co-founded by his father Vernon. For the first time in his adult life, Chris entertained a career outside of music. He even trimmed down his curly locks to make room for a paper hat. This was his first attempt at shadowing his father's legacy.

John Hampton: Chris' dad threw him in one of his Danver's locations, the one over by Memphis State [now University of Memphis]. We would go into that Danver's all the time and make Chris get us hamburgers. He was like, "All right guys, quit screwing with me...yeah, yeah."

Ken Woodley: I'd pick him up from Danver's sometimes and we'd go over to Ardent. That's about the time I played slide guitar and piano on "Though I Know She Lies."

Dale Franklin — Danver's co-worker: It was a happening place. That location was the hottest unit at the time. As fast as you could load the fry baskets and dump them, you were still behind. I worked with Chris at the original Danver's before Shoney's bought it. The owners bought the old Roy Rogers roast-beef chain here in Memphis, which included the rights to use their formula and how they did things. When Chris started, I was a night manager. They came up to me one night and said, "Hey, we got a new guy and he's going to train with you. It's Vernon Bell's son." I thought that was a little scary.

Linda Schaeffer Yarman: Vernon Bell and his business partner Dan Turley started Danver's together. That's where they got the name: They combined their first names.

Robert Johnson: Danver's was sort of an upscale McDonald's—you could actually get a decent meal there. I used to live in an apartment off Poplar behind the Danver's. I can vividly remember Chris in the back with his little hat on, flipping burgers. After he'd clock out, he'd go hang out at the Cockeyed Camel, a restaurant right down the street from his work.

Sara Bell: I was happy Chris was working there. Structure was pretty good for him at the time.

David Bell: Taking the Danver's job was more of a spiritual decision for Chris. He was going to stop giving our father headaches. He decided, "I'll be the good son. I'm going to get an honest job." He felt he'd caused a lot of grief to my parents. Certainly, when you're rushed to the hospital because you've taken a bunch of pills—yeah, he caused a bunch of grief. He was a hippie and rebellious. My poor father. You never know how great someone is until they're gone, what they did, and how spoiled you were because they were always there to take care of whatever messes you were making because they love you. My father was worried about both of us, but with Chris, he was worried about what he would become. Chris wanted to do something responsible and make our father proud. It wasn't that he was just dying to get into this.

Linda Schaeffer Yarman: Chris just tried to fit into the mold of his father by managing the Danver's and going the non-musical route. There would be times I would drop him off at the restaurant. He had to wear a paper hat and he'd always laugh about it. We always had fun. He and I were just very close, especially toward the last three years of his life. He was doing so well towards the end. But Chris was always pensive and sensitive. It had a lot to do with expectations of his life.

Cindy Bell Coleman: I know Daddy's dream was to have one of his boys go into the restaurant business, follow in his footsteps. That wasn't David's dream at all. He wasn't going to have any part of it. Chris wanted Daddy's approval, and he tried in his own fashion, but he wasn't going to be happy doing it. As it turns out, it was our sister Sara who followed in his footsteps. She opened Mortimer's Restaurant in Memphis.

Jody Stephens: I thought it was cool how seriously Chris was taking his Danver's job. He took a lot of pride in doing a good job. A lot more was expected out of him because he was one of the owner's sons. Nepotism can work both ways.

Dale Franklin: One night, Chris and I were working together. He looks out the window and says, "Oh man, my dad!" I said, "What are you talking about?" Chris says, "Look, he's sitting in a car across the street." They had big windows out front. Chris said Vernon was out there making sure he was working.

John Fry: Chris never complained about working there. It was something he did to make some money and to make his dad somewhat happy. Vernon Bell was not a hard man to get along with. I met him many times. He was simply puzzled by the whole music thing.

John Dando: Chris was realizing he might not make it playing music. He was beginning to see reality closing in on him. It must have gone through his head that he didn't have anywhere else to go.

In early 1977, Chris was presented with an opportunity from his father's expanding franchise to move five-and-a-half hours away to Georgia. His mission: open Atlanta's first Danver's and train its new staff on the art of roast-beef slicing. In March, Chris moved from his parents' home to his own rental outside of Atlanta at Pineland Woods Apartments #312, a newly built complex at 3640 Peachtree Corners in Norcross, Georgia. The management job afforded him a shiny, white 1977 Triumph TR7, a small British sports car, and the ability to pay for tennis lessons.

David Bell: He liked it in Atlanta. He enjoyed his time there. Once he was in a responsible job and making some decent money, he could play tennis and do other things that weren't just solely focused on music. He went to a few Atlanta Braves games, things he would have never done before. He wouldn't have cared. He told me he regretted that he never made it to any hockey games. Even the tennis thing was an attempt to do something a little more mainstream—tennis was huge at the time. He found a coterie of Christian friends but was not involved in a specific church. He spent most of his time working out there. At one point he told me, "This Danver's thing is getting serious. They are going to start a Danver's University to train future managers."

Helen Heinle — Friend, Danver's co-worker: I worked for Danver's for a couple years. We were busy all the time. It was just a basic menu, but they had their signature roast beef and these cherry and apple turnovers. The huge salad bar was a big deal back then, too. That was my first real job. I was about sixteen when I started. The store was on Buford Highway in an area by Atlanta called North Druid Hills. It was a four-lane highway with lots of businesses and such. Chris was the night manager and easy to work for. He had a good rapport with his employees. He wanted to make sure the restaurant did well, and it did do well.

After Chris settled in with his new Atlanta clique, made up mostly of his Danver's co-workers, he found time to partake in some low-key shenanigans.

Helen Heinle: He liked to smoke pot, though he never did at work. He only smoked if we were just hanging out. I don't recall him doing anything heavier, like pills or anything like that. He'd have a few beers from time to time. There was a place around the corner from Danver's called the Rusty Nail Pub. We would hang there after work. He would talk about tennis a lot. He was just crazy about it. He loaned me a book called *The Inner Game of Tennis*. It was about how your mindset affects tennis. Another thing with Chris: he was so happy and proud when he got that little Triumph TR7. He drove it back to Memphis every several weeks and would spend a weekend or a few days there.

John Dando: I never understood where all the money for that TR7 came from. His car before that was a Ford Pinto station wagon.

After getting to know each other on-and-off the Danver's clock, Chris and Helen grew closer, enough so that he talked her up to family members back home.

Helen Heinle: I never heard he was gay, bisexual, or anything like that. There was no talk of that in our group of friends. Chris and I weren't really boyfriend and girlfriend, but he liked me a lot. We were good friends. I was about nine years younger than him. We never had any consummation of our relationship. I guess because of the age difference, we were going slow. It was a sweet relationship. I remember writing his name on notebooks. Being a kid in high school, I would doodle "Christopher Branford Bell" and "I love Chris"—things teenagers do.

Chris may have lived hours away from Memphis, but his musical partnership with Tommy Hoehn still managed to grow into a casual but consistent series of collaborations. During a two-week vacation in St. Martin, the pair's first recorded collaboration was a rough take of a co-penned song, one later included on Tommy Hoehn's 1981 I Do Love the Light *LP.*

Tommy Hoehn: I met Chris through Alex in '75. He was out of Big Star and it wasn't too long after *Sister Lovers* was recorded. We became buddies, playing together and working together. I was close friends with Chris.

David Bell: Tommy and Chris convinced John Fry to bring some recording equipment on his small plane to St. Martin. That's where they did the first recording of "Cuba."

John Hampton: They started writing songs together. "Cuba" was one of them. I had to box up a four-track tape machine in a crate, so they could take it to St. Martin with them. John Fry would be the engineer and Chris and Tommy would just sit around and play acoustic guitars.

John Fry: The whole recording session on the beach was a huge pain in the ass. We hauled a Scully four-track analog tape recorder, a four-input Spectra Sonics mixer, several Neumann mics—all overloading the aircraft for what was supposed to be these wonderful Bell/Hoehn sessions in St. Martin. The house had bad electricity and the mic cables caused a constant hum. I had to do a bunch of things to stop it, but the electricity would still frequently go off. They recorded two fairly good songs, "Cuba" and one other, which I can't recall.

David Bell: That was the same trip they ran into Peter Frampton. They talked to him at the casino in Mullet Bay and invited him to come and jam. Frampton didn't show, of course. Chris ran into him again after he stood them up and he apparently laid into him verbally for blowing them off. That was my brother. He didn't care if you were some big star.

As Chris sharpened his restaurateur skills in Atlanta, and jammed with Tommy when he could, Alex Chilton exited Memphis and went to New York City, where he played shows with Chris Stamey in a short-lived band called the Cossacks. Alex may have been low on cash, but while sipping drinks at clubs like CBGB and Max's Kansas City, he discreetly brushed shoulders with rock elites like David Bowie, Iggy Pop, Debbie Harry, and Lou Reed. One photo of the boisterous Nancy Spungen schmoozing at Max's captured a discreet Alex sitting in the background.

Alex Chilton: I was just hanging around in Memphis drinking and hanging out in clubs. So then in the first part of '77, after I made some of those tapes in '75 with Jon Tiven, this record company [Ork Records] in New York called me up and said, "We're going to release these things [as the *Singer Not the Song* EP]. Would you come to New York and play a few dates?" I said, "Yeah, that sounds like fun." I went up there and played and ended up staying there the whole year. I kept on playing a lot of dates and recorded "Bangkok."

Like some of his past dealings with record labels, Alex's partnership with Ork Records, and its owner Terry Ork, quickly soured. In a January 1979 interview with a Memphis newspaper, Alex vented his frustration: "Terry [Ork] is this big, fat queer in New York who haunts the avant-garde circuit and keeps Richard Lloyd in the junk when he can. It was only inevitable he would end up with a record label. Ork said to me, 'Come to New York and we'll take care of you.' I went to New York; they didn't take care of me." The East Coast stint was not a complete failure; however, as it was the catalyst of his crucial introduction to Lux Interior and Poison Ivy of the Cramps. Alex's fertile friendship with the soon-to-be iconic psychobilly-garage-punks led to the band's groundbreaking early recordings.

Alex Chilton: "Bangkok," I guess, was cut after I had seen the Cramps. They made a big impression on me. I saw them play in New York and became a devoted fan. After a month or two, I ran into them at a friend's apartment and said, "Say, you guys are the greatest band I've ever seen. We ought to work together in the studio."

Together, they laid down the Cramps' primitive Gravest Hits *EP in October 1977 at Ardent Studios. A couple years later, they collaborated on the ground-breakingly trashy* Songs the Lord Taught Us *LP at Phillips Recording. The refined production work heard on his Big Star albums was left in the dust in favor of early Sun Records rawness. "I think it makes [the Cramps] feel good to be down here in Memphis—down here where all the music they have collected for so long and like so much came from," Alex told Channel 13 in Memphis during a 1979 television segment on the Cramps' visit to Sam Phillips' studio. "I think for them to be here in Sam's studio makes them feel great." Still, no matter how far he strayed from his glistening power-pop past, Big Star's legacy haunted Alex throughout the birth of the punk-rock scene and beyond.*

Alex Chilton: I went to New York and played some gigs in early '77 and the place was packed. I knew [Big Star] was the reason. When I play my own gigs, Big Star songs make up a very small percentage of my set, for a variety of reasons—one being that a lot of those songs are kind of half-baked and not well crafted. They didn't go through as rigorous a refinement stage as they should have, and a lot of them just seem kind of young.

Over time, especially by the 2000s, Alex appeared to cool his adverse, often indifferent, feelings on Big Star.

Bruce Eaton: When Alex was ready to talk to me in 2009 for the *Radio City* 33⅓ book, he understood that Big Star was an important chapter in his career and largely set the stage for everything he did thereafter, far more so than the Box Tops. But, as he said, "Big Star was one thing. I was something else." When he pursued his solo career in earnest, he felt a bit dogged by expectations that he would recreate the Big Star sound as the Big Star cult grew. Over the years though, the fans came to understand what he was all about, and he came to accept Big Star. There was a happy meeting in the middle somewhere. But I'm sure he got far more enjoyment in playing an obscure R&B song than he did playing "September Gurls."

Just before takeoff to St. Martin, the gang poses for a photo: (L-R) John Fry, Tommy Hoehn, [Tommy's then-wife] Sarah Gratz, [Tommy's friend] Wes Bramlett and Chris Bell.

ARDENT STUDIOS ARCHIVE

John Dando, Big Star's roadie and sound tech, inside the atrium at Ardent Studios.

ARDENT STUDIOS ARCHIVE

Chris Bell performing with the Baker Street Regulars, 1976.

PHOTO COURTESY OF VAN DUREN

Songwriter and bandleader Keith Sykes, 1974.

Solo artist and songwriter Tommy Hoehn poses for a promotional photo.

Alex Chilton and the Cossacks, featuring guitarist Chris Stamey (left),
live at CBGB, 1977.

PHOTO BY EBET ROBERTS

Chris Bell enjoying a drink on a Mississippi River steamboat.

ARDENT STUDIOS ARCHIVE

The name tag Chris wore while managing his father's fast-food restaurant.

BELL FAMILY ARCHIVE

CHAPTER 21

HOME AGAIN — TENNIS: FALL 1977-SPRING 1978

After spending just under a year in Atlanta, Chris transferred back to a Memphis Danver's and resumed living in his parents' house. With no serious musical commitments chewing up his time, Chris went full-tilt into Christianity. His gusto for God was recalled by Alex Chilton in an August 1977 interview with Big Star *magazine. "Chris is managing a hamburger joint that his dad owns a chain of, and wants to turn into the next McDonald's," Alex told Bernie Kugel, the quarterly fanzine's founder. "He goes around the store with all his Jesus doctrine. It's pretty weird."*

David Bell: Chris was very vocal about religion. I would see him with religious tracts. He would speak in tongues, though that is something that occurred within a worship service or a worshipful setting. From the late '60s on, there was the Charismatic Renewal in the Episcopal Church. All of this is based on what's popularly known as the Pentecostal Experience. Whatever Pentecostal churches base their denomination on has to do with gifts of the Holy Spirit, and one of those is speaking in tongues. That was definitely part of Chris' conversion experience.

Cindy Bell Coleman: It seemed to center him. We got a lot closer then. He started going to the Episcopal Church in East Memphis regularly. It was an upswing for him. It's some of my best memories. He was vocal about it with me and wanted me to understand what was going on with him and wanted me to be a part of it.

Linda Schaeffer Yarman: His spiritual aspect was important to him. As a result, I also became a Christian. We had both been wild teenagers, but you knew this was a real transformation and a true one. Chris would take me to the All Saints Episcopal Church. He played guitar for their youth group.

David Bell: Chris worshipped both in and out of church. At a certain point, he would get disillusioned in one church and then go find another.

Tommy Hoehn: I don't know that [Chris] would say he belonged to the church. He certainly participated in it and in several other charismatic Christian churches. Speaking in tongues, that sort of thing—he was real into that. He and I would go to one church. Well, it wasn't a church, actually. It was a little group of older people, perhaps in their sixties or seventies, who met in a house somewhere in East Memphis. These people were laying hands on each other, healing each other. It was very subdued and there was an element of conviction that ran through it unlike most charismatic groups. That's what Chris was involved in. We would play music there. Chris was into some early Christian rock, which was just emerging as an artform back then, with DeGarmo and Key. We did a lot of those early-Christian songs for these elderly people and would witness as they laid their hands on each other. It was a charming experience. Another time, we all went to Florida—myself, Chris, John Fry, and Ken Woodley. We went to a church called St. Andrews by the Sea. It was a small church and people would play tambourines during the service. At this service, there were about fifteen of us and we all sat in a big circle and one person preached. In other words, we would pray for that individual and at the end of the service everyone held hands and sang in tongues very quietly...I'm not a practicing Christian, but that was unusual. It was cosmic, almost as if we were floating above the ground.

Danielle McCarthy-Boles: David Bell and John Fry said Chris was trying to convert both of them. Chris would tell them, "You don't have to check your brain at the door when it comes to the Bible." That was appealing for Chris.

David Bell: He was certainly my teacher in that. I shared the same religious experience with him, to a lesser extent.

John Dando: Chris treaded lightly with me on that because he knew I wasn't going to go that route with him. He didn't try to sell me too hard on it.

Ken Woodley: He told me a couple times I needed to be saved, but that's about it.

Jody Stephens: Chris wasn't evangelical around me. From time to time he certainly did talk about it. It was fine with me. I'm a believer myself. Faith was a large part of the way Chris thought and lived through his adult life. "Try Again" on *#1 Record* seems to be the beginnings of that. Then there's "Look Up" on his solo record. It was a guiding thing for him.

Richard Rosebrough: He was telling me, "You should read *The Screwtape Letters.*" He'd say, "You need to read this book," or "You need to pray to the Lord." Chris saw that as a way to solve our problems. I had some issues and I talked to Chris about it. He said, "Come out to this church and listen to a service, talk to some of the people there, maybe they can help you with what's troubling you." I talked to some guy over there, a total stranger. I told him my story and he started looking it up in the Bible passages and scriptures he could read to me. I thought it was a bunch of bullshit. It wasn't my thing, but Chris did persuade me to get a Bible and to read it. He made me wear a cross around my neck. I gave it the old college try. It lasted about two years and then I thought, "No, I can't do this."

Jon Tiven — Journalist, Prix, record producer, musician: When I went in and did some recording with Tommy Hoehn, I asked Chris if he'd co-produce it with me at Ardent and he was totally into it. He was there co-producing, making decisions. But we did a version of Alex's song "Take Me Home and Make Me Like It," and he didn't want anything to do with that. Chris was skeptical about Alex's lyrical angles. He said to me, "If you sing the words of the devil, you become the devil." He was consumed by religion. But he enjoyed most of the other songs and was involved. Another time, I was in California at the office of Chess Records. I was working for them. I was talking with Alex about Chris' devout belief in God and Alex said, "If you're going to be a rock 'n' roll singer, you have to believe you are the Messiah."

Tommy Hoehn: Chris and Alex befriended each other a little bit at the end...One day, we were all standing in a Quick Stop. Chris was singing to himself, just walking around singing. Alex looked at me and said, "I can't believe this. Chris is such an uptight person and here he is singing in public." He didn't even realize he was doing it. He had found some form of freedom.

Earl Smith's widow, Tommie Dunavant, who met Chris in 1975, said Chris and Earl's shared devotion to Christianity became the center of their longtime friendship.

Tommie Dunavant: Chris was one hundred percent an evangelist. He felt he needed to be. It wasn't a quiet faith. Both Earl and Chris wanted to do the Lord's work and wanted to be the people they felt God called them to be. They thought everyone should believe. One day, I was with them when they had these religious tracts and they were going to give them out downtown outside the Peabody Hotel.

Chris and Earl did go to church together, too. They were evangelical but into modern music — it wouldn't be like old hymns. There had to be good music, or they wouldn't have gone. They believed their love of music could be used by the Lord. Chris also used to sit around and play his own songs for us. Earl sometimes played the bass while Chris was singing and playing. Chris could just break into music. You could give him a topic and he could start playing and singing a song about it — make it up on the spot. I thought of him as my kid brother. Earl and Chris were the same age, but I felt Earl was like the older brother. Chris looked up to him.

Although Chris appeared happier during these final months, religion hadn't relieved all of his troubles and he was still prone to less-severe bouts of depression.

Tommie Dunavant: When Earl and I fell in love and got married in 1976, Chris was the best man at our wedding in Destin, Florida. Chris was a part of the package. Earl was a confidant for him. In a week, Earl would probably talk to Chris three to five times. If Chris wasn't calling Earl, Earl was calling him. He struggled with who he was and what direction he wanted to go in life. Earl is someone he called in the middle of the night when he was upset and wanted to talk with somebody. He would hang up the phone and say, "We need to pray for Chris." But Earl never got stressed with Chris. He loved him to the end, because Earl himself had a lot of struggles. He came from a family of divorces and alcoholism. Earl battled drug addiction, on and off, up to his own death. He was sadly killed in a car wreck about ten years after Chris' accident. But Chris was sensitive, he listened to what people said and sometimes it hurt him. Just when you'd think Chris had his feet on the ground and was doing all right, he'd fly off the handle again.

Beverly Baxter Ross: Chris was always conflicted. About sex, faith, everything. Everything seemed to bring him down, but in his later years he seemed at peace. He'd found his faith. He said, "I've become a Christian, everything is better. I'm much happier and clear."

Lesa Aldridge Hoehn: I never knew Chris to have a boyfriend or anything, but being a homosexual was still not so accepted. We all knew it but didn't go on about it. I thought it was no big deal. I heard he'd found the Lord so he was going to go straight. It's a sad story. I find it hard to believe he'd wake up and say, "I think I'll turn gay, so I can make my life harder." You just are or you're not. Then you throw in that Memphis is at the top of the Deep South, the Bible Belt.

Jon Tiven: When Little Feat played in town, I went with some of my friends. Chris was there with a female date. That sent tongues wagging at Ardent. They couldn't believe Chris was there with a female date. For him to show up with a woman was quite a shocker.

Sarah Gratz — Friend, Tommy Hoehn's ex-wife: There was some talk, but the main talk was, "It's none of your business and nobody cares. Chris is Chris." We just didn't pay any attention to it.

Taking his mind off those lingering inner conflicts was Chris' continued dedication to training on the tennis courts. Chris was enthralled with professional tennis, which boomed in 1978 thanks to the highly publicized rivalry between Björn Borg and John McEnroe.

Richard Rosebrough: He played tennis a lot with his new tennis buddies, but he occasionally showed up at Ardent in his tennis shorts and headband in his sporty little car. I thought the tennis thing was an effort to divorce himself from the studio. Not the music, the studio. He was recreating his life, seeking happiness.

Jody Stephens: We would get together and play tennis by his house out in Germantown. Chris wanted to be good. He was all right, but he aspired to be a tennis pro. He took it seriously. What's weird is, one time he introduced me as a tennis pro to one of his friends. I didn't know he was going to do that. The guy took my hand to see if I had calluses and I did from drumming, not from playing tennis, so the ruse seemed to work.

Linda Schaeffer Yarman: For a while, and this was a lot of fun, Chris and I were playing tennis together at the Racquet Club. At the same time, we were making fun of ourselves, because that was just so status quo. We were hippies trying to hit the tennis circuit. We were laughing at the people we would ridicule, but at the same time we were playing tennis, too.

Ken Woodley: I played tennis with him one time. He wasn't very good. I was not very good, but I was better than him and that's horrible. I had the long helmet hair and the little shorts. Oh, boy! We were the odd couple out there.

John Fry: I could not play tennis. One time down in St. Martin Chris tried to show me how to do it. I just said, "Chris, I can't do this, I don't understand what's going on." I never knew any of the tennis people.

That was another world. I cannot remember his name but one of his tennis buddies was one of the pallbearers at his funeral. I do know that for a little while he took some private tennis lessons from Jim Zumwalt, who is now a big-time music lawyer in Nashville, but back then he was just starting out in Memphis and was the tennis pro at the Memphis Athletic Club.

Jim Zumwalt — Band manager, Tennis coach: In the fall of '73, I turned Elvis and his entourage on to racquetball at my club, sold them all the gear. It was a weird anomaly that Dr. Nichopoulos brought me Elvis Presley, not for music, but for tennis, just like my later encounter with Chris Bell. I met Chris through John Fry because the bands I was managing, Hotdogs and Target, were recording at Ardent. One day, I get a call from Chris and we met at the courts at Hickory Ridge apartments. Here's this guy from the music scene that's driving a Triumph sports car. He was quiet and didn't look like a rock 'n' roller. His look was more of a white-collar, intelligent, suburban kid from a well-to-do family. He was Memphis preppy, not Ivy League preppy. I took him out on the court and showed him the proper grips. I showed him how to swing, hit balls at him, and coached him on the proper technique. As for his skill, it wasn't like teaching a girl, where you have the floppy wrist and all that, but he was slender. It wasn't like dealing with a prodigy with great coordination—he was a musician.

Tommy Hoehn: He thought he would become a tennis pro, but he was terrible. Chris wasn't very athletic. He was a bit frail. Alex, on the other hand, was naturally adept as an athlete.

Barry Jenkins — Tennis partner: Chris and I got to be friends playing tennis. When I knew Chris, I had never heard of Big Star or Chris Bell the musician. We became good friends near the end of his life. He was four or five years older than me. I was still a senior in college and was playing a lot of tennis over at what was then called Memphis State University. He came up, introduced himself and asked me if I would like to play tennis sometime. He had such a winsome way about him, I was happy to spend some time with him. We also played a lot at Colonial Country Club where his father was a big-wig. In the dead of the summer, we would play at least four or five times a week. He even knew some of the tennis pros in town. On the courts, he was a novice, but wanted so much to get good. He would practice, do drills. I was a bit better, maybe a lot better, but we would practice doing serving drills, those sorts of things. Back then, there were huge tennis stars like Jimmy Connors, John McEnroe, and Björn Borg. Chris wanted to be like them. A lot of people's favorite player at the time was Björn because he was winning Wimbledon tournaments. He'd dress like Björn. There was a certain type of Fila headband that only Björn wore and Chris managed to find it. He wanted to be an athlete and he wanted to be healthy. He was into yogurt. I was twenty-one and never even heard of yogurt. It wasn't too popular yet when he made the comment, "Dannon Yogurt has more active cultures." I was like, "What's an active culture?" He did bring up music some. I knew he was into it. I knew he had access to Ardent, but that's about it. Chris talked more about the music he liked. He was really into a group called Uncle Walt's Band. He loaned me one of their demo tapes to listen to. I listened to it until it broke.

Chris' appreciation of Uncle Walt's Band, an Austin via South Carolina outfit, encouraged him to visit Ardent Studios and record a melodious, bare-bones cover of the band's 1974 demo "So Long Baby," a tune written by the group's Deschamps "Champ" Hood. Chris' instrumental version, found on an unlabeled reel years later, was improperly titled "Clacton Rag" and misattributed to Chris on the 2009 Rhino Records' edition of I Am the Cosmos. *Omnivore Records' 2017 edition accurately credited the song to Hood. It shines as a prime example of Chris' precise, graceful playing skills. Adding further backstory to the 1976 instrumental is the voice of his friend Doreen "Dore" Harper, heard at the tail end of the tune. With polite goading from Chris, in her thick English accent, the aged Dore says: "I say, Cecil! How about going down to Clacton and having a bit of a rag?...That is all I am going to say, Christopher!" The playful banter gives some insight into their unlikely friendship.*

Richard Rosebrough: Dore was a key player in Chris' life, but she also developed a close relationship with David, John Dando, and me. She was British and the same age as Chris' mother. She grew up in London and married after World War II in 1945 to Colonel Harper. But her husband passed away, leaving her a widow with no children who lived by herself. She loved hanging around with us at her house in Midtown. It was very platonic. We were friends.

David Bell: Chris met Dore through me. It was later, toward 1969, when Chris first met her. She was just hysterically funny and intelligent. She had sort of a *Monty Python*-style sense of humor.

John Fry: Dore was also very skilled. She was an editor of the Campbell Clinic's *Manual of Orthopedic Medicine*, which, back then, was regarded as the standard book on the subject.

Richard Rosebrough: I was around Dore a lot; we would have a fireside gathering with some tea or wine. She was a little weird, but she was a friend. We would sit around, smoke cigarettes, talk and hang out with her cats, which she loved.

David Bell: We liked having her around, but Dore probably should have gone back to England right after her husband died. Like some English women, she did not assimilate too well to the United States. My mother was sort of like that. They were both proud of their English heritage and were both big influences on Chris and me, especially with Chris because of the English Invasion and the Beatles.

CHAPTER 22

LIKE FLIES — LAST VACATION: APRIL-MAY 1978

On April 4, 1978, Chris got a slight taste of rock stardom when a carload of excited Big Star fans unexpectedly arrived. The trio of admirers had just made a ten-hour road trip from Winston-Salem, North Carolina when they walked into Danver's in search of Chris Bell. With nothing but record sleeves and a few magazine articles to gaze at, the early-twenty-somethings had a lot of queries about Big Star. These weren't just any admirers—they were future dB's members Peter Holsapple and Will Rigby. Also on the trip was their pal Mitch Easter, who went on to front Let's Active and produce R.E.M.'s early albums. At this point, their only solid connection to Memphis was their friend and bandmate Chris Stamey, who was not on this adventure but had collaborated with Alex Chilton in New York City the year prior. They decided to utilize that loose connection and dig into the mystery of Big Star at its roots.

Mitch Easter — Singer-songwriter, guitarist, Let's Active, record producer: There's sort of a concept that some of the first people to champion Big Star were R.E.M., but they heard them ten years after us. We heard them on the radio. R.E.M. and those other bands were bigger than me and Chris Stamey [of the dB's], but we were always carrying the flag. We're just known as very early fans who never stopped talking about them.

Ric Menck: It was nearly impossible to find out any information about Big Star in the pre-Internet age. The first person I met who actually knew something about them was Mitch Easter, because he'd gone to Memphis in search of Alex Chilton and Chris Bell before anyone else. He told me a lot about Chris I didn't know, which helped put his music into perspective.

Mitch Easter: I was living in Chapel Hill and was at the end of college, plus we loved those Big Star records, so we decided on a Memphis trip. We were sort of emboldened to show up like that. Alex had lived in New York, where I met him a year earlier, but he moved back to Memphis, so it didn't seem impossible to hook up with Alex and meet Chris.

Will Rigby: We checked in with Alex as soon as we got there. We all met him before, so he was gracious. He gave us a lot of his time just driving us around pointing out places like American Studios, where they cut "The Letter." Then he took us to Sun Studio on Union Avenue, which was still empty and boarded up. There was a fence behind it and somehow Alex knew there was a hole in it. We crawled through the fence and the building either wasn't locked or missing a door. None of the recording equipment was in there, but Alex showed us where it had been. The window Sam Phillips looked through into the recording room was still there. There was a shell of a car sitting in the middle of the room—it had last been an auto repair place. Alex climbed up on it and got some of the acoustical ceiling tile that was still up there. In the afternoon, he took us down into Mississippi to go get some barbeque. He was nice. I'm sure it helped we were friends with Chris Stamey. In Alex's car, on a shitty little cassette machine, he played us "I Am the Cosmos." It was the first time we had heard it; it hadn't been released yet.

Peter Holsapple: We found Chris through Alex. He gave us the information about Danver's, which one he'd be working at, and we headed over there.

Will Rigby: We just walked up to the counter and they said, "Can I help you?" One of us said, "Is Chris Bell here?" He came out, in his shirt and tie, wearing a little paper hat. He was nonplussed that fans had come to see him at work.

Mitch Easter: Chris walked out and we all thought he looked like Russell Mael from Sparks—that was our first impression. He looked good, looked healthy, but he had this look on his face like, "Really?" He had a shy demeanor, but was nice.

Peter Holsapple: He was a little freaked out that he'd been sought out by Will, Mitch and me. I understand why he was a little uncomfortable. He had three strangers from North Carolina randomly drop by his job to talk to him about the band he wasn't a part of anymore.

Will Rigby: He sat for a few minutes with us at the restaurant in a booth and then he said, "Let's meet up tonight."

Peter Holsapple: We got together with him later that night at the Bombay Bicycle Club [in Overton Square] where we watched him play backgammon with Jon Byrd. Chris seemed like a gentle and genuinely likable guy. Not the total mensch Jody is, but more like that than not.

Mitch Easter: We just sat and talked. I was not wanting to ask the wrong thing or be too annoying. I don't know what his state of mind was, but people often want to sensationalize things and make him out to be a depressed guy who was on the verge of suicide. He certainly did not seem like that. He didn't seem on top of the world, but he didn't appear to be tragically depressed.

Will Rigby: We asked him what bands he was into. He said, "I don't know, rock 'n' roll just went dead for me." We asked him what he liked, he said, "Well, Fleetwood Mac." I get it now, Fleetwood Mac made great pop records, but that's just not what we were wanting to hear from someone who we looked up to.

Mitch Easter: He told us he'd got into playing the acoustic guitar and was musically into the Steve Miller Band and Fleetwood Mac. The fact he cited these two mega-successful radio-star bands blew my mind. It was surprising because we were just getting our punk-rock sensibilities, so we were expecting him to say something a little more underground or weird. I can't remember too much else about the conversation inside, but I remember being on the street and finally getting the courage to ask about the equipment he used *on #1 Record.*

Will Rigby: Being young kids, we go, "What's going on tonight?" Chris says, "Well, Horslips is playing." We were like, "We don't want to see Horslips, we want to see something local." We badgered him a bit and then asked him, "Alex is in the studio tonight, want to go by?" I could tell he didn't want to, but he finally relented and took us by Sam Phillips where Alex was recording. He drove over in his TR7 Triumph.

The session they walked into was for Like Flies on Sherbert, *the first Alex Chilton solo LP. Produced in 1978 and '79 by Jim Dickinson, and engineered by Alex, Richard Rosebrough, and John Hampton, it showcased a complete detachment from the pop music spectrum. Months prior, Alex attended the now legendary Sex Pistols show at the Taliesyn Ballroom in Midtown Memphis. He relished the slovenliness and summoned that untamed spirit on* Like Flies. *There were no boundaries, but one tongue-in-cheek track, "Riding through the Reich" (sung in the tune of "Jingle Bells"), was deemed too offensive by producer Jim Dickinson and was cut from the final track list. The polarizing disc*

*foreshadowed the lo-fi, blues-punk explosion later solidified by primitive bands
like the Gories, Oblivians, Black Keys, and White Stripes. In a July 1980 Rolling Stone review, critic Ken Tucker called* Like Flies *"a small masterpiece of
crudity and split-second invention." He added, "Guitars veer out of tune before
your very ears, and the drums invariably crash along for a few extra beats after
everyone else has stopped playing." Alex's next live band, the Yard Dogs, was an
equally primitive '50s-style rockabilly outfit led by Alex on acoustic guitar and
vocals. The trio, which also comprised guitarist Chris Thomson and percussionist
Richard Rosebrough (or alternately Ross Johnson) on snare drum, busked for
pocket change outside the Mid-America Mall.*

Ken Woodley: Around that time, Chris came up to me holding a record
and said, "This is the new sound." It was the Cars. He also loved ABBA.

David Bell: With the *Like Flies* album and all that, Alex was getting eclectic. Chris didn't think too much of it. He was a lot more mainstream and
a lot more interested in melody.

Richard Rosebrough: Chris said very little that night at Sam Phillips.
He seemed to be uncomfortable. Phillips can be an intimidating place. I
don't know if he heard the entire *Sherbert* album—just hearing one song
is enough to scare you bad.

Mitch Easter: I got the impression Alex and Chris had not seen each
other in a long time; maybe our presence somehow facilitated them
talking again a little bit. It wasn't unfriendly or anything, it just seemed
like they hadn't talked.

Will Rigby: My impression of *Like Flies* was they recorded it fast and
spent a long time mixing it. That was the only time I was ever in the
same room as Jim Dickinson. Alex played us a few tracks: "I've Had It"
and "Girl After Girl." Chris just sat in the chair and didn't say much.
He and Alex just nodded to each other. It was a little tense, but Alex
was nice to us, even then. He took time out to play us songs. He was
proud of them. Dickinson and Richard Rosebrough were sitting behind
the board ignoring us. Chris split pretty quickly, but we hung around
longer and Alex showed us around the building. After Chris left that
studio, I never saw him again.

Mitch Easter: It always worried me that Chris maybe thought all we
wanted to do was get to Alex, because Alex was more famous than him. I
so hope he didn't think that. It was amazing he offered to hang out with
us; he must have been bored enough to do it.

Like Flies on Sherbert *was released in the summer of 1979 after a modest
batch of 500 copies were pressed by Peabody Records, a small label operated by*

Memphis songwriter Sid Selvidge. The cover art, an odd montage of baby dolls piled on a Cadillac hood, was provided by William Eggleston. In 1980, Aura Records reissued the brilliantly messy endeavor. It's since been re-pressed by several labels with varying sequences.

Alex Chilton: It's the summation of my wild period, I guess. The music sounds so untamed and unrehearsed.

Richard Rosebrough: There was a lot of partying going on in those days. Alex's behavior knew no bounds. He'd go out and do anything with anybody, anytime, anywhere. He had a lot of girlfriends. There's a song on the *Like Flies on Sherbert* that goes, "I go from girl after girl, night after night"—that's Alex.

Alex Chilton: It was a speculative project. [No record label] had given us any money to do the thing up front...I just thought I needed to make a record.

Holly George-Warren: Alex had been exploring all kinds of music since he was a kid and that's his exploration of old-timey country [Carter Family], honky-tonk [Ernest Tubb], Cajun, R&B, and soul and his interpretation of roots music. Also, it represented the complete opposite recording technique that was used on *#1 Record*. Rather than seek perfection via overdubs and re-dos, he tried to catch lightning in a bottle.

Alex Chilton: When I conceived of doing the record, I thought maybe Jim and I, and maybe one or two other people, would record. When I turned up for the session, Jim had his whole band there, like Lee Baker and Mike Ladd on guitars and me on guitar, too. Ross Johnson was on drums, there was a bass player and a few other people. I thought, *Hmm, this isn't what I had in mind,* but I didn't say anything. I just thought we should try it and see how it goes...I was out there playing it, I wasn't in the control room listening to it, so I thought, *Man, that must sound terrible.* But when I went in and heard what we had done, it was just incredible-sounding. I like that album a lot still...Most of it was recorded in three nights. "Hey! Little Child" was written and recorded right before the final album mix-down. I re-recorded "Girl After Girl" then too, because I didn't feel I had a sufficient take of it from before.

Ross Johnson — Drummer, Alex Chilton, Panther Burns, solo musician: We started *Like Flies on Sherbert* at Sam Phillips in February 1978 and finished sessions at Ardent the next August. We would begin around noon, after I had already had my liquid breakfast and I would be knocking over mics, doing drum overdubs when [John] Hampton would say, "Come lie down on the couch." No matter what alcohol-fueled fun was going on around him, Chilton always knew what he wanted to go on tape. He liked to do music in a social context, with people coming in and out of the studio, but he never got lost, even when people were spilling drinks on the board or having hissy fits.

Alex Chilton: We had used all the credit we had with any recording studios to get the project done, so I had to slip back into the studio whenever I could...I would get a night and then the next week I would get two nights. Over about a year, I finally got the album mixed.

Upon its release, Like Flies *sold few copies, though, over the years, it's become a sought-after fan favorite.*

Ric Menck: The Chilton record I go to first nowadays is *Like Flies on Sherbert*, which I feel is his masterpiece. Yeah, it's a fucked-up record, but that turns me on. I think the record is more produced than most people think, but that the idea of primitive musical chaos is played up to incredible effect. I don't think it's easy to make a record that sounds like *Like Flies on Sherbet*, one that is compelling and listenable...To my mind, this coincides with the point where his true musical personality begins to surface.

Chris remained distant from the studio. Instead of hunkering down at Ardent, he spent time with John Fry in the sky, flying to tropical destinations. With Fry in the pilot's seat, the pair resumed taking trips to St. Martin. Chris' final trip to the island was in May 1978.

John Fry: A lot of our friends tagged along with us over the years. Earl Smith and his wife made the flight a few times with us, both in light aircraft and on the airline. Sometimes it was larger groups of people. The little airplanes kept getting bigger and bigger. I can remember one trip down there where Tommy Hoehn and his first wife, Sarah, were on the plane. Chris cooked up a scheme to pick up some friends from Atlanta. After we took off in Atlanta, I thought, "I should have added up all the weight, I should have checked the balance, this thing feels squirrely." After we burned off some fuel, we were okay, but it was a white-knuckle flight.

David Bell: Chris had become a licensed private pilot. He'd fly out of Memphis at the small flying service near the main airport. He took me up once for a flight down to Mississippi to visit our step-grandmother for lunch. On the way down, he looked over at me with an evil grin and asked, "Do you want me to stall?" I screamed back at him, "Don't you dare!" I was petrified. Luckily, he had mercy on me.

Tommie Dunavant: One trip to St. Martin, we sat on the beach down from David's house and a hotel called La Samanna. There were airplanes flying over because the hotel was close to the airport. We were drinking piña coladas. Chris was relaxed and happy. He loved the calypso music and steel-drum music on the beach. He was in his element.

Holliday Aldridge: When I bonded with Chris was on the trip to St. Martin in 1976, I went with Jody, we were still dating. Fry and Chris slept on the opposite side of the house on the two twin beds and Jody and I got the master suite. We had to use rain water as our water source. They didn't have a lot of rain, so we had to conserve. It was all low-key, no one getting really drunk or wild partying. Chris cooked for us. He made the best hash browns I've ever had in my life. We would just relax, go to restaurants, hang at the beach and take field trips to the towns to shop. It was calm for the '70s.

Chris' alcoholic, Dilaudid-shooting days were behind him, but his penchant for opiate-based painkillers still lingered in later years — albeit to a much lower degree and weaker caliber of medications.

Holliday Aldridge: We were at the Bells' house in St. Martin and I just had horrible cramps. They all wanted to go out, but I didn't want to, and Jody didn't want to leave me. I was telling him to just go. Then Chris comes out with a Empirin 3 pill, which is aspirin with codeine. He gave me one and suddenly I'm euphoric and don't have cramps. I was on cloud nine and was up for anything.

Tommy Hoehn: [Chris] and I went to St. Martin on one occasion with John Fry. Chris would occasionally dabble in codeine…He would sometimes dabble in that or drink a little bit — we did some of that on the islands.

Even during these mellow, codeine-dosed vacations in St. Martin, Chris dedicated time to spreading the word of Jesus Christ.

John Fry: We were getting ready to fly to St. Martin when Chris acquired — from somewhere — this giant sack of paperback books. They were the Book of John and the Book of Acts. They were sections abridged from the Bible. He said, "We need to carry these down because there's a guy down there who is doing work with some kids and he needs these." I said, "Fine, we'll carry them." I was a pagan at the time, so I was annoyed. I was like, "Oh, another piece of baggage." We got down there and drove from the Bells' house over to Philipsburg, the main town on the Dutch side. Back then it was damn near terrifying. They had this road going over the mountain where we could just fall off the side at any minute. We get over there and he's walking around with this giant paper sack of books. I said, "Where are we taking these?" He said, "I don't know, but this guy is around this area somewhere and I think we'll find him."

Chris Bell vacationing in Dominica, March 1976.

ARDENT STUDIOS ARCHIVE

Chris Bell on a Mississippi River steamboat.

ARDENT STUDIOS ARCHIVE

Chris Bell in St. Martin, 1978.

I said, "You don't know his address, phone number or anything?" Chris said, "No, I don't, but it's fine." Inside my head I'm just cussing. I'm thinking we're on a fool's errand now. About three minutes later, this black guy comes walking down the street and he recognizes Chris and gets this big smile on his face. Chris says, "Oh, there you are. I knew you'd be around here somewhere. We brought these for you." The man pulled them out and at first looked at them a bit suspiciously. Then he realized what they were and just looked at Chris and said, "Yes! Thank you. We can make good use of these." I have not a clue how they knew each other. He was going through a powerful experience. I don't recall when religion first started having an impact on Chris. My recollection is that he'd have periods where he was nurtured by that, and then some dry periods. As time went along, the nurtured periods grew, and the dry periods seemed to disappear. In the last 18 months of his life, he was just solid in his relationship with Christ. All that back-and-forth stuff seemed to have gone away.

Nicky's got the D's.

Oh, D. I had forgotten what you felt like
I wanna take you in my arms
I know you do me

~~Bonnie~~ please
Oh please
Dont hang me up
Oh please
Dont bring me down
oh Please, I know Nicky's Got the D.'s

I read the news I know what goin on

Codiene

Chris Bell's handwritten lyrics for a never-recorded song, "Nicky's Got the D's."

ACT SIX

A LIGHT IN THE DARKNESS

Chris Bell in a Memphis guitar shop.

PHOTO BY JOHN DANDO

CHAPTER 23

CAR, EMI, & AURA — THE FINAL REHEARSAL: SUMMER 1978-1979

Chris arrived at home with work to do. On April 1, 1978, he penned a contract with Car Records, Chris Stamey's tiny, New York City-based record label. The deal was for one picture sleeve vinyl single and "I Am the Cosmos" was slated for the A-side. This deal came four years after the track was recorded at Shoe Productions. For the B-side, Bell suggested "Fight at the Table," but Stamey insisted on the moodier "You and Your Sister," Bell's final duet with Alex Chilton. Stamey started Car Records in North Carolina in 1976 as an outlet to release an EP by his own band, the Sneakers. After he moved to Bleeker Street in Greenwich Village, a few more releases followed. Given the distance between them, Stamey never met Bell in person; instead the two communicated through a series of letters and phone calls. For payment, Stamey mailed a $300 check to Bell, covering a $200 advance and Larry Nix's $100 mastering fee. One artistic suggestion made by Stamey was to speed up "Cosmos" a tad. He felt the track was a bit "draggy." Bell agreed and used vari-speed control to bump up the pitch. From there, the lacquers were shipped to Mastercraft Record Plating in New York and then All Disc in New Jersey pressed a limited edition of roughly 700 copies. It's since been re-pressed twice, but copies of the original pressing often fetch $200-$300 per copy. It was the first and only solo release Bell saw in his lifetime.

David Bell: I didn't find this out until years later, but it was Alex who brought "I Am the Cosmos" to Chris Stamey and said, "Hey, you ought to release this."

Alex Chilton: "I Am the Cosmos" was the best thing he ever did. It needed to be released ever since it was made.

Chris Bell: I prefer it to anything I did with Big Star. It has far deeper personal meaning. I'm really proud of the arrangement.

Richard Rosebrough: Chris didn't directly talk about the lyrics with me, but he did with Dore Harper. A lot of the information about the song I got came from talking with her. She and Chris discussed what it's all about. I honestly don't get it. It's all very abstract and gets into this realm of the Lord, universe and God.

As the solo single arrived in select record shops in July 1978, Car Records issued a one-sheet press release to rock critics, calling Chris' "I Am the Cosmos" his "monstrous masterpiece" and underscoring how the "extremely rare Big Star records" were in high demand and that Chris was "currently discussing his return to the stage with Jody Stephens." ZigZag, a British rock magazine, was among the first publications to review the single in its November 1978 issue:

"Chris Bell was a member of those legends-you-love-to-wish-you-had-loved Big Star, and this seems to be a revamp of one of their old songs. Unsurprisingly reminiscent of ex-colleague Alex Chilton in its fragile quirkiness (oh ho, and here's Alex on the 'B' side too!) ...[This single is] ponderously swamped in guitar-layers and so dense you could cut the sound with a razor as it aches and heaves. I like."

—HUGH JARSE, ZIGZAG

Coinciding with the release was the news that EMI and Stax had agreed to issue #1 Record and Radio City as a double LP. This English-made gatefold sleeve edition came about after demand from fans pushed the prices of the scarce originals to upwards of $50 each—$200 in today's money. In a July 29 postcard from Jody to Chris, the defunct band's drummer modestly gloated about early interest from record shops: "3,500 pre-orders. Not bad." Jody, who was in Paris chasing music leads, witnessed Big Star's growing fandom in European music mags. Days later, on August 1, the fanfare continued when Third was finally issued by PVC Records in the United States and by Aura Records in the U.K. Each featured varying track lists. Two other Third import pressings followed via Les Disques Motors in France, and Powderworks Records in Australia. By the fall of '78, as PVC placed full-page ads for Third in rock publications like Trouser Press, a string of reviews cropped up in notable mags, including Creem, which declared Third a "haphazard masterpiece." Four years after its disintegration, the band's catalog had finally secured some proper distribution, and fans were buying it. Of course, Alex still had no interest in reviving the group. In a late 1978 interview with the Dixie Flyer, Alex voiced concerns about the freshly issued double LP and the industry in general. "None of us [band members] got anything from [EMI-Stax]," he said. "They didn't even send me a copy of the album. I don't know whether they'll pay us or not. Four albums out this summer, *and four singles, and not a penny from any of them." Cashing in on the burst of Big Star buzz seemed unlikely, but not impossible. In an interview with* Dark Star *magazine, Jody remained optimistic. "I'm trying to re-form the original band now, all four of us," Jody told the London-based publication. "It's difficult. Chris is involved with his father's hamburger chain and he's got a tennis habit, too, so he has to support that. He's pretty pressured...but Chris is all for it and so is Andy. Alex is a possible maybe because he's got other things he wants to do... But if the reissues really sell, it might persuade him and maybe we would make some money for a change. But Alex is so unpredictable. We might commit ourselves to a small tour of Europe and see where we go from there."*

David Bell: Chris was still hoping something could happen with his music.

Alex Chilton: I first became aware of it, that there was a real cult of fans around the band, in the later '70s, I guess in 1977.

Drew DeNicola: It was almost like everything was coming back around for him. It was beautiful when those records came out because he at least got to know they were being released.

Jody Stephens: We were excited about it and there were conversations about getting Big Star back together. I was overseas for five months, [and] it seemed like every time I picked up a new *Melody Maker* or *NME*, there was something about Alex or Big Star, even if it was just in the back where people were looking to buy the records...I would have done a reunion tour. I thought it was a good idea with or without Alex. I didn't see Alex not being there stopping it. We could have done it with Chris, and Chris had new material.

Tom Eubanks: Chris was attempting to get back together with Big Star. He called me up at work one morning. He said he and Alex were talking about putting Big Star back together, but Alex had gotten into playing sort of an avant-garde style. Chris said, "We're trying to put Big Star back together, but I've got a problem. Alex doesn't want the instruments to necessarily be in tune or worry about playing in tempo with the drummer." I said, "Well, you've got a real problem. How are you going to recreate *#1 Record* under those circumstances?" He said, "I don't know what we're going to do."

David Bell: Chris left Danver's after about a year and a half. He said, "There's no way I can do this the rest of my life." He felt he'd done the good thing and made a good-faith effort, but in the end, it wasn't for him. He got a job at the Whole Foods General Store.

Advertisement for the EMI/Stax Records double-LP reissue of *#1 Record* and *Radio City*, 1978.

89 Bleecker St.
New York City, 10012
212 254 5315

Dear Chris:

I enclose a $200 check for you as an advance and
$100 for the mastering. You can send the lacquers to
Mastercraft Record Plating, Inc., 609 West 51st Street,
New York City, 10019. Include a note that it is to be
sent to Alldisc. I would also like a safety copy of
the master tape for the files, when you have time.

The contract will be down to you in a few days.
If you think of any clauses you need in the meantime,
let us know. Otherwise, it will be as we discussed.

When you send the photos, give me any information
that you want on the cover. I need publishing information, facts on who played what, who engineered and
produced various mixes, any credits and thanks to's,
and ideas about a cover conception. Charles Parrish
will be doing the art, and you can discuss it with him
if you wnt to. If you want a message around the inside
vinyl, indicate it on the note to Mastercraft. Also,
if you have a bio or any facts for a press release,
send them. In praticular, a post Bg Str capsule history
would be good.

yrs

Chris Stamey

Chris Stamey's 1978 letter to Chris Bell detailing the "I Am the Cosmos" single deal—
the limited Car Records release is seen on the opposite page.

COURTESY OF DAVID BELL

353

The "I Am the Cosmos" single, released by Car Records in 1978.

Big Star's *Third* was recorded in late 1974, but remained unreleased for four years. Above is a 1978 PVC Records advertisement for the first issue of the record.

Ken Woodley: This was an independent store. It was across the street from the Knickerbocker.

David Bell: Back then Whole Foods was a hippie-dippy thing, because only the hippies were interested in healthy food, apparently. Before Whole Foods, Chris worked for a short time as a waiter at some restaurant down on the river, but he wanted to be true to his talent and do what he could with music.

Cindy Bell Coleman: The corporate life was just not for him; he was too creative. He needed to be making music or painting. He was also the boss' son, which is a hard thing to follow. Chris was just a normal kid who was seeking his father's approval, and Daddy had some pretty big shoes to fill.

Linda Schaeffer Yarman: Chris' dad reminded me of my father: all business. That's the thing that drew us together. We both had successful fathers who were wealthy and wanted us to play the game. I didn't want to do it and neither did he. Chris didn't feel he was going to measure up and join the country club or run a restaurant.

Being freed up from Danver's allowed Chris not only more time to plot a Big Star reunion with Jody, but also to further grow his budding musical partnership with Tommy Hoehn. Hoehn had spent time playing in Prix, a mid-'70s group featuring Jon Tiven, which produced two singles in its short lifespan. After Prix unsuccessfully auditioned for Columbia Records in the fall of 1976 at a New York City studio, Tommy returned to Memphis and refocused as a solo artist, issuing "Blow Yourself Up," the now classic power-pop single on Power Play Records. The B-side, "Love You All Day Long," featured Chris on lead guitar. The pair's equal love of the Beatles and British pop made for a seamless sound. Tommy also shared with Chris the discouragement of releasing a failed album. Earlier that year, Losing You to Sleep, *his brilliant debut solo LP on London Records, flopped despite critical praise and full-page ads in* Rolling Stone. *They had plenty to commiserate about, but most importantly, Chris appreciated their songwriting partnership; something he hadn't experienced since his* #1 Record *days. Their sonic kinship seemed promising and, they both relished spending countless hours in the studio. It was a perfect match.*

Lesa Aldridge Hoehn: Tommy mostly liked to write songs and record. London Records picked up his *Losing You to Sleep* album. They flew him up to New York to take the photo on the record and then he didn't book any gigs. I don't know what happened. Maybe he dropped the ball. He was a fine musician and would play by ear. I don't remember him playing as much as the Klitz or Panther Burns did. There were Tommy Hoehn shows, but not as many.

Tommy Hoehn: Chris and I had talked about making a band together. I talked to Ken Woodley a bit about it, too. [The year before], we had co-written a few songs, one named "Cuba." We had done some work on another tune called "Get Away," and several other songs that we worked together on.

Lesa Aldridge Hoehn: Tommy and Chris were working together, writing together and wanted to record. They were doing music together but were also close friends and hanging out a lot.

Sarah Gratz: When I was married to Tommy, we would go out to Chris' house out east. We would sit around and listen to his songs, the latter part of his music. We would go upstairs, and Chris would play some of the things he was doing at Ardent. He and Tommy spent a lot of nights, right before he died, trying to put together some new songs. I don't know if anything ever came of it. It was almost like Chris and Tommy were brothers. It was easy for them to work together. At that time, Chris was trying to find a new sound, but nothing survived from that collaboration.

Even with the torrent of positive energy unexpectedly surrounding his music, as the 1978 holiday season loomed, Chris dealt with a mild bout of seasonal depression.

David Bell: Chris was up and down a little bit over the holidays. He always hated Christmas, and so did I. Christmas always seemed to be depressing, so this was normal. It wasn't anything clinical, he just had the blues a little bit. I was living at my parents' home and so was Chris. Fortune smiled on me. I had been living in Denver for over a year and just decided to come back to Memphis for about six months. I was headed toward a monastery in Michigan, that's actually why I wanted to come back home to visit the family for a while. I wanted to see them before I left, although I soon abandoned that monastery plan. Luckily, I got to spend the last six weeks of his life with him at our parents' home. I've always said I would have hated the world, God and everything else, for the rest of my life if I had not been back home and had those last weeks to be with him before he was killed.

Linda Schaeffer Yarman: I have a haunting memory of Chris asking me to move to England with him. He wanted to just leave. He said, "That would solve all of my problems." We didn't get into what those problems were. I was seriously considering the offer, but I didn't do it. A few months later, he was gone.

John Dando: Chris left himself no way out, he was working without a net. I used to have this terrible premonition that he would never grow old because he had nowhere to go. He had no way out. I just couldn't project him living past his twenties. He just had no way to survive in the future. It was obvious towards the latter part of his life that it was going to be difficult for him to do that.

Steve Rhea: Chris would tell you he didn't expect to live beyond thirty.

Tom Eubanks: He'd always tell me, "You know, I've got to work and work because I have to become a millionaire by the time I'm thirty. If I don't do it by then, it's all over."

Regardless of his inner turmoil, Chris never lost sight of his Christianity, or what he saw as the religion's healing powers.

Tommy Hoehn: Chris was certainly on a spiritual quest. He felt like the Holy Spirit entered him and healed him. He wore glasses, but then he felt like the Holy Spirit had made his vision better. He had an aversion to spaghetti—he thought it was like eating worms—so when we would go out to eat at his parents' restaurant, the Knickerbocker in East Memphis, he would intentionally order spaghetti to show how the power of the spirit was healing him. He'd eat spaghetti and drive without his glasses on.

During his final months, Chris occasionally patronized the now-defunct Maranatha Chapel. However, according to his close friends, it wasn't a positive experience for him.

Tommy Hoehn: His involvement with charismatic Christianity was profound; his involvement with that specific church was casual. He liked the social aspect of it, hanging out...My impression of that church was it did not have an organized clergy. It was a lot of people that ran around individually ministering to people.

Richard Rosebrough: Chris, Earl Smith and Earl's mother would go there. They would all speak in tongues. I went out there once with him. Chris kept bugging me, "You've got to come out here!" Later, I heard some weird stories about that church and how one of the people there was chasing after boys.

Tommy Hoehn: After the church service, one of the individuals came up to us and condemned us for looking like Christ, for having long hair and beards...He said, "You are trying to pray in the image of Christ." He wasn't the leader of the church, he was one of the body...Chris took it to heart, he was very sensitive...We went out to eat later that evening, pretty late, around 1 a.m. There we sat talking and I looked across the aisle and there was this fellow who had been condemning us sitting with someone in drag and they were making out...Chris was pretty disturbed by it. It bothered him. My take was, "Chris, look, it's bullshit. Not the Holy Spirit, but this specific incident is bullshit." I don't know if it was the sexual element or what, but it bothered him...What was even more tragically disillusioning [for Chris] was that his eyes weren't getting better, he wasn't going to be a tennis pro, and probably wasn't ever going to be a heterosexual Chris never came out as a homosexual. He and I were never lovers, but I always knew that Chris at least leaned that way. One thing that tormented him was that he'd become a Christian and that his sexual orientation had not necessarily changed. He certainly made an effort to make it change, but like he made an effort to make his eyes better and the spaghetti taste good, none of that worked. But I don't think that Chris, frankly, was ever sexually involved with another guy after he was born again.

A few days later, Chris arrived at his final rehearsal at Tommy's on December 26, 1978. The get-together started with an early-evening round of jamming with guitarist Gene Nunez.

Gene Nunez — Guitarist, Tommy Hoehn Band, solo: That rehearsal was the second time I had ever met Chris Bell. Chris had not been part of the Tommy Hoehn Band and it wasn't clear to me if he was going to be a part of the band on a permanent basis. The day Chris Bell died, I only saw him in the early afternoon. There was a daytime rehearsal at Tommy's house for a gig on New Year's Eve. We were planning to go play a show at one of the clubs there along Madison, the Overton Square area. Chris showed up and we started around 2 or 3 p.m. We set up in Tommy's living room in Midtown. We were rehearsing "Zero" and some of the things Chris had a hand in co-writing with Tommy. We had some burgers and beer but none of us were drunk. It wasn't a lot of beer and there wasn't anything stronger going on. The Tommy Hoehn Band was known to do some partying, but this wasn't one of those times, at least while I was there. Chris was not intoxicated when I quit for the night. That was at 6 or 7 p.m. Of course, I wasn't around after a certain point on that day. I was shocked when I got the call the next day.

After Gene left, Chris left and met up with Ken Woodley and hung out for a bit. After a few hours, Chris and Ken went to Tommy's for a late-night jam session. Also present that evening was Sarah Gratz and their friend Mike "Wild Willy" Willis.

Ken Woodley: Chris and I had been hanging out, then we met up with Tommy over at his house. He lived off Poplar Avenue on Autumn. We were playing in his living room. We started pretty late. I was on drums and Chris and Tommy were playing guitars.

Tommy Hoehn: We were toying with the idea of making a band...He was rehearsing with myself and Ken. We weren't calling ourselves anything, but we knew we were working up to it and the plan was to cut another record, hopefully with London Records.

Mike Willis — Friend of Tommy Hoehn: That night, Tommy and the guys were just jamming and writing songs. That wasn't unusual, but there was something off that night. Tommy and I hung out with Chris quite a bit over the last year. They'd played music a lot, and Chris was always sober. He never had a drink or smoked with us. That last night, he came in with a big smile on his face and for the first time since I had met him, Chris had a drink and smoked a joint with us.

Ken Woodley: We were *fucked up*. It had something to do with pharmaceuticals.

Tommy Hoehn: Chris showed up with a fifth of Jack Daniel's, which was way out of character...He had also gotten his hands on Mandrax—they were Mexico's version of Quaaludes. Where he got them, I don't know or care, but he had gotten a pretty good number of them. He had taken them, and he was fucked up, walking around talking about how in this world, in this business, you have to become a Superman, existential Nietzsche-type. You have to rise to the occasion to make it in the music business. You have to be all this stuff that is virtually impossible to be. He was clearly frustrated, and he was clearly fucked up. Chris wasn't in recovery, and I didn't perceive this as a relapse, but it felt that way...like, "Chris, what are you doing?" For me, that was normal behavior, but it was odd to see him doing it.

Sarah Gratz: I absolutely do not remember Chris being overly drunk or high. I didn't have a clue, but I heard some undertones of him having things I didn't know about. I do know it was late and they were working hard. He left that night after they finished working on some material.

Ken Woodley: I worked at Ardent and had to be there at 7 a.m., so I said, "I have to go." It pissed them off. They wanted to keep playing. We jammed right up to the last second.

Tommy Hoehn: Chris was very messed up when he left; that may be all there is to it.

At roughly 1:05 a.m., the guys called it a night and Chris split from Tommy's house alongside Ken, who agreed to give Chris a lift to his car.

Tommy Hoehn: Chris left my house and got in the car with Ken. Ken took him back to Ardent. I lived around the corner from there.

John Fry: Chris had parked his car at Ardent before he went to Tommy's, so Ken Woodley drove him over to the studio to pick it up.

Ken Woodley: In my car, Chris didn't say anything. When I dropped him at Ardent, he just said, "I'll talk to you tomorrow." He seemed OK. He didn't go inside of Ardent. He got right in his car and headed home by himself.

Tommy Hoehn: He got in his little white Triumph and took off. He went down Madison, got on Poplar, headed east and wrecked his car somewhere near the Maranatha church.

There's a light in the darkness
It doesn't seem far
Is something the matter?
The throttle's ajar

— CHRIS BELL, "SPEED OF SOUND"

At 1:25 a.m. Chris passed the Grove Park intersection, where he clipped the curb, lost control and left the south side of Poplar, according to a Memphis Police Department report. He then crossed a private driveway and collided head-on with a wooden utility pole.

John Fry: The accident was on Poplar Avenue, a main east-west street. Chris hit the pole, the thing snapped and fell over and crushed the car.

David Bell: He died instantly. There was some sort of report that said excessive speed was not involved. The speed limit there would be forty. The bad thing about those light poles, they were barely off the pavement — very close to the road.

Terry Manning: The rebound force knocked his car back out into the street, and then the pole itself came down on the car and hit him. It happened right in front of the Goldsmith's department store that was there at the time.

Gene Nunez: It was right near the Knickerbocker Restaurant, his father's business on Poplar. This was a couple days after Christmas, so it was a cold night.

Larry Raspberry: There was a couple who witnessed that accident. They stopped to ask if Chris was okay and then watched in horror as that pole fell on him.

Sarah Gratz: I asked Tommy, "Was there anything wrong with Chris when he left our house? Do you think it could have played a part in his accident?" Tommy said, "Well, he might have been taking some pills."

Tommy Hoehn: I don't think Chris committed suicide, but I don't know what happened. I thought he had for a long time. I felt guilty about letting him leave my house.

While the ambulance was still en route, Memphis Police Sergeant George L. Stacy arrived on the scene minutes after the accident and discovered the body of Chris Bell. Across town, Chris' sister Sara rushed to her parents' home.

Sara Bell: I got a call from our father saying Chris had been in an accident. I lived not far from their house, so I said, "I'll be right there." I drove down with them to the hospital. The whole time, I was thinking, "Why is he driving so slowly? Why isn't he speeding? What's going on here?" Then we walked into The MED [Regional Medical Center], and they took us in a room and said, "I'm sorry, your son Christopher didn't make it." It didn't dawn on me that he had died. I'm thinking, "What do you mean he didn't make it? He isn't here yet?" Then I looked at my parents' faces, and I realized what they were saying. I just thought he had been in an accident. I always wondered if Daddy already knew on the way to the hospital and that's why he was driving so slowly. Maybe he knew that once we were taken down to The MED, that would be it.

John Fry: I'll never forget it. I woke up startled, like someone was in the room. I turned a light on. I looked over at the clock. It was around 1:30 a.m. I cut the light off and went back to sleep. About 5:30 or 6 a.m., my phone rang. It was Chris Bell's dad. He told me that Chris had a car accident, and he was dead. The moment I woke up startled was at the exact time of the accident. I'll never forget that.

Jody Stephens: The night Chris died, I came to the studio looking for him. They said he had just left. It was around 1 a.m. or so. I decided to head home and drove down Poplar. When I got to this department store, it's a big intersection, and near there I saw a wreck. At that point in the night I couldn't tell what model of car it was, and I didn't want to deal with it, so I turned off on a side street and took another route home. John Fry called me the next morning and told me Chris had died in a car accident and where it happened. I thought, "Oh, my God. I saw Chris' car with the pole on top of it." I didn't realize it was him.

Given the holiday timing, some out-of-town relatives and friends were still in Memphis, while others were still commuting home. While Vernon Bell handled calling his family, the stoic John Fry offered to notify Chris' friends.

Cindy Bell Coleman: Daddy called at six o'clock in the morning and told me. Basically, I went into shock, and my husband took the phone.

Richard Rosebrough: Dore Harper called me up in the early morning hours and said, "Where's David? Chris has been killed!" We were on the phone for four hours straight. Then Fry called me, dutifully, at 9 a.m. He was the leader.

Ken Woodley: I showed up at Ardent the next morning. John Fry walks in and says, "I've got some bad news." I left and proceeded to drink. I don't like talking about it.

David Bell: Hearing the news was an unfortunate thing for me. I had spent the night at a friend's in Memphis. I had taken my father's step-mother down to Mississippi to drop her off at her home, so I wasn't in touch with anybody. I came home the next morning, and I stopped at the Knickerbocker. I saw a sign on the door about the restaurant being closed. Nobody there said anything to me. I was in the kitchen and I walked into the bar area and a waitress, who I had known for years, came up to me and said, "I don't know what we're going to do without Chris." I thought, *What are you talking about?* I'm sure I had a strange look on my face. That's how I found out. I told the hostess, "Call my parents, tell them I'm on my way home...Something is going on and I don't know anything about it, just tell them I'm coming home." All the way home I thought, *Well, maybe I misunderstood something.*

Tommie Dunavant: Earl and I were back in Memphis for the holidays, so we saw Chris the day before he died. We had lunch with him. Earl and I had been trying to have children and I had some miscarriages, so we talked about life and death. We were still in Memphis when we got the phone call that he had died. It was such a shock; we had just seen him. When I saw Chris, I thought he was acting fine.

John Dando: I was headed home to Memphis that Christmas but didn't get into town until December 26, and I called Chris that day. We were going to get together the next day, but Mr. Bell called me at five o'clock that morning and told me Chris had been killed.

Paul Williams — Alex Chilton's friend, Audiomania Records founder: Alex Chilton and I were hanging out at Alex's house. We stayed up pretty late, probably 2 or 3 a.m. We listened to records all night. Alex kept playing these two records over and over. One of them was "Train Kept A-Rollin'" by Johnny Burnette and the Rock and Roll Trio. The other was "My Way" by Sid Vicious, which was a new record at the time. He had the twelve-inch single. He played each a dozen times. The next morning, I went back over to pick him up. We were going to shop for

45s. He told me right when I picked him up that Chris had died. He was unsentimental about it. He was typical Alex about it, guarding his emotions. I heard that later that night Alex was hanging out with Fry and he did get more emotional about it, but I didn't see any sentiment about that at all from him. He was very much in denial about all of it.

Those who didn't receive a phone call likely read about the fatal wreck in The Commercial Appeal, the daily paper. "Bell, son of Mr. and Mrs. Vernon Bell of Germantown, was an employee of Whole Foods General Store and founder of the old Big Star rock band. He played in several bands after Big Star broke up." The Memphis Press-Scimitar, a now-defunct afternoon paper, also reported the accident. The headline read: "Son of Restaurateur Killed in Car Wreck." A few states away, Chris' former Danver's co-worker and close friend Helen Heinle heard from her co-workers after the news spread to Atlanta.

Helen Heinle: In late 1978, not long before the Christmas holidays, I had just turned eighteen, and he came to see me at my parents' house. I said goodbye to him on the front porch. That was the last time I saw Chris. It was cold outside. He had on a little hat and scarf. We were like, "All right, I'll see you after Christmas." Then the accident happened. I never got closure because I never got to be with his family or go to the funeral.

Sara Bell: I read some letters from Helen to my mother after Chris died. She wrote her several times, which was comforting to her. She told her how much she loved him and how much she missed him.

Helen Heinle: After Chris was killed, I called his house and spoke to one of his sisters on the phone. She told me, "Chris said he thought you two would probably get married one day." I thought that was funny. Chris and I had never talked about that. I felt the same way, but we never discussed it. It did make me feel good. I've often thought, "I wonder what my life would have been like if he had lived." After his car accident, his family sent me a couple little items of his. One was a little carved figure from St. Martin. I still have a sweater of his that he gave me. I've hung onto it all these years, even though it's on the threadbare side now.

Vernon Bell promptly got the funeral affairs in order and had the service set for the day after the wreck, Thursday, December 28. The well-attended service was held at a Memphis church he frequented as a communicant. The traditional memorial closed with a spirited version of the Easter hymn "Jesus Christ Is Risen Today."

John Fry: His funeral was at Saint John's Episcopal Church. I was one of the pallbearers. So was John Dando.

Steve Rhea: I was also a pallbearer with Tommy Hoehn and some other people.

Tom Eubanks: I went over to the funeral home. Of course, it was closed casket.

Terry Manning: It devastated everybody. It was eerie, cold, and overcast the day of the funeral. It was a terrible time.

Linda Schaeffer Yarman: I went to the funeral and sat with Carole. I was doing well but then started crying uncontrollably at the end of the service and ran out. I was embarrassed.

Tommy Hoehn: What I remember of the funeral is not very much. I remember carrying his coffin. I remember telling John Fry that [Chris] had taken drugs and John said to keep that to myself. I did.

Bob Schiffer: I spoke to Andy right after Chris died. Andy was in such rough shape he said he wasn't going to go to the funeral, but he went at the last minute. He was overwhelmed.

Tommie Dunavant: It was surreal. Nobody could believe it was real. Earl was in a daze. He hadn't dealt with it. I remember seeing John Fry's face and seeing Chris' family. It was one of the saddest times of our lives, just the heaviness of what happened. He was so young.

Jody Stephens: When you lose a loved one, the world gets quiet. You get numb. It's an incomprehensible event. It's like trying to get your mind around the universe or around God. It's death.

After the service, a procession of vehicles embarked on the twenty-minute drive northeast to Bartlett, Tennessee for the burial at Memory Hill Gardens Cemetery (now Memphis Funeral Home and Memorial Gardens). Buried with Chris was a copy of #1 Record, which John Fry brought to the funeral home at the request of the family.

Cindy Bell Coleman: The church was packed; there was no room left. Then the procession to the cemetery—you could look back and see cars forever.

Linda Schaeffer Yarman: I went to the gravesite. I had it a little bit more together by then. To this day, when I visit Memphis, there is hardly a time where I don't visit his grave.

John Fry: By odd circumstance, December 28th is Alex Chilton's birthday. Alex was still living in Memphis when this happened. He did not come to the funeral service, but he did come by my house after the burial was over and talked to me for a while. He didn't say why he didn't show up. He just wasn't up for doing that. I can certainly understand that.

Richard Rosebrough: Alex missed the funeral. It was something like he'd overslept or didn't get it together. He said he came to the service, but everyone had left. He was late getting there. I still hold a little grudge about that.

Vera Ellis: When I was dating Alex, my brother was killed in a car accident. Alex didn't go to the funeral and he should have. That would have been the appropriate thing to do. He said, "No, it will bring me down." That's a part of him being obstinate and kind of a jerk. It's like, "Alex, are you afraid you're going to cry?" He didn't want to deal with the emotions.

Jim Dickinson: I was around Alex when Chris died, and it definitely affected him. Of course, you couldn't help but think it could have just as easily had been him driving in the car. A lot of people think Chris committed suicide. I don't know what to say about that. He was more of a mystery in that way than Alex.

Chris Morris: To this day, people wonder if the accident that took his life was premeditated or not. That's thoroughly understandable knowing his history of attempting suicide.

Varying theories have circulated around Memphis for decades about what condition and state of mind Chris was in during those early-morning hours of December 27, and whether it was an accident or intentional. The police report shows Chris' blood-alcohol concentration was tested and he was not intoxicated at the time of the accident. Only a trace amount appeared in the results. If Chris indeed arrived at Tommy's with a bottle of whiskey, the report shows he didn't drink much of it. Chris was also not in possession of any prescription pills or mind-altering narcotics at the scene. Only a bottle of vitamins was found in his car. A toxicology test was never performed.

Rob Jovanovic — Author, *Big Star: The Story of Rock's Forgotten Band*: The police report clearly shows that Bell's car clipped the curb one hundred feet before it swerved off the road and into the pole. If he had planned to commit suicide, as some suspected, there were surely much easier ways to intentionally crash a car.

Richard Rosebrough: The story was out pretty quickly that Chris popped Mandrax. That story has circulated in Memphis for years. I've heard a lot of stories. I was not there. I don't know what he took or what happened, but it's possible that's what happened. Most people feel it was a total accident.

Tom Eubanks: I heard rumors they were doing Quaaludes and Chris likely nodded off.

Richard Rosebrough: Nobody was there, and nobody knows. It's a mystery to everyone.

Tommie Dunavant: I heard that Quaalude rumor just like everybody has heard it. Earl never thought it was suicide. Earl always thought if it was true about the drugs, that Chris never meant to kill himself. He didn't think Chris was capable of copping out on life that way.

Lesa Aldridge Hoehn: Tommy told me Chris' accident was something that always hurt him deeply. Of course, because they were hanging out that night, he'd say, "Could I have done something?"

Days after Chris was interred, John Fry and a few other close friends visited Chris' bedroom. In his closet sat the box of unissued solo tapes. The reels remained untouched for over thirteen years.

John Fry: Some of us were invited out to the Bells' house on Riverdale to go up to his room. His mother put out some of his objects on his bed and said, "If any of you want any of these things, take them." One of them was his tennis racket. Somebody got the Car Records 45 and put it on this tiny record player in the corner and played it. That was the first time I heard "Cosmos." I never heard it until after his death.

John Hampton: I am not a good death person. It doesn't register with me. I have let it sink in for a good long while. I would see his gear around the studio. I would see his guitar sitting there by the amp he played through the other day—then I would have to remind myself, "Oh, yeah. He's not around anymore." For me, it was like that. John, on the other hand, was wrecked.

Richard Rosebrough: Everyone knew it had to hurt John more than anyone else, but you couldn't look at him and tell. John did not show emotion.

Sara Bell: I was teaching school at the time and didn't cope well with any of it. Obviously, with the death of a sibling at such a young age, it was a difficult time.

Cindy Bell Coleman: I don't know how our parents dealt with it. When this happened, I was only twenty-one. Now, I can't fathom losing a child. Chris was just a kid. Of course, I was in my own little world of hurt. It had to have affected my mother more because she didn't ever change his bedroom. She kept it like a time capsule.

Sara Bell: Before Chris died, he was needle-pointing the cover for a kneeler cushion for the Episcopal Church. He was working on this and there were doves all over the cushion. When we were designing his grave marker, we decided to put a dove on it because of that. A few days after the funeral, my parents went down to their home in St. Martin. They would spend January through March down there. When they got there, a dove appeared on the patio. There had never been doves around there, just little finches and island birds, but this dove appeared. It visited them every single day they were there. We have pictures of it on my father's shoulder. My father, and all of us, considered it a sign from my brother that things were alright.

John Fry: Back in the Big Star days, I was a wandering pagan. I didn't believe anything. I was one of these kids that grew up in church but didn't have any real faith or anything. I was like, "That's just garbage they told me when I was a kid and it doesn't make any sense." Well, somebody once wisely said, "If the Bible doesn't make any sense to you, maybe it's because you're reading someone else's mail." That was true for me for a while. Chris had been continuously witnessing to me and telling me that, "Look, John, you need to read your Bible." I didn't want to then, but when Chris died I decided to read it. It's like we say down South: "How do you get the attention of a mule? Hit him between the eyes with a two-by-four." The next Sunday after his accident was my birthday. I got up, went to church, gave my heart to Christ and never looked back.

David Bell: I went back to England in the summer of 1979 for a couple months. I carried a copy of the 45 of "Cosmos" to AIR Studios and gave Geoff Emerick a copy. I was trying to recapture something of that past, the time I spent with Chris over there, but quickly you realize you can't go back. He was gone.

Outside of Memphis, the death of Chris Bell slowly circulated word-of-mouth through fans and a small obituary in Billboard Magazine. *Journalist Max Bell also published a half-page remembrance in* NME's *February '79 issue with a curiously fallacious headline, "Big Star Guitarist Drives Off Cliff." As the Reagan-era commenced, the Chris Bell catalog remained stagnant, forcing his posthumous musical legacy into a decade-plus dormancy. Meanwhile, his small fan base traded dubbed cassettes of his Car Records single and a few leaked solo recordings. Chris' aging parents, who remained in the family's Germantown home, were unaware of their late son's expanding pockets of fanatics.*

Cindy Bell Coleman: I got a call on December 15, 1985 saying Daddy had a heart attack. We took off in the car down Poplar to go to the hospital and saw the ambulance at the end of Riverdale near my parents' house. They had stopped to try to resuscitate him again. They couldn't get him back. He was far too young, only sixty-seven, but, hell, he died the way I want to die. He got up in the morning, smoked a cigarette, had his coffee and a glass of orange juice and then fell over backwards of a heart attack. Poor Momma had to suffer for three years after her stroke. It was terrible. Our mother was in very bad health for quite some time. She passed away November 25, 1992, so she never knew anything about Chris' album.

Two of Chris Bell's close friends: Dore Harper and Richard Rosebrough.

BELL
CHRISTOPHER BRANFORD
1951 ~ 1978

Chris Bell's final resting place.

when I look through your eyes I tend to get better
maybe I'm best advised to keep to myself

I fall every time
though I know she lies, I can't stay away

stars would fall from the skies and I won't forsake you
you've got lust in your eyes but I don't care

~~I fall~~ believing every line
though I know she lies ~~I can't stay away~~

keeping me in the dark
wondering where you are
watching me fall apart

you said take it slow
but I don't know, I don't know –

lie awake in the bed at nights and I worry (ask myself questions
I dont know if it's love but I can't forget you
what can I do

Chris Bell's handwritten lyrics to "Though I Know She Lies," one of the last songs he
ever recorded.

371

The Chris Bell master tape archive at Ardent Studios.

PHOTOS BY NICOLE RICO

This is a Soul Town

Well when I was a whole lot younger
Iused to sit on my own and wonder
Seems like I knew something was wrong
I thought this world was going under

Sometimes I get home at night
Feel OK_- it's alright
I ask myself "Is this Carnal?"
Or should I really be so uptight

He said This is a soul town
T
  They dont call it the Bluff City for nothin
Why dont you turn that guitar down

Chris Bell's handtyped lyrics for unreleased song, "This is a Soul Town."

373

The Panther Burns circa 1979. (l - r): Alex Chilton (guitar), Eric Hill (synthesizer), Ric Ivy (trumpet), Tav Falco (guitar/vocals), Ross Johnson (drums).

PHOTO BY EBET ROBERTS

CHAPTER 24

PANTHER BURNS — SCREAM FOR ALEX CHILTON: 1979-1988

In the weeks following Chris' death, Alex Chilton dug his heels deeper into Memphis's underground and co-founded The Panther Burns as its lead guitarist. The band, fronted by the artfully eccentric Gustavo Antonio, better known as Tav Falco, on guitar and lead vocals, embraced primitive rockabilly and country-blues sounds, and paired them with the crudeness of a '60s garage band. With Tav at center stage, Alex was able to relax and have fun playing a mix of obscure roots-music covers. It would be another fourteen years before a renewed Big Star returned to the stage in Columbia, Missouri.

Tav Falco — Vocalist, guitarist, The Panther Burns, author, photographer: In 1979, I destroyed a guitar on stage with a chainsaw. At that time, audiences, especially at the Orpheum Theatre in Memphis, were not accustomed to such industrial destruction and art damage on stage. It developed into a completely hysterical climax. Alex Chilton was in the audience that night. About a month later, I was throwing a party at my house across the tracks in the Garden District. The bass player from this girl group, the Klitz, called Alex up from my house and talked to him on the phone. Alex said, "What's that I hear in the background? I hear somebody playing guitar? I've never heard anything sound quite like that." She said, "Oh, it's that guy who destroyed the guitar at the Orpheum Theatre, remember?" Alex said, "I'm coming right over." Alex came over, and we stayed up all night playing music. Of course, all I could play was some rudimentary blues, but Alex could play rock 'n' roll. I was impressed. We had a lot of fun. That first night, I didn't realize he sang with the Box Tops. Honestly, I didn't put the Box Tops together with "The Letter." I'd heard "The Letter," but didn't listen to it much. I didn't know who Alex was. Over time, I went over to his house. I saw some Gold Records on the wall and got to know his background. Alex taught me rock 'n' roll, and I turned him on to some blues. Then Alex said, "I know a drummer. If you can come up with a name let's start this band, and I'll play with you for a while."

Alex Chilton: I started playing with The Panther Burns at the beginning of 1979 and I did that steady until about the middle of 1981—then off-and-on from then on. It's all strange low-rockabilly with some blues and off-the-wall stuff, too…The Panther Burns live on and on. They're better than ever now, I'm sure.

After recording 1981's Behind the Magnolia Curtain *LP with The Panther Burns, Alex exited the group, though he made occasional returns to the stage and studio with the band over the years. He was just one of many musicians in Tav's fluid lineup. Meanwhile, in 1982, Jody Stephens recorded one album with the Suspicions, a short-lived pop-rock trio that fizzled soon after its debut. Alex's career also floundered.*

Alex Chilton: After *Like Flies on Sherbert,* I got a little frustrated and said, "I'm tired of making these records and never making any money on them. I'm just going to wait until somebody comes and makes me a proper offer." I was just frustrated. I saw these records coming out and I knew somebody was making some money on them and it wasn't me…I decided [music] wasn't my ticket to financial security. So, I started driving a cab in Memphis and did that for about six months. I was getting nowhere.

With music on the backburner, Alex decided to uproot to New Orleans. While he initially lived in a string of apartments in the Uptown area, he later moved into the carriage house of a mansion in Mid-City. Alex fell in love with the city, eventually buying his own house, and stayed there for the rest of his life.

Alex Chilton: I came down and stayed with a friend of mine in '81 for a while, then came down for Mardi Gras in '82. When I went back to Memphis that year, it was so damn cold and horrible. I said, "This is insane. I'm going back there." I've been here ever since…Memphis [is] interesting in some ways. I don't really have a lot of people there that I care about very much. When I do stay in Tennessee, I've got a place in the country that's closer to Nashville than Memphis. I've just hated [Memphis] for a long time, and it could be that I spent too much time there and have a lot of bad memories. I got off on the wrong foot in that place.

During this big move, Alex decided to shake his lingering battle with alcoholism.

Alex Chilton: In 1972 or '73, I started drinking a lot. I was taking a lot of drugs in the early 1970s, too, but I pretty much quit that in 1975 or 1976, but I was still drinking. When you're taking drugs a lot, sometimes you're drinking just to take the edge off the drugs. When I finally got around to stopping taking drugs, I hadn't even noticed how much I was drinking before that. I didn't even think about that. Then I had a huge drinking habit. I knew I wanted to quit from 1976 on. But long about the end of 1981, I quit drinking.

Holly George-Warren: When I met Alex in 1982, he was just living life in New Orleans, working as a dishwasher and later as a tree trimmer, and staying sober…but his main vice was cigarettes.

Not long after his arrival in the Big Easy, Alex met René Coman, a talented young bassist and New Orleans native who, like Alex, loved both jazz and punk music.

René Coman — Bassist, Alex Chilton, Panther Burns, the Iguanas: I first met Alex in December of 1982 when I was nineteen. Alex didn't have an ongoing musical thing going on in New Orleans. He was just working a few odd jobs. I'd been in music school for a couple years and was dissatisfied with the direction it was going. When I met Alex, he was in the relocating-to-New-Orleans process. He'd been living here for a few months. This was a bit of a sea change for him, but he wanted to leave whatever weirdness that developed in Memphis, and start fresh. He landed a job as a dishwasher at a nice restaurant in the French Quarter called Louis XVI.

Alex Chilton: I got a job as a dishwasher for a year or so, then I worked as a janitor [at Tupelo's Tavern].

René Coman: It was a way for Alex to re-center himself. He wanted to make a big change from hanging around clubs in Memphis and drinking too much. He wanted to stop being around people he felt didn't have his best interest at heart or wanted something from him. He came here to bring it all back close to the vest—live a quiet life and be the captain of his own destiny.

Alex Chilton: I feel a lot freer here…There's a lot of great music in New Orleans, and a lot of great musicians here. I've learned a lot from a lot of the jazz players I've met here. I've learned a lot about the history of rock 'n' roll music and things like that.

René Coman: I was initially recommended as a bassist to Alex because he was throwing a going-away party for a mutual friend at a club called the Beat Exchange. He needed someone to back him up on some songs he wanted to perform at this party. Alex was really into Michael Jackson's *Off the Wall* record, so he wanted to do a couple songs off that record, and some others. On top of that, he also needed someone who could play primitive rockabilly-style music for this group Stanley and the Undesirables. They were friends of Alex's, and he'd produced a recording for them. I was recommended to him as someone who could do both of those things. I didn't have much background on Alex. I wasn't familiar with Big Star. Somebody told me he was the singer in the Box Tops, but I wasn't terribly familiar with their material. We never had the dynamic of me trying to win him over; we hopscotched over that because when I met him I was completely oblivious to his background. I treated him like an equal, not someone who is supposed to be idolized or fawned over. We were just both into old jazz records. He already had them in his repertoire. When I first met him, he could play a bunch of that stuff on guitar. Many of the tunes Alex was doing had a lot of chord changes. He'd show me the songs and we'd work them out. He always played the sophisticated, correct chord changes heard on the records, not the bullshit guitar chord changes you'd find in a fake book. He knew I came from that same background. That was an early thing that resonated with both of us. We'd do "Like Someone in Love." He loved the *Chet Baker Sings* record. We pulled that from his mom's collection during a trip to Memphis.

Alex Chilton: I grew up listening to all the really good jazz that was happening in the early '60s, and before that, too. For me, when fusion started happening, I really was not interested any more. I liked the earlier things.

René Coman: One time, we were walking down Bourbon Street and heard Walter "Wolfman" Washington in a club doing a song called "Save Your Love For Me." Alex goes, "Wow, that's a really cool song." I said, "I know that song. My father has the Nancy Wilson & Cannonball Adderley record that it's on." We went and got the record from my father's house and learned it that night. Alex didn't have a lot of formal training as far as how the theory of music fits together, but he could listen to a recording and hear exactly what was going on and figure it out. He could back into it from the artifact.

Alex Chilton: My dad was a jazz player in Memphis...He was a piano player, in my experience of him, although earlier he was a sax player... When your dad is a musician, sometimes you try to steer clear of what he does, because you don't want to start competing with your dad, because you figure he's so much better than you are. You don't want to fuck up on his turf. Another part of this equation is that just about the same time I moved down here, my dad died, so then nothing was off-limits to me anymore. I could kind of run with a few of the things I learned from him.

By 1984, Alex was not only busy expanding his jazz skills and repertoire, he'd also been roped back into playing some Panther Burns shows.

René Coman: For a short time, Tav Falco moved down to New Orleans, trying to reconstitute The Panther Burns with Alex. They didn't have a permanent bass player at that point, so Alex recommended me. There were some crazy Panther Burns gigs. All the guitars would be turned up to ten, the reverb was turned up to ten, just tons of feedback. Meanwhile, the drummer, Ross Johnson, is laying on the stage with a floor tom between his legs banging on it like a four-year-old. I'd be pumping away on the bass, looking around, thinking, *Holy shit, what's going on?*

The Panther Burns were fixtures at punk clubs across the country, but in the spring of 1984, the band reached a larger audience when it opened for the Clash at two well-attended shows, one at the University of Tennessee in Knoxville, the other at Vanderbilt University in Nashville.

René Coman: The band was tapped to go down and play a couple dates on that North American tour. Alex had to take time off from his job washing dishes to play those dates. Going on the road with The Panther Burns was always sort of an ad hoc situation. We left Memphis on the first day on a used tire we'd just bought. Of course, it blew out and left us on the side of the road. I'd never been on the road for shows before, so it was quite an introduction being involved in something as touch and go as the Panther Burns. Alex kept an eye out for me. We became even closer friends on that Clash trip.

These gigs may have been The Panther Burns' biggest crowd yet, but the Clash-loving college students were bewildered by their primitiveness.

René Coman: They were the headliners in their dressing rooms, and we were not in any dressing rooms. They might have been slightly miffed we showed up so late to the first gig and didn't have equipment. We were like, "Can we use y'all's gear?" They were like, "Uh, what?" They said, "Okay...we guess," after they realized that was the only way we were going to be able to play. These were university auditorium shows, like Vanderbilt University— 3,000-to 5,000-seaters. If you can imagine opening for the Clash at a university that was all Clash fans, the crowds could be a bit intolerant and impatient. The Panther Burns were a provocative group with a provocative sound. When the crowd started to get agitated, we often leaned into that rather than try to placate them or steer it back. We took it as a sign we were getting to them and tried to rile them up even more. That was the first time I ever experienced having an entire room turn on you. We were getting loudly booed by 4,000 people. Then either Alex or Ross threw their hands up in triumph. The rest of the band saw that, and then we all did it. That's when the roar of boos *really* came at us. It washed over the stage. People were throwing things at the stage and screaming. That was a powerful moment for me because the show went as wrong as it could possibly go and we all still walked off stage alive. I thought, *Okay, that's not too bad.*

After The Panther Burns tour, which included a date at the 40 Watt Club in Athens, Georgia, attended by all the members of R.E.M., the party was over. Alex and René, both in need of rent money, worked the same manual labor job at Asplundh, the largest tree-cutting service in the United States. Alex's hiatus from working as a solo artist continued as he spent a year firing up chainsaws.

Alex Chilton: I worked as an urban lumberjack for this company that would cut the trees away from the power lines for a while. That was really dangerous.

René Coman: Alex asked me to be a part of their crew, so I took the job. The cutter would have to get up in the cherry picker and use high-powered chainsaws. We were working thirty minutes outside New Orleans, cutting trees off 50,000-volt powerlines. Between that and the chippers, every aspect of the job was deadly. The saw can kick back into your face. If you cut something, and it hits a powerline, and it touches you, it's going to light you up—drop you.

Alex Chilton: I got canned and then started freelance tree work, a combination of yard gardener and lumberjack. I did that for about six months, and I would play with The Panther Burns every now and then.

René Coman: When we'd get home in the evening from cutting trees, neither of us had a television at the time, but he had instruments to play and a few records. He'd throw on his favorite records, and we'd play along with them at his place. We'd swap back and forth on keyboard and guitar, just entertaining ourselves. One left-field record Alex had was that first Frank Zappa record, the doo-wop record; he liked that a lot, and we played both of those songs. He had the Nelson Slater *Wild Angel* album that was produced by Lou Reed. We'd play on "Telstar" for a little bit, that kind of thing. Alex was not drinking at all. I was kind of drinking a bit, but after I ran into him, that's one of the things we did together. We'd hang out and not drink together. We'd play music, not hang out at bars all night.

Alex Chilton: Yeah, if you're not a drinker, a bar gets old in about fifteen minutes.

Alex may have still been holding out for a legit record deal before he'd return to the studio and cut a solo record, but by the early summer of '84, his love of performing soon landed him in a working cover band.

René Coman: It was shortly after Alex left that tree-cutting job that he got the Bourbon Street gig. We went from one thing to the next. A local drummer Alex knew said, "Come practice with me, I have this set playing covers at this place called Papa Joe's on Bourbon Street." Alex told him, "Yeah, I'd be into it, but I have a bass player I'd like to bring in." We started playing as a trio called the Scores. It was prostitute language—a prostitute turns a trick and calls it a "score." We'd do "Chain Gang," Otis Redding's version of "Satisfaction," and some other off-the-beaten-path R&B music. The drummer and Alex would sing; they split it. We'd worked in a lot of favorites of Alex's. He had a huge repertoire of things he liked and finally was in a situation where he could pull those out. The Panther Burns, the original idea of it, was that Alex would do those songs. The idea was Tav could back him up on some stuff and Alex could back Tav up on some stuff. Alex told me, "I figured out pretty soon it was just going to be me backing Tav up."

The Scores played four-hour sets, four nights a week and usually left with around $20 or $25 per man. The room was often attended by tourists and locals who didn't know who Alex was, but would happily shout requests to him throughout the evening. A few times in the bar band's four-month lifespan, Alex's out-of-town indie-rock friends and loyal fans would show up to watch them perform. They wanted to see the former Box Tops and Big Star frontman in action.

René Coman: In the Papa Joe's days, you'd have the dB's stopping by, or maybe Peter Buck. Even going out with The Panther Burns, some people would show up just because they were huge Alex fans. They were trying to get some piece of the Big Star thing. When the dB's came to town for the Scores gig, Will Rigby walked over to Alex and said, "Hey man, if you ever want to play your own shows on the road, you should call our booking agent, he can probably set you up. His name is Frank Riley and he lives in New York." A couple months into this Bourbon Street gig, we had a slight altercation amongst the band. One night, after the first set, the drummer fired us from this band. We were asked to leave. He'd had enough of us scrutinizing him. That night, we went back to Alex's house, and he grabs Frank Riley's business card. Alex didn't have a phone at his house, so we walked to the pay phone. Alex called up Frank and said, "Do you think you can book us some shows on the road?" Frank said he could. That was the beginning of Alex's return.

Alex Chilton: I [realized], *Maybe I can get by without having a steady job,* and I never had another one again. I was working with [Panther Burns] sporadically again, and then I got my own booking agent and started traveling.

René Coman: By '84, we were going out on the road as Alex Chilton's trio. On those first tours, I'd pretty much road-manage everything. I'd keep track of the money, but there really wasn't a lot to manage. We'd get the list of dates from Frank. We'd show up in the town, go to a local coffee shop, get a newspaper or phone book and look up the address of the club, and then ask someone how to get there. We initially went out with a different drummer, but then Doug Garrison joined us and he stayed on for a long time.

Doug Garrison, a twenty-five-year-old jazz-loving Memphian, was hired by Alex in 1984 and stayed in the trio for a decade. With limited funds, the trio toured the country in Alex's rusty but trusty hooptie.

René Coman: We traveled around in a '73 LeSabre. He'd gotten paid with that car from Stanley Adkins to produce that recording by the Undesirables. The car needed a new transmission. When we were on tour, it had no driver's side window. Alex had a black leather motorcycle jacket that the driver would wear because it would be cold at night. It had no lock on the trunk, so we had a screwdriver we left in the glove compartment we'd use to pop the trunk. There was no radio in the car, so we would sit for long periods of silence, then someone would talk. We'd have twenty minutes of stimulating conversation before it'd die down again. Then another two hours of silence.

Doug Garrison — Drummer, Alex Chilton, Panther Burns, the Iguanas: Like any touring musician, you get burnt out a bit. Alex told me once, "The one thing I don't like about the road is I always know what's going to happen next." We had a schedule and could not deviate from it. At one point, he bought a nice car so he didn't have to worry about it breaking down. He'd bring his girlfriend, so they could do as much side stuff as possible. Alex dated a lot of different women over the years, but when I first met him, he was still with Annabelle Lenderink, a kicky Dutch girl that lived in New Orleans. They spent a lot of time together. They had kind of an intense, up-and-down relationship for a while, then she moved to California.

René Coman: Alex was super fun to hang out with on the road. He had a wide variety of subjects he was an authority on. He was still wild about astrology. He could talk about country music at length. He was very well read and very funny.

Billed simply as Alex Chilton, word of his long-awaited return to the stage gradually spread to fans.

Alex Chilton's trio live, 1986.

PHOTO BY LINDSAY BACH (COURTESY OF RENÉ COMAN)

Alex's backing band: René Coman and Doug Garrison, 1985.

PHOTO BY TAV FALCO

René Coman: It brought out all the Alex Chilton fans who hadn't seen him for a while and wondered what he was up to. He liked meeting and talking to people. He would be very tolerant, but like a lot of people who have experienced a certain amount of admiration and walked away from it not really digging the feeling it gives you, Alex decided if people crossed a certain line that objectified him, then he would lose patience pretty quickly. It goes back to the idea that if Alex thought someone was trying to court him as an idol, he would not interact with them in that manner. He could be dismissive of someone, or at least try to steer them away from that sort of interaction.

Doug Garrison: You had to be smart around Alex, that's all. He didn't suffer the fool and a lot of people were intimidated by that. Some of them likely thought he was aloof or kind of an asshole, but he was actually a really warm person when you got to know him.

René Coman: He was a strong person who liked to be around other strong people. Early on, he said in a flippant way about someone, "Yeah, I know you can take it, but can you dish it out?" He was interested in people who could dish it out. He wasn't looking to be around people he could dominate. He wanted to be around strong people who could stand up to him.

Doug Garrison: He didn't want to get to know every person who approached him. You had to be interesting and not starstruck. I didn't even know who Big Star was when I first met him. That's what he liked about me. The night we first met, I was playing a gig with a jazz pianist named Phineas Newborn Jr. at a William Eggleston photo exhibition at the Brooks Museum of Art. Alex was a friend of William, so he was at the reception. Alex was in between drummers for this trio project, so he said, "We should do a gig." We rehearsed only one time and then played a gig at the Antenna Club in Memphis. The rehearsal for that show was maybe an hour long. We wouldn't even play the whole song, he'd just show me the groove of each song he wanted to do.

That Antenna Club show on November 17, 1984 was played to a crowded room of ecstatic local fans, all curious about what Alex had been up to. It was a glorious homecoming and introduced Memphians to his new sound.

Doug Garrison: We did a lot of his older songs, some interesting old R&B and blues tunes, some jazz and a few originals he was working on. It was a lot of fun because he was a brilliant guitar player. His style was very rooted in Southern soul and R&B music. He really listened to a lot of the old blues guys and other funky-ass players.

Alex Chilton: I listen to a lot of gospel, I listen to a lot of older R&B. Very little that's very new. I guess gospel is my main thing that I listen to these days that other people mostly don't.

Doug Garrison: Because of his taste in music, Alex was a very gritty player, but always very good. He was easy to play with and had a great feel. It never seemed labored, it was all very natural. He could play Bach with René and never miss a note—hit all the octaves and finger-picking parts.

Already a talented guitarist, Alex's playing steadily improved as he remained sober and frequently tested himself by learning new, challenging material. Some of those songs made it into the band's setlists, but he also always made room for at least a few fan favorites.

Doug Garrison: The whole ten years I worked with him, I saw him have maybe two drinks. He was one of the most professional people I have ever worked with. He took gigs very seriously. Any sort of nonsense on stage was usually initiated by some assholes in the audience. Right to the end, he was still playing "The Letter" because people requested it. He'd say, "Sure, man. I'll play that." He loved that song. He was also doing a few Big Star tunes in each set. He felt he'd moved past a lot of those songs, but at every show there were some people who only wanted to hear it, so he'd play some of it.

Alex Chilton: I say let them scream for whatever they want. If I can stomach what they're asking for, then I'll do it. But there are many times when I can't.

Doug Garrison: Luckily, especially in Europe, there were fans who trusted his musicianship enough to just let him play what he wanted to play, and they knew it'd be great. But he enjoyed playing a few of the Big Star tunes. "September Gurls," we played a bunch. "In the Street" we played a lot. If it was an upbeat, rocking Big Star tune he liked, then he'd do it. The lamenting, slow, sad songs—he didn't dig that stuff anymore. The last third of his career, he was really doing what he wanted to do: explore the roots and play funky music.

René Coman: People were amazed we were following "Ubangi Stomp" with some Bach. We'd do a lot of New Orleans R&B, like Chris Kenner's "Sick and Tired" was part of our set from Bourbon Street and we carried it on to the trio. We'd play Slim Harpo's "Te-Ni-Nee-Ni-Nu," another one from Bourbon Street. "Bangkok" was usually in there. We'd do Carole King songs, like "Let Me Get Close to You." We would do maybe one or two Big Star songs. When we first started going on the road, he told me, "We should probably play a few songs from this band I was in, Big Star, because people are going to want to hear some of this stuff. We'll play some of the more prominent numbers." I'd ask him, "Do you want to play me the Big Star record, so I can learn it from there?" He'd say, "Why don't you just let me teach you the song?" To Big Star devotees, they'd think, "God, if you learn it that way, you're missing the whole point." That's the magic, what they created in the studio. But Alex was not hung up on all that. He knew people wanted to hear more Big Star than we were playing, but he is someone who was very self-determined. He'd rather sit down and do nothing than be in a better situation and be told what to do. He'd often say, "Yeah, I'm not going to do that."

Doug Garrison: I don't recall him bringing up Chris Bell, not once. He was not interested in talking about anything Big Star. When he would do an interview at a gig, and they asked him about Big Star, he would turn off. The thing that pissed him off the most were journalists who didn't know their homework and just wanted to talk about Big Star, not knowing he didn't want to talk about that. I saw him really humiliate people for that. But if the reporter was astute and informed, he had the best time in the world.

Alex Chilton: I don't get off on doing interviews, generally. A lot of the people that one talks to doing interviews really have their heads up their asses...The best interviewer that anybody talks to is going to get a few things wrong, and the worst of them are going to get a lot of things wrong. In a way it's just sort of a waste of time.

Paul Williams: As a friend of his, I always got along great with Alex, but he could be hot and cold with other people. To me, he was a sweet guy with a wicked sense of humor. We always just talked about music we liked.

After his return to the indie-rock scene, Alex rubbed shoulders with some of his higher-profile fans who were touring the same circuit, including Paul Westerberg of the Replacements. Paul forever immortalized Alex as a mythical rock legend with a tribute song, "Alex Chilton," which was included on the Replacements' 1987 Pleased to Meet Me LP. Produced at Ardent Studios by Jim Dickinson, the song introduced Alex, and the cult of Big Star, to the youthful mainstream-alternative music generation of the late '80s and early '90s. In fact, the punchy single, which includes the lyrics "I never travel far, without a little Big Star," continues to earn Big Star new fans today, thanks to the Replacements' unwavering legacy. In a 1987 Sire Records-produced promotional interview, Westerberg explained why he penned the song. "We want people to know who Alex is, if you've never heard of Big Star," he said. "[Alex] doesn't need our help, he doesn't want our help, but damnit he is going to get it, whether he likes it or not. He's a great songwriter and he's influenced me...He does exactly what he wants, and he is comfortable with that." Paul and Alex met a few years before the release of Pleased to Meet Me, *and Peter Jesperson, then-manager of the Replacements, was there to witness the momentous encounter that led to the now-classic Alex homage.*

Peter Jesperson: Alex Chilton and I go back a long time. We first met at CBGB, of all places, when he opened for the Replacements in December of 1984. I managed the Replacements, so I was there for the show. Alex was the opening act and, of course, we were hysterical fans and were wondering why he was opening for them. It was the day after they shared a bill at CBGB, and I was going to meet Alex for lunch. It was supposed to be just the two of us. The Replacements and I were staying at a hotel in Times Square. I was getting ready to leave to meet Alex while Paul was still in bed. We had been up late drinking our faces off. I stopped over at his room on my way out and said, "Hey, I'm leaving for a couple hours, but you've got an interview in a couple hours so don't go too far." He was like, "Yeah, yeah. I got it. Leave me alone, I want to go back to sleep." As I started to close the door, he said, "Where are you going so early anyway?" I said, "I'm going to meet Alex Chilton for lunch." He shot out of bed like a rocket and said, "Can I come?" I said, "Of course." Paul got dressed fast. We jumped in a taxi and went down to St. Mark's Place where we were meeting Alex. A lot of Paul's "Alex Chilton" lyrics are about that day. He says something about "checking his stash by the trash at St. Mark's Place." When we met, Alex was standing on the street corner. It was a bizarre experience, but it looked like he was looking through the garbage when we got there.

After that day, Peter and Alex became long-time friends. While on tour, Alex frequently stayed at Peter's house in Minneapolis.

Peter Jesperson: Alex would be in a good mood, then he would turn on a dime. One day, we went out riding bicycles around Lake of the Isles in Minneapolis; there are a lot of lakes right downtown. It was a beautiful spring day in Minneapolis. We got back to my place and he went back to the guest room to change out of biking clothes. I had just bought a bunch of 25-cent records at a garage sale. I found a Charlie Christian record, he was a guitarist. Alex was doing a lot of jazz guitar at the time and rearranging classical music. I thought, *Maybe this Charlie Christian record might appeal to Alex? I'll throw this on.* A minute later, Alex came out of the guest room, came up to me and got right in my face, almost nose-to-nos, and said, "Did you put this on because you thought I would *like it*?" I said, "Well, yeah. Kind of." He said, "I *hate* Charlie Christian." He walked back in the guest room, slammed the door and didn't come out for two hours. That was pretty weird, but for the most part we got along great.

By the mid-'80s, Alex was receiving international praise in popular music magazines. His trio was playing shows from San Francisco to New York and all across Europe.

Doug Garrison: It varied a lot, but we'd usually go out for two or three weeks. A few tours were five weeks, but two weeks was average. We'd play all kinds of places, everything from small clubs to Irving Plaza in New York. We'd play the Rex Club in Paris. There were a few summer festivals here and there, but it was mostly small clubs, like CBGB.

René Coman: We'd stay at people's houses when we could. We did that quite a bit. We would always bring our sleeping bags with us, so we could crash on someone's floor. When we'd get hotel rooms, we'd usually just get one room for the three of us. You'd get a bed to yourself every third night. When we played in Los Angeles, Lux and Ivy came to our gig. We were hanging out afterwards and Alex asks if we can stay at their pad overnight and they say, "Sure!" We go to their place and Ivy is sitting on the lawn smoking a cigarette with the long cigarette holder, wearing some pumps and pedal pushers. Lux is showing us all the used vinyl he just found at a used record store. I was in heaven. I loved the Cramps before I even knew who Alex Chilton was. We had a lot of unforgettable times on the road.

Alex and his bandmates may have spent some days hanging out with alt-rock royalty on the road, but most often the guys passed time by chain-smoking cigarettes across whatever state or foreign country they happened to be in at the time. After a few tours, the musicians were all but tobacco connoisseurs.

René Coman: We all were puffing away. It started off where we smoked Drum, a hand-rolling brand of tobacco. It took too much time to roll a cigarette on stage, so we switched to Pall Mall, a non-filtered brand of cigarettes. Alex and I both smoked those for years. Those were so delicious. We'd be on the road in Europe buying different countries' versions of Pall Malls to see who made the best ones. We also made a special trip to Durham, North Carolina—we were not playing there—just because the Lucky Strike factory was there and so was [the American Tobacco Historic District].

Doug Garrison: There was so much smoking going on, especially in Europe, because the crew would be smoking nonstop, too. We had a saxophone player at one point, he was the only guy in the van who didn't smoke. He was green all the time. I felt bad for him being stuck in a vehicle with us, but I was chain-smoking away myself.

With a long list of songs fully hashed out by 1985, Alex had warmed to the idea of returning to the studio to cut some new solo tracks after a legitimate offer fell into his lap.

René Coman: On that first tour up to New York, we ran into a guy with contacts to New Rose Records. It was a French journalist who happened to be staying at the same apartment we were crashing at. He called up one of the owners of New Rose Records, Patrick Mathé, and he said, "I'd love for you to do a record for me." It was a very organic process. We decided to do some of the covers we'd been playing live, and Alex started writing a few originals. That became the *Feudalist Tarts* EP.

Doug Garrison: Our setlist pretty much ended up being that record. That was the first record I did with him. I played on six records with Alex and he always had a lot of fun in the studio. He enjoyed it and was good at it.

Alex tightened things up during the 1985 sessions held at his old stomping grounds: Ardent Studios.

René Coman: It wasn't a super warm homecoming in every corridor of Ardent. There were some wry smiles here and there. Alex was like, "Fuck you. That's your trip." Ardent just had a modern facility. We had a budget, not a huge budget, but one big enough to go in and do a day of recording, a day of overdubs, and a day of mixing. We did *Feudalist Tarts* in three consecutive days over Easter weekend.

Doug Garrison: Alex liked to have a hand in engineering it, even though he was out on the floor playing. He was always involved with every aspect of the studio. Most of the records I played on with Alex, he wanted to do all the mixing himself.

Alex Chilton: I don't really need somebody else in charge of what I'm doing. It's hard for somebody else to see what you're getting at. Very often, when I get all the music onto the tape, it doesn't resemble any-thing like what I'm getting at. It's only with my careful attention that I turn it into that in the mixing.

Doug Garrison: He had an interesting approach. He would get the mix on the first tune and wouldn't stop until he got all of them mixed. Some-times it would be an all-nighter. Usually, he would start early in the day and wouldn't get out of there until almost twenty-four hours later. He wanted to do it on one ear, he didn't want to come back days later when he was perceiving it differently.

René Coman: He wasn't going for a *Like Flies* vibe. We weren't trying to make something that sounded broken. We were trying to make something that would do well and put us in a position to go and play dates. There was no self-sabotage involved, but Alex was a fan of what he called "maintaining the bloodiness of a recording." That meant you got it on tape early enough in the process and captured the visceral quality of the song. It would sound real and have life to it—not perfect. He didn't work all the blood, or life, out of anything we recorded.

Doug Garrison: Alex came from a lineage of producers in Memphis, guys who keep the sessions really loose hoping for good mistakes to happen. Jim Dickinson was a huge proponent of that: turn the tape machine on and see what happens. That first record I did with Alex, almost everything on there is a first take. It took me aback. I had never worked like that before. He was like that years later, too. When we were in the studio working on *A Man Called Destruction*, I thought we were just running through the songs so the horn players could read their charts. Then we played "Te-Ni-Nee-Ni-Nu" and Alex said, "Okay, are we cool with that?" I didn't even know we were rolling tape. We did about forty songs on that recording day—all the original tunes for the record, and then he just wanted to burn tape and play a bunch of covers. It was bam, bam, bam.

As the new EP hit stores, The Cutting Edge, *MTV's first alternative-music program, aired a four-minute spotlight on Alex. The segment was a welcome promotional push, as Alex was prepping his group for an upcoming tour.*

René Coman: The gigs kept coming. We did a few European tours where we played thirty dates in forty days. We learned "Volare" when we were on the road in Europe that first time. We were going through Italy and Alex started talking about the song. The original was sung by an Italian guy, Domenico Modugno. It was a big hit and the Italians loved it, so we decided to add it to the set.

Doug Garrison: Since we were in Italy, Alex had a local person coach him on the pronunciation of the "Volare" lyrics. He wanted to make sure he got it exactly right. I don't know why he was so fascinated with that song. He had a camp factor in some of his song choices.

Alex Chilton: "Volare" is a great song. When we were in Italy we started playing it and the audiences went crazy for it, so we kept doing it. It's an interesting piece of music. It's an odd, interesting thing. I think actually it's one of the better versions of "Volare" that's ever been done.

René Coman: Alex was the type to say, "Let me teach you this song and maybe we'll play it tonight." We also ran across the Serge Gainsbourg

Let Me Get Close
• Sept. G.
In the Street
Bangkok
Rock Hard
No Sex
Mercy Upon You
Save Your Love
Lonely Weekends
Alligator Man
Make You Mine
Nobody's Fool
→
Look of Love
Lost My Job
B-A-B-Y
Tee Ni Nee Ni Noo
Thank You John
The Letter
Honkin Down the Highway
Hey Little Child
Paradise

A 1985 Alex Chilton trio setlist.

and Jane Birkin song, "Je t'aime...moi non plus." We learned it and started doing it that night. He'd play great songs that nobody was doing, or nobody knew about. He enjoyed that. Mostly Alex would only write original songs when he had something to write for, if he had a record coming up, or if he had a lyrical or musical idea he was fascinated by. I heard him say, "There are so many great songs out there. Why do I have to write new ones?"

Alex Chilton: When I was first making my own records, we were writing a lot of things, and I was writing a lot, experimenting with a lot of things and just trying to find myself as a writer. I felt like there was a time in the mid-'70s when I sort of came of age as a writer and found myself. I stopped experimenting so much then, and started writing much less, because I had a stronger criteria of what I thought a good song was. I haven't been particularly prolific at all in the last ten years. It's not easy for me to write a lot of songs. I work on it sometimes fairly hard.

Alex's original songs and cover choices perplexed some audiences and critics, mainly those hoping he'd return to the Big Star sound. Alex refused to backpedal or compromise.

Alex Chilton: Everybody tells me how difficult I am. I don't know. I just do things the way I want to do things and that's the only way I can work.

Holly George-Warren: Alex was a musical seeker. He didn't like to repeat himself. He'd destroy his previous artistic endeavors by moving on to something else, like the Dadaists, rather than continue to pursue a particular style or sound. He didn't like stasis.

Alex Chilton: I can't say there has always been one vision of something I wanted to do. It changes from day to day, minute to minute, year to year...At every step along the way, the vast majority of people are always telling me I'm doing the wrong thing—now, then, all along the way. Now people tell me, because I don't make music that sounds like Big Star, that I'm making a big mistake. I just say, "To hell with them." This is what I want to do. And I pretty much always have from 1970 on, and I'll continue to do that. If it happens that I can't make a living playing music anymore, then that's the way it's going to be.

Ric Menck: If you were clued in to Alex Chilton when his '80s solo albums were being released, what did you think of them at the time? Honestly, it's not what I wanted to hear from the man, but in trying to understand what Chilton was all about as an artist, I eventually came to adore them. Chilton's '80s records also taught me a valuable lesson. I don't always get what I want, and maybe I shouldn't.

Alex may not have been too excited about Big Star, but a growing number of major-label bands were getting hip to that once obscure back catalog. In 1986, the Bangles laid down a cover of "September Gurls" on its Different Light *LP, their breakthrough, platinum-selling album containing hit singles like "Manic Monday" and "Walk Like an Egyptian." Alex welcomed the financial rewards.*

Alex Chilton: Making money off a thing like the Bangles' record makes up for a lot of things. I guess that my life has been a series of flukes in the record business. The first thing I ever did was the biggest record that I'll ever have. I've been paid for some things that were real successful for no good reasons, and I've not been paid for things that weren't so successful for a lot of good reasons.

In the February 1988 issue of Creem, *however, Alex assured readers he wasn't losing sleep over his chain of not-so-profitable dealings.*

Alex Chilton: You can't live your life staying angry about that stuff. I may be down on something, but that doesn't mean I've got to think about it all the time. It's a lot worse when you're struggling day to day to make ends meet—then you start thinking, *These bastards didn't pay me.* But a little money will grease the skids.

Alex, now in his mid-thirties, was entering smarter, more profitable record deals, and decided to keep that encouraging momentum going. He followed up Feudalist Tarts *with another EP, 1986's* No Sex, *a three-song disc featuring its notorious title track that riffed on the devasting AIDS epidemic. By 1987, Alex had amassed enough originals and covers to fill a full-length solo album: the* High Priest *LP. Released on Big Time Records, the R&B-tinged track list scored airplay on college radio stations across the country and earned him some favorable reviews. Thanks to all the successful tours, Alex was earning the most money he'd made since his Box Tops days. He was now able to rent reliable cars for tours, occasionally hire a driver, and pay his band a decent wage.*

René Coman: About 1987, I stopped playing with the band. When I left is when Ron Easley started playing bass with Alex. He replaced me in the trio and stayed for many years. Alex and I were super close and spent a bunch of time together, but like anybody you spend a lot of time with, there are points that generate friction. You pile up enough of those points and relationships take different paths. Our relationship had run its course. There was too much tension between Alex and I, not for just one reason. It was just being too close and spending too much time together. Alex takes things seriously. That's not a knock on him. He was just a sensitive person who could get his feelings hurt even when no one was trying to hurt his feelings. He was a serious person who took things to heart, possibly more than he ever intended.

ACT SEVEN

WATCH THE SUNRISE

Big Star at their 1993 reunion at the University of Missouri (L to R): Jon Auer, Alex
Chilton, Jody Stephens, and Ken Stringfellow.

COURTESY OF JODY STEPHENS

CHAPTER 25

RYKODISC — THE RISE OF BIG STAR: 1990S-2005

From the late '80s into the early '90s, as grunge overtook hair metal on MTV and the radio, Alex Chilton kept busy touring the world with his trio. All the while, he remained a low-key fixture in his local New Orleans music scene, gigging periodically at local haunts like the Howlin' Wolf. Meanwhile, back in Memphis, Ardent Studios remained focused on recording albums for paying clients; the days of producing pro bono passion projects were long gone. Occasionally, the studio, still owned by John Fry, churned out radio hits. In 1980, Ardent added a third studio. Aside from a string of ZZ Top records engineered by Terry Manning, including 1983's Eliminator, *which sold over 10 million copies, the studio also became a destination for bluesmen like Robert Cray, Johnny Winter, Albert Collins, B.B. King, Jimmie Vaughan, and Stevie Ray Vaughan. By 1987, Jody Stephens, marketing degree in hand, returned to Ardent as its project director. A year later, Jody's Big Star cred helped usher in R.E.M., which produced its* Green *LP in Studio A. Hits like "Stand," "Orange Crush," and "Pop Song 89" topped* Billboard's *Modern Rock chart. Over the following decades, a stream of other notable alternative-rock bands followed suit and booked time at Ardent, including Afghan Whigs, Cat Power, Smashing Pumpkins, the Gin Blossoms, Mudhoney, Archers of Loaf, and two of Jack White's bands: the White Stripes and the Raconteurs. Today, after surviving music industry ebbs and flows, Ardent remains open, and Jody still holds a management position.*

Tim Riley: Some years were slower than others for Ardent, but the overall industry feel is: If you're in Memphis and need a hit, you have to cut something at Ardent.

Big Star's first two LPs (L to R): *#1 Record* (1972, Ardent), *Radio City* (1973, Ardent).

The last two studio albums (L to R): *Third/Sister Lovers* (1978, PVC), and *In Space* (2005, Ryko/Omnivore Recordings).

John Hampton: ZZ Top came here to bathe in the water. They wanted to get away from home, and they believed in the musical vibe that's in the air here. Same with the Vaughans. When Stevie Ray and Jimmie weren't working, they were down on Beale Street listening to local bands.

Andria Lisle: John Fry and producers like Jim Dickinson and John Hampton encouraged experimentation, too. The meter is always running at Ardent, but it still feels laid-back. I remember Primal Scream recording there in the '90s and inviting Nation of Ulysses, who were playing a gig at the Antenna Club, to use their studio after hours. At the same time, Ardent was kind of the establishment. A great side effect of having the studio here has been the less-corporate ethos led by producers like Doug Easley, who built a great alternative to Ardent in the '90s with Easley McCain Recording.

Sherman Willmott: Ardent went through what you could call a rough commercial patch in the late '80s and early '90s. A lot of what they were doing was bad AOR. I'm talking about their studio, not about their private label. Their label wasn't releasing anything at that time. I understand; that was probably the last of the glory days of the music industry, so you take whatever work is out there. That said, at the same time, R.E.M. recorded *Green* there. The Replacements cut *Pleased to Meet Me* at Ardent with Jim Dickinson. You can't take that away from them. You can't judge them for the misses when you've got hits like that. History is going to treat Ardent very well.

Ardent may have been shooting for major-label success stories, but Alex Chilton remained far left of the dial. In 1990, he sought out the Gories, a primitive, Detroit-based garage-punk trio, and produced the group's sophomore LP, I Know You Fine, But How You Doin', *at Easley McCain Recording in Memphis. Alex loved and respected the untamed rawness of the Gories, but that nascent sound didn't overflow onto his own solo records. 1994's* Clichés, *and 1995's* A Man Called Destruction, *remained in the same polished R&B and jazz veins as his previous efforts. Though, he did stretch out and get experimental on the* Cubist Blues *LP, a 1996 collaboration with Ben Vaughn and Alan Vega of Suicide. By the early '90s, after several trips to Glasgow, Alex befriended a poppier band: Teenage Fanclub. He often collaborated with the emerging Scottish band best known for its milestone 1991 LP,* Bandwagonesque, *sometimes referred to by critics as "Big Star's Fourth."*

Bruce Eaton: I think the live radio show he did with Teenage Fanclub is maybe the best example of [Alex's] roots and musical interests tied into one package. There are some live recordings out there of Alex from the '80s and '90s that are also great testimonies to Alex as a solo artist. He certainly didn't fit in any one box.

Andy Hummel: A lot of Big Star's [recognition] was a result of Alex being a part of it. The guy was a star going into it and he didn't exactly fade after it ended. He was always out doing something that somebody found interesting, even when he was just playing old standards in a New York bar in front of fifteen people. But [Big Star's gradual rise to fame is] rather odd. How many bands back in those days went out, gave it a shot, it didn't work out for them and then you never heard from them again? Rock 'n' roll is a weird thing. There's just no figuring it.

An unintentional side effect of Alex's activity in the '80s and '90s was its impact on the slowly intensifying Big Star revival. With the name "ALEX CHILTON" plastered on gig posters across the world, fans were constantly reminded of the long-lost band. Along with the interest in Big Star came some curiosity about the band's unknown founder. Fans saw Chris Bell's face and name on the back of #1 Record. Diehard fans perhaps had a scratchy bootleg cassette with a few of his solo tunes. Some even heard he'd tragically died at twenty-seven in a car wreck. His only released output was #1 Record and the impossible-to-find 1978 "I Am the Cosmos" single, but, soon, Chris would rise from the ashes of anonymity. In 1991, his solo music was introduced to a new batch of youthful ears when This Mortal Coil covered both sides of the Car Records single. Kim Deal of the Pixies led the group's emotional take of "You and Your Sister." The following year, the Posies cut both "Feel" and "Cosmos" for a vinyl single. The word was out about this long-lost songwriter named Chris Bell, but his solo tapes remained shelved. That all changed when Rykodisc, an American record label sometimes referred to as "Ryko," finally sought out David Bell and inked a deal to release a post-humous solo album. The LP, titled I Am the Cosmos, *compiled many of his post-Big Star songs, the same tape reels Chris and David unsuccessfully shopped in 1975. Seventeen years later, it happened without effort. Chris' life may have ended in late 1978, but his musical spirit was reborn in early 1992.*

David Bell: Chris' album finally coming out was totally out of left field. And yet, there's another side of me that thinks it's the most obvious thing in the world—of course this happened. It's inexplicable to have both of those thoughts in my brain at the same time, but that's how it was. Before all that, I had gone into the studio and compiled what later turned into the *Cosmos* album with John Hampton. This was for PVC Records, who had released *Third*. That label was interested in it, but then nothing happened. Through all of that, I never lost the connection I had with Chris. In those twelve years, from the time he died to when there was talk about releasing *Cosmos* as an album with Ryko, anybody who knew me knew about my brother. I didn't shut up about it. When all the interest started coming around, it was like, "Okay, this wasn't a fluke." It wasn't, "Oh, this was a sad story, and then nobody ever heard from him again." It was like somebody stamped my ticket for validation.

Jody Stephens: *I Am the Cosmos* happened after Jeff Rougvie at Rykodisc stepped up and asked if they could release that record. Jeff was a big fan. Before it was released, David Bell and John Fry weren't shopping it to labels. The labels came to them and they decided to go with Ryko.

David Bell: There was a preamble to all of this when I was getting calls from different people who were interested in releasing his solo material. Bud Scoppa was contacting me, asking me to go with Zoo Entertainment. At some point, I talked to John Fry who said, "We're going with Ryko [for the Big Star releases], but you're free to release Chris' music with whomever you like." But, from the beginning, I thought it made more sense to have all three CDs come from the same company. In the end, Ryko could not have done a better job with all of it.

Jeff Rougvie — Record producer, Rykodisc: It was the early '90s when I got involved with the Chris Bell and Big Star releases for Ryko, but I was a fan before that. Around 1990 or 1991 we got word the Chris record was available. This was before we heard Big Star's *Third* and the *Live* record could be a part of the deal, too. I started hustling and figuring out who had it. I ended up talking to John Fry, Jody, and David Bell. Originally, we just went after the Chris Bell record. It was our first target. It came down to us and Sub Pop, but Sub Pop was busy with other projects, and it was dragging on. I developed a relationship with David especially. John and Jody agreed we were the right place for Big Star, and Ryko ended up getting it. That was exciting. It came together easily once we got the deal together. It's because we all knew we were working on something special. We all knew the goal was to honor Chris and put his talent in the proper spotlight.

David Bell: They contacted me and said they were interested in his unreleased music. I went in the studio with [producer, engineer] John Hampton at Ardent and we listened to everything, all the sixteen-track tapes were at Ardent. I said, obviously, "'Cosmos' and 'Sister' are going to be on there." I had never heard a few of the songs until then. Rick Clark delivered some alternate takes. One turned out to be "I Don't Know," which is really "Get Away" in a different guise.

Jeff Rougvie: Originally, I wanted to include multiple versions of "You and Your Sister" and all of that. But we pulled back on including all those tracks, the ones later included on the two-disc Rhino Handmade deluxe edition. That's how we ended up with the Ryko album. They dug up a lot of tapes. David was great and there for some of the actual recordings, so he knew what everything was.

I Am The Cosmos original CD cover artwork
(Rykodisc, 1992).

Big Star *Live* 1974 CD cover artwork
(Rykodisc, 1992).

Adam Hill: Chris never officially signed off on a completed record, but the Rykodisc record is very close to Chris' vision. The mastering job wasn't the best, but it was okay for the time. All those mixes Chris was alive for, except for "Though I Know She Lies."

Jeff Rougvie: I was not in the studio with them calling the shots. My motto has always been, "Don't stick your nose in if people know what they want to do." If they have questions, they'll ask. They put all of it together from the tapes Chris left behind, and Ardent and John Fry have always kept good track of everything. Working with Ardent was fantastic. They took the tracks, dumped them on a DAT tape and sent it to us mixed. Together we figured out the final form of the record and then David sent us a bunch of pictures. I can't imagine a better album cover.

David Bell: That 1972 photograph we used for the cover really captures his disposition at that time. I cropped it so it'd look like he was floating in the air. I shot it with a Comica 35mm and used slides. Just about everybody was taking slides back then because the resolution was superior.

Jeff Rougvie: We figured out the track list and got the liner notes together. It was an honor having David write the liner notes. You can tell he really loves his brother and was excited it was finally going to be available.

David Bell: Jeff, who was most helpful to me, asked me to write the liner notes and then I wrote a little mini book. Something pulled that right out of me. It was an organic thing. I think I'd been waiting to write this for a long time and then suddenly there was a reason to. It came out so naturally.

Jeff Rougvie: When we got the liner notes from David, his first pass at it was pretty intense and a little unwieldy. He and I spent quite a while, a few weeks, going back and forth and getting them in shape, so it was a little more straightforward. It was an emotional thing for David. Like most, I hardly knew anything about Chris, so it was exciting to read and understand everything they'd done—all the traveling, the disappointments, and playing in little clubs across Europe.

John Fry: Frankly, I did not have enough involvement on the Ryko release of Chris' album. It's been a source of regret. It came at a busy time at Ardent. Even by that time, the early '90s, the only two songs I'd heard were "Cosmos" and "Sister." I had never heard the rest of the material. It's probably hard for anyone to believe that, but it's the truth. To my shame, when we put all this together for Ryko, I never listened to the sequence. I just said, "They want to put it out, so round up the tapes and get it ready."

That was the early '90s, the days when no one realized how much people were going to be interested in these records. Then after Ryko issued the CD, it was years later before I really listened to the album. You may put that down to neglect or being super busy. You may put it down to simply being scared of hearing it. By "scared" I mean, I'd heard "Cosmos" and "Sister"—the emotions that came to me from hearing those...I didn't work on the Ryko release much, but since then, I've insisted that everything new comes from the best original analog sources. It took us a while to realize what treasures we had in our custody.

The release of I Am the Cosmos *secured Chris Bell's status as an indie-rock pioneer overnight. With the '90s rock boom hitting its stride, Chris' songbook of moody, proto-alternative tunes gelled with the DIY-rock culture. Critically, the album received positive ink in a pile of rock magazines, including March 1992's review in* Rolling Stone *by Parke Puterbaugh. "Like Chilton, the late Chris Bell was no stranger to emotional turmoil, judging from the twelve songs (plus three alternate versions)...I Am the Cosmos offers a bevy of shimmering, angst-ridden pop, including the frantic rocker 'Get Away' (which recalls Big Star's raucous 'Don't Lie to Me'); the colorful and catchy 'Make a Scene'; an acoustic jewel entitled 'You and Your Sister'; and the utterly transcendent 'I Am the Cosmos,' a lush, spine-tingling number in which megalomania and vulnerability come together in these unfathomable lines: 'Every night I tell myself I am the cosmos/I am the wind/But that don't get you back again.'"*

Jeff Rougvie: *I Am the Cosmos* was a big success and exceeded our expectations. It remains a hugely important project to me. The Chris record is one my favorite things I've ever worked on—more than the Bowie catalog, more than the Elvis Costello catalog.

Ric Menck: When they finally issued a full album of Bell's solo material on Ryko, I remember thinking it was one of the most important releases of my lifetime. We had all been waiting so long for more of Chris' material to surface. It was everything we could have hoped for.

Mark Deming: Years before, I'd heard his Car Records single, so I was psyched when the album finally came out. I was thinking, *Wow, a whole album of this!* Once I heard it, I was knocked out, but also surprised. The Car Records single suggested the album was going to be a return to the sound of *#1 Record*, but it was something rather different. It was darker, more personal, more revealing and rougher around the edges. It flew in the face of the argument that Alex was the sloppy rock dude and Chris was the polished pop guy.

Cindy Bell Coleman: Being his sister, I am so far removed from Chris' music. David knows about it, but I was still amazed. I thought, *That was*

my brother who played back in the backhouse—what's all of this? I am fascinated by it. When his music first started hitting, I thought, *Why couldn't
this have happened when he was alive? Why did it happen so much later?*

On February 21, 1992, the same day I Am the Cosmos *CDs and cassettes hit
stores, Ryko dropped two other Big Star discs, including* Live, *the post-Bell,
1974 performance recorded in New York for WLIR. Alongside that was a reissue
of* Third/Sister Lovers. *With oversight from Jim Dickinson, the disc presented
a new sequence and two previously unissued covers. That same year, Fantasy
Records, which had acquired much of the Stax catalog, released one CD with* #1
Record *and* Radio City *back to back. From there, the often-bootlegged catalog
of Big Star became accessible and with greater clarity than ever before.*

Jeff Rougvie: Everyone was excited about it. I even got an out of the
blue phone call from Alex Chilton one day about the releases. He called
and said, "Thanks a lot for doing this, it has really meant a lot to me,"
which completely goes against a lot of stories I've heard about him. I
never expected to hear from him. I'll never forget it.

Sherman Willmott: At my store, Shangri-La Records in Memphis, a big
part of our focus was Memphis music, and [Big Star] were a big part of
that. We loved them and sold as many records and shirts as we could
get our hands on. Then Rykodisc did all those re-issues and Fantasy
Records did the CD with the first two records on it. Once those reissues
started coming out, we could easily sell their music. Before that, it was
hard to find anything Big Star.

Jeff Rougvie: It's funny, at the time, the higher-ups at Ryko didn't think
the Big Star and Chris Bell records were going to make much of an
impact. I was cautiously optimistic. Then, of course, we ended up getting a lead review in *Rolling Stone* and everyone from R.E.M. came out
and said how much they loved them. It turned into a pretty big deal and
everything did better than I expected. There was also a groundswell of
other things happening at the same time, with Teenage Fanclub getting
big in the U.S. and other bands that were heavily influenced by Big Star.
It felt like a right time for the music, but also there were those notable
musicians out there, who, unprompted, would talk about the records
and how great they are. Those bands were just as excited as we were.
They'd been chasing after scraps for years just trying to figure out the
pieces to the puzzle. We sort of got all the pieces almost all at once.

*While the trio of 1992 Rykodisc releases caused a buzz throughout the music
industry, the following year saw the true, unexpected rise of Big Star as offers
from promoters and labels floated in. One bid proposed a concert reuniting Alex
and Jody. That idea soon morphed into a full-on reunion show. Alex surprisingly*

agreed and stayed on board throughout the planning process, however, neither Andy Hummel or John Lightman took part. The April 25, 1993 concert, held at the University of Missouri in Columbia, was a monumental occasion. It had been eighteen years since Big Star's last show. A contract to release the concert as a live album arrived via Zoo Entertainment, a now-defunct BMG imprint that was concurrently working on Tool's debut LP. Released in September 1993, Big Star's Columbia: Live at Missouri University 4/25/93 *became the first newly recorded Big Star output in nearly two decades. The concert was a part of the University of Missouri's annual Springfest, which included a daylong lineup of eight bands playing inside a large tent outside the campus arena. The idea to lure Big Star onto the lengthy bill was initiated by the university's campus radio station KCOU's promotions director Jeff Breeze and its general manager Mike Mulvihill.*

John Dando: Some college-promotion people organized the reunion gig for Big Star in Missouri. They were the same type of people who promoted Big Star back in the original days. On a lark, they got in touch with Jody to see if Big Star would reunite and play at their college.

Andy Hummel: That reunion deal is something of a mystery. Jody called me beforehand and I was initially very interested. The next I heard about the whole deal was after it happened, which I recall being a little pissed about.

Alex Chilton: I don't know. I haven't talked to Andy [since about 1975]. I think Jody has spoken to him every now and then, but I haven't.

Andy Hummel: Later, Jody said that he had tried to contact me and was told I wasn't interested. And that is certainly possible. My career was in very high gear at the time and it may have just been a miscommunication, with secretaries taking messages and all. As a practical matter, I don't know how I would have done it anyway.

Jody Stephens: Mike Mulvihill called at the right moment. I guess we were all just feeling good and cooperative. I would never have thought it would work. When I got the call, I thought an easy way out of it would be to say, "If Alex will do this, I'll do it," thinking Alex probably wouldn't do it, given all I'd heard about Alex's sentiments about Big Star...When the opportunity came around to do a few Big Star songs and Alex agreed to do it, it was shocking to me.

Alex Chilton: Well, it was proposed to me as something different than a Big Star reunion. Some people like Paul Westerberg and some others were being bandied about as people that were going to be there, and they just wanted to get a lot of people like them and me together on a stage. I said, "Sure, I'm not doing anything that day. I'll be there." Jody was one of the people they mentioned.

Jody Stephens: I was cautiously excited. I hadn't played in a long time, so I had to get my chops back.

Alex Chilton: The next thing I knew, all these people were asking me, "Gosh, I hear there's going to be a Big Star reunion." I said, "Well, I hadn't heard about that." But then this record company jumped in, and said, "If there's going to be a Big Star reunion, then we'd really like to record it and here's this much money." And I said, "There's going to be a Big Star reunion." One of the conditions of doing that record was I said, "It's fine for you to record it. After we're finished with the performance, if it turns out well, then we'll use it, but if it doesn't turn out well, then we won't use it and you won't pay us." But it turned out well enough for me.

After some deliberation about who would fill the shoes of Chris Bell and Andy Hummel, Jody recruited guitarist Jon Auer and bassist Ken Stringfellow of the Posies, an emerging, Seattle-based alternative power-pop band signed to DGC Records. The year prior, the Posies had gained rock cred when Ringo Starr released a cover of their 1990 single "Golden Blunders."

John Dando: Jody got the Posies guys to play the gig with them. It was that show that got the final incarnation of Big Star playing together.

Jon Auer — Guitarist, vocalist, the Posies, Big Star, Big Star's Third: I remember coming home to an answering machine message; Jody called and told us it was going to happen.

Ken Stringfellow — Bassist, vocalist, guitarist, keyboardist, the Posies, Big Star, Big Star's Third: The root of it goes back to us being super fans. In 1990, we looked into recording at Ardent Studios and discovered Jody Stephens worked there. It kind of blew our minds to think he was a real, living and breathing person. We didn't end up recording at the studio, but we stayed in touch with Jody and he became a fan of our work. Jody also noticed we did some incredible covers, in terms of replicating the sounds of Big Star.

Jon Auer: Ken and I have this harmonizing thing going on. We can do justice to those harmonies in ways that even the original Big Star couldn't do live.

Alex Chilton: [The Posies] had recorded a couple of Big Star tunes, and I heard that they did it very well. I said, "Okay, we'll give them a try." We got together with them in Seattle and rehearsed one time, and I knew in five minutes that they were perfect for the gig.

Jody Stephens: After Bud Scoppa [at Zoo Entertainment] and producer Jim Rondinelli caught wind of the show and wanted to record, they got us a little advance money. It wasn't much, but enough to travel to Seattle and rehearse for a couple days with Jon and Ken. It was the first time I'd played with Alex since 1978.

Ken Stringfellow: The first Big Star rehearsal in Seattle started off a bit odd. We walked in and were just standing there awkwardly in front of Alex, a character we'd been hearing nothing but insane rumors about. He has quite a bit of legend about his behavior. Was he difficult? Was he really "a man called destruction?" So we're standing there awkwardly and not shaking hands. That was Alex's thing: He didn't shake hands. We're one foot inside the door right now. Then Alex, very thoughtfully, methodically and slowly, unwrapped this purple handkerchief he was wearing around his neck cowboy style. He proceeded to blow his nose for like two minutes. It seemed like forever. We were losing our shit. He probably knew we were. Then we started jamming, and it was great.

Jon Auer: Alex was not super dictatorial at this rehearsal. It's not like he didn't care, but he wasn't trying to run the show. He wanted to make it as easy as possible. Whatever songs he didn't want to do, we ended up singing on. We'd suggest a song and if he didn't want to do it, he'd say, "Be my guest."

By the day of the University of Missouri show, the band had about twenty songs on the setlist. "In the Street" sat at the top. Other fan favorites, like "Thirteen" and "September Gurls," also made the cut. Alex's love of covers came through with two T. Rex singles and a take on Leiber and Stoller's "Kansas City," among others. Four songs into the set, in front of a couple hundred awestruck fans, Chris Bell was remembered when Jon Auer led a spot-on version of "I Am the Cosmos."

Jody Stephens: I was a bit nervous and excited. Feeling lucky it had all come together. It was a pretty improbable event. It even came down to the weather that day. There was a storm and we were lucky it didn't coincide with our performance. I'm not sure we could have performed during it, and we certainly couldn't have recorded it. I rehearsed with Jon and Ken after we arrived in Columbia, but it seems Alex had a gig the night before and showed up the day of...After Alex showed up, I thought, *Wow, this is really going to happen.*

Peter Jesperson: When Big Star did the reunion show in '93 with the two Posies guys, I thought it'd be like traveling to Mecca—people from all over the world coming by plane, boat, or train. I was living

Jon Auer prepares for Big Star's performance on *the Tonight Show with Jay Leno,* Halloween 1994.

COURTESY OF JODY STEPHENS

Jon Auer, Alex Chilton, and Ken Stringfellow on stage at the University of Missouri reunion show.

COURTESY OF JODY STEPHENS

A 1992 one-sheet for Ryko's CD reissues of *Third/Sister Lovers*, *Live*, and Chris Bell's debut solo album. Twenty-six years later, Peter Buck's quote still rings true, proving the material to be more influential than ever.

CHRIS BELL
I Am The Cosmos

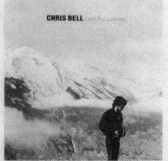

	CD	CASSETTE
CATALOG #	RCD 10222	RACS 0222
BAR CODE#	14431-0222-2	14431-0222-4
LIST PRICE:	$13.98	$9.98

- **THIS IS ONE OF THE GREAT LOST RELEASES OF THE SEVENTIES.** The existence of hissy 10th generation tapes of these sessions have been coveted by fans throughout the years and now this material is finally available the way it was intended to be. **Chris Bell's** talents for writing catchy, melodic pop songs are showcased on **I AM THE COSMOS**.

- **Chris Bell** contributed to the first two **Big Star** releases and then went off on his own to pursue a solo career. Unfortunately, he died in a car crash in 1978 and his solo album was never released. Chris' total recorded output was limited to one single (*I Am The Cosmos/You and Your Sister*) that came out on **Chris Stamey's** Car label in 1978.

- The last release by 4AD's supergroup **This Mortal Coil, BLOOD** featured covers of both songs found on the original Chris Bell Single.

- **I AM THE COSMOS will receive a 3 1/2 star rating in the February 18th Rolling Stone**

TRACK LIST: *I Am The Cosmos, Better Save Yourself, Speed Of The Sound, Get Away, You and Your Sister, Make a Scene, Look Up, I Got Kinda Lost, There Was A Light, Fight At The Table, I Don't Know, Though I Know She Lies, I Am The Cosmos (Slow Version), You And Your Sister (Country Version), You And Your Sister (Acoustic Version)*

Ryko press release one-sheet for the 1992 release of the *I Am The Cosmos* album, finally available for the first time anywhere.

in Minneapolis then, so I drove down Highway 61 to Columbia. I got to the show and was standing around listening to the opening act in the tent where the stage was set up. After they finished, the emcee said, "Up next, Big Star!" I almost caved in. My knees almost gave out. I never thought I'd hear those words in my life. It was a huge deal to me, but it was a bit of an odd show. Alex wasn't really singing in a committed fashion like he came to in later years. He was kind of uncooperative and surly. He had Ken and Jon sang some of the songs he used to sing. That was a little weird. He did some interesting covers, like Todd Rundgren's "Slut."

Jody Stephens: I don't remember anything negative. I was just excited to play those songs again. It rocked. At one point, Alex said "Follow me," and launched into "Duke of Earl," which he hadn't rehearsed with us, but he proceeded to nail the falsetto parts. It blew my mind. There was a lot of nervous energy on my part. There was some intensity, but it was a damn good time.

Peter Jesperson: After they were done, I wandered around the backstage area and saw the four of them lined up against some road cases. A guy from the label was there snapping some pictures. Alex maybe stood still for about ninety seconds. He was not into it. Alex saw me and gave me a little nod and, pretty quickly, walked away and said, "Do you have your car here? Let's get out of here. I'm really sick of this." We drove back to his hotel and hung out and went to dinner, which was nice because we hadn't seen each other for a while. The next morning, when he was getting ready to go back to New Orleans, he called and asked if I wanted to have breakfast. I went and picked him up and grabbed something to eat. Then he says, "I don't have to catch this plane for another hour and a half or so, can we just drive for a little bit so I can smoke a joint?" I said, "Absolutely. No problem." I just got on some road and started driving. I wasn't smoking but he was.

We got to the outskirts of town. It was getting pretty rural. I said, "I better turn around and head back towards the city. I don't want to get lost out here." We just randomly turned off the road and pulled into a little street. I was backing around when Alex grabs my arm and said, "Wait, look at that!" He pointed at a street sign that said Cosmos Place. We both kind of went, "Wow...that's weird." That spurred a conversation about Chris. We talked about the Beatles and Big Star's affection for the Beatles. A couple of the things he said really stuck with me. He said their favorite Beatles album was the *Second Album*. Which, if you know anything about the Beatles, is an American compilation of British singles and EPs. It's kind of an odd one to be a favorite; I thought that was cool. He said the Big Star guys had a theory that the Beatles mixed the bass and the drums together, which gave the Beatles such a powerful rhythm section. I don't know if that's true or not, but it's interesting they were thinking about things like that. Alex was just looking out the window, with a half-grin on his face, talking about all this. Maybe it was the pot, or he was just happy, but he got a little wistful. It's interesting, because he had been sort of publicly dismissive about Chris in some ways, and in this conversation, it was very apparent to me his fondness for Chris and what they did together was quite deep and quite strong.

Other reunion shows followed, including a spot in a tent at the 1993 Reading Festival in England, which included big names like The Flaming Lips, Blur, Rage Against the Machine, Stone Temple Pilots, and The Breeders. Big Star toured Europe and Japan before returning to the U.S. for select dates and a Halloween 1994 performance of "In the Street" on The Tonight Show with Jay Leno. *The lineup stayed together for seventeen years, until Alex died in 2010.*

Jody Stephens: We did the Columbia show in April, then went to Europe in August. We did about five dates over there. There was the Lowlands Festival in the Netherlands, the Clapham Grand in London, the Reading Festival, played the University in Glasgow...we played a little pub called the Duchess of York in Leeds—that was awesome. The stage was maybe two inches off the ground. There was a microphone and then the audience. There was nothing between us. It was a little bitty stage, but it was one of the best times I ever had playing a gig because within five feet you could see the expressions on people's faces and there was a killer energy.

Ken Stringfellow: Adding in new songs to play came up sometimes. Alex said, "We need some more rockers." I said, "What about 'You Can't Have Me' and 'Kizza Me' from *Third*?" Alex was like, "Yeah, we should do those, they'd be great. Those will grab people." So, a few months later, at the next show we were doing in Spain, our last show in Europe, at soundcheck we'd all been talking about trying "Kizza Me." I learned it, Jon learned it, Jody knew it. We got to soundcheck and started playing the song. We started with those opening chords, but then the verse started and Alex just didn't sing. The song went along, we kept playing. Then Alex sort of wanders over to his amp, noodles with a couple things, put his guitar down and walked off. It was like he went blank or something. It was like we'd never discussed it. It was weird. It's not like he was weird to us after that, but it was clear that subject was closed.

Jon Auer: Alex wasn't into the more precious and pristine aspect of Big Star. He was more into fucking things up, having a good time and surprising people.

Ken Stringfellow: We're talking about songs like "What's Going Ahn?" or "You Get What You Deserve." He thought those were like high school poetry. He wouldn't play "Big Black Car." Alex was already invested into the style he was into: a mix of R&B and jazz. He pushed songs in that direction whenever possible with his guitar playing and whatnot. After our first rehearsals, we never really added any more old Big Star songs to the setlist—ever. He was like, "The songs I'm playing are the only ones I can live with. The rest of the songs are just crap I wrote when I was a kid."

Jody Stephens: There were maybe two shows a year, maybe five a year, with the exception of a couple years where we played more.

Alex Chilton: Well, these gigs, they pay very well—I mean, I am trying to make a living. And it's not unenjoyable, either. I think last year we probably played ten gigs. We went to Japan and played five or six gigs in America…We charge a lot of money for them when we do them. So, if it comes up five or ten times in a year, that's tolerable to me. I can do it five or ten times and enjoy it. Doing it more than that, I don't know if I really would enjoy it.

Ken Stringfellow: We never really traveled together on the road. All our shows were one-offs, so we typically flew in separately. We were always flying from different places to assemble wherever the show was, in London, San Francisco, Minneapolis, or wherever. Alex was pretty quiet and liked to hang out in the hotel room. He wasn't out socializing much.

Alex may have been willing to perform his old Big Star songs for fans, but he never mustered patience for overly chatty Big Star fanatics.

Ken Stringfellow: It would shut him down totally. If you would talk to him about anything other than Big Star and how great they were, he'd actually be really conversational. He'd talk about gardening or the Civil War. He'd talk about astrology for hours.

Jon Auer: The exception to that rule would be when we toured Japan. He really opened up. He found something really charming in Japanese fans, in their appreciation. He made time for them in ways I never saw him do for any other fans ever.

Ken Stringfellow: Perhaps it was because he knew he'd never see them again. They wouldn't show up on his doorstep. Later on, when I was tour manager, I basically just kept people away. It was just nicer to have nobody around backstage. But, every once in a while, somebody I knew would try to talk to Alex—they'd been dying to nerd out about Big Star. Alex would literally not say a word and walk away.

Alex's years of heavy substance abuse were long behind him, but dealing with overzealous fans on the road was a bit more tolerable after a few puffs backstage.

Ken Stringfellow: He drank a little bit when we first started playing; he'd drink some Heineken. Later, he didn't drink at all, but he was always smoking tons of pot. Lots of pot. An astronomical amount of weed.

Jon Auer: We played the House of Blues in Los Angeles in 1994. We did two shows in one night. The early show was great, but between the shows he fucking smoked a ton of pot. We came out and started playing "In the Street." He walks over to his amp to try and adjust something and just stood there for a whole verse and a chorus just staring at his amp with the guitar just squealing feedback full blast. This kind of shit actually happened, but there were some nice moments, too. We had an afternoon where Alex drove me around Memphis and showed me all these cool spots, places Elvis went as a kid. He would often come to Paris just to hang out. If he had a show in Europe, he'd stay in Paris for a bit afterwards. We'd have dinner, hang out and talk about music. I definitely approached the subject of Chris Bell with Alex, but he didn't have much to say, other than he was a sweet guy who had some troubles and was emotional. He didn't go into any real depth about it. We'd talk about a lot of things, but very little about the Big Star days.

Ken Stringfellow: With the Box Tops, he was happy to tell us how much he thought a lot of it sucked. How much he hated touring England with the Box Tops in the '60s, and how much England sucked. That was a big thing for him. Alex was more willing to talk about what he was listening to at the time—he'd get on these kicks and he'd really want to play it for you. For a while, he was really into Lothar and the Hand People and he'd play that record for anyone who'd listen. Around the time we met him, he was releasing his *Clichés* album. I think that sums up his listening world—Nina Simone and that kind of thing.

Big Star 1994 reunion tour set list.

COURTESY OF JODY STEPHENS

Big Star arrives in Japan, 1994.

COURTESY OF JODY STEPHENS

Big Star live in Japan, 1994.

COURTESY OF JODY STEPHENS

Big Star performs July 1, 2009 in Hyde Park, London. (L-R) Jon Auer, Ken Stringfellow, Jody Stephens, and Alex Chilton.

PHOTO BY MARCELO COSTA / SCREAM & YELL MAGAZINE

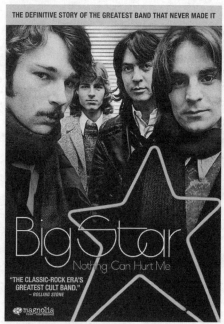

THE DEFINITIVE STORY OF THE GREATEST BAND THAT NEVER MADE IT

Big Star

Nothing Can Hurt Me

"THE CLASSIC-ROCK ERA'S
GREATEST CULT BAND."
– ROLLING STONE

magnolia

(above) The reunited Box Tops, late
'90s (L-R) Gary Talley, Alex Chilton,
Bill Cunningham, Danny Smythe.

PHOTO COURTESY OF BILL CUNNINGHAM

(left) *Big Star: Nothing Can Hurt Me,*
the 2012 documentary (Magnolia
Pictures), earned the band legions
of new fans across the globe.

Jody Stephens, the last surviving member of Big Star's original lineup, May 2016.
Jody has also worked in management at Ardent Studios since 1987.

PHOTO BY NICOLE RICO

Alex Chilton riffs with Jon Auer backstage at a 1994 Big Star gig.

CHAPTER 26

IN SPACE — WHAT'S GOING AHN:
LATE '90S-2018

Even when Big Star finally became a hot commodity in the 1990s, Alex Chilton never abandoned his solo act. His band played periodically to both small and large crowds. In July 1995, following the release of his A Man Called Destruction *solo LP, Alex's band performed a funky take of "Lies" on NBC's* Late Night with Conan O'Brien. *Three years later, on August 23, 1998, the teen-comedy* That '70s Show *debuted on FOX with a cover of "In the Street" as its theme song. The Emmy-winning show, now in syndication, lasted eight seasons and was viewed by an average ten million viewers each week. The stream of royalty checks boosted his profile and provided a financial cushion for the self-made Alex Chilton.*

Ron Easley — Musician, guitarist bassist, Alex Chilton trio, Panther Burns: Touring [with Alex] was always a gas. Over the years, our touring evolved from all of us piling into Alex's old Buick LeSabre and sleeping in the same motel room, all the way to me having my own car and traveling as I chose, booking my own rooms, taking in the sights along the way and just showing up at the gigs. We played the usual club circuits in most areas of the country. The biggest tour was with Counting Crows [1994], back when they were hot. Altogether, our trio's touring went on for two solid decades and change.

Sherman Willmott: Alex went from playing solo at the 300-person capacity Antenna Club with his trio to playing with Big Star at the New Daisy Theatre, which seats over a thousand. He didn't play as frequently after Big Star's reunion. He was making more money playing fewer, but better, shows.

Alex Chilton: I also do oldies dates that revolve around the Box Tops sometimes. And that's fun too, especially getting together with all these old '60s bands at those kinds of shows. I think last year [1994], I probably did five or six of them. I get to play with Ronnie Spector and people like that.

In the fall of 1996, after the original 1967-68 Box Tops lineup reunited, the revived blue-eyed soul band played nostalgia shows across the country for years to come. In December 1998, the group even released a final album, the Tear Off! *LP. The record, stacked with soulful cover tunes, was recorded at Easley McCain Recording in Memphis and released via Last Call Records. The classic lineup included Alex on vocals and guitar, lead guitarist Gary Talley, keyboardist John Evans, bassist Bill Cunningham, and drummer Danny Smythe.*

Bill Cunningham: The Box Tops reunion started out pretty casual. I just wanted to work on some songs I'd been listening to. I wanted to play, but I hadn't touched an instrument in about seventeen years. On a whim, I called Alex up and said, "Do you want to do something together in the studio? I haven't played in one in years." He said, "Yeah, sure. Who should we get?" Originally, I thought it might just be Alex and me, but then I suggested all the original Box Tops guys. He agreed, they all agreed, and it took off from there. We showed up in Memphis and basically recorded each track in one take. Only one was two takes. It was all just live first takes and spontaneous. That's the *Tear Off!* LP. Word got out we were in the studio and some people tried to talk us into a tour. I was busy with work, so I said, "Maybe we can try ten or twelve dates a year," which is about what we stuck to. We went out to Los Angeles for the first gig. We played the House of Blues for Dan Aykroyd. He heard we were back together and called for us immediately.

Bernie Kugel: The last time I saw Alex it was with the reunited Box Tops. They played here in Buffalo at this venue called Melody Fair, which is closed now. It was basically a place for older people in a rural area to go see bands from back in the day. Tommy Roe opened the show, did a great set and was nice as can be. Then Chilton and the Box Tops show up, they drive up in a car. Big Star people kind of know about the sometimes-nasty Alex Chilton vibe, but seventy-year-old rural Buffalo people didn't know about the Chilton persona. He introduced a song and said, "This is a song that was popular in the 1800s and judging by the look of this audience, I'd say a lot of you were around for it."

Bill Cunningham: We had a blast at these shows. The Box Tops fans did too. Once or twice someone called out a Big Star number and Alex would say, "That's the wrong group." He tried to keep Big Star and the Box Tops separate.

While Alex refused to pander to his vocal Big Star fans, he would sometimes surprise them. Twelve years after Big Star reunited in Columbia, Missouri, Alex, at fifty-four, once again agreed to something no fan ever thought possible: a new Big Star studio album. In Space, *released in 2005 by Rykodisc, brought Alex and Jody together at Ardent Studios for the first time since their notorious* Third *sessions. Along with them were Jon and Ken, who shared songwriting duties. Producer and engineer Jeff Powell, along with help from assistant Adam Hill, produced the twelve-track disc. Given Alex's disdain for repeating himself, the original songs did not attempt to recreate the pristine Big Star sound, to the dismay of some fans and critics. AllMusic critic Mark Deming, who gave the album three-out-of-five stars, said: "In* Space *is an album that should appeal to anyone who digs Alex Chilton; however, anyone expecting a Big Star album is going to be more than a bit puzzled by most of these tunes." Pitchfork critic Stephen M. Deusner shared a similar opinion: "For all its bright spots,* In Space *is not much more than adequate power pop. It's hard to judge the album on its own terms and almost impossible to shake the fact that it would sound better with another band's name on the spine, one that didn't invite hopeless comparisons to* #1 Record, Radio City, *and* Third/Sister Lovers."

Ken Stringfellow: The theme for *In Space* was that we'd write and record a new song each day we were in the studio.

Jody Stephens: On the first two Big Star albums, we'd rehearsed them to some extent before we cut them—*Third*, not so much. But the approach was a lot different on *In Space*. The two songs I wrote with Jon Auer, they came to me the night before. We finished it in the morning and cut it that afternoon at Ardent. The same thing happened the next night. Alex or Jon would come up with a riff, we'd bang around and jam on it for a minute and see what we could come up with.

Adam Hill: On the first day, Alex showed up and started handing out, he'd transcribed two or three pieces by this 15th century composer named Georg Muffat. He was way into transcribing these pieces for a four-piece band. He starts handing out the music. Jody doesn't read music. Ken kind of reads music. Jon, to a lesser degree. But they all just jumped in and had a go at it. One of them, "Aria, Largo," ended up on the record. I know they recorded at least one other one, a slower tempo piece that was just gorgeous. He wasn't trying to drive people away, it was just genuinely what he wanted to do. He didn't want to make Big Star records. That was thirty years ago.

Jon Auer: Alex was still into a lot of the more primitive recordings. For *In Space*, he brought in this crappy microphone to use because he thought it was great-sounding. There were times Ken and I spent a long time working on something, a more layered approach. He'd be like, "What are you doing? Let's keep it moving." Alex didn't really take the lead to start on that either. It made you realize that, back in the day, Big Star was a real collaboration. When we were making that record, he was like, "Okay, what are your ideas?" He was looking to us to start. I think the first thing he contributed was "Do You Wanna Make It," which is just a 1-4-5 progression, jammy kind of thing. Ken and I were left to write things that might be construed as being closer to Big Star-ish. There would be things he'd be excited about, but he could be cantankerous. He'd be like, "What do you got? Why don't you have a bridge? What are we doing with this?"

Adam Hill: It was very collaborative. If Alex had something, he'd jump in. If he didn't, he'd hang back. But, overall, everything ultimately passed the gate of Alex. Nobody was cowering, but everybody wanted Alex to show up the next day. They wanted him to see it through and be cool with it. It was his show, whether he was running it or not.

Jon Auer: Alex would reject some ideas. There was something Ken and Jody came up with and he didn't like it. I think it was just the mood he was in, not that it was a bad idea. But with this song "Dony," which opens the record, it was cool because suddenly he got really into it and wanted to write some words. Next thing you know, he's in the booth and we're coaching him on vocals. He was like, "What do you want me to do?" Either he'd be enthusiastic about it, or he wouldn't play it. You could see when he was into the idea by the fact that he'd join in. When we first joined the band in 1993, we suggested doing "I Am the Cosmos." Alex was like, "I think I know how that goes." We started playing and he joined in. That was his endorsement.

While Big Star enjoyed its efficacious second wind, steadily gigging throughout the '90s and 2000s, Ardent Studios had also undergone a fruitful resurgence as a revived record label. Ardent Records, dormant since the Third/Sister Lovers-era, picked up in 1995 as a Christian music label. While Ardent also issued some one-off solo LPs by Alex Chilton, its roster of emerging religious acts, like the Grammy-winning rock band Skillet, proved to be the breakout successes.

John Fry: Since launching the Christian label, we've made 36 albums on artists like Todd Agnew, whose debut record *Grace Like Rain* sold close to 300,000 copies. His first single sold 1.5 million.

John Hampton: Ardent has somewhat of a sordid reputation, so [the Christian label] has been a positive thing. They help give this place a good vibe. On the other hand, Jack White told me part of the reason he initially came here was because I'd done the Cramps.

John Fry: We've really been blessed in doing [the Christian label]. We've gotten to associate with great people, we've gotten to proclaim a message that, I think, is the most important one in the world.

Steve Rhea: Ardent was more successful as a Christian label than they ever were in terms of releasing their own secular records. It was through Chris Bell that John Fry became a born-again Christian, and then, through John, so many others were born-again. The contemporary Christian label that Ardent became in later years all flowed from that.

John Hampton: Chris' death definitely left a hole at Ardent. It's hard to describe, but he still has a presence here. We have a couple of younger engineers who have been influenced by Chris' playing on Big Star records. One of them, Adam Hill, keeps coming at me with, "Hey, check this out!" And he's perfectly copping one of Chris' guitar licks. Adam never even knew Chris Bell.

During its successful run in the religious market, by 2008, the Ardent team was prompted by Rhino Records rep Cheryl Pawelski to delve into its archive of Big Star tapes. Rhino's proposal called for the first-ever holy grail boxset on the band, compiling never-before heard rehearsals, alternate mixes, demos and live performances in one package. Released in September 2009 as Keep an Eye on the Sky, *the four-CD, 98-track set of rarities spans the pre-Big Star days of 1968 through the* Third *sessions and Chris Bell's solo era. The project was produced by a team of players and producers, including Pawelski, Alec Palao, Andrew Sandoval, John Fry, and Adam Hill. After its release, the extensive liner notes, penned by Memphis-based author Robert Gordon, won a 2009 Grammy Award for Best Album Notes. In a September 2009 review,* Pitchfork *called it "the one reissue that finally gets Big Star right." While producing* Keep an Eye on the Sky, *the Rhino team also penned a deal with David Bell to press a new edition of* I Am the Cosmos. *This would be the first Chris Bell release since Judith Beeman, founder of the Big Star fanzine* Back of a Car, *issued a limited flexi-disc release of "Country Morn" in 1995. Released on Rhino's subsidiary Rhino Handmade, the deluxe* Cosmos *not only offered up new liner notes and an extended track list, but also inspired John Fry to return to the recording console after a decades-long hiatus from the studio.*

Adam Hill: Up to that point, Fry basically hadn't engineered anything since about when Chris Bell died. He recorded a Scruffs record and is credited on a Tommy Hoehn record that came out in 1980. This was pretty much his last hurrah in the studio.

John Fry: In 2008 or so, when we started work on the Rhino Handmade *Cosmos*, that is when I first truly started listening to and working on Chris' solo music. My Lord, did we work on that deluxe edition. The audio on Rhino's *Cosmos* reissue is very good. It's the best mix we could do using the original analog tapes.

Cheryl Pawelski — Record executive, former Rhino Records producer, co-owner Omnivore Recordings: There was plenty to do on both projects, so Alec Palao took lead on the *Cosmos* expanded Handmade project while Andrew Sandoval and I concentrated a little more on the Big Star boxed set. I had to do some internal dancing to keep that boxed set alive within the company at the time. While most of the staff at Rhino were huge Big Star fans, there were some folks that neither knew nor cared, and weren't exactly convinced [the releases] would do anything sales-wise. But the biggest thing about all the Big Star-related records I've been involved in making, is how unusually passionate everyone is who contributes to them.

Adam Hill: For *Keep an Eye on the Sky*, Fry came to me and said, "We need to find out what's all on these tapes." He hadn't put them on a machine since he recorded them. A majority of the work was me transferring tapes, making rough mixes and telling everybody what was there. It wasn't a bad gig. I was on the clock and transferring Big Star tapes, finding gold, like rare acoustic demos of "Life Is White" and "What's Going Ahn," and reporting back to Fry. It was fun as hell.

Alec Palao — Record producer, *Keep an Eye on the Sky, I Am the Cosmos* re-issue: My role as reissue producer in the expanded Rhino Handmade reissue of *I Am the Cosmos* came as a result of my close work with the Big Star and Ardent catalog, including *Thank You Friends: The Ardent Records Story* CD for Ace Records, and also the Big Star box *Keep An Eye On The Sky*. Both, of course, included tracks by Chris. In the process, I had spent much time discussing Ardent's back catalog with John Fry, and we both agreed that *I Am the Cosmos* could stand a sonic upgrade. Fry was committed to making it sound the very best it could. He had not been involved with the mastering on the original Ryko issue, and it showed. There was also additional material that had been overlooked or undiscovered at the time of that release, that's why Cheryl Pawelski green-lit an expanded two-CD version.

David Bell: I came into Ardent a few times during the *Cosmos* reissue. When Alec Palao came to Memphis, I stopped at the studio and listened to some tapes with him, but it was mainly Adam Hill and John Fry working on it.

Adam Hill: While working on that *Cosmos* reissue, Fry got a little flustered at first because he wasn't familiar with EQ on the Neve board, but once he got used to the console, he was up and running. We still have a lot of the same outboard gear he used on the original recordings. It's like riding a bike. He got the same acoustic guitar sounds on that Neve that he got back in the '70s on the Spectra Sonics. The lesson with that is, "It's a poor craftsman who blames his tools." People who know what they're doing have the sound in their heads. They use the gear to chase it and find it.

Alec Palao: Studio archivist Adam Hill and myself made exhaustive trawls through the vaults in Memphis, so we had at hand many of the different takes of Chris' masters. We also had additional material by his early bands like Icewater and Rock City, and tracks with other artists such as Nancy Bryan and Keith Sykes. Adam also accessed Chris' personal stash of tapes from David Bell, which had further alternate versions and mixes.

Adam Hill: Chris' tapes were a fucking mess to varying degrees. He would just go in and be focused on something and work on it a lot, but you don't erase things you're not using, you just mute it when you're not mixing. So, in some cases, we had to separate the wheat from the chaff, hopefully figure out what Chris' intent was. There'd be something going one direction on the tape, then you'd get halfway through and half of the tracks would start running backwards, which means he flipped the tape over and recorded something that way. On "Cosmos," he had a lot of overdubs—one of them he tried to make the notes of the solo hang on longer. He would crossfade what he'd originally done with the new guitar. There was all this shit on there. We'd pull up the multi-track and go, "No, he didn't mean for that guitar to be in the final mix." I mean, the "Cosmos" tape has a twelve-string guitar on there, almost doing a bluesy lick. He was just fucking around for a take. That's why Richard Rosebrough was so great to have around. He worked with Chris. He had a better idea of his intent than I did, and I want to get as close to the intent as I can. Another key person was Alec Palao; he was the driving force behind the *Cosmos* reissue. He wrote the technical liner notes and remixed all the bonus tracks, like "Looking Forward."

Alec Palao: I surveyed all the material and decided to keep the first disc as a linear listen: the album that never was. For many listeners, it already was via the Ryko disc, albeit with a slight reshuffling of tracks. I moved the bonus versions to disc two and added the best of the extras. It all fell together quite easily and neatly.

Adam Hill: Basically, the first disc is all mixes Chris did himself or oversaw. They're all '70s mixes. Then on disc two, all the bonus material, we didn't have to remix much of that. Thomas Eubanks has a great quarter-inch tape of the final mixes of the Rock City material and that's where we got a few things. We did a remix of Rock City's version of "Try Again," which was eight-track. The remixes we did were things that only existed on multi-track and there was no stereo mix for. In a few instances, they were simply mixes Fry wanted to do.

John Fry: One of the things was simple: We included an eight-track version of "Cosmos," so people could hear how it started. Then it's like, "We'll use this song ['Better Save Yourself'] because it's got strings, but you can't hear them in the first mix, so let's make that more prominent on this mix."

Adam Hill: Fry was very keen to better feature Bill Cunningham's "Better Save Yourself" string arrangements; he thought they hadn't gotten their due on the original. We had a full sixteen-track with all the strings and everything. The mix is really thick. There's that cloudiness to Chris' solo music, but John was eager to feature the double bass, cello and a lot of low strings—add some gravitas to Chris' lyrics. The heavy subject matter of the song really struck Fry.

Alec Palao: During all this, John Fry told me this in an email: "This is likely to be the last time I get an opportunity to be involved with Chris' music," and "I am glad to do whatever it takes for Chris. He will be pleased, if folks up there even care about things like this. For further information, read *The Great Divorce* by C. S. Lewis."

John Fry: I don't think there's a day that's gone by in thirty years that I haven't thought about him. And it's often in context of hearing something and thinking, "Oh, this is good, Chris would've loved this." Or, "This really stinks, Chris would've hated that." Or, "Gosh, Chris would've come up with a good joke about this."

Adam Hill: After all the *Cosmos* work was finished, Fry called me and said, "Do you know how hard that was for me? I'd look up and expect to see Chris on the other side of the glass." The day we did the last mix, we wrapped up around 5 p.m. at Ardent. He told me, "I walked out the side door of the studio. The sun was setting." It was his way of saying he got some closure. He was able to draw a little peace.

Upon its release, the deluxe I Am the Cosmos *set was a bit overshadowed by the Big Star box. It did, however, receive a burst of acclaim. A Pitchfork review asserted that Chris had "amassed more than enough strong material to make him a cult hero, almost akin to an American analog of Nick Drake, another struggling songwriter lost too soon but unearthed and embraced later." The review, penned by critic Joshua Klein, proclaims: "Away from Big Star, Bell's solo work proves him Chilton's equal, or at least equally inclined toward a sort of melancholy but melodic proto power-pop." As* Keep an Eye on the Sky *flew out of record stores and exceeded Rhino's sales expectations, Alex continued to spend most of his time in New Orleans at his home at 1228 N. Prieur Street, which suffered only minor damages during the devastation of Hurricane Katrina in 2005. Alex, who ignored evacuation orders, was ultimately rescued from his rooftop. After the floodwaters settled, he returned home and, in the following years, married fellow musician Laura Kersting Chilton.*

Doug Garrison: New Orleans is a small town. He would show up at my gigs, and I would play with him occasionally on the odd chance he had a local gig and needed a drummer. He wouldn't want to bring his New York drummer down for a little club gig. We'd go out for dinner. After the hurricane, we'd hang out occasionally. We talked about how surreal it was and he told me how he wished he hadn't stayed. Everyone that stayed regrets it, for obvious reasons. There was no electricity, no places to get food. The whole place was under water for three weeks. It's kind of arbitrary, but if your house took on water depended on how high your foundation pilings were. Luckily Alex's house was raised. It was a little one-story cottage in the Tremé. It was not big and about 100 years old, which is typical for houses in central New Orleans. The last time I saw him, he seemed in pretty good health. He just didn't know he had a bad ticker. He smoked like crazy. That was his downfall, as much as anything.

John Lightman: I went down to New Orleans to visit Alex and I brought some pot with me. He had a friend stop by who brought him two or three cigarettes. He was never able to quit smoking. Alex struggled hard with it. He was trying to quit, that's why his friend brought him just a couple, so he wouldn't go buy a whole pack and smoke them up. I'm sure that made his heart work a lot harder. Knowing Alex, he probably had symptoms and warning signs before the event and neglected to go to the doctor. When I'd visit him, we'd drive around in his car and his gas tank would be on empty. We'd be riding around on fumes and I'd say, "Alex, don't you want to stop and throw a few bucks in the tank?" He'd say, "No, it's okay." He was just nonchalant about things most people wouldn't be nonchalant about.

On November 18, 2009, four months before his death, Alex took the stage with Big Star one last time before an enthusiastic crowd in New York at the Brooklyn Masonic Temple.

Ken Stringfellow: That Brooklyn show was interesting for several reasons, especially since it became the last show. It was like this whole new leaf of Alex that was really surprising. Alex had a tough few years before that. This was 2009. Katrina and its aftermath had been a real nightmare for him. He had some health issues around that time. He had some dental work done around the time of Katrina and it got infected. He just couldn't get rid of the infection—his body just wasn't in the greatest shape. It made him really cranky. He was civil enough to us, in general, but you could tell he was miserable. That lasted a couple years, but around that show everything changed. He kicked that infection. He felt tons better and had way more energy. He was happy and charming again. He got married. All of these amazing things happened. I will say, that Brooklyn show stands out to me as a unique example of Alex actually enjoying the fact that people loved Big Star's music. I think he was finally able to let go of the fact that Big Star didn't meet his expectations commercially or artistically, but he was able to say, "I don't get it, but people love this music. I was a part of it and if it works for them, it works for me." He was really happy at that show, watching people sing along. Not only happy, but I could tell he was touched. That was never the case before that.

Jody Stephens: [*Rolling Stone* writer] David Fricke came to that last show. I came off the stage and around to an exit door and saw him. The audience was filing through there and I said hello to everyone as they left. I finally got in the hall and talked to David for a minute. It all seemed pretty cool. Before Alex passed away, I saw Big Star continuing—there wasn't an end in sight. There was something special about it all. The next show would have been SXSW.

Nine days after his final Big Star show, on Thanksgiving 2009, Alex arrived in Niagara Falls for his final performance with the Box Tops.

Bill Cunningham: Niagara Falls was a great show at the Bear's Den, a casino with great acoustics. That night before we played the show, Alex and I went up to my hotel room to work up a new original number. We worked it out real fast and played it in the green room for our drummer Danny and a few others. Alex wanted to do it that night as a duet, but I wanted to wait and get it right, so we didn't do it. That's one of my big regrets. I said, "No, let's wait until the next gig," which was already booked. We had something booked in Washington for 2010. PBS was also talking to us about playing the special on '60s groups.

I talked to Alex about that three days before he passed. He said he wasn't feeling well.

Alex played his very last show, a swiftly planned benefit for Doctors Without Borders on January 24, 2010. In front of 100 or so local onlookers at the Big Top, a New Orleans art gallery and performance space, Alex churned out a thirty-minute solo set of what he loved most: old-time covers and favorites from his own discography. Around this time, he also crossed paths with his old friend, René Coman.

René Coman: I ran into Alex on the street in New Orleans. I was coming out of a gig I just played. I hadn't run into him in a couple years. I hear, "Hey, René." I was like, "Wow! Alex, I didn't expect to see you here." I was pushing my gear down the street, getting it loaded back in my car. He seemed happy to see me and I was happy to see him. It's funny because, during that conversation, I said, "Hey, what's going on with Big Star? I can't pick up a *Rolling Stone* magazine without seeing something written about you guys or someone name-checking you." Alex got this pained look on his face. I said, "You don't want to talk about this, do you?" He smiled and said, "No, I'd rather not." We stood in the street and talked about other things for about thirty minutes or so. It was nice. That was the last time I saw him. Six weeks later he passed away.

On March 17, 2010, while mowing the lawn at his New Orleans home, Alex called his wife Laura at work and complained of chest pains, chills, and shortness of breath. He had suffered several bouts of the symptoms in weeks prior but avoided the doctor's office, in part, because he didn't have health insurance. Laura raced home from work and immediately rushed Alex to Tulane Medical Center. During the eight-minute drive he said, "Run the red light!" and then lost consciousness in the car, just blocks from the hospital. Alex was pronounced dead shortly after he arrived at the emergency room. He was fifty-nine years old.

Ron Easley: As soon as Alex died, I moved quickly to hold a memorial gathering at Minglewood Hall here in Memphis. I was determined to have this be a quiet memorial for the man, not a Big Star promotion. It fell to me to emcee the event and was a very nice gathering...Laura Chilton and I played one song with flute and guitar: "Theme from Rosemary's Baby." I called many people to the stage who were a part of Alex's life and career. Other than a few remarks from U.S. Congressman Steve Cohen, there were no eulogies.

Alex's passing was reported by major news outlets like Rolling Stone, The New York Times *and* Entertainment Weekly. *By April 3, 2010, Big Star hit the* Billboard *charts for the first time ever. The* #1 Record/Radio City *CD (Fantasy Records) quickly sold 3,000 copies and reached No. 48 on the Top Pop*

Catalog Albums chart. Meanwhile, Big Star's scheduled SXSW performance, three days after his passing, carried on as a makeshift Alex Chilton tribute at Antone's in Austin. The SXSW panel initially planned to discuss the history of Big Star and the Keep an Eye on the Sky *box set turned into a ninety-minute celebration of Alex's life. Jody Stephens, Jon Auer, and Ken Stringfellow led a long cast of guest singer-songwriters at a concert dedicated to Alex's Big Star songbook. Guest musicians quickly learned and rehearsed their favorite Alex tunes in hotel rooms and backstage areas. They included Curt Kirkwood of the Meat Puppets, Chris Stamey, Amy Speace, M. Ward, Mike Mills, John Doe of X, Sondre Lerche, and Evan Dando of the Lemonheads. Making the memorial show extra special was a rare performance from Andy Hummel, who flew in from Texas. It was his first on-stage performance with Jody in thirty-five years. The emotional peak of the evening came before the music even started, when a heartfelt letter penned by Laura Chilton was read by publicist Heather West. The crowd of mourning fans listened carefully, as Laura (who was not in attendance) offered a rare glimpse into the quiet final days of Alex Chilton.*

Even though Alex left this world way too soon, I feel so fortunate to have been his friend and wife. I would like to say a few things about his relationship with music and also speak of what he was about as a person.

He was an individual who did what he pleased. However, he was also the most considerate and sincere person I've ever known. He loved life and people and usually befriended the underdogs. He saw beauty in what other people would just dismiss—old rickety houses about to fall down; he would say, 'Now that's a great house worth buying.' He would spend ten minutes chatting with a homeless person on the street and always helped them out with some money. He was a good listener and was very compassionate. He was extremely generous—always giving time, energy, and money to his friends with a no-strings-attached attitude.

There is one aspect to his personality that seemed to define how he approached and interpreted life and that is a consistent tendency to be absolutely clear in expression and communication. His mind worked analytically; he had a low tolerance level for vagueness and carelessness. His relationship with music was all about analysis. When listening and appreciating a piece of music, whether it be a Beach Boys tune or a Bach partita, he was able to pay attention to individual elements simultaneously: harmony, rhythm, melody, meter, etc. I believe this is why he loved working in the studio producing records. He spoke a lot about John Fry teaching him how to do work in the studio, and how he enjoyed playing around with the different elements. The one thing he was absolutely proud of was producing the Cramps records. He would play them at home and just talk and talk about the experience. He was also quite proud of the Detroit garage band the Gories—both his work with them and the band itself. He was very excited for them now that they are playing shows again.

At home in New Orleans, Alex lived a simple and relaxed life. He watched a lot of TV while fooling around on the keyboard and guitar. We played music together, both classical and pop. He rode around town on his bike and loved to strike up conversation with whoever he came across. For the past few years, when I lived with him, he listened and played classical Baroque music, Scott Joplin rag tunes, and '60s pop music. Names that often came up include the following: Carole King, Petula Clark, Brian Wilson, the Byrds, Teenage Fanclub, Frederick Knight, the band Free, George Frideric Handel, Georg Muffat, Haydn, and the baroque-performance group Musica Antiqua Köln. There are dozens more, but these names come to mind as I'm writing this.

The final point I would like to draw attention to was he valued spontaneity. This would seem to contradict his insistence on analysis and accuracy, but somehow, he managed to be both at the same time. Honestly, this remains a mystery to me and is probably why he has been described as a genius and a musician's musician. I am only speculating on this, but I am thinking it is probable.

I will miss him forever and will honor him by maintaining and developing what I've learned from him: compassion, spontaneity, honesty, directness, generosity, an excellent listener and enthusiasm about what life has to offer. He had a blasé attitude towards death—it didn't interest him. The same goes for sleep; he just said the other day that he wished he could be awake 24/7—life was too interesting, and he didn't want to waste it sleeping. I laughed at that, but I knew he was serious. On that note, I need to end this little essay and go take a nap. Here's what Alex would say: "'Night, Shug."

— LAURA CHILTON, MARCH 2010

On May 15, 2010, what was initially booked as a Big Star concert with Alex at the Levitt Shell in Memphis, turned into another memorial concert featuring the remaining members of Big Star and special guests. At the hometown tribute, Mike Mills of R.E.M. sang lead on "Jesus Christ," Brendan Benson tackled

"September Gurls," and John Davis of Superdrag delivered a raucous perfor-
mance of "Don't Lie to Me." Andy Hummel, then battling through the final
stages of a two-year bout with cancer, did not attend. On July 19, 2010, four
months after Alex's death, Andy passed away at his home in Weatherford, Texas.
Like Alex, he was fifty-nine. Jody was now the last surviving member of Big
Star's original lineup. Despite 2010 being a tragic year for the band, a Big Star
documentary already in production kept filming interviews across Memphis and
beyond, capturing never-before-heard stories. Ultimately released as Big Star:
Nothing Can Hurt Me *by Magnolia Films, the film was spearheaded by Dan-*
ielle McCarthy-Boles and earned critical praise following its 2012 premiere.

Danielle McCarthy-Boles: [Memphis-based writer] Robert Gordon
said, "I will put you in touch with John Fry at Ardent who really does
hold the key to the kingdom, so to speak, the gateway for everything
Big Star." He called John and vouched for me. Maybe it's because I was
young and wasn't looking to do a tell-all tabloid version of it. We set up
our first shoot in June of 2007. If it wasn't for John, the movie would've
never happened. If John Fry believed in you, you'd have all the support
you could possibly need. When he was shepherding this film, if we had
a moment of doubt, he'd build us back up. It was remarkable. He was
great at finding and supporting talent, but also very humble about his
own talents.

Jim Dickinson: That Ardent sound has come a long way from Granny's
sewing room. Any musical tradition this city has now would've dried
up and blown away after Stax went out of business if it hadn't been for
John Fry. Anybody creating music in Memphis today is doing it because
of him.

Tim Riley: Fry wasn't out beating his drum. Anybody that was anybody
in Memphis knew the contribution he made to the Memphis music community. Fry gave so much back to Memphis. He was instrumental in
getting equipment for the Stax Museum. He was always a behind-the-
scenes kind of guy.

John Fry: I spent a good deal of time with the folks who made the documentary. It started after the producer Danielle called up with this idea.
She started interviewing people back then, before Drew DeNicola got
involved as director.

Drew DeNicola: I got involved in the film in 2009 and the real shooting
started in 2010.

John Fry: Fortunately, Drew came on board — that was a good thing
that happened. There were many people that passed away after they

were interviewed for that film. A lot of memories would have been lost forever, starting with Jim Dickinson and going on from here.

Aside from the deaths of Alex and Andy, others close to Big Star passed during the making of Nothing Can Hurt Me, *including Tommy Hoehn, Jim Dickinson, Carole Ruleman Manning, and Steve Rhea. The extensive interviews, conducted with those closest to the band, preserved large sections of Big Star's once fuzzy history. Even with little footage of the original band, through vivid stories and countless photos, the doc shined more light on the band than ever before, though dredging up those old memories was not easy for everyone involved.*

Drew DeNicola: John Dando was a major find for the documentary. When we talked to him, at first, he said, "This is really sad stuff for me. I don't know if I really want to do this. That was a very difficult time for me." A lot of people said that, but Dando was someone who was still carrying the depression and darkness from that time.

Richard Rosebrough: That Big Star documentary probably came really close to killing John Fry. It really took everything out of him. That was probably the toughest thing Fry ever had to do. Of course, he wanted to make it happen. He had his personal reasons for putting it out and all that effort into it. He wanted to promote Big Star, but he also wanted to promote Chris.

Drew DeNicola: The Chris Bell part of the Big Star documentary really, really took off with the movie much more than I ever expected. There are people out there who are just Chris Bell fans, and they became fans by seeing this movie. A lot of that came from Netflix streaming it. That was the best distribution the film could have. I learned a lot about the film biz from that. It was Netflix that allowed the movie to just sit there and be discovered over a long period of time. It became a sleeper hit.

Following its release, on May 4, 2013, Big Star re-entered the mainstream charts when the film's double-LP soundtrack, released by Omnivore Recordings, reached No. 20 on Billboard's Soundtrack chart. It later made No. 22 on the Tastemakers Album chart. With a wave of encouraging buzz around the documentary, the filmmakers, which also included director Olivia Mori, embarked on a series of screenings at theaters across the country and overseas. Sometimes, John Fry attended and participated in panel discussions, notably a sold-out event at the Doc NYC fest. While fun and therapeutic, the process was indeed a tough one for Fry, though he preferred not to dwell on it too much, as he said during a Q&A at the 2012 London Film Festival:

John Fry: For better or for worse, I am probably more than four decades into this thing, from first meeting Chris Bell, Jody, Andy, and Alex during his Box Tops days...It has been an interesting experience.

Certainly, there is a tragic aspect to this, but I don't dwell entirely on that because [Big Star] has enjoyed a surprising amount of recognition and ongoing success. I mean, it's not megabucks...but it's gratifying for me to see this music I had a very small part in dealing with...has got fans that are in their young teens now. These kids will come up to me and know more about what I did in the '70s than I know. It's a pretty amazing story. Every time you think it's over with, you turn around and the next thing turns up.

Robert Gordon: Big Star has always been the pride of Ardent, whether it was known or unknown at the time. Back in those days, the guys knew how great the records sounded because it couldn't be denied. If the public didn't recognize that, it was the public's loss.

John Dando: Fry wanted that hit group. I suppose he got it, it's just taken thirty or forty years to happen, and most of the band is not alive anymore. All things considered, Fry probably threw more into Big Star than anything he's done in his life.

Richard Rosebrough: In the early days after *#1 Record* and the Cargoe record, it became apparent that Big Star was not going to become an overnight success. I said, "Well, how long are you going to stay with this, John?" He said, "I really want to give everything its own good chance to fail." I thought that probably meant a few years. Here we are, over forty years later, and he still believed in that record. He wasn't going to let it fail.

In the years following the film's release, the early Ardent family suffered more losses with the deaths of John Hampton, Richard Rosebrough, and John Dando. John Fry passed away December 18, 2014, at his Germantown home. He was sixty-nine years old. Today, Ardent Studios still operates out of 2000 Madison Avenue, and a glowing neon star hangs just inside the main entrance.

Vera Ellis: It was a blood clot that Fry had. They were going to the doctor that morning. They were getting dressed to go to the doctor, and John was taking a long time. My sister Betty, his wife, went to check on him and found him on the floor. He wasn't feeling great, but it was unexpected completely. Betty was in a state of shock for a while. Fry played Big Star music at his house all the time. I mean, *all the time,* and right up to the end. John put his heart and soul into Big Star. That is more of his legacy than all of Ardent put together.

Greg Reding: John Fry was the educator. He was so much about teaching, that's one of the reasons I recently started teaching at the School of Rock in Germantown. Fry told us, "If you have gifts and knowledge and you don't pass it on, then it will die with you. But if you pass it on to the next generation, then you will live forever." After he passed away, and I was sitting at the sanctuary at his funeral service, I looked around and thought, "Half of these people, at least, have been touched and taught by him." That man lives.

While Big Star ended the day Alex passed away, Jody still periodically gets behind the kit and performs the band's songbook across the country as "Big Star's Third." With bandleader Chris Stamey, Jon Auer, and Ken Stringfellow on board, the fluid group also comprises (in part) Mike Mills, Luther Russell, Mitch Easter, Ira Kaplan of Yo La Tengo, and Wilco's Jeff Tweedy and Pat Sansone.As of 2017, Big Star's Third has played everywhere from Central Park in New York and the Wilshire Ebell Theatre in Los Angeles, to the First Avenue nightclub in Minneapolis. An April 2016 show, recorded and filmed at the Alex Theatre in Glendale, was issued in 2017 as Thank You, Friends: Big Star's Third Live... And More, *a live album and concert film. Among a long cast of contributing musicians, the double album features notable spots from Robyn Hitchcock and keyboardist Benmont Tench of Tom Petty and the Heartbreakers. In remembrance of Chris Bell, Chris Stamey takes the lead on "I Am the Cosmos." For Jody, who still loves performing, it's been a surprising blessing.*

Jody Stephens: Chris Stamey came up with the idea [for Big Star's Third] when Alex was still alive; it was sometime in October or November 2009. Stamey emailed John Fry and me the idea. I remember thinking it was a pretty ambitious idea. I didn't know if it'd be feasible, for one, and not too practical. At any rate, he was talking about a number of players who'd have to be flown in, the hiring of a string section and then the intent was to get guests from the city we happen to be playing. It required a lot of organizational skills, a lot of tenacity, perseverance and money. I'm thinking, Stamey is a talented guy, but this was a lot to expect anyone to do. Stamey thought about asking Alex, but it just didn't seem like it was going to work. Fry and I just forgot about it. Then, Alex passed away and it took on a whole new meaning. We had to keep this music in front of people, and it was a great way to honor Alex. He passed away in March and we played our first show on December 10, 2010. As of 2017, we've done at least sixteen shows and it's always a blast. Nobody is in it for the money. Mike Mills is awesome to work with. He's in it for a good time. He's only missed one show, and that's because he had an ear infection.

Aside from live concerts commemorating the band's catalog, a stream of notable literary releases trickled in throughout the 2000s. After author Rob Jovanovic's Big Star: The Story of Rock's Forgotten Band *arrived in stores in 2005, journalist Bruce Eaton penned an in-depth look at the* Radio City *LP for 33 1/3 in 2009. Five years later, Holly George-Warren unveiled the first-ever Chilton biography,* A Man Called Destruction: The Life and Music of Alex

Chilton... *Then, in late 2016,* Isolated in the Light, *a hardcover photo book featuring 1970s images of Big Star, was issued by First Third Books. The excavation of the Big Star vaults didn't stop either. In 2010, after Cheryl Pawelski left Rhino Records and co-founded Omnivore Recordings, the Grammy-winning imprint quickly became the home for Big Star's music, and a series of deluxe reissues followed, including Chilton's* 1970 Sessions, *the* Complete Third *set and the first vinyl issue of Big Star's* Live At Lafayette's Music Room. *With the steady stream of reissues, it was hard for fans and rock critics to forget about Big Star or Chris Bell, especially in 2017, when Omnivore dug deeper than ever into the Bell archive. From that, came the* Complete Chris Bell *box set, a six-LP set containing most of his solo work and a never-before-heard 1975 audio interview with British journalist Barry Ballard. That same year, the label also released a sonically enhanced vinyl edition (and expanded CD set) of* I Am the Cosmos, *which had gone out of print.*

David Bell: It's been a steady-building kind of thing. For twenty-five years or so now, since the beginning with Ryko, there'd be activity with Chris' music, then there'd be a lull. The next thing I knew, Big Star would have an appearance on *The Tonight Show*, there would be more interest, then there would be a lull. Then people are calling me to say, "We need you to re-up on the publishing for *#1 Record* because these people are doing a television show and want to use 'In the Street' as its theme." There's a few years that go well, then there's another lull. In 2004, I get a call saying, "They want to honor Big Star at the Memphis Hero Awards. Would you please accept for your brother?" Then there'd be a lull. Then, in 2008, the producers of *Nick and Norah's Infinite Playlist* chose "Speed of Sound" for its opening film credits, which was just amazing to see. After that, Rhino came around and did the Handmade edition in 2009. Then there was a lull. Then the Big Star documentary came out, and everything blew up again. A few years later, in 2017, Omnivore produced many releases on Chris, more than ever before. I don't think any of it is overkill. To have his music come out and be as successful as it's been, years after he passed away, I'm just happy as a lark for anybody to have whatever they want. I've wondered for several years: *When is the golden goose going to die? Is the golden goose going to live forever?*

Cheryl Pawelski: When it came time to look at the Chris Bell material for Omnivore, I thought it was an opportunity that hadn't quite existed before because all these releases I had planned were now coming after the documentary and after all the Big Star's Third live shows. We thought Chris' profile had increased and we were right. The releases are doing well and I'm so pleased to keep Chris Bell's music in print for the old fans, but also the ones just discovering it.

Today, the home Vernon Bell built in Germantown remains in the family, though much of the acreage surrounding it was split up, sold and developed. Chris' sister Sara continues the Bell restaurateur legacy as the longtime proprietor of Mortimer's Restaurant, a Memphis establishment named after their late father's middle name. As an additional nod to Vernon, the restaurant serves many items from the old Knickerbocker menu. Chris' memory is also honored in Mortimer's "Big Star Section," a popular stop for fans on Big Star-themed road trips.

Sara Bell: I own Mortimer's, but my son Christopher Jamieson, who is named after my brother, runs the restaurant with me. He'll eventually take over. It's become known as the Big Star bar in Memphis. I have paintings, pictures and albums hanging on the walls. There are people who come into the restaurant and say, "What's the Big Star connection here?" When I say, "Well, he was my brother," this look comes over their face and they go, "You're kidding, really? I'm such a huge fan!"

David Bell: Today, in our family, Chris is uniformly revered as the late great, rock-star uncle. They didn't really understand that for quite a while, but once you had a song on *That '70s Show*, once you're on television, that's when it clicked. It was a large step. Every time there's a family gathering, everyone wants to know what's up with Chris.

Sara Bell: It's very rewarding because it was so heartbreaking to see Chris' disappointment through all of it while he was with us. But I try to think of the positives. Back when I was still in my twenties, I taught school for about ten years. The first year, Chris brought in his guitar and played for my class. We sat in the classroom and listened while he played. This one little girl in particular, Amy, just thought he was a Beatle. She jumped, clapped, and screamed. She was only about six years old at that time, but she was just so excited, like he was a star. To this day, I can picture Chris playing his guitar and just smiling because it was so cute. He just had this big grin on his face. She wound up being one of those students that I sort of kept up with. Amy went on to become an attorney and moved to Nashville. After meeting her husband in law school, she sent me an email about how her and her future husband were talking about music, and her husband told her he loves Big Star. Amy said, "Oh, my gosh! That was my first-grade teacher's brother. Chris Bell came and played for our class and I just thought he was wonderful." Sadly, Amy died not long ago from Lou Gehrig's disease. Her husband posted on Facebook last week that he'd played a Chris Bell song for his little five-year-old and he said, "Oh, dad! Is this the Beatles?" He said, "No. This is better, it's Big Star and your mother saw him play." He tries to keep their mother in their thoughts by telling them stories, so he relayed the story about Chris. That's a roundabout way to say it, but there are many ways it touches my life. It's wonderful. Every day somebody says something that keeps Chris alive for me.

David Bell: I've often heard, "This must be bittersweet for you, since Chris isn't here to witness it." But that's not the case. Getting to write the liner notes about Chris for the Ryko CD in '92, where I probably said too much, was very cathartic for me. Then twelve years after his car accident was a whole other kettle of fish. It was a long, long mourning period. But since then, it's been nothing but joy. With my brother and his latter-day celebrity, it's just been extraordinary. I have absolutely no doubt that Chris is quite aware of all this. It doesn't make sense to everybody, but there have been too many instances where I'm looking over my shoulder or up in the air, and think, "You're orchestrating stuff! How is this coming about?" If Chris was still here, he would've seen himself as Vincent van Gogh. We were both big lovers of Van Gogh and his brother, Theo. I often put myself in Theo van Gogh's shoes. This person you love can irritate the shit out of you and drive you to distraction, but also thrill you beyond measure with what they do. Chris would happily see himself as the artist who got his recognition all these years later. For me, in this life, I got to say, "See, Chris, I told you so!" Here it is, over forty years later, and the music is better known than it ever was. Over the past ten or fifteen years, it's just been like shooting texts back and forth with him, like, "Did you see this?" It's been wonderful. Luckily, since he was killed, I've never felt any huge distance between my brother and myself. I don't ever have to visit his headstone. I don't go out there. That's where I'd get upset. There is nothing there of him for me. Chris is much more present in my mind.

During production of the 2009 *I Am The Cosmos* deluxe edition, the gang poses for a shot at Ardent Studios. (L-R) Adam Hill, Jody Stephens, Richard Rosebrough, and David Bell.

PHOTO COURTESY OF ADAM HILL

Cast of Voices

Holliday Aldridge: Jody Stephens' ex-girlfriend, Lesa Aldridge's sister

Lesa Aldridge Hoehn: Vocalist/guitarist, the Klitz, Alex Chilton's ex-girlfriend

Jon Auer: Bellingham, Washington native. Guitarist, vocalist, the Posies, Big Star, Big Star's Third

Al Bell: Record executive, Stax Records co-owner, no relation to Chris Bell

Chris Bell: Guitarist, vocalist, songwriter, the Jynx, Christmas Future, Icewater, Rock City, Big Star, solo, Baker Street Regulars (aka Walk 'n' Wall), Keith Sykes Band. Engineer, Ardent Studios

David Bell: Older brother, Chris Bell's manager from 1974-75. Manages the musical estate of Chris Bell

Max Bell: British journalist, rock critic, no relation to Chris Bell

Sara Bell: Sister, restaurateur, owner of Mortimer's Restaurant in Memphis

Mark Boone: Michigan-based musician, Uprising. Opened for Big Star in April 1974 in East Lansing, Michigan

Mike Brignardello: Guitarist, bassist, Baker Street Regulars, Giant, Nashville session player

Alex Chilton: Vocalist, guitarist, songwriter, Box Tops, Big Star, Panther Burns, solo. Producer, the Cramps, Chris Stamey, the Gories, The Royal Pendletons, Lorette Velvette, among others. Deceased (1950-2010)

Rick Clark: Musician, bassist, Tommy Hoehn, Prix, Alex Chilton, record producer, journalist

Cindy Bell Coleman: Sister

René Coman: New Orleans native. Bassist, Alex Chilton trio, Panther Burns, the Iguanas

Bill Cunningham: Bassist, keyboardist, multi-instrumentalist, the Jynx, the Box Tops. Classical musician, Memphis Symphony, White House Orchestra. Performed on Stax Records sessions, arranged the string section on "You and Your Sister"

John Dando: Friend, sound engineer, Big Star road manager, Ardent Productions employee. Deceased (1950-2014)

Clive Davis: New York native. Record executive producer, former CBS/Columbia president. Penned distribution deal between Stax Records and CBS, which impacted Stax subsidiary Ardent Records

Mark Deming: Michigan-based music critic, AllMusic Guide

Drew DeNicola: New York-based film director and editor, *Big Star: Nothing Can Hurt Me* director. Jacksonville, Florida native

Jim Dickinson: Producer, musician, Ardent Studios. Recorded and/or performed with many artists, including Big Star, Alex Chilton, Ry Cooder, the Replacements, Rolling Stones, and Bob Dylan. Deceased (1941–2009)

Van Duren: Musician, songwriter, solo, Baker Street Regulars, Walk 'n' Wall, Loveland Duren

Tommie Dunavant: Friend, Earl Smith's widow

Ron Easley: Musician, guitarist, bassist, Alex Chilton trio, Panther Burns, solo. Brother of Doug Easley (of Easley McCain Recording in Memphis)

Mitch Easter: Winston-Salem, North Carolina native. Musician, songwriter, guitarist, vocalist, Let's Active, Big Star's Third. Producer of early R.E.M. titles

Bruce Eaton: Buffalo, New York-based Journalist, author of Radio City 33 1/3. Played bass and guitar for Alex Chilton on early solo dates in Buffalo, Toronto and New York

Vera Ellis: Friend, Alex Chilton's ex-girlfriend, John Fry's sister-in-law

Tom Eubanks: Vocalist, guitarist, songwriter, Rock City, solo. AKA Thomas Dean Eubanks

Tav Falco: Vocalist, guitarist, Panther Burns front man. Author, photographer. Now Paris, France resident

Drew Fortune: Los Angeles-based journalist, author. Omaha, Nebraska native

Dale Franklin: Danver's Restaurant co-worker, Memphis location

John Fry: Ardent Records founder. Engineer, producer, Big Star's executive producer. Deceased (1944-2014)

Doug Garrison: Memphis native, long-time New Orleans transplant. Drummer, Alex Chilton trio, Panther Burns, the Iguanas

Holly George-Warren: New York-based journalist, editor. Author, *A Man Called Destruction: The Life & Music of Alex Chilton*, among other titles

Leo Goff: Bassist, the Jynx, solo

Robert Gordon: Memphis-based journalist, author, film director. Won a 2011 Grammy Award for his *Big Star: Keep an Eye on the Sky* liner notes

Sarah Gratz: Friend, ex-wife of Tommy Hoehn

Ben Hamper: Michigan-based radio host and author

John Hampton: Musician, drummer, Baker Street Regulars. Engineer, producer, Ardent Studios

Claude Harper: British engineer, Apple Studios, Château d'Hérouville

Helen Heinle: Georgia native. Close friend, co-worker, Danver's Restaurant, Atlanta location

Adam Hill: Musician. Engineer, Ardent Studios, Big Star archivist

Tommy Hoehn: Vocalist, pianist, songwriter, solo, Prix. Deceased (1953-2010)

Peter Holdforth: British concert promoter, Jim Lord's manager. Booked Chris Bell in 1975, London

Peter Holsapple: Winston-Sale, North Carolina native. Musician, songwriter, dB's, R.E.M. sideman. Now a Durham, N.C. resident

Barney Hoskyns: British music critic, journalist, author

Andy Hummel: Classmate, MUS, UT. Bassist, keys, Chessmen, Swinging Sensations, Icewater, Rock City, Big Star. Later relocated to Weatherford, Texas. Mechanical engineer, Lockheed Martin. Deceased (1951-2010)

Barry Jenkins: Friend, tennis partner, musician

Peter Jesperson: Minneapolis, Minnesota native. Record executive, Twin/Tone Records co-founder, A&R. The Replacements' first manager. Now a Los Angeles resident

Robert Johnson: Guitarist, songwriter, Alamo, Isaac Hayes, solo

Ross Johnson: Musician, drummer, Alex Chilton solo, Panther Burns, solo

Rob Jovanovic: British journalist, author, *Big Star: The Story of Rock's Forgotten Band*, among other titles

John King: Publicist for Ardent Records, Big Star. Founded the Rock Writers' Convention

Bernie Kugel: Buffalo, New York-based musician, the Good, Mystic Eyes. Publisher, *Big Star* zine publisher

John Lightman: Bassist, became Big Star's second bassist in 1974

Andria Lisle: Memphis-based journalist, co-author of *Waking Up in Memphis*

Jim Lord: New Jersey native. folk musician, songwriter, solo. Hired Chris Bell as a sideman in 1975

Carole Ruleman Manning: Friend, photographer, Ardent Studios' art designer. Deceased (1951-2010)

Terry Manning: Producer, engineer, Ardent Studios, Compass Point Studios. Photographer. Musician, Lawson & Four More, Goatdancers, Christmas Future, Rock City, solo

Danielle McCarthy-Boles: New York-based film producer and publicist, *Big Star: Nothing Can Hurt Me* producer. Fernandina Beach, Florida native

Ric Menck: Champaign, Illinois native. Drummer, Matthew Sweet. Songwriter, vocalist, Velvet Crush, the Springfields, Choo Choo Train. AKA Eric Menck

Bob Mehr: Memphis-based journalist, author of *Trouble Boys: The True Story of the Replacements*

Mike Mills: Georgia native. Bassist, vocalist, songwriter, R.E.M., Big Star's Third

Chris Morris: Los Angeles-based journalist, music critic. Chicago native

Rick Nielsen: Rockford, Illinois native. Guitarist, songwriter, Cheap Trick

Larry Nix: Mastering engineer, Ardent Studios, Stax Records

Gene Nunez: Guitarist, Tommy Hoehn Band, solo

Michael O'Brien: Classmate, MUS, UT. Award-winning photographer, shot early Big Star promos

Alec Palao: London native, San Francisco transplant. Writer, musician. Record executive, ACE Records, Omnivore, Light in the Attic. Curated 2008's *Thank You Friends: The Ardent Story* CD, co-produced 2009's *I Am the Cosmos* re-issue for Rhino

Cheryl Pawelski: Los Angeles-based record executive. Former Rhino Entertainment, Omnivore Recordings co-founder. Produced many records, including a series of Chris Bell, Alex Chilton and Big Star-related projects throughout the 2000s

Dan Penn: Alabama native, moved to Memphis in 1966. Relocated to Nashville in the '70s. Producer of the Box Tops and many others. Songwriter, worked solo and alongside musical partner Spooner Oldham

Larry Raspberry: Vocalist, guitarist, songwriter, the Gentrys, Alamo, Larry Raspberry & the Highsteppers. Relocated to southern California in 1983

Phillip Rauls: Photographer, record promoter, Stax, worked Radio City LP promotions

Greg Reding: Pianist, guitarist, the Hot Dogs, the Memphis All-Stars

Steve Rhea: MUS classmate. Drummer, guitarist, vocalist, songwriter in Christmas Future and Icewater. 1970s-era Ardent Records promotions employee, later became a banker and financial planner. Deceased (1949-2012)

Tim Riley: Record executive, Ardent Studios

Will Rigby: North Carolina native. Drummer, songwriter, the dB's, solo

Ira Robbins: New York-based journalist, editor, publisher, *Trouser Press* co-founder

Richard Rosebrough: Drummer, Alamo, Dolby Fuckers, Alex Chilton, session player. Engineer, Ardent Studios and Sam Phillips Recording Service. Drummer on most of Chris Bell's solo material. Deceased (1949-2015)

Beverly Baxter Ross: Friend. Actress. Vocalist, studio singer

Jeff Rougvie: Massachusetts native. Record producer, Rykodisc, oversaw 1992's *I Am the Cosmos* and Big Star re-issues

Bob Schiffer: New York native. Friend, UT classmate

Bud Scoppa: Los Angeles native. Journalist, music critic, *Rolling Stone* magazine. A&R executive, Zoo Entertainment, spearheaded Big Star's *Columbia: Live At Missouri University 4/25/93* LP

Peter Schutt: Bassist, Christmas Future, MUS classmate

Jody Stephens: Drummer, Big Star, Icewater, Rock City, Baker Street Regulars, Suspicions, Big Star's Third, Those Pretty Wrongs, Ardent Studios management

Gary Stevens: Friend, MUS classmate

Ken Stringfellow: Bellingham, Washington native. Guitarist, vocalist, keyboardist, bassist, the Posies, Big Star, Big Star's Third. Record producer

Matthew Sweet: Lincoln, Nebraska native. Musician, songwriter, solo

Keith Sykes: Kentucky native, longtime Memphis transplant. Vocalist, guitarist, songwriter, solo

Jon Tiven: New Haven, Connecticut native. Journalist. Musician, record producer, Prix, Alex Chilton, Tommy Hoehn. Now a Nashville resident

John Tobler: British record executive, CBS Records, music journalist

Peter Tomlinson: New Jersey native. Music critic, zine publisher, musician

Warren Wagner: Producer, engineer, Shoe Productions founder, "I Am the Cosmos" engineer

Ivo Watts-Russell: British record executive, 4AD Records founder. Musician, This Mortal Coil. Now a Santa Fe, New Mexico resident

Paul Williams: Alex Chilton's friend, Audiomania Records founder

Mike Willis: Friend. AKA "Wild Willy"

Sherman Willmott: Shangri-La Records founder, Shangri-La Projects

Ken Woodley: Multi-instrumentalist, vocalist, Paris Pilot, Alamo, solo. Bassist, keyboardist on much of Chris Bell's solo material. 1970s-era Ardent employee

Linda Schaeffer Yarman: Close friend, ex-girlfriend of Andy Hummel

Pete Yorn: New Jersey native. Singer-songwriter, solo, Pete Yorn & Scarlett Johansson. Now a Los Angeles resident

Jim Zumwalt: 1970s band manager of Target, the Hot Dogs. Chris Bell's tennis coach. Nashville-based music, entertainment attorney

Acknowledgements

Since the interview process for *There Was A Light* started in 2013, I've been able to interview dozens of Chris Bell's friends, family members and fans. Without their time, photos, materials and memories, this book would not exist — so "thank you!" to everyone interviewed in this book.

Some of these folks also answered countless follow up questions over the years, including David Bell, John Fry, Richard Rosebrough, Van Duren, Terry Manning, Jody Stephens and Bill Cunningham, to only name a few.

Another prime example of an ongoing source is Big Star archivist Adam Hill — he has been a tremendous friend and support system since the beginning of the process. From digging up tedious facts about recording sessions to road tripping with me across state lines to interview Chris Bell's bassist Ken Woodley, Adam pushed me to try harder and keep going. His time was greatly appreciated. I'd also like to thank Addison Hare, who helped me navigate Ardent Studios' massive archive of photos and press materials.

Much gratitude goes out to Steve Miller and Berl Schwartz for reading (scary) early drafts of this oral history — and they didn't even send me an invoice. I'd also like to thank my editor, Katie Moulton, for having a great eye and never missing deadlines.

Special thank you to the entire *Big Star: Nothing Can Hurt Me* team, including Drew DeNicola, Danielle McCarthy Boles and Olivia Mori. As noted at the front of the book, the hours of raw interview footage shot by their crew were vital to this project. Their hard work preserved many priceless memories from those no longer with us.

I'd also like to acknowledge my entire family, including my mother Elaine and my sisters — Sarah, Angie, and Rachael — who've all been patient with me as I've spent countless evenings and weekends toiling away on this project.

Unfortunately, my father Richard Michael Tupica isn't around to see this. But while he was here, he never stopped asking me about the Chris Bell book — even though he was more of a Simon & Garfunkel kind of guy.

I could go on, but instead, THANK YOU to all of these people:

Jacob Hoye, Post Hill Press, Christian Fuller, Sara Bell, Brittain Coleman, Vicky Bell, Virginia Bell, Christopher & Ashley Jamieson, Christiana Coleman Helvie, Cindy Bell Coleman, Anna Bolton, HoZac Books, Magnolia Pictures, September Gurls Productions, Ardent Studios, Todd Novak, Brett Cross, Barry Ballard, Max Bell, Bert Murihead, Tom Hutchison, Diana Stephens, Frank Bruno, Brian Edwards, Dorothy Cotie & Steve Daniels, the Lights, Warren Wagner, Bud Scoppa, José & Rita Rico, Monica Rico, Bill Webb Jr., The Posies, Jason Gross, Jeff Rougvie, Nathan Webber, Cheryl Pawelski, Omnivore Recordings, Cary Baker, Patti Hummel, Mark Deming, Keith Spera, Thomas Dean Eubanks, Keith Sykes, Tav Falco, Rob Jovanovic, Holly George-Warren, Paul Lester, Judith Beeman, Miriam Linna and Billy Miller, Barry McLuskie, Bob Mehr, Greg Roberson, Rock's Back Pages, Robert Gordon, Barney Hoskyns, Frank Campagna, Dan Shumake, Jonathan Pretus, Chris Gafford, Rick Steff, Alex Szegedy, George Szegedy, Hans Faulhaber, Ken and Susan Woodley, Hannah Szegedy, and all the members of the Big Star Fan Group on Facebook.

Last, but not least, thanks to every rock journalist who has ever written about Big Star. Their research made *There Was A Light* possible. Without the trail of bread crumbs left by stacks of old music magazines, perhaps Big Star would've been lost forever.

There Was A Light **editors**: Jacob Hoye, Nicole Rico, Hannah Szegedy, Katie Moulton, Todd Novak.

Source Index

A sincere "thank you" to the following writers, publications and filmmakers:

Gordon Alexander — *Dixie Flyer*

Martin Aston — *Melody Maker, OOR, MOJO*

Barry Ballard — *Omaha Rainbow*

Leslie Jones Barker — WRAS-FM interview, thesoundreflector.tumblr.com

David Bell — *I Am the Cosmos* liner notes (Rykodisc)

Max Bell — *Dark Star, NME*

Steve Burgess — *Dark Star*

Larry Crane — *Tape Op*

Clive Davis & Anthony DeCurtis — *The Soundtrack of My Life* (Simon & Schuster)

Harold DeMuir — *CREEM*

Bruce Eaton — *Big Star's Radio City, 33 1/3 series* (Bloomsbury Publishing)

Dawn Eden — *The Bob*

Entertainment Tonight — *"The Letter" segment*

Holly George-Warren — *A Man Called Destruction: The Life and Music of Alex Chilton, from Box Tops to Big Star to Backdoor Man* (Penguin Books)

Robert Gordon — *It Came From Memphis* (Atria Books), Randall Lyon outtake

Jason Gross — *Perfect Sound Forever*, perfectsoundforever.com

Russel Hall — Gibson.com

John Hampton—*Random Ramblings of the Musical Mind* blog

Barney Hoskyns — *MOJO*

Joss Hutton— *Bucketfull of Brains, Perfect Sound Forever*

Rob Jovonavic— *Big Star: The Story of Rock's Forgotten Band*

Chris Junior — *Goldmine*

Bernie Kugel — *Big Star* (fanzine), *Bomp!*

David Less — *PressPlay: A Tribute to John Fry and John Hampton* (video)

Paul Lester —*Melody Maker*

Miriam Linna — Unpublished Alex Chilton interview

Andria Lisle — *Memphis Flyer*

Kristine McKenna — *LA Weekly*

Bob Mehr — *The Commercial Appeal*

Bert Murihead — *Fat Angel*

Larry Nager — *Rockumentary: 40 Years of Your Favorite Records, 1966-2006* (video)

Alec Palao — *Thank You Friends: The Ardent Records Story* liner notes (Big Beat Records)

Robin Platts — *DISCoveries*

Sandy Robertson — *Sounds*

Josh Rosenthal — *Buzz Magazine*, *The Record Store of the Mind* (Tompkins Square Books)

James Rotondi — *Guitar Player*

Jeff Rougvie — *I Am the Cosmos* liner notes (Rykodisc)

Steve Scariano — *Bomp!*

Bud Scoppa — *Rolling Stone, Phonograph Record*

Jon Scott — WMC-FM radio

September Gurls Productions crew — *Big Star: Nothing Can Hurt Me* interviews, outtakes

Keith Spera — *OffBeat Magazine*, offbeat.com

Philip Stevenson — *Tape Op*

Jon Tiven — *Circus, Rock*

Ken Tucker — *Rolling Stone*

Epic Soundtracks — *What A Nice Way To Turn Seventeen*

Jonathan Valania — Tommy Hoehn interview

Mike Wilson — *PressPlay: A Tribute to John Fry and John Hampton* (video)

Peter Zaremba — MTV's *The Cutting Edge* (video)

Portions of album reviews appear courtesy of the following publications:

AllMusic (TiVo), Billboard, Cashbox, Creem, Fusion, Phonograph Record, Pitchfork Media, Rolling Stone and ZigZag

BIBLIOGRAPHY

All sources are from print or online publications, except where noted.

Alexander, Gordon. "So You Want to Be A Rock and Roll Star." *Dixie Flyer*, January 1979.

Aston, Martin. "Alex Chilton: Alex's Wild Years." *Melody Maker*, November 2, 1985.

Aston, Martin. "Alex Chilton and Big Star." *OOR*, Fall 1992.

Aston, Martin. "Out of Time." *MOJO*, Issue 192, November 2009.

Ballard, Barry. "Chris Bell Talking About Himself and Big Star." *Omaha Rainbow*, Issue 7, 1975.

Barker, Leslie Jones. "Alex Chilton utters over 5,000 Words in One Sitting." Georgia State University's WRAS radio interview transcript, Conducted Dec. 14, 1987, thesoundreflector.tumblr.com. 2017. (Interview Transcript)

Bell, David and Jeff Rougvie. "*I Am the Cosmos.*" Rykodisc, February 1992. (Album Liner Notes)

Bell, Max. "Big Star." *Dark Star*, No. 11, October 1977.

Big Star: Nothing Can Hurt Me. Raw interview footage and film outtakes. Directed by Drew DeNicola, Olivia Mori, produced by Daniel McCarthy-Boles. (Used courtesy of John Fry/Ardent Studios). September Gurls Productions/Magnolia Films, 2012. (Audio/Video)

BFI London Film Festival, "*Big Star: Nothing Can Hurt Me* panel discussion." John Fry quote, October 2012. (Panel Discussion Video)

Burgess, Steve. "Big Star: What's Goin' Ahn." *Dark Star*, No. 16, August 1978.

Chilton, Laura. "SXSW letter written by Laura." March 20, 2010.

Crane, Larry. "40 Years in the Trenches: John Fry's life-long career running Memphis' Ardent Studios." *Tape Op*, Issue 58, March/April 2007.

Davis, Clive with Anthony DeCurtis. "*The Soundtrack of My Life.*" New York: Simon & Schuster, 2013. (Book)

Demuir, Harold. "From Memphis to Venus and Back Again!" *CREEM*, February 1988.

Eaton, Bruce. *Big Star's Radio City (33 1/3).* New York: Bloomsbury Publishing, 2009. (Book)

Eden, Dawn. "Mr. Postman." *The Bob*, May-June 1987.

Entertainment Tonight. "Segment on 'The Letter.'" CBS, 1987. (Video)

George-Warren, Holly. *A Man Called Destruction: The Life and Music of Alex Chilton, From Box Tops to Big Star to Backdoor Man.* New York: Penguin Books, 2014. (Book)

Godfrey, Kevin (aka Epic Soundtracks). "Alex Chilton." Conducted October 16, 1985. *What A Nice Way to Turn Seventeen*, No.6, July 1986.

Gordon, Robert. "Randall Lyon interview." *It Came From Memphis* book outtake, November 1993 (Unpublished Interview).

Gross, Jason. "Big Star — Andy Hummel." perfectsoundforever.com. *Perfect Sound Forever*. July 2001.

Hall, Russell. "The Gibson Classic Interview: Alex Chilton." Gibson.com. *Gibson Guitars*. September 4, 2010.

Hampton, John. "An Evening with Chris Bell." jhampton.com. *Ramblings of the Musical Mind*, April 19, 2010.

Harris, Steve. "Alex Chilton interview." June 3, 1994. (Audio Interview)

Hoskyns, Barney. "The Stars that Fell to Earth." *MOJO*, Issue 75, 2000.

Hutton, Joss. "Dan Penn and Spooner Oldham #1: 'Spend a Little Time with the Old Folks'." *Bucketfull of Brains*, 1999.

Hutton, Joss. "Jim Dickinson: Home Cooking." perfectsoundforever.com, *Perfect Sound Forever*, January 2002.

James, Rotondi. "Big Star's Reluctant Legend." *Guitar Player*, September 1994.

Jovonavic, Rob. *"Big Star: The Story of Rock's Forgotten Band."* London: Jawbone Press, 2013. (Book)

Junior, Chris. "Big Star: The Power Pop Band that Should Have Been Huge." *Goldmine*, Issue 520, June 30, 2000.

Kugel, Bernie. "A Self-Made Man." *Big Star*, No. 2, August 1977.

Less, David and Mike Wilson. "PressPlay: A Tribute to John Fry and John Hampton." Levitt Shell YouTube channel, April 2015. (Video)

Lester, Paul. "Big Star: 'Whatever Was There, I Drank It Or Took It...'" *Melody Maker*, August 21, 1993.

Linna, Miriam. "Alex Chilton interview." Norton Records, 2000. (Unpublished Interview Transcript)

Lisle, Andria. "40 Years of Ardent." *Memphis Flyer*, October 26, 2006.

McKenna, Kristine. "Big Easy Star." *LA Weekly*, March 29, 2000.

Mehr, Bob. "Chris Bell's passion for music still rings true." *The Commercial Appeal*, December 28, 2008.

Murihead, Bert. "The Legend of Chris Bell and Big Star." *Fat Angel*, No. 14, Winter 1976.

Nager, Larry. "Rockumentary: 40 Years of Your Favorite Records, 1966-2006." Last Train to Memphis, 2006. (Video)

Palao, Alec. *"Thank You Friends: The Ardent Records Story."* Ace/Big Beat Records, 2008. (Album Liner Notes)

Platts, Robin. "From Memphis to Columbia: An Interview with Jody Stephens of Big Star." *DISCoveries*, January 1996.

Robertson, Sandy. "Alex Chilton: Getting The Cramps Between The Box Tops And Big Stardom." *Sounds*, December 31, 1977.

Josh Rosenthal, "1987 Buzz Magazine interview with Alex Chilton." *The Record Store of the Mind*. New York: Tompkins Square Books, 2015. (Book)

Scariano, Steve, and Bernie Kugel. Power Pop. "Alex Chilton," *Bomp!, Special Issue: Power Pop!, March 1978.*

Scott, Jon. "Radio interview with Alex Chilton & Andy Hummel." WMC-FM, 1972. (Radio Interview)

Spera, Keith. "Alex Chilton Lets Them Scream." *OffBeat Magazine*, offbeat.com, May 1, 1995.

Stevenson, Philip. "Roll, Jordan, Roll: A conversation with legendary Memphis producer Jim Dickinson." *Tape Op*, Issue 19, September/October 2000.

Tiven, Jon. "Big Star: Step Right Up and Get Your Americana." *Rock*, March 25, 1974.

Tiven, Jon. "Big Star: No Glam, Just Rock and Ram." *Circus*, May 1974.

Valania, Jonathan. Tommy Hoehn interview. 1999. (Unpublished Interview Transcript)

Zaremba, Peter. "Alex Chilton interview." MTV's *The Cutting Edge*, 1985. (Video)

* All source material in *There Was A Light* remains copyright and property of the writer and/or publication and may not be reprinted or reproduced without the owner's authorization.

INTERVIEW DETAILS

Interviews with the following sources were conducted by Rich Tupica between 2013 and 2018:

Holliday Aldridge, Lesa Aldridge Hoehn, Jon Auer, David Bell, Max Bell, Sara Bell, Mark Boone, Mike Brignardello, Rick Clark, Cindy Bell Coleman, René Coman, Bill Cunningham, Mark Deming, Drew DeNicola, Van Duren, Tommie Dunavant, Ron Easley, Mitch Easter, Bruce Eaton, Vera Ellis, Tom Eubanks, Tav Falco, Drew Fortune, Dale Franklin, John Fry, Doug Garrison, Holly George-Warren, Leo Goff, Robert Gordon, Sarah Gratz, Ben Hamper, John Hampton, Claude Harper, Helen Heinle, Adam Hill, Peter Holdforth, Peter Holsapple, Barney Hoskyns, Barry Jenkins, Peter Jesperson, Robert Johnson, Bernie Kugel, John Lightman, Andria Lisle, Jim Lord, Terry Manning, Danielle McCarthy-Boles, Ric Menck, Bob Mehr, Chris Morris, Rick Nielsen, Gene Nunez, Michael O'Brien, Alec Palao, Cheryl Pawelski, Larry Raspberry, Phillip Rauls, Greg Reding, Tim Riley, Will Rigby, Ira Robbins, Richard Rosebrough, Beverly Baxter Ross, Jeff Rougvie, Bob Schiffer, Bud Scoppa, Peter Schutt, Jody Stephens, Gary Stevens, Ken Stringfellow, Matthew Sweet, Keith Sykes, Jon Tiven, John Tobler, Peter Tomlinson, Warren Wagner, Ivo Watts-Russell, Paul Williams, Mike Willis, Sherman Willmott, Ken Woodley, Linda Schaeffer Yarman, Pete Yorn and Jim Zumwalt.

Important: Three Chris Bell interviews appear in *There Was A Light*, all were conducted in London (1975) and appear courtesy of: Barry Ballard (*Omaha Rainbow*), Max Bell (*Dark Star*) and Bert Murihead (*Fat Angel*). Thank you eternally to those writers for allowing Chris Bell's voice to exist in this oral history.

Other Archival interview notes:

All Carole Ruleman Manning, Mike Mills and John Dando interviews appear courtesy of the *Big Star: Nothing Can Hurt Me* crew, who conducted the interviews. All Steve Rhea quotes also appear courtesy of *Big Star: Nothing Can Hurt Me*, aside from a few mined from the *Thank You Friends: The Ardent Story* liner notes (those are detailed in the chapter citations). All Andy Hummel quotes, except where noted in the citations, also appear courtesy of *Big Star: Nothing Can Hurt Me*.

All Al Bell, John King, Larry Nix and Ross Johnson quotes appear courtesy of Andria Lisle and originally appeared in her terrific "40 Years of Ardent" story in the *Memphis Flyer*, circa 2006.

All Dan Penn quotes are courtesy of Joss Hutton/*Bucketfull of Brains*, while all Tommy Hoehn quotes appear courtesy of Jonathan Valania.

ARCHIVAL INTERVIEW CITATIONS

PROLOGUE:

"When FOX came up": Larry Nager. *Rockumentary.*

"What brought that all about": Robin Platts, *DISCoveries.*

"I'm continually surprised": Martin Aston, *OOR.*

CHAPTER ONE:

"When I was little I had": Leslie Jones Barker, Chilton interview.

"Elvis? Never laid eyes": Leslie Jones Barker, Chilton interview.

"I loved British music": Dawn Eden. *The Bob.*

"The first time that public schools": Miriam Linna, Chilton interview.

CHAPTER TWO:

"Some of the older bands": Miriam Linna. Chilton interview.

"I was about thirteen years old": Miriam Linna, Chilton interview.

"I couldn't play or anything": Miriam Linna, Chilton interview.

CHAPTER THREE

"The Box Tops was originally called": Sandy Robertson, *Sounds*.

"We kept working together": Leslie Jones Barker, Chilton interview.

"I got with the band and": Jon Tiven, *Rock*.

"We recorded it in March": Leslie Jones Barker, Chilton interview.

"I started singing it softly": *Entertainment Tonight*, CBS.

"It was No. 1 for four weeks": Leslie Jones Barker, Chilton interview.

"The first song [Alex] did at Ardent": Larry Nager, *Rockumentary*.

"We must have played": Epic Soundtracks, *What A Nice Way to Turn 17*.

"I went out to California": Epic Soundtracks, *What A Nice Way to Turn 17*.

"My early interest was": Alec Palao, *Thank You Friends* notes.

"We had a little pirate radio": Larry Nager, *Rockumentary*.

"We built a studio in my house": Alec Palao, *Thank You Friends* notes.

"The studio was in a separate": Andria Lisle, *Memphis Flyer*.

"The original equipment was": Larry Crane, *Tape Op*.

"I read everything I could get": Larry Nager, *Rockumentary*.

"When we decided that we": Alec Palao, *Thank You Friends* notes.

"My dad was in the building-material": Larry Nager, *Rockumentary*.

"The next step in the garage": Larry Nager, *Rockumentary*.

"My friend Bobby Fisher called": Alec Palao. *Thank You Friends* notes.

"One night, Jimmy Crosthwait": Andria Lisle, *Memphis Flyer*.

"The thing that occasioned": Larry Nage,. *Rockumentary*.

"When Grandview was being sold": Alec Palao, *Thank You Friends* notes.

"We had already ordered a Scully": Alec Palao, *Thank You Friends* notes.

"I wish I could say we had a real": Larry Nager, *Rockumentary*.

"Manning and I became engineers": Andria Lisle, *Memphis Flyer*.

"I was the first employee": Alec Palao, *Thank You Friends* notes.

"Dickinson came along as": Alec Palao, *Thank You Friends* notes.

"We just had the one studio": Larry Crane, *Tape Op*.

"My first connection to Stax was": Larry Nager, *Rockumentary*.

"Another early customer was Pepper": David Less, *PressPlay*.

"That was mostly '66": Larry Crane, *Tape Op*.

"The good thing about the jingle": Alec Palao, *Thank You Friends* notes.

"Along with the jingles": Andria Lisle, *Memphis Flyer*.

"There was a fella named": Larry Nager, *Rockumentary*.

CHAPTER FOUR

"They played a lot of Hendrix": Jason Gross, *Perfect Sound Forever*.

"In our senior year": Jason Gross, *Perfect Sound Forever*.

CHAPTER FIVE

This chapter contains only author interviews and Andy Hummel interviews courtesy of *Big Star: Nothing Can Hurt Me*.

CHAPTER SIX

"Alex felt that they were": Alec Palao, *Thank You Friends* notes.

"[My cover of] 'Sugar, Sugar'": Dawn Eden, *The Bob*.

"In the late 1960s, at": Alec Palao, *Thank You Friends* notes.

"['Neon Rainbow"] was right": Leslie Jones Barker, Chilton interview.

"They kept presenting me": Dawn Eden, *The Bob*.

"The Box Tops actually played": Jon Tiven, *Rock*.

"When the Box Tops first started": Dawn Eden, *The Bob*.

"The only reason I stayed": Jon Tiven, *Rock*.

"My initial interest in Alex": Joss Hutton, *Perfect Sound Forever*.

"One day, I finally got fed up": Steve Harris, Chilton interview.

"I guess it was about 1969": Leslie Jones Barker, Chilton interview.

"I wouldn't say I 'stormed'": Leslie Jones Barker, Chilton interview.

"I held little classes to": Alec Palao, *Thank You Friends* notes.

"There were six people": Chris Junior, *Goldmine*.

"The overriding thing": Alec Palao, *Thank You Friends* notes.

"I can see Chris walking": Alec Palao, *Thank You Friends* notes.

"I was still in high school": Robin Platts, *DISCoveries*.

"Steve Rhea was at this first": Robin Platts, *DISCoveries*.

"I didn't see myself as": Alec Palao, *Thank You Friends* notes.

"We had trouble with gigs": Steve Burgess, *Dark Star*.

"We were doing Free": Steve Burgess, *Dark Star*.

"I can remember covers": Robin Platts, *DISCoveries*.

"We had several names": Steve Burgess, *Dark Star*.

CHAPTER SEVEN

"I would play around": Leslie Jones Barker, Chilton interview.

"There were still a lot of bluegrass": Dawn Eden, *The Bob*.

"I wanted to get to the point": Gordon Alexander, *Dixie Flyer*.

"I was confused. I didn't": Jon Tiven, *Rock*.

"I didn't have a high": Alec Palao, *Thank You Friends* notes.

"When we went in the": Alec Palao, *Thank You Friends* notes.

"Jody, once he did his": Alec Palao, *Thank You Friends* notes.

"These earlier projects": Alec Palao, *Thank You Friends* notes.

"Alex and Chris recognized": Chris Junior, *Goldmine*.

"Chris asked me to": Bruce Eaton, *Radio City (33 1/3)*.

"He asked me to join his": Leslie Jones Barker, Chilton interview.

"We thought he'd make": Jon Tiven, *Circus*.

"It was a band that got": Leslie Jones Barker, Chilton interview.

"The band, except for Alex": Jon Scott, WMC-FM.

"The name Big Star was": Steve Harris, Chilton interview.

CHAPTER EIGHT

"We practiced together about three": Jon Scott, WMC-FM.

"I totally enjoyed hearing": Alec Palao, *Thank You Friends* notes.

"Chris and I would have some": Bruce Eaton, *Radio City (33 1/3)*.

"Chris had a tremendous": Alec Palao, *Thank You Friends* notes.

"We played [the songs]": Jason Gross, *Perfect Sound Forever*.

"I learned to write": Epic Soundtracks, *What A Nice Way to Turn 17*.

"What I loved about the": Robin Platts, *DISCoveries*.

"I just sort of did what": Russell Hall, *Gibson Guitars*.

"They were oriented toward": Steve Harris, Chilton interview.

"'In The Street' is": Epic Soundtracks, *What A Nice Way to Turn 17*.

"Most of the songs [on *#1 Record*]": Jon Tiven, *Rock*.

"That was all mine": Leslie Jones Barker, Chilton interview.

"On looking back at that": Steve Scariano, *Bomp!*.

"I remember making up": Martin Aston, *OOR*.

"If you're writing anything": James Rotondi, *Guitar Player*.

"It was Chris' idea": Russell Hall, *Gibson Guitars*.

"Certainly, [Chris and I]": Steve Harris, Chilton interview.

"It was out of fashion": Robin Platts, *DISCoveries*.

"I was very into Todd": Jon Tiven, *Rock*.

"Chris added a real pop": Robin Platts, *DISCoveries*.

"The Byrds' [influence] came": Martin Aston, *OOR*.

"We thought we had": Alec Palao, *Thank You Friends notes*.

"Once we began working": Andria Lisle, *Memphis Flyer*.

"We felt like we could": Jon Scott, WMC-FM.

"Chris was in charge": Jason Gross, *Perfect Sound Forever*.

CHAPTER NINE

"We were busy, so we": Larry Crane, *Tape Op*.

"He engineered all three": Steve Burgess, *Dark Star*.

"We cut the basic tracks": Gordon Alexander, *Dixie Flyer*.

"I guess we were the ultimate": Martin Aston, *OOR*.

"Alamo would come to": Chris Junior, *Goldmine*.

CHAPTER 10

"His producing was agonizing": Jason Gross, *Perfect Sound Forever*.

"He was somebody whose": Josh Rosenthal, *The Record Store of the Mind*.

"Chris and I worked well": Bruce Eaton, *Radio City (33 1/3)*.

"Outside the studio, Alex": Bruce Eaton, *Radio City (33 1/3)*.

"I was drinking a lot and": Martin Aston, *OOR*.

"It was a trying time": Jason Gross, *Perfect Sound Forever*.

CHAPTER 11

"It took too long. About six": Jon Scott, WMC-FM.

"Counting getting the thing": Jon Scott, WMC-FM.

"We have a lot of strange": Jon Scott, WMC-FM.

"At the time, I didn't": Alec Palao, *Thank You Friends* notes.

"Stax was primarily into R&B": Chris Junior, *Goldmine*.

"Alex was the focal point": Steve Burgess, *Dark Star*.

"We weren't part of any scene": Martin Aston, *OOR*.

CHAPTER 12

"I had conversations with Al": Clive Davis, *"The Soundtrack of My Life."*

"[Stax] made this deal": Larry Crane, *Tape Op*.

"One thing was, [Big Star]": Alec Palao, *Thank You Friends* notes.

"Stax Records could never sell": Steve Harris, Chilton interview.

"I heard about airplay": Chris Junior, *Goldmine*.

CHAPTER 13

"As the *#1 Record* effort": Bruce Eaton, *Radio City (33 1/3)*.

"Chris, Andy and I got": Russell Hall, *Gibson Guitars*.

"Looking back, [Ardent] was": Alec Palao, *Thank You Friends* notes.

"Chris was a bright, seemingly": Jason Gross, *Perfect Sound Forever*.

"I never knew anything about": Kristine McKenna, *LA Weekly*.

"There were some pretty bad": Paul Lester, *Melody Maker*.

"Chris was having": Epic Soundtracks, *What A Nice Way to Turn 17*.

"Chris had a way of being so cryptic": Bruce Eaton, *Radio City (33 1/3)*.

"I was very concerned": Jon Tiven, *Rock*.

"I'm a pretty self-centered": Paul Lester," *Melody Maker*.

"When Alex went to New York": Joss Hutton, *Perfect Sound Forever*.

"There are several schools": Kristine McKenna, *LA Weekly*.

"Some people have tried": Russell Hall, *Gibson Guitars*.

"Any problems I ever had": Russell Hall, *Gibson Guitars*.

"We all saw it coming": Chris Junior, *Goldmine*.

CHAPTER 14

"I remember Chris coming to": Bruce Eaton, *Radio City (33 1/3)*.

"Chris leaving the band": Jason Gross, *Perfect Sound Forever*.

"Somehow, Chris got": Epic Soundtracks, *What A Nice Way to Turn 17*.

"My brother was near": David Bell, *I Am the Cosmos* notes.

"Everything seemed to." David Bell, *I Am the Cosmos* notes.

"Working as a trio after": Jon Tiven, *Circus*.

"Alex had actually formed": Steve Burgess, *Dark Star*.

"Those late-night": Alec Palao, *Thank You Friends* notes.

"I mean, when [Chris]": Russell Hall, *Gibson Guitars*.

"There was a dormant": Steve Burgess, *Dark Star*.

"It was sloppy, but": Steve Burgess, *Dark Star*.

"We decided to stay together": Steve Burgess, *Dark Star*.

"[Back then] you would tag": Holly George-Warren, *A Man Called Destruction*.

"Ardent was saying": Epic Soundtracks, *What A Nice Way to Turn 17*.

"On *Radio City*, [Chris]": Epic Soundtracks, *What A Nice Way to Turn 17*.

"['Back of a Car'] has Chris": Bruce Eaton, *Radio City (33 1/3)*.

"We made an arbitrary": Russell Hall, *Gibson Guitars*.

"We started from scratch": Bruce Eaton, *Radio City (33 1/3)*.

"The doing of *Radio City*": Bruce Eaton, *Radio City (33 1/3)*.

"Alex and I did lots of": Bruce Eaton, *Radio City (33 1/3)*.

"I don't think [*Radio City* is]": Leslie Jones Barker, Chilton interview.

"The music business is a funny": Martin Aston, *OOR*.

"We kept up the tradition": Bruce Eaton, *Radio City (33 1/3)*.

"If there was ever a Big Star": Bruce Eaton, *Radio City (33 1/3)*.

"I'm not sure what was all": Steve Harris, Chilton interview.

"I know that CBS": Steve Harris, Chilton interview.

"We got more press but sold": Steve Burgess, *Dark Star*.

"We got no money from": Steve Burgess, *Dark Star*.

"We live in a restored": Jason Gross, *Perfect Sound Forever*.

"That tour was like": Robin Platts, *DISCoveries*.

CHAPTER 15

All interviews conducted by author, except the Steve Rhea quote ("He was totally a broken guy"), courtesy of *Big Star: Nothing Can Hurt Me*.

CHAPTER 16

"During the course of four": David Bell, *I Am the Cosmos* notes.

"Many people I grew up with": Kristine McKenna, *LA Weekly*.

"[I told Chris], 'We should": David Bell, *I Am the Cosmos* notes.

"At this point, it was more": David Bell, *I Am the Cosmos* notes.

"Several Italian industrialists": David Bell, *I Am the Cosmos* notes.

"The next morning we took": David Bell, *I Am the Cosmos* notes.

"On our last day at AIR": David Bell, *I Am the Cosmos* notes.

"He felt he had arrived": David Bell, *I Am the Cosmos* notes.

CHAPTER 17

"Certainly, Stax wasn't": David Less, *PressPlay*.

"Alex and Jody had already": Alec Palao, *Thank You Friends* notes.

"In my life, I've never": Martin Aston, *Melody Maker*.

"The other members of Big Star": Martin Aston, *OOR*.

"The third record was": Steve Harris, Chilton interview.

"[*Third*] was just something": Chris Junior, *Goldmine*.

"Each of the [Big Star] records": Steve Harris, Chilton interview.

"I was kind of puzzled": Robin Platts, *DISCoveries*.

"The record is about the decomposition": Joss Hutton, *Perfect Sound Forever*.

"I was coming to a period of": Leslie Jones Barker, Chilton interview.

"I had always felt when": Leslie Jones Barker, Chilton interview.

"Chris was a mimic": Barney Hoskyns, *MOJO*.

"The first two albums were": Martin Aston, *OOR*.

"The crazier it was, the more": Andria Lisle, *Memphis Flyer*.

"['Holocaust' is] just": Leslie Jones Barker, Chilton interview.

"We would record a song": Robin Platts, *DISCoveries*.

"[Dickinson] just did this": Leslie Jones Barker, Chilton interview.

"Maybe I was a little brutal": Alec Palao, *Thank You Friends* notes.

"Dickinson's a genius": Leslie Jones Barker, Chilton interview.

"People have accused me": Alec Palao, *Thank You Friends* notes.

"['Jesus Christ'] was fairly": Epic Soundtracks, *What A Nice Way to Turn 17*.

"What's cool about ('Kanga Roo')": Dawn Eden, *The Bob*.

"[One night at Ardent] we were drunk": Martin Aston, *OOR*

"Alex's big complaint": Alec Palao, *Thank You Friends* notes.

"I hung in there just to get": Andria Lisle, *Memphis Flyer*.

"I know that last Big Star record": Joss Hutton, *Perfect Sound Forever*.

"Chilton was having issues": Andria Lisle, *Memphis Flyer*.

"We did a live broadcast in Memphis": Steve Burgess, *Dark Star*.

"Heroin? Oh no": Paul Lester, *Melody Maker*.

"There was a clear point": Robin Platts, *DISCoveries*.

"We made test pressings": Alec Palao, *Thank You Friends* notes.

"Ardent had ceased": Leslie Jones Barker, Chilton interview.

"Everybody knew Stax was": Philip Stevenson, *Tape Op*.

"Stax was gone then": Chris Junior, *Goldmine*.

"I think Jerry Wexler": Leslie Jones Barker, Chilton interview.

"John tried to sell this": Steve Burgess, *Dark Star*.

"We couldn't sell it": Alec Palao, *Thank You Friends* notes.

CHAPTER 18

"Chris had the modern": Robert Gordon, Randall Lyon interview.

CHAPTER 19

"Chris did a lunchtime": David Bell, *I Am the Cosmos* notes.

"Chris returned to": David Bell, *I Am the Cosmos* notes.

"I don't know whether he": Russell Hall, *Gibson Guitars*.

"One lucrative night at": David Bell, *I Am the Cosmos* notes.

"The pub gigs": David Bell, *I Am the Cosmos* notes.

"Jody liked the idea": David Bell, *I Am the Cosmos* notes.

"I made a contract with Ardent": Leslie Jones Barker. Chilton interview.

"I was getting really": Epic Soundtracks, *What A Nice Way to Turn 17*.

"I just laid up between": Leslie Jones Barker, Chilton interview.

"Post-Stax, there were": Alec Palao, *Thank You Friends* notes.

"I got to the place later": Larry Crane, *Tape Op*.

"*Third* was the last record": Joss Hutton, *Perfect Sound Forever*.

CHAPTER 20

"In the background, there": David Bell, *I Am the Cosmos* notes.

"One of Chris' million": John Hampton, *Ramblings of the Musical Mind*.

"As Van approached Chris": John Hampton, *Ramblings of the Musical Mind*.

"The gig went from there": John Hampton, *Ramblings of the Musical Mind*.

"I was just hanging around": Leslie Jones Barker, Chilton interview.

"'Bangkok,' I guess": Epic Soundtracks, *What A Nice Way to Turn 17*.

"I went to New York and played": James Rotondi, *Guitar Player*.

CHAPTER 21

All interviews conducted by author, except Tommy Hoehn quotes, courtesy of Jonathan Valania.

CHAPTER 22

"It's the summation of my wild": Martin Aston, *Melody Maker*.

"It was a speculative project." Leslie Jones Barker, Chilton interview.

"When I conceived": Epic Soundtracks, *What A Nice Way to Turn 17*.

"We had used all the credit." Leslie Jones Barker, Chilton interview.

CHAPTER 23

"'I Am the Cosmos' was the best": Martin Aston, *OOR*.

"I first became aware": Steve Harris, Chilton interview.

"I was around Alex when Chris": Barney Hoskyns, *MOJO*.

"The police report": Rob Jovonavic, *Big Star: The Story of Rock's Forgotten Band*.

"Nobody was there": Chris Junior, *Goldmine*.

CHAPTER 24

"I started playing with": Leslie Jones Barker, Chilton interview.

"After *Like Flies on Sherbert*": Leslie Jones Barker, Chilton interview.

"I came down [to New Orleans]": Keith Spera, *OffBeat Magazine*.

"In 1972 or '73": Steve Harris, Chilton interview.

"I got a job as a dishwasher." Leslie Jones Barker, Chilton interview.

"I feel a lot freer here": Peter Zaremba, MTV's *The Cutting Edge*.

"I grew up listening": Keith Spera, *OffBeat Magazine*.

"My dad was a jazz player": Keith Spera, *OffBeat Magazine*.

"I worked as an urban": Leslie Jones Barker, Chilton interview.

"I got canned": Leslie Jones Barker, Chilton interview.

"Yeah, if you're not a drinker": Keith Spera, *OffBeat Magazine*.

"I [realized], 'Maybe I can get'": Keith Spera, *OffBeat Magazine*.

"I listen to a lot of gospel": Keith Spera, *OffBeat Magazine*.

"I say let them scream": Keith Spera, *OffBeat Magazine*.

"I don't get off on doing": Keith Spera, *OffBeat Magazine*.

"I don't really need somebody": Keith Spera, *OffBeat Magazine*.

"'Volare' is a great song": Leslie Jones Barker, Chilton interview

"When I was first making": Keith Spera, *OffBeat Magazine*.

"Everybody tells me how": Harold DeMuir, *CREEM*.

"I can't say there has always": Steve Harris, Chilton interview.

"Making money off": Dawn Eden, *The Bob*.

"You can't live your life staying": Harold DeMuir, *CREEM*.

CHAPTER 25

"ZZ Top came here": Andria Lisle, *Memphis Flyer*.

"That reunion deal is": Jason Gross, *Perfect Sound Forever*.

"I don't know. I haven't": Keith Spera, *OffBeat Magazine*.

"Later, Jody said that": Jason Gross, *Perfect Sound Forever*.

"Mike Mulvihill called": Robin Platts, *DISCoveries*.

"Well, it was proposed": Keith Spera, *OffBeat Magazine*.

"The next thing I knew": Keith Spera, *OffBeat Magazine*.

"[The Posies] had recorded": Keith Spera, *OffBeat Magazine*.

"Well, these gigs, they pay": Keith Spera, *OffBeat Magazine*.

CHAPTER 26

"Since launching the Christian": Andria Lisle, *Memphis Flyer*.

"Ardent has somewhat of": Andria Lisle, *Memphis Flyer*.

"We've really been blessed": David Less, *PressPlay*.

"I don't think there's a day": Bob Mehr, *The Commercial Appeal*.

"Even though Alex left": Laura Chilton, "SXSW letter."

"That Ardent sound has come": Andria Lisle, *Memphis Flyer*.

*All sourced material remains property of the writer and/or publication and may not be reproduced or reprinted without authorization of the copyright holder.

PHOTO CREDITS

During my research for this book, quite a few people were helpful and gracious with their images. From the start, John Fry gave me full access to the Ardent Studios archive of Big Star and Ardent-related photos. I cannot thank him and the Ardent staff enough for accommodating me while I was at the studio scanning old photos and digging into beautiful scans of never-before seen images. Those photographs, some shot by Fry himself, helped put faces to the names in this oral history. Other photos featured in *There Was A Light*, many shot by Big Star's circle of friends, show every side of Chris Bell and his bandmates — their work cannot be praised enough.

A very special thanks goes out to Michael O'Brien, whose *#1 Record*-era photos are some of the most iconic shots of Big Star — it's an honor to have his work included. You may want to check out more of his work at obrienphotography.com. Equal praise goes out to the late, great Carole Manning, who was pointing cameras at Chris Bell when he was still cutting his teeth in garage bands.

Of course, David Bell's countless shots of Chris in Europe (circa 1975) are works of art and it's a privilege to include them here.

One last shout out to Ebet Roberts, who captured Alex Chilton doing what he did best: performing music he loved. More of her work is showcased at ebetroberts.com.

Photo Credits and Copyright Notes:

More Photography Credits:

Beyond Chris' family, there are so many others who offered up courtesy photos and scans. Each deserves thanks: The Athens State University Archive, Frank Bruno, Cindy Bell Coleman, René Coman, Bill Cunningham, Van Duren, John Fry, Adam Hill, Tom Hutchison, Memphis University School Archive, Richard Rosebrough, Peter Schutt, Jody Stephens, Diana Stephens, and Keith Sykes.

SONG LYRICS:

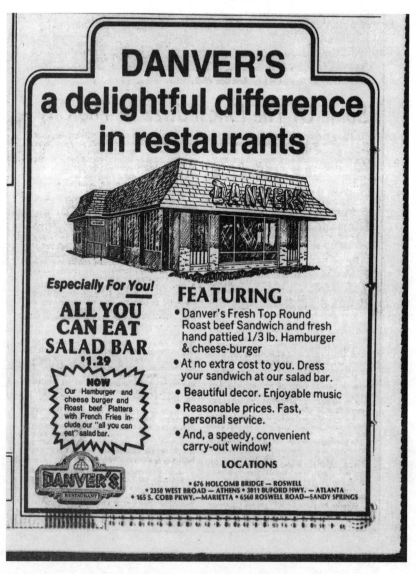

1978 Danver's print advertisement.

Chris Bell recording a guitar track at Ardent Studios.

Alex Chilton riding down a Memphis street.

BY ANDY HUMMEL

Chris Bell in London 1975.

PHOTO BY DAVID BELL

About the Author

Rich Tupica is a Lansing, Michigan-based journalist and music critic whose work has been published in national and international publications, including *UNCUT*, *Record Collector*, *American Songwriter*, and *Ugly Things Magazine*. Locally, he has worked for multiple Michigan newspapers, reporting both entertainment and hard news stories.